T5-AFL-755

Women, Business and the Law 2014

Removing Restrictions to Enhance Gender Equality

Table of Contents

Foreword 1

About *Women, Business and the Law* 3

Key Findings 8

Spotlight on Violence Against Women 24

The Default Marital Property Regime and Women's
Entrepreneurship: The Case of Chile 29

Constitutional Reform and Women's Rights:
The Case of Kenya 33

Laws on Sexual Harassment and Domestic
Violence in South Asia 36

References 39

Data notes...44

Economy Tables..69

Pilot Data Tables.......................................167

Acknowledgments 181

Foreword

One of the foremost development priorities of our century is ensuring gender equality. Empowering every citizen to contribute all of her or his talents to achieving today's overarching economic goals —boosting productivity, competitiveness, and sustainable growth—is essential to fulfilling the World Bank Group's mission: ending extreme poverty by 2030 and promoting shared prosperity in every developing country.

The ideal of equality before the law and equality of economic opportunity is not just wise social policy: It's smart economic policy. When women and men participate in economic life on an equal footing, they can contribute their energies to building a more cohesive society and a more resilient economy. The surest way to help enrich the lives of families, communities and economies is to allow every individual to live up to his or her fullest creative potential.

In this latest edition of *Women, Business and the Law*, the World Bank Group underscores our commitment to carefully analyzing evidence and building knowledge about priorities that deserve the sustained attention of lawmakers and policymakers. Using objective criteria to gather data from 143 economies worldwide, this report establishes a detailed fact base on the many ways in which the law has been used to establish differences on the basis of gender, generally to the detriment of women. As this year's data show, many societies have made progress, gradually moving to dismantle ingrained forms of discrimination against women. Yet, a great deal remains to be done.

This year's report analyzes trends across six indicators: Accessing institutions, Using property, Getting a job, Providing incentives to work, Building credit, and Going to court. It also adds a new pilot indicator on Protecting women from violence. Like previous editions, this year's report examines laws, regulations, and institutions that treat women differently. That can be found in ways that make it more difficult for them to earn an income, make decisions about property or start a business—and ultimately deny them opportunities for economic advancement and personal growth. In turn, those roadblocks impede social mobility, undermine competitiveness, and restrain economic growth.

The latest data help clarify the magnitude of the challenge society still faces in our quest to ensure equality. By informing the policy dialogue about the current state of gender inequality, this report aims to promote steps that can help countries create conditions for building a stronger economy: establishing a pro-growth business environment and adopting inclusive social policies.

Ensuring that half the world's population has the opportunity to lead more productive, more fulfilling lives will help promote shared prosperity across the world. By strengthening productivity, we can accelerate job creation and provide more people with pathways out of poverty, thus advancing the entire global development agenda. I hope you'll join me in welcoming this latest edition of *Women, Business and the Law*, which highlights the progress that is already being made, and the challenges that we must still confront, as we promote equal opportunity for all.

Dr. Jim Yong Kim
President
The World Bank Group

About *Women, Business and the Law*

Though legal gender parity has improved around the world, major differences remain. Many laws, regulations and policies on entrepreneurship and employment continue to prevent women from improving their own and their families' well-being by working or running a business.

Datasets such as the World Bank Group's *Enterprise Surveys* and *Doing Business* have led the way in providing information on the challenges that all firms and entrepreneurs face in starting and expanding their businesses and creating jobs.[1] But women entrepreneurs and workers often face additional constraints in starting businesses and navigating the workforce.

How can governments improve regulations to benefit women entrepreneurs and workers? Answering this question requires understanding many factors, from access to education and healthcare to social and cultural norms. One important factor is how laws, regulations and institutions differentiate between women and men, affecting women's incentives or capacity to set up and run a business or to work. *Women, Business and the Law 2014* is the third in a series. It provides data on legal and regulatory barriers to women's entrepreneurship and employment in 143 economies.

What does this report cover?

Gender differences in the law are only one of many factors that affect women's economic opportunities—but they are an important factor that governments can directly influence. *Women, Business and the Law 2014* provides seven indicators of gender differences in formal laws and institutions:

- **Accessing institutions** explores women's legal ability to interact with public authorities and the private sector in the same ways as men. This indicator provides disaggregated information on 11 categories of legal ability, highlighting differences between married and unmarried women. This edition expands the data coverage to examine gender differences in getting national identity cards. Information has also been added on the use of quotas to increase women's representation on corporate boards and in national parliaments and local governments.

- **Using property** analyzes women's ability to own, manage, control and inherit property. This edition expands the data coverage to include women's ownership rights in the marital home and whether legislation accounts for nonmonetary contributions such as unpaid care for children or the elderly.

- **Getting a job** assesses restrictions on women's work, such as prohibitions on working at night or in certain industries. This indicator also covers laws on work-related maternity, paternity and parental benefits and on retirement ages. This edition examines data on industry restrictions in greater detail to provide more nuanced information on where women face more onerous barriers.

- **Providing incentives to work** examines personal income tax liabilities, taking into account tax credits and deductions available to women relative to men. This indicator covers taxation as well as public services such as childcare and education.

- **Building credit** identifies minimum loans tracked by private credit bureaus and public credit registries and assesses bureaus and registries that collect information from microfinance institutions. This edition expands the data coverage to examine economies where credit registries and bureaus collect information from retailers and utilities.

- **Going to court** examines access to small claims courts and data on whether women's testimony in court is given the same evidentiary weight as that of men. This edition includes additional data on the number of women justices—including chief justices—in supreme courts.

- **Protecting women from violence** examines laws on domestic violence against women and the existence and scope of laws on sexual harassment.

The first three indicators capture legislation with direct gender dimensions and are based on a reading of laws from the perspective of women. These indicators also examine areas of laws with indirect gender dimensions. For example, laws may have gender-neutral text but can affect women more in practice.

The Providing incentives to work indicator examines explicit gender differences in tax laws as well as the existence of public services, such as childcare, that are not gender differentiated but are more likely to favor women.

The Building credit and Going to court indicators examine ease of access to credit bureaus and courts to assess the indirect effects that credit reporting and dispute resolution mechanisms have on women, who are more likely to rely on nontraditional financial services.[2] Each indicator was constructed based on data availability, economic relevance and variation in regulation across economies.

The Protecting women from violence indicator is being piloted in this report. Data have been collected for 100 economies on the laws, regulations and institutions that deal with domestic violence against women and sexual harassment. This pilot indicator represents a partial effort in both the number of economies covered and the scope of the data collected. For example, when using the data it is important to look beyond criminalization to also consider laws authorizing and funding prevention programs and services for survivors of violence. This indicator is a first step toward quantifying the global legislative framework on domestic violence and sexual harassment and offers comparable baseline data. This report includes a separate section highlighting findings from this pilot indicator (box 1.1).

Laws on domestic violence and sexual harassment are further explored in a case study on South Asia. A second case study focuses on marital property regimes in Chile and examines the evolution of women's legal capacity and property rights in Latin America. A third case study looks at the implementation of constitutional reforms benefiting women in Kenya. Kenya was the top reformer in the previous edition of *Women, Business and the Law*.

The *50 Years of Women's Legal Rights* database (available on the *Women, Business and the Law* website at http://wbl .worldbank.org) indicates how 100 economies have reformed in the Accessing institutions and Using property indicators over the past 50 years. The database makes it possible to examine how some economies have improved women's economic opportunities and why others have lagged behind.

The *Women, Business and the Law* indicators add to a number of sets of global gender indicators including:

- The Women's Economic Opportunity Index, published by the Economist Intelligence Unit, examines 26 indicators for 128 economies to understand regulations and practices affecting women entrepreneurs and workers. These indicators include both policy variables, such as measures of the regulatory environment, and outcome variables, such as measures of educational attainment. The index presents a mix of objective and expert-based indicators.

- The Global Gender Gap Index, published by the World Economic Forum, examines gender inequalities in 135 economies using criteria based on economics, politics, education and health. This index uses mainly quantitative outcome variables such as the ratio of female to male labor force participation.

- The Social Institutions and Gender Index provides a composite measure of gender equality for 86 economies based on the Gender, Institutions and Development Database produced by the Organisation for Economic Co-operation and Development (OECD). This index includes 12 indicators on social institutions based on expert assessments of what happens in practice beyond the legal framework. The indicators focus on policy and input variables, such as inheritance regulation, and outcome variables, such as access to credit.

- The United Nations Gender Inequality Index provides a composite measure of gender disparity for 148 economies. This index includes five indicators across three areas: reproductive health, empowerment (as measured by educational attainment and parliamentary

---

BOX 1.1   VIOLENCE AGAINST WOMEN

A life free of violence is a basic human right. There are also substantial economic benefits to preventing violence.

The 1994 U.S. Violence Against Women Act provided $1.6 billion for programs over five years. A cost-benefit analysis of the act estimates that over that period it saved $16.4 billion in averted costs of property losses, healthcare, police and victim services, lost productivity, reduced quality of life and premature deaths. The act's net benefits are estimated at $14.8 billion.

In 2003 Colombia's government spent $73.7 million in direct costs to prevent, detect and offer services to survivors of domestic violence, an amount equal to 0.6% of the national budget. The same year, the indirect costs of domestic violence—including forgone income for victims and government revenue not received due to higher unemployment—were estimated at about 4% of GDP.

Around the world violence against women—including domestic violence and sexual harassment—affect the lives of millions. But the global cost of violence against women remains unknown. Conservative estimates include costs of healthcare and lost wages for victims, decreased productivity for businesses, government first responder services and access to justice. Better protecting women from violence is essential for them to enjoy rights and allows them to take advantage of economic opportunities.

Source: Violence against Women Act, Pub. L. No. 103-322, tit. IV, 108 Stat. 1902 (1994); Clark and others 2002; Sánchez and others 2004.

representation) and the labor market. The indicators are based on quantitative outcome variables. The index was introduced in the United Nations Development Programme's *Human Development Report 2010*.

These indexes take different approaches to developing gender indicators and present different views of the position of women in society. But overall there is a lack of internationally comparable gender-disaggregated data. Moreover, such data are rarely updated, limiting the possibility of analyzing variations over time.[3] *Women, Business and the Law* and the *50 Years of Women's Legal Rights* database complement the above indexes by adding a time-series element to examine legal differences between women and men.

In addition, *Women, Business and the Law* is the only global dataset measuring gender gaps in policies using quantitative, objective data. The dataset does not include qualitative assessments. Outcome variables, such as female labor force participation rates, also do not form part of the dataset, though they are used for the analysis in the report.

What does this report not cover?

Equal opportunities for women in business and the workplace depend on the interplay of various economic, social and cultural factors. For example, unless women have opportunities to get an education or develop their skills, equal rights to entrepreneurship and employment can mean little. Equalizing rights to work might not result in more women entering the workforce if they are still expected to be the primary caregivers for their children and access to childcare is limited. Other factors such as infrastructure—for example, safe transportation—might also affect women's ability and desire to work in certain locations or at night.

Women, Business and the Law recognizes that many issues affect women's economic opportunities but focuses on one in particular: the formal legal and regulatory environment that determines whether women can open their own businesses or work. Not everything of importance is covered by each indicator. For example, while the Accessing institutions indicator includes laws covering gender-based quotas in parliaments, it does not include information on quotas for electoral lists—an important factor in determining women's representation in political institutions.

The report focuses on laws governing the formal economy. Though most women in developing economies start businesses or work in the informal economy, one of the main goals of this project is to define features of the formal economy that prevent women from making the transition from informal to formal. But all the indicators, other than Getting a job and Providing incentives to work, cover regulations that affect women in both the informal and formal economies.

Customary law can exist in parallel with formal legal regimes. Where such legal systems exist together, customary law can determine a woman's rights in marriage or to property and inheritance, often granting women rights different from those they would receive under the statutory legal system. *Women, Business and the Law* tries to partially cover customary law by examining its constitutional treatment. In particular, the report analyzes whether customary law is exempt from constitutional provisions on nondiscrimination and equality. But the actual application of customary law is not covered due to its often uncodified status and the resulting difficulties in defining its rules.

While focusing on written legislation, the report recognizes the often large gaps in implementation between laws on the books and actual practice: women do not always have access to the equality that exists for them in formal laws. Identifying legal differences is one step toward better understanding where women's economic rights might be restricted in practice. Of the countries covered by the report, only the Islamic Republic of Iran, Sudan and the United States are not parties to the United Nations Convention on the Elimination of All Forms of Discrimination Against Women.[4] Thus it would seem that most women in the economies covered should have access to formal equality. But as the report shows, that is not always the case.

The report's focus on formal law is consistent with the idea that facilitating the entry of women into the workforce involves improving the regulatory environment for women, stimulating business and job creation and making businesses and the overall economy more competitive. Assessing the potential benefits of equality—and when and how legal differences based on gender help or harm outcomes for women—requires additional analysis.

Why this focus?

Women, Business and the Law builds on the growing body of research and empirical evidence that stresses the importance of the legal and institutional framework in shaping women's economic rights and opportunities and improving gender equality. Research has called into question the notion that economic growth alone increases gender equality. Continuous policy commitments to gender equality might be required to achieve it.[5]

Gender equality favors a variety of positive development outcomes. In Colombia women who own property are in a better bargaining position at home, where they are more likely to be able to move freely, negotiate the right to work and control their income.[6] Women's access to land has also been linked to gains in family welfare, including children's health.[7]

Moreover, unequal rights for women have adverse effects on women entrepreneurs.

In economies where husbands can prohibit their wives from working, women are less likely to have formal accounts, savings or credit. The same is true in economies with a higher prevalence of violence against women. But if married women can choose where to live in the same way as married men and are not legally required to obey their husbands, they are more likely to use formal financial products.[8]

The gender asset gap, which has been well documented, can also undermine women's bargaining power and capacity to engage in economic activities.[9] Access to formal credit relies heavily on asset-based lending.[10] A recent survey of banks in Ghana found that they strongly prefer land and buildings as collateral.[11] If women have unequal property rights, they are constrained in their ability to use property as collateral, limiting their access to credit.[12] Where that is the case, reputation collateral such as records of successful loan repayments to microfinance institutions or retailers may help women build their credit histories and ultimately access finance.

Workplace and labor regulations also affect women's opportunities and outcomes. Restrictions on the hours that women can work or the industries where they can work can limit their ability to get the jobs they want. In Taiwan, China, working hour restrictions reduced the number of hours that women work, while maternity benefits increased women's labor force participation.[13]

But personal income tax liability can affect workers' decisions about how much or whether to work. Women, particularly those who are married, are more negatively affected by income tax rules.[14] In contrast, childcare subsidies such as tax credits and the availability of childcare increase women's participation in the labor force.[15]

Legal formalities and litigation costs—direct and incidental—discourage poor people—regardless of their gender—from accessing courts.[16] Even for relatively simple disputes, legal formalities are associated with less contract enforcement, longer cases and perceptions of lower-quality justice.[17] One-stop shops such as small claims courts can improve access to justice for men and women.[18]

How to use these data

Women, Business and the Law can be used to raise awareness, inform policy discussions on gender differences in laws and prod policy makers to take actions strengthening women's economic rights and opportunities. The report is also designed for researchers, as it can be used to further research at the economy level and across economies on links between gender-based legal differences and outcomes for women. *Women, Business and the Law* and the *50 Years of Women's Legal Rights* database can be used together to study these links over time.

Data and methodology

The data in this report cover April 2011 to April 2013, were collected between September 2012 and April 2013 and are current as of April 2013. The report's indicators were constructed using responses from country practitioners with expertise in family and labor law including lawyers, judges, academics and members of civil society organizations working on gender issues. Their responses were verified against codified sources of national law including constitutions, marriage and family codes, labor laws, passport procedures, citizenship rules, inheritance statutes, tax regulations, land laws, gender equality laws, civil procedure rules, electoral laws and social security codes. The pilot Protecting women from violence indicator also examines criminal laws and procedures and laws on violence against women. Where possible, these laws are provided on the *Women, Business and the Law* website. In addition, *Doing Business 2014* surveys were used to develop the Building credit indicator.

As noted, *Women, Business and the Law* covers 143 economies. For two of the report's indicators, Accessing institutions and Using property, the *50 Years of Women's Legal Rights* database provided information on legal reforms for 100 economies, and this report presents analysis using both datasets. More detailed data on each economy, including time-series data and links to the sources used, are available on the *Women, Business and the Law* website at http://wbl.worldbank.org.

Several assumptions were made about the situation of women in this report's sample of economies. For example, it is assumed that they live in each economy's largest city for business. This assumption might make a significant difference in federal economies, where laws affecting women can vary by state. In addition, where several sets of personal law apply, setting out different rights and obligations for different groups of women, the data focus on the most populous group of women. A detailed explanation of the report's methodology and recent changes to it—including all the questions asked and assumptions made—is provided in the Data notes. The methodology for historical data is presented on the *Women, Business and the Law* website.

Feedback is welcome on all aspects of the report and can be offered through the *Women, Business and the Law* website.

Endnotes

1 See World Bank, *Enterprise Surveys*, http://www.enterprisesur-veys.org; and World Bank Group, *Doing Business*, http://www.doingbusiness.org.

2 Coleman and Carsky 1996; Coleman 2000; Orser, Hogarth-Scott and Riding 2000.

3 Gaye and others 2010.

4 The United States has signed but not ratified the convention.

5 Duflo 2012.

6 Friedemann-Sánchez 2008; Deere and León 2001, 2003b.

7 Allendorf 2007; Duflo 2003.

8 Demirguc-Kunt, Klapper and Singer 2013.

9 Deere and León 2003b; Quisumbing and Hallman 2005; Deere and Doss 2006.

10 IFC 2011.

11 Law and Development Partnership 2011.

12 IFC 2011.

13 Zveglich and van der Meulen Rodgers 2003.

14 Eissa 1995; Eissa and Hoynes 2004; Eissa, Kleven and Kreiner 2008.

15 Averett, Peters and Waldman 1997; Baker, Gruber and Milligan 2008.

16 Gloppen and Kanyongolo 2007.

17 Djankov and others 2003.

18 UN Women 2011.

Key Findings

In the past 50 years women's legal status has improved all over the world. But many laws still make it difficult for women to fully participate in economic life—whether by getting jobs or starting businesses. Discriminatory rules bar women from certain jobs, restrict access to capital for women-owned firms and limit women's capacity to make legal decisions. Gender differences in laws affect both developing and developed economies, and women in all regions.

Highlights from *Women, Business and the Law 2014*

- Almost 90% of the 143 economies covered by *Women, Business and the Law 2014* have at least one legal difference restricting women's economic opportunities.

- Twenty-eight economies have 10 or more legal differences for men and women in the areas covered by *Women, Business and the Law*. Among these, 25 are in the Middle East and North Africa and Sub-Saharan Africa.

- The *50 Years of Women's Legal Rights* database has made it possible to take two *Women, Business and the Law* indicators (Accessing institutions and Using property) backward in time for 100 economies for 50 years. The results are striking: more than half of the restrictions in these two indicators in place in 1960 had been removed by 2010.

- Over the past 50 years, economies in Sub-Saharan Africa and Latin America and the Caribbean have reformed the most in Accessing Institutions and Using property.

- Over the past two years the most reforms have occurred in Côte d'Ivoire, Mali, the Philippines and the Slovak Republic for the six indicators measured by *Women, Business and the Law*.

- But many restrictions remain. In 15 economies husbands can object to their wives working and prevent them from accepting jobs.

- In 79 economies laws restrict the types of jobs that women can do. The most extensive restrictions on women's employment are in Eastern Europe and Central Asia. And some benefits, when taken to a certain threshold, can undermine women's labor force participation. For example, in economies where the cumulative duration of paid maternity and parental leave available for mothers exceeds two years female labor force participation is lower.

- Policies encouraging women to join and remain in the labor force are associated with less income inequality.

- Women are more likely to have accounts at formal financial institutions in economies with a default full community of property or partial community of property marital regime than in economies with a default separation of property marital regime.

- New data explore legal quotas on the share of women on corporate boards, in parliaments and local governments, and serving as judges on constitutional courts. The data find that 6 economies have quotas for women on boards of publicly listed companies and 12 have legal quotas for women in parliaments. Among the 123 economies covered by *Women, Business and the Law* that have constitutional courts or court-like bodies, women are represented on all but 19.

- Of the economies measured, 76 have established explicit legislation addressing domestic violence but only 32 have specific provisions on sexual harassment in schools. Even less prevalent is legislation on sexual harassment in public spaces—only 8 of the 100 economies examined have enacted such laws.

How common are gender differences in laws?

Women, Business and the Law measures restrictions on women's employment and entrepreneurship as well as incentives for women's employment in 143 economies. The dataset captures 21 legal differences for unmarried women and 26 for married women that affect women's economic opportunities, for a total of 47 differences across five indicators (box 2.1).

Of the 143 economies covered by *Women, Business and the Law*, 128 have at least one difference between women and men according to this simple measure (figure 2.1). The 28 economies with 10 or more legal differences are in the Middle East and North Africa (14 economies), Sub-Saharan Africa (11), East Asia and the Pacific (2) and South Asia (1).

The 15 economies with no legal differences between women and men in the areas measured are Armenia, Canada, the

Dominican Republic, Estonia, Hungary, Kosovo, Mexico, Namibia, the Netherlands, New Zealand, Peru, Puerto Rico (U.S.), the Slovak Republic, South Africa and Spain.

Some methodological considerations

The measure of legal gender differences is constructed by adding the restrictions on married and unmarried women together. Five restrictions that only apply to married women are counted once, while 21 restrictions that apply to married or unmarried women are counted twice, for a total of 47 restrictions. For example, only married women can be legally required to obey their husbands, while both married and unmarried women may be legally prohibited from working in certain jobs. The measure of legal gender differences can sum to a whole number or a decimal for any economy because the question on job restrictions has eight sub-questions that examine specific restrictions on women's work. Thus each sub-question is equal to one-eighth.

Of all the questions covered by *Women, Business and the Law*, only 47 are included in this measure. Twenty-two questions are included because they contain explicit gender-based differences. Three questions pertain to constitutional rights: the absence of a nondiscrimination clause in the constitution with gender as a protected category, the validity of customary law even if it is contrary to constitutional nondiscrimination and equality, and the validity of personal law even if it

FIGURE 2.1 NUMBERS OF GENDER LEGAL DIFFERENCES VARY BY ECONOMY

Number of legal restrictions

■ 0   ■ 0 < # < 3   ▨ 3 ≤ # < 5   ▨ 5 ≤ # < 10   ■ ≥10

Source: Women, Business and the Law database.

is contrary to constitutional nondiscrimination and equality. These questions were selected because of the importance of specific constitutional protections on nondiscrimination for gender equality and assume that customary and personal laws might include gender-based legal differences. One question pertains to the absence of legal recognition for nonmonetary contributions to marital property. This question was selected based on the assumption that women are more

---

BOX 2.1 LEGAL DIFFERENCES FOR MARRIED AND UNMARRIED WOMEN

Women, Business and the Law examines differences by comparing men and women of the same marital status on the following 21 areas:

1. Applying for a passport
2. Traveling outside the home
3. Traveling outside the country
4. Getting a job or pursuing a trade or profession without permission
5. Signing a contract
6. Registering a business
7. Being "head of household" or "head of family"
8. Conferring citizenship on their children
9. Opening a bank account
10. Choosing where to live
11. Obtaining a national identity card

12. Having ownership rights over property
13. Having inheritance rights over property
14. Working the same night hours
15. Doing the same jobs
16. Enjoying the same statutory retirement age
17. Enjoying the same tax deductions or credits
18. Having their testimony carry the same evidentiary weight in court
19. Absence of a gender or sex nondiscrimination clause in the constitution
20. Validity of customary law if it violates the constitution
21. Validity of personal law if it violates the constitution

In addition, the dataset captures five other areas applicable only to married women:

22. Being legally required to obey their husbands
23. Being able to convey citizenship to their non-national husband
24. Administering marital property

25. Having legal recognition for nonmonetary contributions to marital property
26. Having inheritance rights to the property of their deceased husbands

---

likely to perform activities that benefit the household but are not paid for, such as childcare.

The questions which are not part of this measure can be divided into three sets. First, questions that are not gender differentiated but may disproportionately affect women because of the types of businesses they are concentrated in—such as businesses that are smaller, more likely to be home-based and more likely to operate in the informal sector. Second, questions describing legal frameworks, such as marital property regimes, that are gender neutral. Third, questions from the pilot indicator on Protecting women from violence that are presented separately. The questions are not weighted by their importance to women or by the number of women affected. For example, prohibitions on women working in mines can affect women more intensely where mining is a major industry, but may matter less in economies where it is not—while requirements for married women to get their husbands' permission to travel outside the home affect all married women.

How common are legal incentives encouraging women to work?

Governments also institute policies that encourage women to work and make it easier for them to do so. Such policies can range from nondiscrimination in hiring to maternity and paternity leave regimes to quotas encouraging women's participation in economic life. *Women, Business and the Law* examines 12 such legal provisions (box 2.2).

Of these, 10 directly relate to promoting women's employment—including quotas, benefits associated with maternity and paternity leave and women-specific tax deductions. The other 2 involve equalizing the treatment of women and men in the workplace through equal remuneration for work of equal value and nondiscrimination in hiring practices.

FIGURE 2.2 LEGAL DIFFERENCES AND INCENTIVES FOR WOMEN TO WORK DIFFER WIDELY

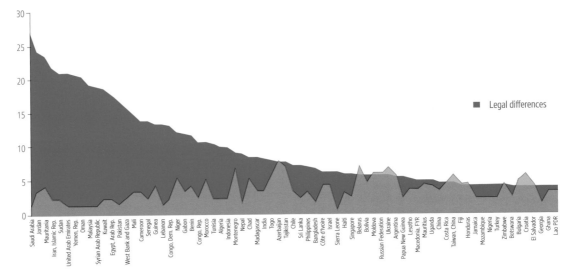

Source: Women, Business and the Law database.

These incentives represent an initial cataloguing of government policies that can encourage women's economic participation. But they are not an exhaustive list of government policies promoting women's economic opportunities.

When incentives for women to work are mapped against legal differences in women's economic opportunities as measured by *Women, Business and the Law*, economies with the most legal differences tend to provide fewer incentives (figure 2.2).

Hungary, the Slovak Republic and Spain have no legal differences and six or more incentives. Oman, Saudi Arabia, the United Arab Emirates and the Republic of Yemen have more than 20 differences and fewer than two incentives.

How have restrictions on women's legal rights changed over time?

Gender-based restrictions on women's legal capacity and property rights have fallen in recent decades. The *50 Years of Women's Legal Rights* database has made it possible to take two *Women, Business and the Law* indicators (Accessing institutions and Using property) backward in time for 100 economies for 50 years. The results are striking: more than half the restrictions in these two indicators in place in 1960 had been removed by 2010 (figure 2.3).

Sub-Saharan Africa had the most restrictions in 1960—and by 2010 had implemented the most reforms. For example, in 1960 South African women in customary unions were deemed legal minors, with their husbands as guardians. The 1998 Recognition of Customary Marriages Act reformed this by ensuring that women in customary unions had full status and capacity, including the ability to acquire and dispose of assets, enter into contracts and litigate.

Most economies examined in Latin America and the Caribbean had removed the gender legal differences measured since 1960. Between 1960 and 2010 significant reforms occurred in Argentina, Bolivia, Brazil, Colombia, Peru and Paraguay. Until 1988 in Brazil the husband was the head of household, giving him sole legal ability to represent the family, choose the family domicile and administer marital assets as well as his wife's separate assets. Since then women have had equal recognition in these areas.

Economies in East Asia and the Pacific covered by *Women, Business and the Law* also made significant reforms in the areas examined. These include Indonesia's 1974 Law on Marriage, which replaced the 1874 Dutch Civil Code and granted married women greater rights, including the ability to open individual bank accounts.

In Eastern Europe and Central Asia the communist influence on legal systems resulted in few gender differences in women's property rights and legal capacity as measured by the Using property and Accessing institutions indicators. The differences that did exist in 1960 had been removed by 2010. The OECD high-income economies covered had also removed the measured differences by 2010.

Incentives

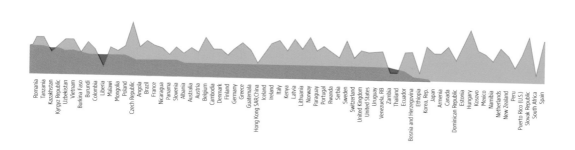

The Middle East and North Africa and South Asia have changed the least since 1960 in the areas covered. Though some constraints have been removed in both regions, many restrictions remain. One example of reform in the Middle East and North Africa is the changes that occurred in Morocco in 1996, when the Commercial Code was amended to allow married women to engage in commercial activities without the permission of their husbands. In 2004 the passage of a new Family Code also equalized the right of both spouses to make household decisions.

Yet additional legal barriers have been introduced. In 1994 the Republic of Yemen removed the constitutional provision on nondiscrimination. Moreover, after the reunification of Yemen in 1990, gains in women's rights made in the Arab Republic of Yemen (in the south) were reversed. The Islamic Republic of Iran also saw reversals in legal protections. The 1975 Family Protection Law equalized the right to work for both spouses, but in 1979 the law was reversed—once again allowing husbands to keep their wives from working. After 1979, laws were also put in place limiting women's economic opportunities. For example, women judges were no longer allowed to impose sentences, limiting their ability to work in the judiciary. In addition, women faced restrictions on their mobility that had not been in place before.

A more recent reversal in legal rights occurred in the Arab Republic of Egypt, where the removal of constitutional non-discrimination based on gender has led to a discussion on the relationship between legal rights and gender equality.

Reformers in South Asia include Nepal, which in 2002 reformed its General Code to allow, among other things, unmarried daughters under 35 to inherit property. But the reform did not cover married daughters regardless of their age.

Over time some of the measured legal restrictions have become nearly obsolete. Since 1960, 18 of the economies examined have lifted requirements that married women must have their husbands' permission to initiate judicial proceedings: Angola (1996), Argentina (1968), Austria (1975), Benin (2002), Bolivia (1975), Brazil (1962), the Dominican Republic (1978), Indonesia (1963), Lesotho (2006), Mozambique (2004), Namibia (1996), Paraguay (1987), Portugal (1966), Rwanda (1988), South Africa (1998), Spain (1981), Switzerland (1984) and Zimbabwe (1982).[1]

Yet these restrictions still exist in the Democratic Republic of the Congo. According to articles 450 and 451 of the Family Code, married women require spousal permission to sue in civil matters unless the suit is against their husbands. And under Liberia's Code of Civil Procedure a married woman who brings action in court must have her husband joined as a party to the suit. Only if the action is against her husband or she is suing in connection with a business she operates can she file independently.

Legal restrictions remain on the books in other areas. An example is the requirement that husbands give their wives permission to work. *Women, Business and the Law 2014* found that 15 economies still have this restriction. Yet many

---

FIGURE 2.3 EVOLUTION OF RESTRICTIONS OVER TIME IN 100 ECONOMIES

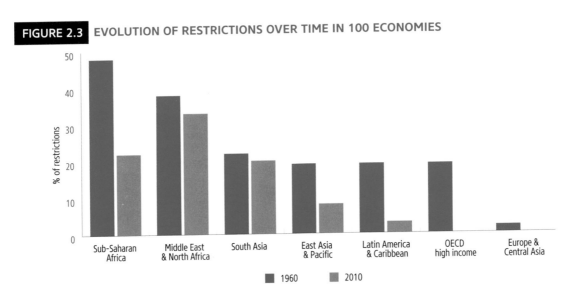

Source: *50 Years of Women's Legal Rights* database; Hallward-Driemeier, Hasan and Rusu forthcoming.
Note: Where data are unavailable for 1960, the first known value is used.

economies have removed it. Since 1960 at least two dozen economies have curtailed husbands' legal power to restrict their wives from working, including France (1965), Indonesia (1974), Morocco (1996), Peru (1984), South Africa (1998) and Turkey (2001).[2] And in the past two years Côte d'Ivoire, Mali and Togo have reformed such laws.

Where are relationships between women and the law changing?

Over a two-year period ending in April 2013, *Women, Business and the Law* recorded 59 legal changes in 44 economies on its six established indicators (table 2.1). Of these changes, 48 increased gender parity, 11 were neutral to gender parity and none reduced gender parity.

Who reformed the most?

Côte d'Ivoire, Mali, the Philippines and the Slovak Republic each increased gender parity in two *Women, Business and the Law* indicators. Côte d'Ivoire reformed in the Accessing institutions and Providing incentives to work indicators. Previously in Côte d'Ivoire only husbands could decide on the family residence and could legally stop their wives from working if they deemed that the work was not in the interests of the family. Husbands were also the legal heads of household. A 2013 reform allows both spouses to choose the family residence and stop the other from working if they deem it against family interests. Moreover, both husbands and wives can legally be the head of household. These reforms in the Accessing institutions indicator also had tax

implications that were captured by the Providing incentives to work indicator. Married women who previously could not claim tax deductions for their children or husbands because they were barred from being legal heads of household can now claim the same deductions as married men, reducing their overall tax burden and increasing their incentives to join the workforce.

Mali abolished differences that allowed husbands to prevent their wives from working, which were captured by the Accessing institutions indicator, and introduced equal inheritance rights for spouses, triggering the Using property indicator.

The Philippines lifted restrictions on night work for women, as captured in the Getting a job indicator, and has a new credit bureau with no minimum loan amount that also collects information from microfinance institutions, as reflected in the Building credit indicator.

The Slovak Republic increased the percentage of wages paid during maternity leave from 55% to 65%, affecting the Getting a job indicator. It also raised the maximum amount of a small claim, allowing additional claims to be processed by small claims courts and triggering changes in the Going to court indicator.

Changes by indicator

For the Accessing institutions indicator, in addition to the changes made in Côte d'Ivoire and Mali, Togo enacted a new Family Code giving both spouses the right to choose

TABLE 2.1	**IN RECENT YEARS MANY ECONOMIES MADE CHANGES INCREASING OR NEUTRAL TO GENDER PARITY**		
Women, Business and the Law indicator	Changes increasing gender parity	Changes neutral to gender parity	Changes reducing gender parity
Accessing institutions	Botswana; Côte d'Ivoire; Jamaica; Mali; Syrian Arab Republic; Togo; Zimbabwe		
Using property	Mali		
Getting a job	Belgium; Bolivia; Chile; China; Colombia; Ethiopia; Hungary; Italy; Lithuania; Malawi; Mexico; Montenegro; Norway; Philippines; Poland; Slovak Republic; Slovenia; Ukraine; Venezuela, RB; Vietnam	Belgium; Finland; Hungary; Italy; Latvia; Lithuania; Malaysia; Netherlands; Poland; United Kingdom	
Building credit	Algeria; Angola; Cambodia; Egypt, Arab Rep.; Ethiopia; Ghana; Kenya; Lao PDR; Macedonia, FYR; Mauritius; Philippines; Tajikistan; Vietnam		
Providing incentives to work	Côte d'Ivoire; Israel		
Going to court	Latvia; Netherlands; Slovak Republic; Uganda; United Kingdom	Malaysia	

Source: Women, Business and the Law database.

the family domicile. The new code also allows each spouse to object to the profession of the other. Under the previous code only husbands could do so.

Botswana and the Syrian Arab Republic enacted new constitutions including nondiscrimination clauses with gender as a protected category. Jamaica enacted a constitutional amendment adding a gender equality clause and a non-discrimination clause with gender as a protected category. Zimbabwe also enacted a new constitution under which customary law is no longer exempt from constitutional protections on nondiscrimination.

For the Getting a job indicator, 20 economies made changes toward gender parity. In addition to the changes in the Philippines and the Slovak Republic, Belgium extended the length of parental leave and Chile introduced it. China, Colombia, República Bolivariana de Venezuela and Vietnam increased the number of days for maternity leave, and Bolivia and Mexico introduced paid paternity leave. Mexico also adopted legislation prohibiting the dismissal of women for being pregnant, and Montenegro adopted legislation requiring employers to give women their jobs back after returning from maternity leave. It also adopted 365 days of paid parental leave, 45 of which are reserved for the mother (while decreasing the length of maternity leave). Norway extended the length of paid parental leave and increased the quota of parental leave reserved for fathers.

Hungary's new Labor Code removed women-specific restrictions in employment, instead providing employment protections for all workers. The previous code prohibited employing women and young people for work that could have detrimental effects on their physical condition or development. The new Labor Code provides protection against harmful jobs for both women and men regardless of their age. Slovenia removed night work restrictions on women. Italy and Ukraine raised and equalized retirement and pensionable ages for women and men. Lithuania and Poland are gradually increasing and equalizing retirement ages, and Slovenia is doing the same for retirement and pensionable ages. Ethiopia and Malawi introduced retirement and pensionable ages for women and men.

For the Going to court indicator, four economies reformed in addition to the Slovak Republic. Latvia and Uganda introduced small claims procedures, and the Netherlands and the United Kingdom raised the maximum for small claims.

For the Building credit indicator, 12 economies recorded positive reforms in addition to the Philippines. Algeria eliminated the minimum loan amount for inclusion in the credit registry, which now includes information from microfinance institutions. In Angola, Mauritius and Vietnam public credit registries now also include information from microfinance institutions, as do private credit bureaus in Egypt, Kenya, Ghana and the former Yugoslav Republic of Macedonia. Cambodia and Tajikistan have new credit bureaus with no minimum loan amounts that also collect information from microfinance institutions. The Lao People's Democratic Republic has a new credit registry that includes information from microfinance institutions. In Ethiopia loans of any amount are now included in the credit reporting system.

For the Providing incentives to work indicator, reforms occurred in Côte d'Ivoire (discussed above) and Israel, whose Cabinet approved free education to all children 3 and older. Previously free education was provided only for children above the age of 5.

Finally, 11 economies made changes that were neutral to gender parity but still affect the *Women, Business and the Law* indicators. Italy introduced a day of paternity leave on an experimental basis for 2013–15, and Latvia temporarily reduced the percentage of wages paid during maternity and paternity leave. Lithuania gave parents more options in terms of the length of parental leave they could choose and the percentage of wages received. In Hungary paternity leave used to be paid by the government but is now paid by employers. Belgium and Finland increased pensionable ages, Malaysia increased its retirement age and made procedural changes to its small claims courts and the Netherlands is gradually increasing retirement and pensionable ages. These four economies have maintained existing gender parity. Poland raised the pensionable age for women from 60 to 62 but maintained unequal pensionable ages for men and women. Meanwhile, the United Kingdom adopted the Employment Equality (Repeal of Retirement Age Provisions) Regulations, phasing out pensionable ages for women and men.

Why do relationships between women and the law matter?

Regulatory restrictions on women's economic participation are associated with real economic outcomes. *Women, Business and the Law* and World Bank Enterprise Surveys data show that lower legal gender parity is associated with fewer women participating in the ownership of firms (figure 2.4).

Using the Gini coefficient of inequality as a proxy, *Women, Business and the Law* data show that policies encouraging women to join and remain in the labor force are associated with less income inequality (figure 2.5). Ensuring that women are encouraged to work helps promote shared prosperity around the world.

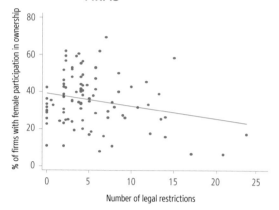

FIGURE 2.4 GENDER-BASED LEGAL RESTRICTIONS ARE ASSOCIATED WITH LOWER FEMALE PARTICIPATION IN OWNERSHIP OF FIRMS

Source: Women, Business and the Law database; World Bank *World Development Indicators* database; World Bank Enterprise Surveys, http://www.enterprisesurveys.org/.

Note: The figure is based on 94 economies for which data are available. The negative relationship between legal restrictions and the percentage of firms with female participation in ownership is statistically significant at the 5% level even after controlling for 2011 income per capita. The regression analysis of this relationship includes 70 economies for which data are available. These statistical relationships cannot be interpreted as causal.

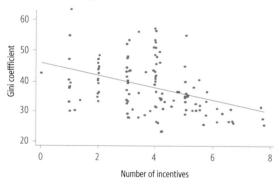

FIGURE 2.5 ECONOMIES THAT PROVIDE MORE INCENTIVES FOR WOMEN TO WORK HAVE GREATER INCOME EQUALITY

Source: Women, Business and the Law database; World Bank *World Development Indicators* database; All the Ginis dataset, updated October 2012, http://econ.worldbank.org/projects/inequality; Milanovic 2005.

Note: The figure is based on 120 economies for which data are available. A Gini coefficient of 0 indicates perfect equality and a Gini coefficient of 100 indicates maximum inequality. The negative relationship between incentives and the Gini coefficient is statistically significant at the 5% level even after controlling for 2011 income per capita, welfare (income or consumption/expenditure, gross or net) and the recipient unit (household or individual) to which the reported Gini refers. The regression analysis of this relationship includes 74 economies for which data are available. These statistical relationships cannot be interpreted as causal.

Legal gender equality matters for women's economic opportunities. It matters for women's access to finance and entrepreneurial activities. And it matters for increasing equality of opportunity in economies. Whether by easing restrictions on women's employment and business activities or by adopting policies increasing women's ability to take up economic activities, gender equality is smart economics.

Where do things stand on women and the law globally?

Around the world, economies tend to cluster their legislative choices by region, partly because economies are likely to have similar legal histories and share some sociocultural norms and values.

OECD high-income economies and those in Eastern Europe and Central Asia do not impose many legal restrictions on women as measured by the Accessing institutions and Using property indicators. But economies in Eastern Europe and Central Asia have pervasive restrictions on women's employment, as measured by the Getting a job indicator.

In Latin America and the Caribbean and East Asia and the Pacific explicit legal gender differences are less common in the areas measured by the Accessing institutions and Using property indicators. But they still exist in some economies including Ecuador, Honduras, Indonesia, Malaysia and the Philippines.

Explicit legal gender differences are more common in the Middle East and North Africa, South Asia and Sub-Saharan Africa, both in Accessing institutions and Using property. All 14 economies covered in the Middle East and North Africa have at least one legal differentiation in both Accessing institutions and Using property, as do all five economies covered in South Asia. Of the 36 economies covered in Sub-Saharan Africa only 6—Angola, Burkina Faso, Ethiopia, Namibia, South Africa and Zimbabwe—have no legal differentiations in these areas. Moreover, benefits such as paternity leave, designed to share child-raising responsibilities and free women's time to work outside the home, are rare in these three regions. In fact, none of the economies covered in South Asia offers any paternity leave.

The following sections examine new data and regional trends in the *Women, Business and the Law* indicators.

Accessing institutions

Lack of autonomy to interact with government institutions or conduct official transactions restricts women's ability to conduct basic transactions.

A husband's legal veto power

To determine whether women and men have the same capacity to operate in and access the business environment, *Women, Business and the Law* examines 11 actions that women might have to take to earn an income.[3] Some are directly related to women's abilities to function in the business environment, such as being able to take a job or pursue a profession. Others, such as the ability to travel outside the home or country, are indirectly related. But each can affect a woman's ability to function without hindrance in the business environment. Each action is examined separately for married and unmarried women. The data show that most restrictions apply only to married women (table 2.2).

In 29 economies husbands are the legally designated heads of households. That means that husbands control key decisions such as choosing the family residence or obtaining official documents. In 19 of the economies where husbands are the legal heads of households, they also choose the family residence.

In 15 of the 143 economies covered by *Women, Business and the Law*, husbands can prevent their wives from working. In Guinea a husband may object to his wife's employment if his objection is based on the interests of the family. A wife can go to court and have her husband's objection overturned, but must prove to the court that his objection is unjustified.

Vestiges of history remain codified in certain economies simply because legislation such as the Code Napoléon was adopted wholesale and not regularly reviewed or updated. The notion of head of household, for example, was removed from France's Civil Code in 1970 but persists in many civil codes throughout West Africa.

Other restrictions are holdovers from history as well. Niger's Family Code still only allows women to open bank accounts to deposit funds that their husbands gave them if banks first

| TABLE 2.2 | IN MANY ECONOMIES MARRIED WOMEN DO NOT TAKE SOME ACTIONS THE SAME WAY AS MARRIED MEN |

Action	Economies where married women do not perform the action the same way as married men
Be head of household	Benin; Burundi; Cameroon; Chad; Chile; Congo, Dem. Rep.; Congo, Rep.; Gabon; Guinea; Honduras; Indonesia; Iran, Islamic Rep.; Jordan; Madagascar; Mali; Mauritania; Morocco; Nicaragua; Niger; Oman; Philippines ; Rwanda; Saudi Arabia; Senegal; Sudan; Togo; Tunisia; United Arab Emirates; Yemen, Rep. (29)
Choose where to live	Benin; Burkina Faso; Cameroon; Chad; Congo, Dem. Rep.; Congo, Rep.; Gabon; Guinea; Haiti; Iran, Islamic Rep.; Jordan; Kuwait; Malaysia; Mali; Nicaragua; Niger; Oman; Rwanda; Saudi Arabia; Senegal; Sudan; Syrian Arab Republic; United Arab Emirates; West Bank and Gaza; Yemen, Rep. (25)
Apply for a passport	Benin; Botswana; Cameroon; Congo, Rep.; Egypt, Arab Rep.; Fiji; Gabon; Haiti; Iran, Islamic Rep.; Jordan; Kuwait; Malawi; Oman; Pakistan; Saudi Arabia; Sudan; Uganda; United Arab Emirates; Yemen, Rep. (19)
Confer citizenship on her children	Guinea; Iran, Islamic Rep.; Jordan; Kuwait; Lebanon; Madagascar; Malaysia; Mali; Mauritania; Nepal; Oman; Saudi Arabia; Sudan; Syrian Arab Republic; United Arab Emirates; West Bank and Gaza (16)
Get a job without permission	Bolivia; Cameroon; Chad; Congo, Dem. Rep.; Gabon; Guinea; Iran, Islamic Rep.; Jordan; Kuwait; Mauritania; Niger; Sudan; Syrian Arab Republic; United Arab Emirates; West Bank and Gaza (15)
Obtain a national identity card	Benin; Cameroon; Egypt, Arab Rep.; Mauritius; Oman; Pakistan; Saudi Arabia; Senegal; Togo (9)
Travel outside the home	Iran, Islamic Rep.; Jordan; Kuwait; Malaysia; Oman; Sudan; Syrian Arab Republic; West Bank and Gaza; Yemen, Rep. (9)
Travel outside the country	Oman; Saudi Arabia; Sudan; Syrian Arab Republic (4)
Open a bank account	Congo, Dem. Rep.; Niger (2)
Register a business	Congo, Dem. Rep.; Pakistan (2)
Sign a contract	Congo, Dem. Rep. (1)

Source: Women, Business and the Law database.

notify the husbands. But women can open bank accounts in their own names if they have their own jobs, in which case their husbands do not have to be notified. Such legal provisions used to be common throughout Europe. Complicated provisions such as these can create confusion among financial institutions, which might simply require all married women to get permission from their husbands before opening bank accounts even when not legally bound to do so.

Women in leadership positions

Women, Business and the Law 2014 expands the data coverage on Accessing institutions to better examine women's ability to access the institutions of public and economic life. The data now cover legal quotas on the share of women on corporate boards and in parliaments and local governments.[4]

The principle of equity is at the core of arguments in favor of gender quotas. Quotas can enable a more equitable representation of women in leadership positions, improving their descriptive representation—which may translate into more equitable representation of women's interests in decision making. This aims to improve women's substantive representation.

Six economies have established quotas for women on boards of publicly listed companies. These quotas vary. Rwanda's constitution sets a minimum of 30% for women and men on boards of publicly listed companies. In 2010 Iceland set a 40% quota for women's representation on corporate boards, and in 2011 Belgium and Italy established 33% quotas. France's Law 2011-103, enacted in January 2011, established a 20% quota, to be progressively raised to 40%.

Norway led the way on this issue in 2002, when its secretary of state for trade and industry proposed voluntary quotas for increasing women's representation on corporate boards. The goal was to reach average representation of 40% by 2005, up from 6%. By the deadline the average had only increased to 25%, so parliament amended the Public Companies Act—making quotas mandatory and establishing a new deadline of 2008. The quotas were to be enforced first by fines, then deregistration from the Oslo Stock Exchange and, finally, dissolution. By 2008 more than 80% of listed firms had complied.

Critics of the Norwegian experience have stressed the limits of corporate board quotas. In addition to the argument that governments should not determine the composition of corporate boards, critics pointed out the lack of diversity among female board members after a small number of senior women accumulated a large share of the new board appointments. The relatively few qualified women available to serve on boards when quotas were introduced in Norway led to the emergence of private initiatives to train women to serve on

boards. Thus the initial lack of diversity among female board members might be a transitional issue.

Of the 143 economies measured by *Women, Business and the Law*, 12 have legal quotas for women in parliaments. The proportion of women in parliaments is 6 percentage points higher in these economies than in economies without legal quotas.[5] Though this represents a small number of economies, the result suggests that quotas may be an effective policy tool for increasing female representation in parliaments.

Decisions by legislative bodies with more women may qualitatively differ from those by institutions with fewer women involved in decision making. A study of 265 village councils in two states in India where a third of the positions of council head had been reserved for women since 1993 found that leaders invest more in infrastructure directly relevant to the needs of their gender.[6]

Women's participation in parliaments might also affect government spending priorities. One cross-country study that analyzed government spending over more than 35 years found that economies with gender quotas spent more money on social services and welfare than economies without them.[7] Moreover, women's participation in parliaments might affect their labor force participation rates. Analysis based on *Women, Business and the Law* data shows that female labor force participation rates are higher in economies with legal quotas for women in parliaments.[8]

Beyond improving equity in representation and policy outcomes, quotas might help allocate women's talents more efficiently. The public and practical demonstration of those talents may, in turn, change gender-biased attitudes and social norms, and reveal role models who foster other women's aspirations. In the Indian state of West Bengal the 1993 quotas for female village councilors changed expectations and beliefs about what women can achieve. In villages administered by female councilors, parents expressed higher aspirations for their daughters' educations and occupations. Adolescent girls also attained higher education levels and spent less time on domestic chores.[9]

Using property

The importance of land ownership goes beyond capital accumulation. Access to and control over land provides income and reinforces bargaining power and agency. Moreover, the ability to leverage property as collateral is important for both female and male entrepreneurs. But regional and local gender asset gaps persist in property ownership, particularly for major assets.[10]

Unequal inheritance regimes are one cause of gender imbalances in assets. In 98 economies equal inheritance rights were related to a higher likelihood of women having formal bank accounts and credit.[11] Another reason for gender asset gaps may be the structure of marital property regimes. A marital property regime determines the system of property ownership and management between spouses during the course of a marriage and at its dissolution through death or divorce (box 2.3).

Full and partial community of property regimes implicitly recognize the importance of nonmonetary contributions to the household, such as childcare and household labor, by presuming joint ownership of assets. This approach allows the spouse with lower or no income to acquire greater wealth both during marriage and upon its dissolution.

Deferred full or partial community property regimes recognize the importance of nonmonetary contributions at the end of a marriage (either through death or divorce) by equalizing each spouse's share of wealth at that time. This approach protects the spouse with lower or no income at the dissolution of a marriage, but not during its course.

Separation of property regimes leave the spouse with lower or no income at a disadvantage in terms of wealth accumulation both during marriage and at its dissolution.

A study on gender asset and wealth gaps in Ecuador, Ghana and the Indian state of Karnataka used household asset surveys to estimate married women's share of couples' wealth. It found that in Ecuador married women owned 44% of couples' wealth, in Ghana they owned 19% and in Karnataka the owned 9%. The much larger share of couples' wealth held by married women in Ecuador was explained by the fact that it has a partial community of property regime, where most assets are owned jointly by wives and husbands. Married women's smaller share of couples' wealth in Ghana and Karnataka was largely explained by their separation of property regimes, where assets are not jointly owned.[12]

Marital property regimes can also relate to married women's financial inclusion. Under full and partial community regimes, assets such as bank accounts, savings, stocks and bonds are generally legally presumed to be jointly owned. But women married under a separation of property regime must rely solely on assets they earn themselves, as well as their bargaining power in the household.

Women, Business and the Law and the World Bank's Global Financial Inclusion (Global Findex) database show that in economies with a default full community of property regime, there are on average 10 percentage points more female-owned accounts at formal financial institutions than in economies with a default separation of property regime (figure 2.6). One reason is that economies with full community of property regimes may have more joint accounts between wives and husbands. Available data do not make it possible to disaggregate joint accounts from individual ones.

Some separation regimes have enacted legislation protecting spouses earning less or no incomes, recognizing the

---

BOX 2.3	MARITAL PROPERTY REGIMES

The default marital property regime—the one governing the property relationship of every married couple unless they opt for an alternative—defines how each spouse can use, buy or sell property. Among the economies covered by *Women, Business and the Law* there are four common marital property regimes:

- *Full community of property.* All assets and income brought into a marriage, as well as those acquired during it, apart from inheritances or gifts to one spouse, are considered joint property. If a marriage ends, these assets are divided equally. Joint assets are also divided equally upon the death of either spouse. This regime is the default in 6 economies.

- *Partial community of property.* Assets acquired before marriage are considered the property of the acquirer. Assets and income acquired during marriage, apart from inheritances or gifts to one spouse, are considered joint property. If a marriage ends, each spouse retains ownership of their own assets. Assets acquired during the marriage are divided equally. Such assets are also divided equally upon the death of either spouse. This regime is the default in 65 economies.

- *Deferred full or partial community of property.* The rules of full or partial community of property apply at the time of a marriage's dissolution (either by death or divorce). Prior to this time, the rules of separation of property regimes apply. This regime is the default in 16 economies.

- *Separation of property.* All property acquired by spouses before and during their marriage remains separate property. Each spouse has sole control of their assets. This regime is the default in 46 economies.

Source: Women, Business and the Law database.

FIGURE 2.6 WOMEN ARE LESS LIKELY TO HAVE FORMAL ACCOUNTS IN SEPARATION OF PROPERTY MARITAL REGIMES

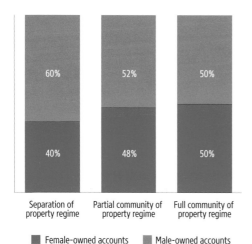

60%	52%	50%
40%	48%	50%

Separation of property regime | Partial community of property regime | Full community of property regime

■ Female-owned accounts   ■ Male-owned accounts

Source: Women, Business and the Law database; Global Financial Inclusion (Global Findex) 2012 database; World Bank World Development Indicators database.

Note: The figure includes data on 110 economies for which data are available and presents average values.

importance of nonmonetary contributions to the household. Of the 46 economies covered by *Women, Business and the Law* with separation of property regimes, 10 have legislation expressly recognizing nonmonetary contributions: Australia; Hong Kong SAR, China; Ireland; Jamaica; Kenya; Malaysia; Tanzania; the United Kingdom; the United States; and Zambia.

Getting a job

All the economies covered by *Women, Business and the Law* have labor regulations that differentiate between women and men. Some of these differences may facilitate women's workforce participation—while others may prevent it. Differences in how women and men are treated under labor law can affect women's incentives and abilities to get the jobs of their choice.

One common reason given by policy makers for restricting women's access to certain jobs is the desire to protect them. Historically these measures stemmed from the perceived need to protect women's physical integrity and reproductive capacity. In 1908 the U.S. Supreme Court upheld an Oregon state statute that limited the workday to 10 hours for women employed in any mechanical establishment, factory or laundry. The court held that, notwithstanding the

"freedom of contracts" guaranteed by the U.S. constitution, women's physiques and the performance of maternal functions required workplace protections.[14] After this decision, other states enacted similar protective legislation, such as maximum hour and minimum wage laws, health and safety regulations and prohibition of night work and certain occupations.

With rapid changes in social mores and the incorporation of women into the global workforce, many such restrictions no longer serve their original purpose. Better safety standards and technology also raise the question of whether such protections are still needed for women—particularly women who are not pregnant or nursing—but not men.

Restrictions on women's work

To better understand gender-specific job restrictions, the Getting a job indicator examines jobs where women are more likely to face employment restrictions. *Women, Business and the Law* records eight areas of work where women face partial or complete employment bans: mining, construction, metalwork, factory work, jobs requiring lifting objects above a certain weight, jobs considered too hazardous for women, jobs considered too arduous for women and jobs considered morally inappropriate for women (box 2.4).

Though the definition of jobs considered morally inappropriate for women suffers from a lack of specificity, the opposite may be true of other gender-based job restrictions. Economies in Eastern Europe and Central Asia, for example, have detailed and lengthy lists of jobs prohibited for women (table 2.3).

Of the 143 economies covered, 79 restrict women who are not pregnant or nursing from doing all the same jobs as men. Restrictions on working hours, sectors and occupations limit the range of jobs that women can hold and can lead to occupational segregation and women's confinement to low-paying sectors and activities.[15] In fact, many of the jobs prohibited for women are in highly paid industries such as mining and manufacturing.

This has real implications for women's earnings potential. The Russian Federation had a high gender earnings differential during its transition to a market economy largely because of occupational segregation by gender. That segregation was related more to gender-based job restrictions in Soviet-era labor regulations than to gender differences in education or the higher incidence of part-time work among women. Because of their maternity and childcare functions, women were considered a specific labor force barred from "unsuitable" occupations and encouraged to concentrate in healthcare, education, light industry and white collar jobs.[16]

Restrictions on the types of work that women pursue can also hurt firms and an economy's overall competitiveness. The pool of qualified candidates for open positions is artificially halved, reducing the likelihood of getting the most talented people for the jobs. Analyzing the number of restrictions on women's work in the eight areas examined shows that having more restrictions is associated with lower labor force participation by women (figure 2.7).

Maternity and parental benefits and women's employment

Though restrictions on women's work may lead to fewer women working, other areas of labor legislation—such as parental leave regimes—can increase women's participation in the workforce. Parental benefits enabling mothers, fathers or both to take paid or unpaid time off to care for a child following birth can foster a more equitable division of childrearing responsibilities in the family. This in turn can give women greater opportunities for career advancement. *Women, Business and the Law* measures the length of paid and unpaid maternity, paternity and parental leave and the rate at which it is paid.

More women participate in the labor force in economies with longer fully paid maternity and parental leave available for new mothers.[17] But too much leave can undermine women's labor force participation. In economies where the cumulative

---

| BOX 2.4 | JOBS LEGALLY DEEMED MORALLY INAPPROPRIATE FOR WOMEN |

Some economies prohibit women from working in jobs legally deemed harmful to their moral character. Though this is an explicit restriction in labor codes, jobs that are "morally harmful" to women are often not defined objectively but left to employers to determine. Working at night can fall into this category if employers feel working at night is morally harmful to women. Bolivia's General Labor Law prohibits women from working in "occupations that harm their morality and good customs" but does not define what that means, leaving it to employers to interpret.

Labor codes can also conflate jobs that are morally inappropriate for women with those that are morally inappropriate for children without explaining what such jobs may entail. An example is Mauritania's Labor Code, which prohibits the employment of children under 18, women and pregnant women for tasks that exceed their strength or might harm their health, physical integrity or moral conduct. Where women and children are treated the same way under labor law, it may make employers more likely to feel that women are incapable of carrying out particular jobs.

Source: FAO 1994.

| TABLE 2.3 | NUMBER AND EXAMPLES OF JOBS PROHIBITED FOR WOMEN IN SOME ECONOMIES IN EASTERN EUROPE AND CENTRAL ASIA |

Economies	Number of specific jobs from which women are barred	Examples
Belarus	252	Diver; porter; lumberjack; carpenter; stonecutter; repairer of wagons; transporting timber; tractor-driver; direct firefighting and emergency response; aircraft mechanic (technician) of radio equipment; pouring steel; laying concrete and asphalt; cross-border driver of vehicles with 14 or more passengers or trucks weighing more than 5 tons; processing of fish and seafood involving hand-mixing fish in salting tanks.
Kazakhstan	299	Snowmobile driver; metal welder; machinist for diesel trains, locomotives, and electric multiple unit trains; railway fitter; operating cranes at sea; stoker of ship operating on solid fuel; drilling for oil and gas for developmental and exploration purposes; rubber-mixing equipment operator; blaster in mines; calibrator of pipes on the press; concrete products carver; presser of raw materials and fibers during initial processing of cotton; rescuer in gas emergencies; lumberjack.
Russian Federation	456	Truck driver in agriculture; freight train conductor; deckhand (boatswain, skipper, assistant skipper and sailors of all denominations) on ships of all types of fleets as well as floating docks and cranes for loading grain, cement, coal and other dusty cargo; worker in integrated teams and longshoreman engaged in loading and unloading in ports and harbors; woodworker; installer of antennas at high places; mining rig operator; operator of chemical treatment of wells; lift machinist in oil and gas industry; bulldozer machinist; plumber involving the repair of sewer networks; metal and alloy smelter; driver of loading machine; pipe, furnace and flue cleaner; controller of speed of train wagons.

Source: Women, Business and the Law database

Key Findings

FIGURE 2.7 **RESTRICTIONS ON JOBS OPEN TO WOMEN CAN REDUCE THE NUMBER OF WOMEN IN THE WORKFORCE**

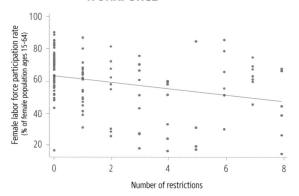

Source: Women, Business and the Law database; World Bank *World Development Indicators* database.

Note: The negative relationship between the number of restrictions on women's work and the female labor force participation rate is statistically significant at the 5% level even after controlling for 2011 income per capita. This relationship is based on regression analysis involving 103 economies for which data on 2011 income per capita are available. The figure is based on 139 economies for which data are available. These statistical relationships cannot be interpreted as causal.

duration of paid maternity and parental leave available for mothers exceeds two years, female labor force participation is lower.[18]

There are several possible reasons. Because women tend to take most or all of their leave entitlement, long periods of leave might cause their skills to deteriorate or become less relevant, slowing their earnings and career progression. They might also lose touch with their professional network, which can reduce their opportunities for career advancement. Finally, employers may be less willing to hire women who they suspect will take long maternity leaves in the near future.

These findings are consistent with a study of the labor market effect of paid leave in 30 OECD economies. Looking at paid leave duration and female employment rates between 1970 and 2010, the study finds that extending paid leave results, on average, in higher female employment rates as long as the leave is less than two years. Additional weeks of leave have a negative impact on female employment and the gender employment gap.[19]

Going to court

Women's access to justice can be hindered by limits on their representation in judicial institutions. The United Nations

estimates that globally women account for 27% of all judges.[20] Evidence is emerging that women judges can make a difference in outcomes of cases where gender is a salient issue. For example, an analysis of U.S. federal appellate cases in 1999, 2000 and 2001 found that a judge's gender mattered in cases involving sex discrimination or sexual harassment. Plaintiffs were twice as likely to win when a women was on the panel deciding such cases. The data showed both that women judges were significantly more likely than their male counterparts to find for the plaintiff in such cases and that having a woman on the panel increased the probability that male judges would support the plaintiff.[21]

Where gender equality is guaranteed in the constitution, constitutional reviews—that is, supervising implementation of the constitution and jettisoning incompatible laws—allow challenges to discriminatory provisions in areas of law such as the civil code, family law and criminal law. In 2004 South Africa's Constitutional Court decided that the rule of primogeniture in customary law, under which the eldest son inherits the family land, was unconstitutional because of its discriminatory impact on African women and children—arguably the most vulnerable groups in society.[22] Over the years most economies have established institutional mechanisms to conduct constitutional reviews. These reviews vary across economies and legal traditions. To examine women's representation in constitutional reviews as judges and chief justices, *Women, Business and the Law* examines courts or court-like bodies mandated to conduct such reviews.

Among the 123 economies covered by *Women, Business and the Law* that have constitutional courts or court-like bodies, women are absent from 19: Cameroon; the Democratic Republic of Congo; Egypt; El Salvador; Hong Kong SAR, China; the Islamic Republic of Iran; Jordan; Kuwait; Lebanon; Mauritania; Moldova; Pakistan; Panama; Peru; Senegal; Thailand; Uruguay; the United Arab Emirates and the Republic of Yemen.

On the other hand, women judges preside over constitutional reviews in 16 economies: Bosnia and Herzegovina, Canada, Costa Rica, Croatia, Gabon, Ghana, Ireland, Jamaica, New Zealand, Niger, Nigeria, the Philippines, Sierra Leone, the Slovak Republic, República Bolivariana de Venezuela and Zambia.

Women account for 10% or less of the members of constitutional courts in nine economies: Belgium, Chile, Hungary, India, Italy, Morocco, Nepal, Turkey and United Kingdom. In 71 economies women make up between 11% and 33% of institutions in charge of constitutional reviews. In18 economies women represent between 34% and 50% of constitutional judges. And in six economies—Bolivia, the Kyrgyz Republic, Latvia, Sierra Leone, Slovenia and Zambia—women account for more than 50% of members of constitutional courts.

Building credit

Establishing a good credit history can help entrepreneurs access finance. Lenders rely on credit histories to distinguish diligent clients from those with late payment records or defaulting loans. Borrowers who build and maintain good credit histories are rewarded with enhanced reputation collateral, giving them the ability to qualify for larger loans and lower interest rates.[23]

Several factors can affect women's ability to build credit histories. Where public credit registries and private credit bureaus only record loans above a certain threshold, they might exclude small borrowers like female entrepreneurs. Where credit registries and bureaus do not record loans from microfinance institutions—for whom women make up a large share of borrowers—the good repayment histories of microfinance clients cannot be leveraged. Finally, where information from nonbank institutions such as retailers and utilities is not used to assess borrowers' creditworthiness, it excludes those who lack traditional banking relationships, many of whom are women.

Of the 143 economies covered by *Women, Business and the Law*, only 6 do not have a public credit registry or private credit bureau (the Democratic Republic of Congo, Jamaica, Lesotho, Malawi, Sudan and Tanzania). Among the 136 economies with credit reporting institutions, 16 have minimum loan thresholds higher than 1% of income per capita. In this group thresholds range from 49% of income per capita in Lebanon and 87% in Bangladesh to more than 20 times income per capita in Nepal and Niger.

Among the 104 low-income, lower-middle-income and upper-middle-income economies covered, microfinance institutions share credit information with public registries or private bureaus in 67. For example, in 2002 Nicaragua's microfinance institutions began sharing such information through Sin Riesgos, a credit bureau promoted by the Nicaraguan Association of Microfinance Institutions (ASOMIF). By 2004 the Law on Bank Secrecy allowed commercial banks, which already shared information through the public credit registry, to access potential clients' credit histories from private credit bureaus. Today commercial banks can access Sin Riesgos records of microfinance clients and assess their creditworthiness and eligibility for conventional loans.

Across all income groups, credit bureaus and registries also collect information from retailers in 40 economies and from utilities in 30. In Rwanda two mobile phone companies and an electricity and gas company have shared information with the country's credit bureau since 2011. On the other hand, the five economies in South Asia covered by *Women, Business and the Law* have credit reporting institutions, but none collects information from retailers or utilities. Overall, in 25 of the economies measured both retailers and utilities provide information to credit reporting institutions.

Conclusion

Evidence is emerging on the value of reforms improving women's legal parity. In 2000 Ethiopia revised its Family Code, which had been in place since 1960. Among other things, the reform eliminated a husband's right to deny his wife permission to work and required the consent of both spouses in the administration of marital property.

Though the reform has now been implemented throughout Ethiopia, it was first introduced in three regions and two charter cities. Two nationally representative surveys, one before the reform and the other five years later, allowed researchers to estimate the reform's impact. Where the reform was followed, women's labor force participation and work outside the home increased. Women were also more likely to work full-time and in higher-skilled jobs.[24]

Similarly, in 1994 two states in India—Karnataka and Maharashtra—reformed the Hindu Succession Act, giving women and men equal rights to inherit joint family property. This change altered the control of assets in families and increased parental investments in their daughters.[25]

The findings from these studies are consistent with analysis of similar reforms. For example, around the turn of the 20th century most U.S. states reformed legislation affecting married women's ability to own and administer property and conduct legal transactions. And state census data showed that expanding women's economic rights through legal reform led more girls to attend school.[26]

There is growing evidence showing the links between women's legal rights and economic opportunities. *Women, Business and the Law 2014* provides a rich body of data that can generate further research and policy action in this area. This report has shown that although much progress has been made in recent decades in gradually dismantling many of the legal restrictions which have hampered women from more fully contributing to national prosperity, there is a large unfinished agenda of reform. In too many economies across all regions the law is still being used to hold women back, to silence their voices and limit their actions—imposing large tangible costs linked to these constraints on women's freedom. Gender equality is important not only for fairness and equity, but also for economic efficiency and is at the center of creating a more prosperous world.

Endnotes

1 *50 Years of Women's Legal Rights* database.

2 *50 Years of Women's Legal Rights* database.

3 One action was added for *Women, Business and the Law 2014*: Can a woman get a national identity card in the same way as a man?

4 *Women, Business and the Law 2014* covers only mandatory quotas for a certain number of seats reserved for women and not quotas for women on candidate lists.

5 The results of the regression analysis of this relationship are statistically significant at the 5% level even when controlling for 2011 income per capita. The analysis includes 103 economies for which data are available and shows that legal quotas are positively correlated with the proportion of seats held by women in parliaments. These statistical relationships cannot be interpreted as causal.

6 Chattopadhyay and Duflo 2004.

7 Chen 2010.

8 The relationship is statistically significant at the 10% level even when controlling for 2011 income per capita. The regression analysis includes 103 economies for which data are available.

9 Beaman and others 2012.

10 Deere and León 2003a; Quisumbing and Hallman 2005; Deere and Doss 2006.

11 Demirgüç-Kunt, Klapper and Singer 2013.

12 Deere and others 2012.

13 The Global Financial Inclusion (Global Findex) database's variable "Account at a formal financial institution, female (% age 15+)" is not disaggregated by marital status. In the analysis of the relationship between marital property regimes and accounts at a formal financial institution it is assumed that all women are married.

14 Muller v. Oregon 208 U.S. 412 (1908).

15 World Bank 2011.

16 Oglobin 1999.

17 The regression analysis shows a positive relationship that is statistically significant at the 5% level even when controlling for 2011 income per capita. The analysis includes 114 economies for which data are available. These statistical relationships cannot be interpreted as causal.

18 The results of the regression analysis of this relationship are statistically significant at the 10% level even when controlling for 2010 income per capita. To analyze this relationship, 2010 income per capita was used as a control variable, as opposed to 2011, due to missing 2011 data on 11 economies that drive the results. The analysis includes 103 economies for which data are available. The variable "paid maternity leave and parental leave available for the mother" includes the number of days of leave paid at various rates, as opposed to the number of days of leave paid at 100% of wages used in the previous relationship. These statistical relationships cannot be interpreted as causal.

19 Thévenon and Solaz 2013.

20 UN Women 2011.

21 Peresie 2005.

22 South Africa Constitutional Court 2004.

23 Miller 2003.

24 Hallward-Driemeier and Gajigo 2010.

25 Deininger, Goyal and Nagarajan 2010.

26 Geddes, Lueck and Tennyson 2012.

Spotlight on Violence against Women

In 1983 Maria da Penha Fernandes was shot by her husband. Two weeks after she returned from the hospital, he tried to electrocute her. She survived but was left paralyzed. Criminal charges were filed and the case took almost 20 years to wind through the Brazilian courts. When her husband was finally sentenced in 2002, he served only two years.

The Inter-American Commission of Human Rights held the Brazilian government responsible for failing to take action against perpetrators of domestic violence. In response, in 2006 the Brazilian government enacted the Maria da Penha Law—the first Brazilian law providing comprehensive measures addressing domestic violence. This was a milestone in the country's fight against gender-based violence.[1]

Laws protecting women from domestic violence have evolved in the wake of cases such as that of Maria da Penha. But violence against women is still widespread around the world. Globally, the World Health Organization estimates that 35% of women have experienced physical or sexual violence.[2]

Effects and economic repercussions of violence against women

Aside from its obvious negative psychological and social effects, violence against women undermines their autonomy and enjoyment of fundamental rights and freedoms. It coerces preferences, behaviors and actions and poses obstacles to women's economic empowerment by restricting their capacity to make choices. Accepting job offers, pursuing university degrees or investing in new business ventures all become out of reach to a woman facing violence in her home or workplace.

Beyond the costs to individual women, violence also has macroeconomic repercussions. These include higher costs

---

BOX 3.1   DEFINING DOMESTIC VIOLENCE AND SEXUAL HARASSMENT

Domestic violence is gender-specific violence commonly directed against women, occurring in the family and interpersonal relationships. Interpersonal relationships can include partners who do not live together or are not married. The violence can be in the form of physical, emotional or psychological, sexual, or financial or economic abuse.

- *Physical violence* is any behavior that offends a woman's bodily integrity or health.

- *Emotional or psychological violence* is any behavior that causes emotional damage and reduces self-worth or self-esteem (or both) or that aims at degrading or controlling a woman's actions, behaviors, beliefs and decisions by means of threat, embarrassment, humiliation, manipulation, isolation, constant surveillance or pursuit, insult, intimidation, blackmail, ridicule, exploitation or any other behavior that damages a woman's psychological health.

- *Sexual violence* is any behavior that forces a woman to witness, maintain or participate in unwanted sexual contact or behavior by means of intimidation, threat, coercion or use of force, including sexual assault, marital rape or forcing any type of sexual activity without consent.

- *Financial or economic violence* is any behavior involving deprivation of financial or economic resources, including disposition, retention or subtraction of money or property or other means making or attempting to make a woman financially dependent by maintaining control over financial resources.

Sexual harassment is any unwelcome sexual advance, request for sexual favor, verbal or physical conduct or gesture of a sexual nature or any other behavior of a sexual nature that might reasonably be expected or be perceived to cause offense or humiliation to another. Such harassment may be but is not necessarily of a form that interferes with work, is a condition of employment or creates an intimidating, hostile or offensive work environment.

Source: United Nations General Assembly 1993; United Nations Economic and Social Council 1996; UNHCR 2005; United Nations 2008 ; U.S. Department of Justice 2013 ; John Hopkins University School of Advanced International Studies Protection Project and Suzanne Mubarak Regional Centre for Women's Health and Development 2010.

for healthcare and justice systems and lost productivity in local businesses. Though estimates vary across economies and there are legitimate debates about the methodologies used, the annual costs of domestic violence run as high as $19.8 billion in Sweden[3] and $2.9 billion in Spain.[4] In Fiji domestic violence cost an estimated 7% of GDP in 2002,[5] while a 2009 study in Canada found that violence against women cost criminal and civil justice systems $379 million a year.[6]

Other studies covering losses from premature death and lower productivity related to domestic violence show similar effects. A U.S. study estimated costs from injuries and deaths at $5.8 billion in 1995, while in Canada the loss of tax revenues due to death, lost time at work and incarceration exceeded $77 million a year.[7] Moreover, the impact of violence against women can extend into future generations. In Nicaragua 63% of children of abused women had to repeat a school year and left school an average of four years earlier than other children.[8]

Laws protecting women from violence

Women can function more freely in society and the business world when not faced with the threat of violence. *Women, Business and the Law 2014* includes pilot data for a new indicator on Protecting women against violence. Though there are many forms of violence against women, this indicator covers the existence and scope of national laws on domestic violence and sexual harassment in 100 economies.[9]

The data examine laws on physical, emotional or psychological, sexual, and financial or economic abuse in the context of domestic violence, as well as on sexual harassment in employment, public places and educational facilities (box 3.1).

Domestic violence

Women, Business and the Law data show that 76 of the 100 economies covered have laws on domestic violence. This is the case in all 9 economies covered in East Asia and the Pacific and in 17 of the 18 economies covered in Latin America and the Caribbean, with Haiti being the exception.

Four of the five economies covered in South Asia have laws on domestic violence, with Pakistan being the exception. Laws on domestic violence also protect women in 11 of the 15 economies covered in Eastern Europe and Central Asia, 17 of the 26 in Sub-Saharan Africa and 16 of the 17 OECD high-income economies, with Canada being the exception. Though most Canadian provinces have passed legislation on the matter, Ontario—home to the country's main business city, Toronto—has yet to do so. Intrafamily violence can be prosecuted under general criminal law in Ontario, but no specific provisions on domestic violence exist.[10]

Laws on domestic violence are less prevalent in the Middle East and North Africa. Out of 100 economies covered, 24 economies have no laws on domestic violence (figure 3.1).

Of the 100 economies measured, 76 include specific provisions on physical violence, 69 include provisions on emotional or psychological violence, 57 cover sexual violence, and 47 address financial or economic violence.[11] Only 44 economies have provisions covering all four types of violence.

FIGURE 3.1 ROUGHLY 25% OF THE ECONOMIES MEASURED HAVE NO LAWS ON DOMESTIC VIOLENCE

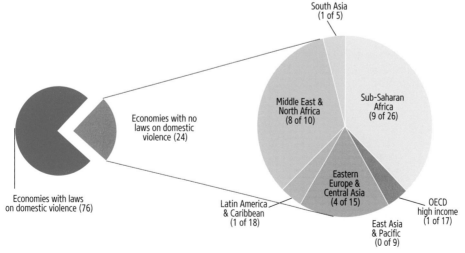

Source: : Women, Business and the Law database.

For example, Chile's Intrafamily Violence Act and Italy's Law on Measures against Violence in Family Relations do not address sexual and financial abuse. Other economies have drafted but not enacted such legislation. Haiti is working on a draft comprehensive law on the Prevention, Sanction and Elimination of Violence against Women, and Lebanon's Parliament is considering a draft bill on domestic violence that was introduced in 2010.[12]

A number of the economies measured by *Women, Business and the Law* have no laws on domestic violence despite well-documented problems. In the Russian Federation 600,000 women a year suffer from domestic violence according to official estimates. Yet after many years of discussion, no legislation exists to address it.[13]

Mechanisms that support victims and denounce aggressors can make laws more effective. Colombia's law on gender violence stipulates that victims of domestic violence cannot withdraw their complaints and that people other than victims can report incidents.[14] Similarly relevant is the role of institutions in preventing and punishing crimes. Mexico's General Law on Women's Access to a Life Free of Violence lays out specific responsibilities for federal, state and municipal governments to address matters such as victim assistance.[15]

Abuse also affects unmarried women.[16] According to *Women, Business and the Law* data, 68 economies protect women in intimate partner relationships. All the economies covered in East Asia and the Pacific and all but one in Latin America and the Caribbean include such provisions. Of the

17 OECD high-income economies covered, 15 protect women in nonmarital relationships. That is also the case in 4 of the 5 economies covered in South Asia and 10 of the 15 economies covered in Eastern Europe and Central Asia. But only 13 of the 26 economies covered in Sub-Saharan Africa and none in the Middle East and North Africa include provisions protecting women in intimate partner relationships.

Sexual harassment

Between 40% and 50% of women in the European Union have reported sexual harassment in the workplace.[17] In Japan, the Republic of Korea, Malaysia and the Philippines 30% to 40% of women suffer sexual harassment in the workplace.[18] And an Australian survey found that two-thirds of the sexual harassment reported by women occurred in the workplace.[19]

In addition to endangering the well-being of workers, sexual harassment undermines careers, the ability to work, work climate and motivation.[20] Its effects also extend to employers. Staff taking sick leave or resigning to escape harassment has a direct impact on firms' profitability.[21]

Women, Business and the Law examines whether economies formally protect women from sexual harassment in employment. The data show that 78 of the 100 economies covered have laws addressing sexual harassment in employment (table 3.1). But another 8 economies (Argentina, Jordan, Nepal, Singapore, Sierra Leone, Syrian Arab Republic, Tunisia, Yemen, Rep.) have laws on sexual harassment, but fail to specifically address sexual harassment within employment.

TABLE 3.1   LAWS ON SEXUAL HARASSMENT IN EMPLOYMENT VARY BY REGION

Region	Economies with laws on sexual harassment in employment
East Asia & Pacific	Cambodia; China; Fiji; Malaysia; Mongolia; Philippines; Thailand
Eastern Europe & Central Asia	Albania; Armenia; Azerbaijan; Bosnia and Herzegovina; Croatia; Latvia; Lithuania; Macedonia, FYR; Romania; Russian Federation; Serbia; Turkey; Ukraine; Uzbekistan
Latin America & Caribbean	Bolivia; Brazil; Colombia; Costa Rica; Ecuador; El Salvador; Honduras; Mexico; Nicaragua; Panama; Paraguay; Peru; Uruguay; Venezuela, RB
Middle East & North Africa	Algeria; Morocco
OECD high income	Australia; Canada; Chile; Denmark; Finland; France; Germany; Italy; Korea, Rep.; Poland; Portugal; Spain; Sweden; Switzerland; United Kingdom; United States
South Asia	Bangladesh; India; Pakistan; Sri Lanka
Sub-Saharan Africa	Angola; Benin; Burkina Faso; Congo, Dem. Rep.; Côte d'Ivoire; Ethiopia; Kenya; Lesotho; Madagascar; Malawi; Mauritius; Mozambique; Namibia; Niger; Rwanda; Senegal; South Africa; Tanzania; Uganda; Zambia; Zimbabwe

Source: Women, Business and the Law database.

The data also cover whether sexual harassment is subject to criminal sanctions. In 2004 Turkey reformed its Penal Code to criminalize sexual harassment, with increased penalties if the offense is driven by undue influence based on employment hierarchy or by taking advantage of working in the same location as the victim.[22] Labor-related sexual harassment is criminalized in 52 of the 100 economies examined by *Women, Business and the Law* (figure 3.2).

Sexual harassment in education can also affect women. In Malawi, for example, half of schoolgirls surveyed reported sexual harassment at school.[23] Specific laws may help lower such figures by requiring educational facilities to prevent and address sexual harassment. However, laws on sexual harassment in educational facilities are less prevalent than those covering employment. Of the 100 economies covered, 32 offer specific protection against sexual harassment in education—none of which are in the Middle East and North Africa (table 3.2).

Sexual harassment in public places, including on the street and public transportation, can lead women to change their habits, avoid certain places or restrict their movement.[24] A 2011 survey in London found that 43% of women between 18 and 34 had experienced sexual harassment in public spaces.[25] Laws may increase awareness of this issue and promote safety for women in public spaces.[26] Only 8 of the economies measured by *Women, Business and the Law* have laws on sexual harassment in public spaces: Benin, Ethiopia and Zambia in Sub-Saharan Africa, Bangladesh and Pakistan in South Asia, Fiji in East Asia and the Pacific, Ecuador in

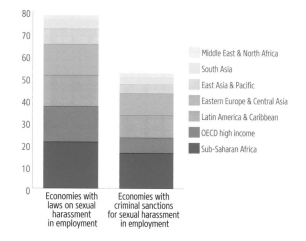

FIGURE 3.2 LAWS INCLUDING CRIMINAL SANCTIONS FOR SEXUAL HARASSMENT IN EMPLOYMENT, BY REGION

Legend:
- Middle East & North Africa
- South Asia
- East Asia & Pacific
- Eastern Europe & Central Asia
- Latin America & Caribbean
- OECD high income
- Sub-Saharan Africa

Source: Women, Business and the Law database.

Latin America and the Caribbean and Canada among OECD high-income economies.

Absence of legislation

Economies with laws on domestic violence are also likely to have provisions on sexual harassment, and vice versa, as in 69 of the economies covered (figure 3.3). But 7 economies

TABLE 3.2 FEW ECONOMIES HAVE SPECIFIC PROVISIONS ON SEXUAL HARASSMENT IN EDUCATIONAL INSTITUTIONS AND PUBLIC PLACES

Region	Economies with laws on sexual harassment in educational facilities	Economies with laws on sexual harassment in public places
East Asia & Pacific	Fiji; Philippines	Fiji
Eastern Europe & Central Asia	Albania; Bosnia and Herzegovina; Croatia; Macedonia, FYR	None
OECD high income	Australia; Finland; Korea, Rep.; Poland; Spain; Sweden; United Kingdom; United States	Canada
Latin America & Caribbean	Argentina; Bolivia; Costa Rica; Ecuador; El Salvador; Honduras; Mexico; Nicaragua; Peru; Uruguay; Venezuela, RB	Ecuador
Middle East & North Africa	None	None
South Asia	Bangladesh; Sri Lanka	Bangladesh; Pakistan
Sub-Saharan Africa	Benin; Ethiopia; Kenya; Mauritius; Zambia	Benin; Ethiopia; Zambia

Source: Women, Business and the Law database.

FIGURE 3.3

MOST ECONOMIES HAVE LAWS ON DOMESTIC VIOLENCE, SEXUAL HARASSMENT OR BOTH—BUT SOME HAVE NEITHER

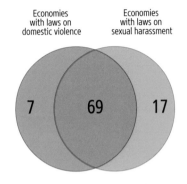

Economies with laws on domestic violence | Economies with laws on sexual harassment | Economies with no laws on domestic violence or sexual harassment

7   69   17

Cameroon
Egypt, Arab Rep.
Haiti
Iran, Islamic Rep.
Lebanon
Mali

Source: Women, Business and the Law database.

have no legislation in either area.[27] Where no specific laws exist, crimes such as assault or battery are still prosecuted under general criminal law. But specific laws on violence against women provide a clear framework addressing its elements and include mechanisms to protect and support women seeking assistance.

The way forward

The dataset for the pilot Protecting women from violence indicator takes a first step toward answering questions on the scope and coverage of laws on domestic violence and sexual harassment. It covers one piece of the picture but does not include the full range of issues involved in preventing and protecting women from violence.

Other critical areas that are not covered include provisions preventing forced or early marriage and sanctions on marital rape.[28] Budgetary commitments to ensure implementation of laws, orders of protection, legal aid and specialized services for victims of violence are equally important areas that are not yet sufficiently measured or understood.

Endnotes

1   Rodriguez de Assis Machado and others 2012.

2   WHO: Global and Regional Estimates of Violence against Women: Prevalence and Health Effects of Intimate Partner Violence and Nonpartner Sexual Violence, http://apps.who.int/iris/bitstream/10665/85239/1/9789241564625_eng.pdf

3   Enval and Erikssen 2004; UN Women 2013.

4   Day, McKenna and Bowlus 2005.

5   UN Women 2013.

6   Zhang and others 2009.

7   Day, McKenna and Bowlus 2005.

8   UN Women Virtual Knowledge Centre to End Violence Against Women and Girls: Costs and Consequences, http://www.endvawnow.org/en/articles/301-consequences-and-costs-.html

9   The full list of economies covered can be found in the data notes.

10 Ontario passed the Domestic Violence Protection Act in 2000, but it was never proclaimed in force and was repealed in 2009. *Women, Business and the Law's* methodology examines applicable laws in the main business city of the economy in question. In federal economies both federal legislation and state or provincial level laws may be applicable. Though no law specifically addresses domestic violence in Ontario, most forms of domestic violence—such as intrahousehold assault—are prohibited under the Criminal Code of Canada, which applies in all Canadian provinces and territories. More information on these laws is available at http://www.justice.gc.ca/eng/pi/fv-vf/laws-lois.html/

11 Tunisia has aggravated penalties for physical abuse between spouses, but no laws or provisions covering domestic violence generally.

12 Human Rights Watch 2013.

13 BBC News 2013 http://www.bbc.co.uk/news/world-europe-21474931

14 Law 1257 to guarantee women the right to live free from violence.

15 Immigration and Refugee Board of Canada 2013.

16 UN Women 2010.

17 http://www.un.org/womenwatch/osagi/pdf/shworkpl.pdf

18 UN Women Fast Facts: Statistics on Violence against Women and Girls, http://www.endvawnow.org/en/articles/299-fast-facts-statistics-on-violence-against-women-and-girls-.html/

19 Australian Human Rights and Equal Opportunity Commission survey cited in Advocates for Human Rights, Stop Violence Against Women, Prevalence of Sexual Harassment, http://www.stopvaw.org/prevalence_of_sexual_harassment/

20 EU 1998.

21 European Union Commission Recommendation of 27 November 1991 in Advocates for Human Rights, Stop Violence Against Women, Effects of Sexual Harassment, http://www.stopvaw.org/effects_of_sexual_harassment/

22 Criminal Code of Turkey, http://legislationline.org/documents/action/popup/id/6872/preview/

23 http://www.un.org/womenwatch/daw/vaw/launch/english/v.a.w-consequenceE-use.pdf

24 Institute for Women's Policy Research, http://www.iwpr.org/blog/2011/04/08/more-research-needed-to-help-prevent-street-harassment/

25 YouGov survey of 1,047 Londoners commissioned by End Violence Against Women Coalition cited in http://www.rawstory.com/rs/2012/05/25/study-43-percent-of-women-experienced-street-harassment-in-britain/

26 Bowman 1993.

27 Saudi Arabia passed a law on domestic violence in August, 2013, outside the period of coverage of this report.

28 The pilot dataset does not include a specific question on legislation criminalizing marital rape, though most laws on sexual violence include marital rape.

The Default Marital Property Regime and Women's Entrepreneurship:

The Case of Chile

Like many Chilean couples, when Sonia Arce and Patricio Salinas were married in 1976, they did not opt out of the default marital property regime of *sociedad conyugal* (marital society). Established in the mid-1800s, this system grants the husband full administrative rights over all joint property as well as both his and his wife's personal property.[1]

Marital regimes define how each spouse can use personal or joint property during marriage. They also determine how assets will be divided upon divorce or death. Couples who want to choose an alternative arrangement must first be aware of the default regime and then go through the process of opting out.

In 1983 Sonia Arce and her husband separated. Because Chile did not recognize divorce at the time, separation was her only option.[2] In 1993 and 1994 Arce and her siblings inherited property upon the death of their parents. They decided to sell the property. But because of the marital property regime in Chile that applied to her assets, Arce was legally required to obtain her estranged husband's permission for any transaction regarding her personal property.[3]

Property rights within marriage and women's participation in the economy

The structure of marital property regimes can help explain gender gaps in access to capital for women. For instance, analysis using data from *Women, Business and the Law* and the Global Financial Inclusion Database (Global Findex) shows that in economies where women marry under *full community of property*—a regime in which all property, including that acquired by each spouse before and during marriage, becomes joint property—a higher percentage have bank accounts in formal financial institutions. Analysis also reveals that women borrow less from financial institutions in economies where women have fewer formal property rights. On average, there are 9 percentage points fewer women with loans in economies where women do not have the same property rights as men.[4]

Administrative rights over personal and joint property within marriage are especially important. Most legal systems have adopted default marital property regimes that grant both spouses the same ability to administer and control their property without any restrictions. However, in five economies measured by *Women, Business and the Law*,

the husband alone administers marital property under the default regime. In Latin America and the Caribbean, Chile is the only economy that grants husbands this right. The other four economies are in Sub-Saharan Africa: Cameroon, the Democratic Republic of Congo, the Republic of Congo and Côte d'Ivoire.

These restrictions in Chile are at odds with the progress made over the past two decades in creating a stable macroeconomic environment supportive of private sector activity. Not only has Chile reduced the incidence of extreme poverty to the lowest levels in the region, but it has managed to do so in a context of sound fiscal management, while maintaining very low levels of public indebtedness. Moreover, Chile has also progressed significantly in promoting women's political participation. In 1949 Chilean women were granted the right to vote and acquired eligibility for public office. That paved the way for a rate of more than 50 percent of women voting by 1989 and for Chile to elect its first female president in 2005.

Property rights of married women in Latin America and the Caribbean

In many cases unequal provisions on control of marital property are the legacy of former colonizers. In Latin America most economies trace their legislation to the Spanish Civil Code, which itself was strongly influenced by the French *Code Napoléon*.

A common feature of civil codes in Latin America during the 19th century was the limited legal capacity of married women, who were subject to *marital power*. Andrés Bello, author of the 1855 Chilean Civil Code, defined marital power as "the sum of rights that the law gives to the husband over the person and property of his wife."

This language was reproduced in civil codes across the region.[5] The concept of marital power limited married women's capacity to administer property and rendered husbands as decision makers over all property within marriage.

During the late 19th and early 20th centuries, some Central American economies—where family and property law derived from Spanish law but were also influenced by German legislation—reformed their laws and adopted *deferred community of property regimes* as the default. In this arrangement, married women administer their separate property but are protected at a marriage's dissolution by a presumption of community, allowing for equal division of joint property between spouses.

Many of the economies that recognized marital power also reformed their laws. In Latin America, reforms eliminating marital power were enacted by Mexico in 1917 and by Colombia in 1932 (figure 4.1).[6] In Argentina initial steps toward granting married women greater rights occurred in 1926, but it was not until 1968 that marital power was repealed. More recently, Spain removed marital power in 1975,[7] Peru in 1984, Paraguay in 1992, and Panama in 1994.[8]

Most economies in Latin America have repealed marital power. However, some still retain provisions favoring the husband's property rights over the wife's. For example, Ecuador allows the husband's decision to prevail when spouses disagree over the disposition of property.

Chile's legislative framework

Marital property regimes have evolved significantly in Chile over time, granting women greater protections and options for administering property within marriage. With the enactment of the Chilean Civil Code in 1855, husbands retained administrative power over all property within marriage, however a partial protection was granted to a married woman's personal property, whereby it could not be sold without her consent. But this protection did not extend to initiating transactions such as leveraging the property for loans, which were still under the husband's control.

In 1925, new legislation introduced *separation of property* as an optional marital property regime, allowing each spouse administrative control over their own property. With the introduction of the new regime, sociedad conyugal became the default.[9] In 1943, married women were granted greater protections under sociedad conyugal, acquiring administrative control over assets they acquired through work independently from their husbands.[10]

Chile ratified the United Nations Convention on the Elimination of All Forms of Discrimination Against Women in 1989 and repealed marital power at that time, recognizing the full capacity of married women.[11] However, provisions in the Civil Code regulating the default marital property regime and granting husbands administrative rights over their wives' personal property remained in effect.

In 1994, *participation in the accrued value of assets* was adopted as a third marital property regime allowing married women greater options.[12] This regime assumes that during the marriage the husband and wife have separate assets but, as those assets appreciate, both spouses benefit from the increased value of each other's property. Under this arrangement, each spouse retains administrative rights over his or her own assets.

FIGURE 4.1 REMOVAL OF RESTRICTIONS ON MARRIED WOMEN'S PROPERTY RIGHTS IN SPAIN AND 19 ECONOMIES IN LATIN AMERICA AND THE CARRIBEAN

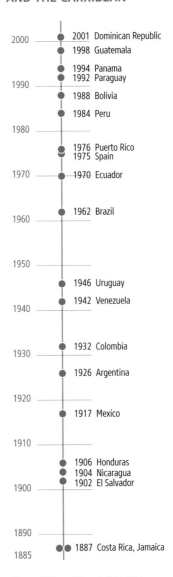

2000	2001 Dominican Republic
	1998 Guatemala
	1994 Panama
1990	1992 Paraguay
	1988 Bolivia
	1984 Peru
1980	
	1976 Puerto Rico
	1975 Spain
1970	1970 Ecuador
1960	1962 Brazil
1950	
	1946 Uruguay
1940	1942 Venezuela
1930	1932 Colombia
	1926 Argentina
1920	
	1917 Mexico
1910	
	1906 Honduras
	1904 Nicaragua
1900	1902 El Salvador
1890	
1885	1887 Costa Rica, Jamaica

Source: 50 Years of Women's Rights database.

Couples in Chile can choose from any of the three marital property regimes. But *sociedad conyugal* remains the default if another selection is not made. According to statistics for 2012 from the Chilean Civil Registry, 55% of Chilean women married under *sociedad conyugal*. Another 43% chose the separation regime and less than 3% opted for the participation in the accrued value of assets regime.

Of the three regimes, only *sociedad conyugal* designates the husband as the administrator of joint assets and his wife's assets—except what she earns through separate employment. The law limits a husband's capacity to manage his wife's property by requiring that he get her consent for major transactions such as alienating or encumbering real property that belongs to the *sociedad conyugal*. The Civil Code also establishes that the wife does not have any rights to the joint assets.[13] Therefore her husband can originate any transaction involving those joint assets. Article 1750 of the Civil Code specifies that "the husband is, with regards to third parties, the owner of all joint assets as if those and his own personal assets conform one patrimony." Consequently, a husband's creditors can take action to recover debts not only against his assets but also the joint marital assets and the personal assets of his wife administered by him.[14]

What does women's entrepreneurship look like in Chile?

Data from Chile's Ministry of Economy reflects that one of every three entrepreneurs is a woman, 42% of whom are married or cohabiting. The average income of women entrepreneurs is one fourth that of male entrepreneurs. Nearly 60% of women who decided to become entrepreneurs said they did so out of necessity, compared with 33% of men.

Six out of ten women's enterprises are informal and 76% of women entrepreneurs' main source of funding for business

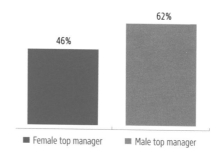

FIGURE 4.2 USE OF IMMOVABLE ASSETS AS COLLATERAL BY CHILEAN FIRMS

Source: World Bank Enterprise Surveys (www.enterprisesurveys.org)

startup is personal savings, suggesting little access to finance.[15] More male managed firms use immovable assets such as land and buildings as collateral when applying for loans than do female managed firms (figure 4.2).

Only 4.5% of small, medium-size and large firms in Chile have female top managers, making Chile the economy with the lowest percentage of female top managers in Latin America and the Caribbean (figure 4.3).

Arce v. Chile

Over the last three decades, there has been an ongoing debate on married women's inability to administer property under the default marital property regime. During the early 1990s Parliament drafted legislation to change this policy, but there was no concrete outcome. In the meantime, women like Sonia Arce have continued to get married under the default marital regime, often without realizing the economic implications of doing so.

FIGURE 4.3 WHAT SHARE OF CHILEAN FIRMS HAVE FEMALE TOP MANAGERS RELATIVE TO OTHER LATIN AMERICAN AND CARIBBEAN ECONOMIES?

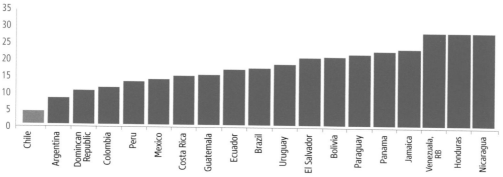

Source: World Bank Enterprise Surveys (www.enterprisesurveys.org)

In Arce's case, not only was she unable to control her own property, but due to her legal situation, her siblings were also prevented from selling their joint inheritance. Arce could have applied to the courts to obtain permission to sell, but she decided to take another course of action.[16] In 2001 she filed a complaint against the Chilean state at the Inter-American Commission on Human Rights.[17]

In 2007 the parties reached an agreement that has yet to be implemented.[18] As part of the settlement, the government of Chile agreed to take all necessary measures to end the legal discrimination against women resulting from the default marital property regime.

In 2011 a proposal was submitted to Parliament repealing husbands' full administrative rights over property under the sociedad conyugal regime. The proposal would eliminate the concept of the husband as head of the sociedad conyugal, providing that spouses shall decide who will administer joint property and, in the absence of agreement, shall be co-administrators. The proposal also requires that each spouse retain administrative power over their personal property, eliminating a husband's power over his wife's personal property under the default regime. In addition, in cases where spouses decide that the husband will administer joint property, the wife will continue to administer assets acquired through her separate work. Approval of the proposed amendments are still pending before Parliament's House of Representatives and Senate.

Endnotes

1 Civil Code of Chile, art.135.

2 Law 10.947, known as Nueva Ley de Matrimonio 2004.

3 Civil Code of Chile, art.1749.

4 Almodóvar-Reteguis, Kushnir and Meilland 2012.

5 Deere and León 2005.

6 Deere and León 2001; Corte Constitucional de Colombia, Sentencia C-068/99.

7 Gobierno de España 1975.

8 Deere and León 2001.

9 Decreto de Ley 328 (1925), art. 8.

10 Civil Code of Chile, arts. 1749 and 1752.

11 Decreto de Ley 18.802 (1989).

12 Decreto de Ley 19.335 (1994).

13 Civil Code of Chile, art. 1752.

14 Civil Code of Chile, art. 1750.

15 Ministry of Economy of Chile 2013.

16 Civil Code of Chile, art. 138.

17 *Sonia Arce Esparza v. Chile*, Caso 071/01, Informe No. 59/03, Inter-Am. C.H.R., OEA/Ser./L/V/II.118 Doc. 70 rev. 2 en 213, 2003.

18 Acuerdo de Solución Amistoase, Caso 12.433 *Sonia Arce Esparza v. Chile* 2007, http://www.humanas.cl/wp-content/uploads/2003/10/Acuerdo_de_Solucion_Amistosa.spdf /

Constitutional Reform and Women's Rights:

The Case of Kenya

Constitutional reform is an effective way to adopt sweeping changes to women's legal position in society. Kenya's 2010 Constitution provides an example of an effective, and comprehensive, legislative reform benefitting women.

Women's groups played a key role in raising women's issues with the Committee of Experts drafting the Constitution. They also lobbied members of Parliament, carried out civic education campaigns and hosted National Women's Strategy Meetings. Their tactics were largely successful and the Kenyan Constitution includes several broad changes equalizing women's position in society.[1]

One of the most significant reforms for women was including customary law—the traditional rules governing personal status and communal resources—in constitutional protections for equality and nondiscrimination. Since independence in 1963, the Kenyan Constitution has prohibited discriminatory laws. In 1997 Parliament included gender as a constitutionally protected category. But customary law was not subject to this protection, so women still faced discrimination on matters of family status and property rights.[2] For example, "wife-inheritance" continued, requiring a widow to marry an in-law in order to retain access to her dead husband's land and ensuring that the land remained within the family's male lineage—a practice known as patrilineal inheritance.[3] Another significant reform in the new Constitution set quotas for women's parliamentary representation.

Customary law and nondiscrimination in Sub-Saharan Africa

While nondiscrimination and equality are guaranteed under many national constitutions, some contain a *clawback* provision, which establishes that nondiscrimination or equality need not apply where customary law is involved. Where clawback provisions exist, as in Zambia, Lesotho and Botswana, the state will abide by and enforce customary law, even if it is in violation of other constitutional provisions.

In order to capture a variety of constitutional approaches, *Women, Business and the Law* examines three areas of constitutional protection: equality, nondiscrimination and nondiscrimination on the basis of gender.

All Sub-Saharan economies covered by *Women, Business and the Law* have either constitutional provisions providing for equality before the law or a nondiscrimination provision in their constitutions (figure 5.1). Constitutional provisions on gender-based nondiscrimination are less common.

Constitutional provisions on customary law

Until 2010 Kenya's Constitution allowed customary law to prevail in matters of marriage, property and inheritance and exempted it from enshrined principles of nondiscrimination and equality. This allowed customary practices such as patrilineal inheritance to continue without constitutional recourse.[4]

Kenya is among the 25 economies in Sub-Saharan Africa covered by *Women, Business and the Law* which recognize customary law in their constitutions. Of these 18 require that customary law conform to constitutional principles of equality and nondiscrimination. However, in Botswana, Chad, Ghana, Lesotho, Mauritius, Sierra Leone and Zambia, customary law need not conform to constitutional provisions on nondiscrimination or equality.

Constitutions that explicitly prohibit discrimination on the basis of gender would be expected to be sensitive to discriminatory customary practices; however 27% of such

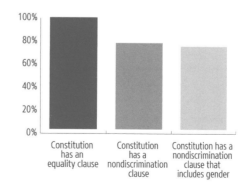

FIGURE 5.1 CONSTITUTIONAL EQUALITY AND NONDISCRIMINATION IN SUB-SAHARAN AFRICA

Source: Women Business and the Law.

economies still exempt customary law from the constitution's nondiscrimination provisions (figure 5.2).

Constitutional protections for women and implementing legislation

After the passage of the Constitution, Kenyan women's rights advocates focused their efforts on enacting implementing legislation to ensure that momentum did not dissipate.

Quotas

One key innovation of the Kenyan Constitution is political quotas for women. Article 27 provides that not more than two-thirds of the members of elective or appointive bodies shall be of the same gender. This affects the judiciary, the legislature, and local governments. There are a variety of arguments in favor of political quotas for women. The justice argument—women represent half the population and have the right to half the seats. The experience argument—women have different experiences that ought to be represented. The interest group argument—women and men have partly conflicting interests and women should therefore represent women's interests. The role model argument—women in parliament are role models, paving the way for other women.[5]

Bodies such as the UN Entity for Gender Equality and the Empowerment of Women advocate the use of quotas to expand women's participation in parliament.[6]

In the Rwandan Parliament, which has the highest proportion of women in the world, women parliamentarians have been active in initiating gender-sensitive laws, improving gender-based government oversight, and forming a caucus to ensure continued women's representation.[7] A study in Rajasthan showed that, once a policy of reserving a third of all council seats and council presidencies for women was implemented, the types of public goods provided in reserved and unreserved village councils differed markedly, with leaders investing more in infrastructure directly relevant to the needs of their gender.[8]

To the consternation of many women's rights activists, Kenya's highest court ruled against implementing a gender quota in parliament ahead of the 2013 elections. Instead, the quota is to be implemented progressively by 2015.[9] Currently there are 65 women in the 350-seat National Assembly, and 18 in the 68-seat Senate. Once the quota is implemented, at least 116 women will have seats in the National Assembly and at least 22 women will be members of the Senate.[10]

Legislation to implement quotas in the judicial system has already been put in place to increase the number of women judges (table 5.1).

Land

Kenya's Constitution is already translating into realities on the ground through reforms in land legislation. Under the Land Registration Act 2012, a wife has an overriding interest in her husband's land, even if she is not noted in the register (table 5.2). The law also gives interest in land to a spouse who has contributed to its productivity, upkeep and improvement.

In the tribal community of Ol Pusimoru, for example, Sara Otione has positively benefited from these reforms. When she separated from her husband, he initially refused to give her a share of their land. Then civil society organizations conducted trainings in rural communities including Otione's, to educate tribal elders on women's newly acquired rights. Subsequently, Otione's husband agreed to share a portion of the family land with her and she is now able to grow food to feed her children and pay for their school fees.[11] The challenge going forward is to ensure that communities are aware of the reforms and are motivated to act on them.

The potential to be a model for reform

Kenya's constitutional reforms have major potential for increasing women's economic empowerment. Customary practices which treated women differently from men are already being set aside, as the newly instituted procedures for land registration demonstrate. It is likely that such changes

---

FIGURE 5.2 SUB-SAHARAN ECONOMIES THAT PROHIBIT GENDER-BASED DISCRIMINATION TREAT CUSTOMARY LAW DIFFERENTLY

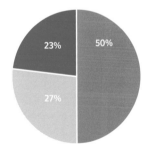

■ Customary law is not recognized in the Constitution

□ Customary law is valid even if it violates constitutional provisions on gender-based discrimination

■ Customary law is invalid if it violates constitutional provisions on gender-based discrimination

Source: Women Business and the Law.

TABLE 5.1	PROGRESS OF WOMEN'S RIGHTS IN THE JUDICIARY IN KENYA
2010 Constitution	**Article 171** ensures women's representation on the Judicial Service Commission.
	Article 27 (6) provides for affirmative action measures and ensures that not more than two-thirds of the members of elective or appointive bodies shall be of the same gender.
Implementing law	**Judicial Service Act No. 1 of 2011** provides that the Commission and the Judiciary shall be guided by considerations of social and gender equity and the need to remove any historical factors of discrimination; it establishes a National Council on the Administration of Justice no more than two-thirds of whose members shall be of the same gender.

TABLE 5.2	PROGRESS OF WOMEN'S LAND RIGHTS IN KENYA
2010 Constitution	**Article 60** ensures the elimination of gender discrimination in law, customs and practices related to land and property in land.
	Article 68 requires revision of land laws to promote gender equality and protect the interests of wives and widows.
Implementing law	**Land Act 2012** prohibits discrimination in land transactions and protects rights to the matrimonial home. It also recognizes customary land rights and local community initiatives in settlement of land disputes, provided they comply with the Constitution.
	Land Registration Act 2012 recognizes spousal rights over matrimonial property as an overriding interest in land, requires joint registration, grants an interest in land to a spouse who has worked the land and requires lenders to inquire as to spousal consent.
	Environmental and Land Court Act No. 19, 2011 obligates courts to consider the elimination of gender discrimination in laws, customs and practices relating to land.

would not have been possible without a constitutional mandate, ensuring that women of all tribal backgrounds, education levels and civil status have equal opportunities on a par with men.

In Sub-Saharan Africa, new Constitutions have also been enacted in Botswana (2012) and Zimbabwe (2013). The Constitution of Botswana added gender as a prohibited ground for discrimination, but continues to exempt customary law. Zimbabwe, by contrast, has followed course with Kenya and no longer exempts customary law from nondiscrimination.

It is rare for constitutions to provide the level of depth on women's rights that is the case in Kenya. However, as legislation implementing these mandates is enacted and translates into realities on the ground, the potential for better economic outcomes for women increases.

Endnotes

1 Maingi 2011.

2 Hallward-Driemeier and Hasan 2012.

3 Harrington and Chopra 2010.

4 Harrington and Chopra 2010.

5 Quota Project, "Quotas—A Key to Equality?" http://www.quotaproject.org/about_research.cfm/.

6 UN News Centre, 2012, "Women's Political Participation Must Be Accelerated through Quotas—UN Official," http://www.un.org/apps/news/story.asp?newsid=41445&cr=un#.Ufpm5qLW6Ck/.

7 Gurirab, Theo-Ben, and Pia Cayetano, 2010, "Women in Politics—The Fight to End Violence against Women," UN Chronicle, http://www.un.org/wcm/content/site/chronicle/home/archive/issues2010/empoweringwomen/womeninpoliticsfightviolenceagainstwomen/.

8 Chattopadhyay and Duflo 2004.

9 Ngugi 2012.

10 Inter Parliamentary Union 2013.

11 Espinosa 2012.

Laws on Sexual Harassment and Domestic Violence in South Asia

In 1997 the case of Vishaka v. State of Rajasthan marked a turning point in addressing sexual harassment in India. It was also a watershed case for South Asia, influencing sexual harassment legislation in Bangladesh and Pakistan.

The *Vishaka* case recognized sexual harassment in the workplace after a social worker in a village in Rajasthan was gang-raped at work. After this incident India's Supreme Court established guidelines making it compulsory for employers to provide grievance mechanisms for sexual harassment.[1] Though the guidelines were considered "binding and enforceable," they did not include strong enforcement mechanisms.

In 2007 the Indian government introduced a bill prohibiting sexual harassment in the workplace.[2] The Sexual Harassment of Women at Workplace (Prevention, Prohibition and Redressal) Act, passed in April 2013, stipulates that women should not be subjected to sexual harassment in the workplace, in transportation to and from work and in dwelling places. The Criminal Law (Amendment) Act was also promulgated in 2013, introducing a section to the Penal Code defining sexual harassment and making it a crime.

Sexual harassment

The *Vishaka* case has been used as a reference point throughout South Asia, including in the 2008 case of *Bangladesh National Women Lawyers Association v. Government of Bangladesh*. Like in the Indian case, in the wake of this case Bangladesh's Supreme Court established binding and legally enforceable guidelines on sexual harassment. But legislation following the guidelines is still pending.

Pakistan also took into account the *Vishaka* case when pushing for the 2010 Protection against Harassment of Women at the Workplace Act.[3] Though this act only provides for administrative penalties ranging from fines to dismissal, in 2009 Pakistan's Penal Code was amended to include provisions and sanctions on sexual harassment in the workplace.

The five South Asian economies examined by *Women, Business and the Law* (Bangladesh, India, Nepal, Pakistan and Sri Lanka) all have provisions and criminal sanctions against sexual harassment. But Nepal does not have criminal sanctions for sexual harassment specific to the workplace and under current laws in Bangladesh there are criminal sanctions for sexual harassment in only some workplaces but not in others. For example, there are no criminal sanctions for sexual harassment in government offices (figure 6.1).[4]

In addition, only Bangladesh and Pakistan specifically legislate against sexual harassment in public places. Bangladesh's Dhaka Metropolitan Police Ordinance establishes a penalty for harassing women "in any street or public place." An amendment to section 509 of Pakistan's Penal Code determines that sexual harassment "might occur in public places including,

---

FIGURE 6.1 **LAWS ON SEXUAL HARASSMENT VARY IN FIVE SOUTH ASIAN ECONOMIES**

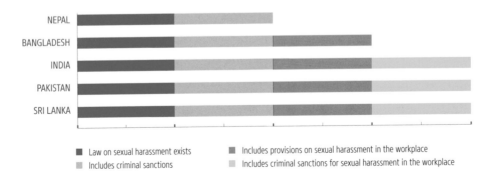

- ■ Law on sexual harassment exists
- ■ Includes criminal sanctions
- ■ Includes provisions on sexual harassment in the workplace
- ■ Includes criminal sanctions for sexual harassment in the workplace

Source: Women, Business and the Law database.

but not limited to, markets, public transport, streets or parks, or it might occur in private places including, but not limited to, work places, private gatherings, or homes."

Another relevant issue addressed by only two of the economies studied is sexual harassment in educational facilities. Sri Lanka's Prohibition of Ragging and Other Forms of Violence in Educational Institutions Act of 1998 was enacted following public outcry over three brutal deaths in 1997 caused by ragging—a form of abuse toward new students in educational institutions.[5] Bangladesh's guidelines against sexual harassment also include specific provisions to ensure a safe environment for students.

Domestic violence

The past 10 years have seen several economies in South Asia enact legislation on domestic violence. Of the five covered by *Women, Business and the Law*, Pakistan is the only one that has yet to enact legislation on domestic violence. The Domestic Violence (Prevention and Protection) Bill is pending approval to become law.

India's Protection of Women from Domestic Violence Act and Sri Lanka's Prevention of Domestic Violence Act, both enacted in 2005, were regional frontrunners in domestic violence legislation. These were followed by Nepal's Domestic Violence (Offence and Punishment) Act in 2009 and Bangladesh's Domestic Violence Prevention and Protection Act in 2010.

India's Protection of Women from Domestic Violence Act addresses the immediate needs of victims of domestic violence,

including protection, shelter and financial relief. It extends to other women living in the family household and stipulates that a woman who is the victim of domestic violence has the right to remain in the household regardless of who owns it. Moreover, the act explicitly and clearly defines domestic violence to include physical, sexual, emotional and economic abuse and encompasses threats of such abuse.

Nearly all the laws on domestic violence in the South Asian economies covered include provisions on physical, sexual, emotional and financial abuse and protect women in nonmarital relationships. The exception is Sri Lanka's domestic violence law, which does not include protection for women against financial abuse (figure 6.2).

The global economic impact of violence against women

In addition to its personal and social ramifications, violence against women imposes economic costs. Though there are no comprehensive figures either globally or for South Asia, country studies have shown that violence against women has significant economic impact.

Domestic violence costs Australian businesses more than $870 million a year due to decreased productivity and reduced work hours.[6] Public and private institutions are also affected because of the costs to hospitals, clinics, courts, law enforcement agencies and welfare organizations.[7] In the United Kingdom in 1996, physical, sexual and psychological abuse in one London borough alone resulted in about $7.8 million in police, civil justice, housing, shelter, social service and healthcare costs.[8]

What promotes legislative reform?

Around the world, as in South Asia, laws have been enacted to explicitly recognize violence against women as a form of discrimination and violation of rights. Economies have included specific provisions in criminal codes, antidiscrimination and gender equality laws, labor codes and other acts to protect women from various types of violence.

But protective legislation for women can vary greatly in degree and scope. Though some economies have enacted legislation covering violence against women in comprehensive and integrated frameworks—such as Ecuador's Act Against Violence towards Women and Families, the U.S. Violence Against Women Act and Zambia's Anti-Gender-Based Violence Act—others have taken a more piecemeal approach, using standalone provisions. Senegal's Penal Code, for example, was amended in 1999 to include an article stating that "one who has deliberately injured or struck

| FIGURE 6.2 | IN THE SOUTH ASIAN ECONOMIES STUDIED, ONLY PAKISTAN HAS NO LAW ON DOMESTIC VIOLENCE |

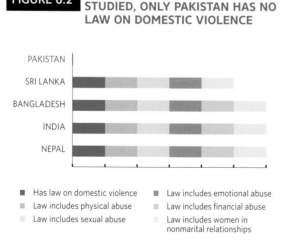

Source: *Women, Business and the Law* database.

or committed any violence or assault against his spouse shall be punished by imprisonment of one to five years and a fine of 50,000 to 500,000 francs if the violence results in illness or incapacity of more than twenty days."

International commitments have led some economies to pass comprehensive legislation or reform laws to encompass certain forms of violence. After the 1993 United Nations Declaration on the Elimination of Violence Against Women and the 1994 Inter-American Convention on the Prevention, Punishment and Eradication of Violence Against Women, several countries—including Bolivia, Colombia, Costa Rica, El Salvador, Honduras, Jamaica, the Republic of Korea, Malaysia and Peru—passed laws on violence against women. Before 1993 only the United Kingdom and the United States had such legislation, and it focused on family violence. Other economies have enacted strong legislation on violence against women in the wake of high-profile incidents such as *Vishaka v. State of Rajasthan*.

Endnotes

1 *Vishaka v. State of Rajasthan* (Air 1997 Supreme Court 3011).

2 *OneWorld South Asia*, 2011, "Groundbreaking Laws Change Women's World," http://southasia.oneworld.net/archive/global headlines/groundbreaking-laws-change-womens-world#. UiiJpzasg18

3 *OneWorld South Asia*, 2011, "Groundbreaking Laws Change Women's World," http://southasia.oneworld.net/archive/global headlines/groundbreaking-laws-change-womens-world#. UiiJpzasg18

4 Bangladesh's Labour Act of 2006 includes provisions and sanctions for sexual harassment in employment, but the act does not apply to a variety of workplaces including government offices.

5 Ashokbharan, Nalliah Kumaraguruparan, 2010, "Ragging in Universities and the Prohibition of Ragging and Other Forms of Violence in Educational Institutions Act, No.20 of 1998," http://nkashokbharan.wordpress.com/2010/05/05/ragging-in-universities-and-the-prohibition-of-ragging-and-other-forms-of-violence-in-educational-institutions-act-no-20-of-1998/

6 Henderson 2000.

7 Social Policy and Development Centre 2012.

8 Stanko and others 1998.

References

Acuerdo de Solución Amistosa. 2007. "Caso N° 12.433 Sonia Arce Esparza v. Chile." http://www.humanas.cl/wp-content/uploads/2003/10/Acuerdo_de_Solucion_Amistosa.pdf.

Allendorf, Keera. 2007. "Do Women's Land Rights Promote Empowerment and Child Health in Nepal?" *World Development* 35 (11): 1975–88.

Almodóvar-Reteguis, Nayda, Khrystyna Kushnir and Thibault Meilland. 2012. "Mapping the Legal Gender Gap in Using Property and Building Credit." World Bank, Washington, DC.

Access Economics. 2004. "The Cost of Domestic Violence to the Australian Economy: Part I." Prepared for the Australian government's Office for the Status of Women, Sydney. http://www.fahcsia.gov.au/sites/default/files/documents/05_2012/cost_of_dv_to_australian_economy_i_1.pdf/.

Averett, Susan L., H. Elizabeth Peters and Donald M. Waldman. 1997. "Tax Credits, Labor Supply and Child Care." *Review of Economics and Statistics* 79 (1): 125–35.

Beaman, Lori, Esther Duflo, Rohini Pande and Petia Topalova. 2012. "Female Leadership Raises Aspirations and Educational Attainment for Girls: A Policy Experiment in India." *Sciencexpress* (January). http://www.hks.harvard.edu/fs/rpande/papers/Female%20Leadership%20Raises%20Aspirations%20Science%202012.pdf.

Bowman, Cynthia Grant. 1993. "Street Harassment and the Informal Ghettoization of Women." *Harvard Law Review* 106 (3): 517–80. http://www.jstor.org/stable/1341656.

CEDAW (Committee on the Elimination of Discrimination against Women). 1992. "General Recommendation No. 19: Violence against Women (Eleventh Session, 1992)." United Nations Document A/47/38, Office of the High Commissioner for Human Rights, Geneva.

———. 2001. "Consideration of Reports Submitted by States Parties under Article 18 of the Convention on the Elimination of All Forms of Discrimination against Women: El Salvador." Convention on the Elimination of All Forms of Discrimination against Women, United Nations, New York. http://www.unhchr.ch/tbs/doc.nsf/0/636963da9e43261fc12572be0035eee7/$FILE/N0158971.pdf/.

Chattopadhyay, Raghabendra, and Esther Duflo. 2004. "Women as Policy Makers: Evidence from a Randomized Policy Experiment in India." *Econometrica* 72 (5): 1409–43.

Chen, Jin-Lu. 2010. "Do Gender Quotas Influence Women's Representation and Policies?" *European Journal of Comparative Economies* 7 (1): 13–60.

Chile Ministry of Economy and Tourism. 2013. "Características del emprendimiento femenino." Santiago.

Civil Registry of Chile. 2012. "Estadísticas con enfoque de género." https://www.registrocivil.cl/f_estadisticas_enfoque_de_genero.html.

Clark, Kathryn Andersen, Andrea K. Biddle and Sandra L. Martin. 2002. "A Cost-Benefit Analysis of the Violence against Women Act of 1994." *Violence against Women* 8 (4): 417–28.

Coleman, Susan. 2000. "Access to Capital and Terms of Credit: A Comparison of Men and Women Owned Small Businesses." *Journal of Small Business Management* 38 (3): 37–52.

Coleman, Susan, and Mary Carsky. 1996. "Understanding the Market of Women-Owned Small Businesses." *Journal of Retail Banking Services* 18 (2): 47–49.

Constitutional Court of South Africa. 2004. "Bhe and Others v Khayelitsha Magistrate and Others." Johannesburg. http://www.saflii.org/za/cases/ZACC/2004/17.html.

Day, Tanis, Katherine McKenna and Audra Bowlus. 2005. "The Economic Costs of Violence against Women: An Evaluation of the Literature." Expert Brief Compiled in Preparation for the Secretary-General's In-Depth Study on All Forms of Violence against Women, United Nations, New York.

Deere, Carmen Diana, and Cheryl R. Doss. 2006. "The Gender Asset Gap: What Do We Know and Why Does It Matter?" *Feminist Economics* 12 (1&2): 1–50.

Deere, Carmen Diana, and Magdalena León. 2001. "Empowering Women: Land and Property Rights in Latin America." University of Pittsburgh, Pittsburgh, PA.

———. 2003a. "Brecha de género en la propiedad de la tierra en América Latina." *Estudios Sociológicos* 22 (65).

———. 2003b. "The Gender Asset Gap: Land in Latin America." *World Development* 31 (6): 925–47.

———. 2005. "Liberalism and Married Women's Property Rights in Nineteenth-Century Latin America." *Hispanic American Historical Review* 85 (4): 627–78.

Deere, Carmen Diana, Abena D. Oduro, Hema Swaminathan and Cheryl Doss. 2012. "Property Rights and the Distribution of Wealth in Ecuador, Ghana and India." Working Paper 13, Gender Asset Gap Project, Centre of Public Policy, Indian Institute of Management, Bangalore. http://genderassetgap.iimb.ernet.in/site/uploads/File/Working%20Papers/159_WP13.pdf

Deininger, Klaus, Aparajita Goyal and Hari Nagarajan. 2010. "Inheritance Law Reform and Women's Access to Capital: Evidence from India's Hindu Succession Act." Policy Research Working Paper 5338, World Bank, Washington, DC.

de Mel, Suresh, David McKenzie and Christopher Woodruff. 2008. "Returns to Capital: Results from a Randomized Experiment." *Quarterly Journal of Economics* 123 (4): 1329–72.

Demirguc-Kunt, Asli, and Leora Klapper. 2012. "Measuring Financial Inclusion: The Global Findex Database." Policy Research Working Paper 6025, World Bank, Washington, DC.

Demirguc-Kunt, Asli, Leora Klapper and Dorothe Singer. 2013. "Financial Inclusion and Legal Discrimination against Women: Evidence from Developing Countries." Policy Research Working Paper 6416, World Bank, Washington, DC.

Djankov, Simeon, Rafael La Porta, Florencio Lopez-de-Silanes and Andrei Shleifer. 2003. "Courts." *Quarterly Journal of Economics* 118 (2): 453–517.

Duflo, Esther. 2003. "Grandmothers and Granddaughters: Old Age Pension and Intra-Household Allocation in South Africa." *The World Bank Economic Review* 17 (1): 1–25.

———. 2012. "Women Empowerment and Economic Development." *Journal of Economic Literature* 50: 1051–79.

EC (European Commission). 1998. "Sexual Harassment in the Workplace in the European Union." Directorate-General for Employment, Industrial Relations and Social Affairs, Brussels. http://www.un.org/womenwatch/osagi/pdf/shworkpl.pdf.

Eissa, Nada. 1995. "Taxation and Labor Supply of Married Women: The Tax Reform Act of 1986 as a Natural Experiment." NBER Working Paper 5023, National Bureau of Economic Research, Cambridge, MA.

Eissa, Nada, and Hillary Williamson Hoynes. 2004. "Taxes and the Labor Market Participation of Married Couples: The Earned Income Tax Credit." *Journal of Public Economics* 88: 1931–58.

Eissa, Nada, Henrik Jacobsen Kleven and Claus Thustrup Kreiner. 2008. "Evaluation of Four Tax Reforms in the United States: Labor Supply and Welfare Effects for Single Mothers." *Journal of Public Economics* 92 (3–4): 795–816.

Enval, E., and A. Erikssen. 2004. "Costs of Violence against Women." National Board of Health and Welfare, Stockholm.

FAO (Food and Agriculture Organization). 1994. "The Legal Status of Rural Women in 19 Latin American Countries." Economic and Social Development Department, Rome. http://www.fao.org/docrep/u5615e/u5615e03.htm.

Freidenvall, Lenita. 2003. "Women's Political Representation and Gender Quotas: The Swedish Case." Working Paper Series 2003, Department of Political Science, Stockholm University.

Friedemann-Sánchez, Greta. 2008. "Ensamblar flores y cultivar hogares: trabajo y género en Colombia." Instituto Colombiano de Antropología e Historia, Bogotá.

Fueyo Lunari, Fernando. 1985. "Problemática general del régimen patrimonial del matrimonio." *Revista de Derecho y Jurisprudencia* 82.

Gaye, Amie, Jeni Klugman, Milorad Kovacevic, Sarah Twigg and Eduardo Zambrano. 2010. "Measuring Key Disparities: The Gender Inequality Index." Human Development Report Research Paper 2010/46, United Nations Development Programme, New York.

Geddes, Rick, Dean Lueck and Sharon Tennyson. 2012. "Human Capital Accumulation and the Expansion of Women's Economic Rights." Cornell University, Ithaca, NY. http://www.deanlueck.net/wp-content/uploads/2012/05/JLE-_7180-Geddes-Lueck-Tennyson_Revised_March-16-2012.pdf.

Gloppen, Siri, and Fidelis Edge Kanyongolo. 2007. "Courts and the Poor in Malawi: Economic Marginalization, Vulnerability and the Law." *International Journal of Constitutional Law* 5 (2): 258–93.

Gobierno de España. 1975. "Ley 14/1975, de 2 de mayo, sobre reforma de determinados artículos del Código Civil y del Código de Comercio sobre la situación jurídica de la mujer casada y los derechos y deberes de los cónyuges." Documento BOE-A-1975-9245, Ministerio de la Presidencia, Madrid. http://www.boe.es/buscar/doc.php?id=BOE-A-1975-9245.

Hallward-Driemeier, Mary, and Ousman Gajigo. 2010. "Strengthening Economic Rights and Women's Occupational Choice: The Impact of Reforming Ethiopia's Family Law." World Bank, Washington, DC.

Hallward-Driemeier, Mary, and Tazeen Hasan. 2012. "Empowering Women: Legal Rights and Economic Opportunities in Africa." World Bank, Washington, DC.

Hallward-Driemeier, Tazeen Hasan and Anca Rusu. Forthcoming. "Women's Legal Rights over 50 Years: Progress, Stagnation or Regression?" World Bank, Washington, DC.

Harrington, Andrew, and Tanja Chopra. 2010. "Arguing Traditions: Denying Kenya's Women Access to Land Rights." World Bank, Washington, DC.

Henderson, Monika. 2000. "Impacts and Costs of Domestic Violence on the Australian Business/Corporate Sector: Report to Lord Mayor's Advisory Group." Cited in Victorian Community Council Against Violence, 2004, "Family Violence IS a Workplace Issue: Workplace Models to Prevent Family Violence," Melbourne.

Human Rights Watch. 2003. *World Report* 2003. New York.

———. 2013. "Lebanon." In *World Report* 2013. New York. http://www.hrw.org/world-report/2013/country-chapters/lebanon?page=2/.

IFC (International Finance Corporation). 2011. "Strengthening Access to Finance for Women-Owned SMEs in Developing Countries." Washington, DC.

Immigration and Refugee Board of Canada. 2007. "Mexico: The New Federal Law to Combat Violence against Women (2007)." Research Directorate, Ottawa. http://www.refworld.org/docid/469cd68d8.html.

John Hopkins University School of Advanced International Studies Protection Project and Suzanne Mubarak Regional Centre for Women's Health and Development. 2010. "Model Law against Domestic Violence." Washington, DC. http://www.protection-project.org/wp-content/uploads/2010/11/Model_Law_On-Violence-Against_Women_Domestic_Violence-FINAL.pdf/.

Law and Development Partnership. 2011. "Access to Credit for Women Entrepreneurs in Ghana: Gender Perspective of Secured Lending Initiatives." London.

Maingi, Grace. 2011. "The Kenyan Constitutional Reform Process: A Case Study on the Work of FIDA Kenya in Securing Women's Rights." *Feminist Africa: Legal Voice: Special Issue* 15: 63–82.

Milanovic, Branko. 2005. *Worlds Apart: Measuring International and Global Inequality.* Princeton, NJ: Princeton University Press.

Miller, Margaret J. 2003. "Credit Reporting Systems around the Globe: The State of the Art in Public Credit Registries and Private Credit Reporting Firms." In *Credit Reporting Systems and the International Economy*, edited by Margaret M. Miller, 25–60. Cambridge, MA: MIT Press.

Morrison, Andrew R., and María Beatriz Orlando. 1999. "Social and Economic Costs of Domestic Violence: Chile and Nicaragua." In *Too Close to Home: Domestic Violence in Latin America*, edited by Andrew R. Morrison and María Loreto Biehl, 51–80. Washington, DC: Inter-American Development Bank.

Oglobin, Constantin. 1999. "Oglobin, C. G. 1999. "The Gender Earnings Differential in the Russian Transition Economy." *Industrial and Labor Relations Review* 52: 602–27"

Orser, B., S. Hogarth-Scott and A. L. Riding. 2000. "Performance, Firm Size and Management Problem Solving." *Journal of Small Business Management* 38 (4): 42–58.

Peresie, Jennifer L. 2005. "Female Judges Matter: Gender and Collegial Decisionmaking in the Federal Appellate Courts." *Yale Law Journal* 114: 1759–90. http://yale-lawjournal.org/images/pdfs/211.pdf.

Programa de las Naciones Unidas para el Desarrollo, Chile. "Reducción de la Pobreza y la Desigualdad, Tasa de Pobreza e Indigencia 1990–2011." Santiago. http://www.pnud.cl/areas/ReduccionPobreza/datos-pobreza-en-Chile.asp.

Quisumbing, Agnes R., and Kelly Hallman. 2005. "Marriage in Transition: Evidence on Age, Education, and Assets from Six Developing Countries." In *The Changing Transitions to Adulthood in Developing Countries*, edited by Cynthia B. Lloyd, Jere R. Behrman, Nelly Stromquist and Barney Cohen. Washington, DC: National Academies Press.

Rheinstein, Max, and Mary Ann Glendon. 1977. "West German Marriage and Family Law Reform." *University of Chicago Law Review* 45: 519.

Robb, Alicia, and Susan Coleman. 2008. "The Impact of Financial Capital on Business Performance: A Comparison of Women- and Men-Owned Firms." Kauffman Foundation. Kansas City, MO. http://www.ssrn.com/abstract=1400742/.

Rodriguez de Assis Machado, Marta, José Rodrigo Rodriguez, Flavio Marques Prol, Gabriela Justino da Silva, Marina

References

Zanata Ganzarolli and Renata do Vale Elias. 2012. "Law Enforcement at Issue: Constitutionality of Maria da Penha Law in Brazilian Courts." *International Journal of Human Rights* 9 (16): 61–84. http://www.surjournal.org/eng/conteudos/pdf/16/miolo.pdf.

Sabarwal, Shwetlena, and Katherine Terrell. 2008. "Does Gender Matter for Firm Performance? Evidence from Eastern Europe and Central Asia." Policy Research Working Paper 4705, World Bank, Washington, DC.

———. 2009. "Access to Credit and Performance of Female Entrepreneurs in Latin America." *Frontiers of Entrepreneurship Research* 29 (18).

Sanchez, Fabio et al. 2004. "Los costos de la violencia intra-familiar en Colombia." Bogota: Universidad de los Andes, Centro Estudios sobre Desarrollo Economico.

Social Policy and Development Centre. 2012. "The Socio-economic Cost of Violence against Women: A Case Study of Karachi." Research Report 5, Gender Research Programme, Karachi.

Stanko, Elizabeth A., Debbie Crisp, Chris Hale and Hebe Lucraft. 1998. "Counting the Costs: Estimating the Impact of Domestic Violence in the London Borough of Hackney." Cited in Carrie L. Yodanis, Alberto Godenzi and Elizabeth A. Stanko, 2000, "The Benefits of Studying Costs: A Review and Agenda for Studies on the Economic Costs of Violence against Women." *Policy Studies* 21 (3): 263–76.

Thévenon, Olivier, and Anne Solaz 2013. "Labour Market Effects of Parental Leave Policies in OECD Countries." OECD Social, Employment and Migration Working Papers 141, Organisation for Economic Co-operation and Development, Paris.

UNDP (United Nations Development Programme). 2010a. *Human Development Report* 2010. New York.

———. 2012. "International Human Development Indicators: Labour Force Participation Rate, Female-Male Ratio (Ratio of Female to Male Shares)." New York. http://hdrstats.undp.org/en/indicators/48906.html.

UNFPA (United Nations Population Fund). 2005. *State of the World's Population.* New York.

United Nations. 1996. "Report of the Fourth World Conference on Women, Beijing, 4–15 September 1995." New York. http://www.un.org/womenwatch/daw/beijing/pdf/Beijing%20full%20report%20E.pdf.

———. 2006. "Violence against Women: Forms, Consequences and Costs." Fact Sheet from "Ending Violence against Women: From Words to Action. Study of the Secretary-General."

New York. http://www.un.org/womenwatch/daw/vaw/launch/english/v.a.w-consequenceE-use.pdf.

———. 2010. "Violence against Women." In *The World's Women.* New York. http://unstats.un.org/unsd/demographic/products/Worldswomen/WW2010%20Report_by%20chapter(pdf)/violence%20against%20women.pdf.

United Nations Department for Economic and Social Affairs. 2010. *Handbook for Legislation on Violence against Women.* Division for the Advancement of Women, New York. http://www.un.org/womenwatch/daw//vaw/handbook/Handbook%20for%20legislation%20on%20violence%20against%20women.pdf.

United Nations Economic and Social Council. 1996. "Framework for Model Legislation on Domestic Violence." Commission on Human Rights, Geneva. http://www.unhchr.ch/Huridocda/Huridoca.nsf/0/0a7aa1c3f8de6f9a802566d700530914.

United Nations General Assembly. 1993. "The UN Declaration on the Elimination of Violence against Women." New York. http://www.un.org/documents/ga/res/48/a48r104.htm/.

UNHCR (United Nations High Commissioner for Refugees). 2005. "Policy on Harassment, Sexual Harassment, and Abuse of Authority." Geneva. http://www.un.org/womenwatch/osagi/UN_system_policies/(UNHCR)policy_on_harassment.pdf.

UN Women (United Nations Entity for Gender Equality and the Empowerment of Women). 2009 . "Good Practices in Legislation to Address Harmful Practices against Women." Vienna. http://www.un.org/womenwatch/daw/vaw/v-egms-gplahpaw.htm.

———. 2011. *Progress of the World's Women* 2011–2012: In Pursuit of Justice. New York. http://progress.unwomen.org/pdfs/EN-Report-Progress.pdf.

———. 2012a. "Virtual Knowledge Centre to End Violence against Women and Girls: Consequences and Costs." New York. http://www.endvawnow.org/en/articles/301-consequences-and-costs-.html.

———. 2012b. "Virtual Knowledge Centre to End Violence against Women and Girls: Fast Facts: Statistics on Violence against Women and Girls." New York. http://www.endvawnow.org/en/articles/299-fast-facts-statistics-on-violence-against-women-and-girls-.html.

U.S. Department of Justice. 2013 "What Is Domestic Violence?" Office on Violence against Women, Washington, DC. http://www.ovw.usdoj.gov/domviolence.htm.

Viera Mondragón Gregorio. 2000. "Efectos que produce el matrimonio (primera parte)." *Revista de la Escuela Libre de Derecho de la Universidad de Puebla* 3. http://www.juridicas.unam.mx/publica/librev/rev/revjurdp/cont/3/art/art5.pdf.

WHO (World Health Organization). 2005. *Multi-country Study on Women's Health and Domestic Violence against Women: Initial Results on Prevalence, Health Outcomes and Women's Responses*. Geneva. http://www.who.int/gender/violence/who_multicountry_study/summary_report/en/index.html.

———. 2013. "Global and Regional Estimates of Violence against Women: Prevalence and Health Effects of Intimate Partner Violence and Nonpartner Sexual Violence." Department of Reproductive Health and Research, Geneva. http://apps.who.int/iris/bitstream/10665/85239/1/9789241564625_eng.pdf.

World Bank. 2011. *World Development Report* 2012: *Gender Equality and Development*. New York: Oxford University Press.

World Bank Group. 2012. *Women, Business and the Law 2012: Removing Barriers to Economic Inclusion*. Washington, DC.

World Learning STAR Network. 2004. "For More Women in Entrepreneurship: Analysis of Survey Results of Women Entrepreneurs in BH." Brattleboro, VT.

Yodanis, Carrie L., Alberto Godenzi and Elizabeth A. Stanko. 2000. "The Benefits of Studying Costs: A Review and Agenda for Studies on the Economic Costs of Violence against Women." *Policy Studies* 21 (3): 263–76.

Zhang, Ting, Josh Hoddenbagh, Susan McDonald and Katie Scrim. 2009. "An Estimation of the Economic Impact of Spousal Violence in Canada, 2009." Department of Justice Canada, Ottawa, Ontario. http://www.justice.gc.ca/eng/rp-pr/cj-jp/fv-vf/rr12_7/rr12_7.pdf.

Zveglich, Joseph E., and Yana van der Meulen Rodgers. 2003. "The Impact of Protective Measures for Female Workers." *Journal of Labor Economics* 21 (3): 533–56.

Data Notes

Women, Business and the Law examines laws and regulations that affect women's ability to earn an income, either by starting and running their own businesses or by getting jobs. When it comes to women's rights, different economies reflect different cultural norms and values in their legislation. This report does not judge or rank countries, but provides objective data to inform dialogue and research about women's economic rights.

Covering 143 economies, *Women, Business and the Law* provides easily comparable data covering the following six areas:

- **Accessing institutions**—explores women's legal ability to interact with public authorities and the private sector in the same ways as men;

- **Using property**—analyzes women's ability to access and use property based on their ability to own, manage, control and inherit it;

- **Getting a job**—assesses restrictions on women's work, such as prohibitions on working at night or in certain jobs. This indicator also covers laws on work-related maternity, paternity, parental benefits, retirement ages, equal remuneration for work of equal value and nondiscrimination in hiring;

- **Providing incentives to work**—examines personal income tax credits and deductions available to women relative to men, and the provision of childcare and education services;

- **Building credit**—identifies minimum loan thresholds in private credit bureaus and public credit registries, and tracks those which collect information from microfinance institutions, utilities and retailers;

- **Going to court**—considers the ease and affordability of accessing justice by examining small-claims courts, as well as a woman's ability to testify in court and the incidence of women on constitutional courts.

A seventh topic area on legislation covering certain types of violence against women is being piloted for 100 economies:

- **Protecting women from violence**—examines the existence of legislation on domestic violence and sexual harassment.

Since the publication of *Women, Business and the Law 2012* there have been methodological changes in the six indicators, both in the number of questions covered and in the way the previously existing questions were analyzed. The principal methodological changes are summarized at the end of this chapter and footnoted throughout the text. The questions for the seventh topic are wholly new.

The report builds on the experience of the *Doing Business* project in developing objective indicators of impediments to entrepreneurship and employment for women. *Doing Business* analyzes regulations in 189 economies that apply to a business throughout its life cycle, including start-up and operations, trading across borders, paying taxes and resolving insolvency. As in the *Doing Business* project, *Women, Business and the Law* strongly emphasizes written law.

The *Women, Business and the Law* indicators were initially created by examining legislation to see what laws most affected women's business rights. Legislation across the legal spectrum was found to affect women's economic potential, either directly or indirectly. The indicators capture laws that directly differentiate between men and women, as well as laws that indirectly have a greater impact on women, given the likelihood that they are small business owners or microfinance clients. The pilot indicator on Protecting women from violence examines the existence and scope of legislation providing protective measures for women in the areas of domestic violence and sexual harassment.

To condense such a large volume of disparate information, broadly based legal questions were posed to local legal experts to determine in what areas women and men have the same or different rights. In addition to survey data from local legal experts, the *Women, Business and the Law* project also consulted constitutions, gender equality laws, marriage and family codes, labor and employment laws, passport procedures, citizenship rules, inheritance statutes, tax regulations and social security codes to determine the sources of gender differentiation in the law. Responses from *Doing Business 2014* surveys on Getting credit were also used. Criminal codes, domestic violence laws and legislation on violence against women were consulted for the pilot indicator. The data from the *Women, Business and the Law* surveys were checked for accuracy by referencing primary legal sources, resulting in revision or expansion of the information collected.

The *Women, Business and the Law* methodology has several useful characteristics:

- It is transparent and uses factual information derived directly from laws and regulations;

- Because standard assumptions are used when collecting the data, comparisons are valid across economies;

- The data identify both potential obstacles to women in business and legislative sources that can be changed as a result of this new information.

The report's focus on written legislation does not disregard the often large gap between laws on the books and actual practices, recognizing that women do not always have access to the equality they are entitled to by law, even though data on formal legal differentiation provides a first step to identifying potential challenges for women in the areas studied.

The report team welcomes feedback on the methodology and construction of this set of indicators and looks forward to improving both its coverage and scope. All the data, legal sources and questionnaires used to collect the data are publicly available at: http://wbl.worldbank.org/.

The following 103 questions[1] were asked about the six main topics across 143 economies, producing a total of 14,729 data points. An additional 15 questions were asked about the pilot topic on Protecting women from violence across 100 economies for an additional 1,500 data points, making a total of 16,229 data points. Each question is followed by information on how the answers were standardized and made comparable across all economies. Assumptions, where used, are also listed.

Accessing institutions

Assumptions

It is assumed that the woman:

- Resides in the main business city of the economy being examined;

- Has reached the legal age of majority; if there is no legal age of majority, the woman is assumed to be 30 years old;

- Is sane, competent, in good health and has no criminal record;

- Is a lawful citizen of the economy being examined;

- Where the question assumes the woman (or man) is married, the marriage is monogamous and registered with the authorities;

- Where the question assumes the woman (or man) is unmarried, she (or he) has never been married;

- Where the answer differs according to the legal system applicable to the woman in question (as may be the case in economies where legal plurality exists), the answer used will be the one applicable to the majority of the population.

The answers to the questions below are based on codified law and not the implementation or practice of that law. Therefore, customary law is not taken into account, unless the customary law has been codified. The only exceptions to this rule are case-law systems, also known as "common law systems."[2] The questions on the status of customary law within the legal framework refer to its existence and place within the hierarchy of legislation, but do not assess its content. Reciprocal restrictions that govern the conduct of both spouses are not covered; therefore, this indicator only measures restrictions that govern the conduct of the wife, but not the husband.

Constitutional rights

This sub-topic focuses on the constitutional treatment of customary law, gender equality and nondiscrimination. It includes seven questions:

1. Is there a nondiscrimination clause in the Constitution?

- For the answer to be "Yes" the Constitution must utilize either the word discrimination or the word nondiscrimination;

- The answer is also "Yes" even when there is a "clawback" provision granting exceptions to the nondiscrimination clause for certain areas of the law such as inheritance, family and customary law;

- The answer is "No" if there is no nondiscrimination provision;

- The answer is also "No" if the nondiscrimination language is present in the preamble of the Constitution, but not in an article of the Constitution; or if there is merely a provision stipulating that the sexes are equal, or the sexes have equal rights and obligations—considered to be an equality clause;

- The answer is also "No" if there is merely a provision stipulating that people are equal before the law, but no provision dedicated to nondiscrimination;

- The answer is also "No" if there is merely language negating privileges based on categories, such as "There shall be no privileges based on birth, sex, class or religion;"

- The answer is also "No" if the Constitution makes reference to an international treaty that addresses discrimination but does not have its own nondiscrimination provision;

- The answer is also "No" if the Constitution does not ban discrimination, but includes measures such as empowering congress to enact laws fostering nondiscrimination.

2. If there is a nondiscrimination clause in the Constitution, does it explicitly mention gender?

- The answer is "Yes" if the Constitution explicitly includes gender or sex as protected categories for nondiscrimination;

- The answer is also "Yes" even when there is a "clawback" provision granting exceptions to the nondiscrimination clause for certain areas of the law such as inheritance, family and customary law;

- The answer is "No" if there is no nondiscrimination provision, or if there is a nondiscrimination provision that does not include gender or sex as protected categories;

- The answer is also "No" if the nondiscrimination language that includes sex is present in the preamble of the Constitution, but not in an article of the Constitution; or if there is merely a provision stipulating that the sexes are equal or the sexes have equal rights and obligations—considered to be an equality clause;

- The answer is also "No" if there is merely a provision stipulating that the sexes are equal before the law, but no provision dedicated to nondiscrimination;

- The answer is also "No" if there is merely language negating privileges based on sex;

- The answer is also "No" if there is merely a provision entitling both sexes to fundamental rights without use of the word discrimination, but with use of phrases such as "without regard to sex" or "whatever his sex."

3. Does the Constitution guarantee equality before the law?

- The answer is "Yes" if there is an equal protection or a general equality provision in the Constitution, and where it is generally applicable to "all citizens" and does not specify women as a protected category;

- The answer is "No" if there is no equal protection or general equality provision in the Constitution.

4a. Is customary law recognized as a valid source of law under the constitution?

- The answer is "Yes" if the Constitution explicitly recognizes customary law;

- The answer is also "Yes" if the Constitution makes reference to methods by which customary law will be brought in line with constitutional principles, or by which customary law is to be determined, or to requirements that customary chiefs be consulted prior to enactment of legislation;

- The answer is "Yes" if the Constitution allows laws applicable before the coming into force of the Constitution to continue to have the force of law—if the economy had a robust system of customary law in place at the time;

- The answer is "No" in the absence of explicit constitutional recognition of customary sources or systems of law;

- This question does not include customary contractual terms, or other forms of implied usage.

4b. Is personal law recognized as a valid source of law under the Constitution?

- The answer is "Yes" if the Constitution explicitly recognizes personal or religious law;

- The answer is also "Yes" if the Constitution makes reference to methods by which personal law will be brought in line with constitutional principles, or by which personal law is to be determined, or if the Constitution recognizes religious systems of law or religious sources of law;

- The answer is also "Yes" if the Constitution allows laws applicable before the Constitution came into force to remain valid—that is, if the country had a robust system of personal law in place at the time;

- The answer is "No" in the absence of explicit constitutional recognition of religious sources or systems of law.

5a. If so, is it [customary law] invalid if it violates constitutional provisions on nondiscrimination or equality?

- The answer is "Yes" if customary law is considered to be invalid if it violates other provisions of constitutional law;

- The answer is also "Yes" if the Constitution makes reference to methods by which customary law will be brought in line with constitutional principles on nondiscrimination or equality;

- The answer is also "Yes" if the Constitution establishes that customary laws or rights are guaranteed equally to men and women;

- The answer is "No" if customary law takes precedence over constitutional provisions on nondiscrimination or equality;

- The answer is "N/A" if there are no constitutional provisions on nondiscrimination or equality, or if customary law is not explicitly mentioned as a valid source of law under the Constitution.

5b. If so, is it [personal law] invalid if it violates constitutional provisions on nondiscrimination or equality?

- The answer is "Yes" if personal or religious laws are considered to be invalid if they violate other provisions of constitutional law;

- The answer is "No" if personal or religious law takes precedence over constitutional provisions on nondiscrimination or equality;

- The answer is also "No" if religious law is declared to be the basis of all legislation and there is a supremacy clause in the constitution;

- The answer is "N/A" if there are no constitutional provisions on nondiscrimination or equality or if personal or religious laws are not considered valid sources of law under the Constitution.

Quotas

This sub-topic focuses on the existence of quotas for corporate boards, parliaments and local governments. It includes three questions, which capture mandatory quotas, specifying the number of seats reserved for women:

6. What are the legal quotas for women on corporate boards?[3]

- Proportions are entered in percentage terms, e.g., 40%;

- N/A means there is no quota;

- Voluntary or recommended quotas are not included in the scope of this question.

7. What are the legal quotas for women representatives in parliament?[4]

- Proportions are entered in percentage terms, e.g., 40%;

- N/A means there is no quota;

- Voluntary or recommended quotas, or quotas for women on candidate lists are not included in the scope of this question. If the parliament has two chambers and the law specifies a quota for one of the chambers, but not the other, then the answer reflects the quota only for the chamber that has a quota.

8. What are the legal quotas for women representatives in local government?[5]

- Proportions are entered in percentage terms, e.g., 40%;

- N/A means there is no quota;

- Voluntary or recommended quotas or quotas for women on candidate lists are not included in the scope of this question.

Rights of married and unmarried women

This sub-topic addresses whether a woman can engage in a set of legal transactions in the same way as a man. It also addresses whether there are differences due to the marital status of the woman. Married and unmarried men and women may not be able do things in the same way when, for instance, women require permission or an additional signature in order to complete a certain transaction, or when they must provide additional documentation not required of men, such as a marriage license or proof of name change. Differences related to property transactions are taken into account in the Using property topic only. Accessing institutions does not count this type of difference.

This sub-topic includes 22 different questions across 11 transactions, including transactions that are legal in nature and those that relate to women's freedom of movement.

In the data tables, the 22 questions for Accessing institutions are condensed into 11 questions with two possible answers each, one for married and one for unmarried women. The questions are as follows:

9a. Can an unmarried woman apply for a passport in the same way as an unmarried man?

- The answer is "Yes" if, upon reaching the legal age of majority, all civil acts may be completed and there are no differences in the way an unmarried woman or man may get a passport;

- The answer is "No" if an adult unmarried woman needs the permission or signature of a guardian to apply for a passport.

9b. Can a married woman apply for a passport in the same way as a married man?

- The answer is "Yes" if upon reaching the legal age of majority, all civil acts may be completed and there are no differences in the way that a married woman or man may get a passport;

- The answer is "No" if an adult married woman needs the permission or signature of her husband in order to apply for a passport;

- The answer is also "No" if any additional documentation is required of a married woman that is not required of a married man; e.g., if a marriage certificate is required specifically for married women but not for married men.

10a. Can an unmarried woman obtain a national ID card in the same way as an unmarried man?[6]

- The answer is "Yes" if there are no inequalities in the process for obtaining a national identity card;

- The answer is "No" if unmarried women require additional signatures, such as those of fathers or guardians, which unmarried men do not require;

- The answer is "No" if unmarried women must indicate the name of a father or guardian, but unmarried men are not required to do so;

- The answer is "No" if identity cards are optional for women, but required for men;

- The answer is "N/A" if there is no national identity card.

10b. Can a married woman obtain a national ID card in the same way as a married man?[7]

- The answer is "Yes" if there are no inequalities in the process for obtaining a national identity card;

- The answer is "No" if married women must provide marriage certificates, while married men are not required to do so;

- The answer is "No" if married women require additional signatures, such as those of fathers or guardians, which married men do not require;

- The answer is "No" if married women must indicate the name of their spouse, but married men are not required to do so;

- The answer is "No" if identity cards are optional for women, but required for men;

- The answer is "No" if the identity cards of married women display the name of their spouse, but the identity cards of married men do not;

- The answer is "N/A" if there is no national identity card.

11a. Can an unmarried woman travel outside the country in the same way as an unmarried man?

- The answer is "Yes" if no restrictions exist on unmarried women traveling alone internationally;

- The answer is also "Yes" if the Constitution guarantees freedom of movement or the right to leave and reenter the country and no restrictions exist on unmarried women traveling internationally;

- The answer is "No" if permission or additional documentation is required for unmarried women to leave the country; however, this permission must be separate from that required to get a passport, an area covered in a separate question.

11b. Can a married woman travel outside the country in the same way as a married man?

- The answer is "Yes" if no restrictions exist on married women traveling alone internationally;

- The answer is also "Yes" if the Constitution guarantees freedom of movement or the right to leave and reenter the country, or if men and women have the same rights inside of marriage, and no restrictions exist on married women traveling internationally;

- The answer is "No" if permission or additional documentation is required for married women to leave the country; however, this permission must be separate from that required get a passport, an area covered in a separate question;

- The answer is also "No" if the law requires a married woman to accompany her husband out of the country if he so wishes.

12a. Can an unmarried woman travel outside her home in the same way as an unmarried man?

- The answer is "Yes" if no restrictions exist on unmarried women traveling alone domestically;

- The answer is also "Yes" if the Constitution guarantees domestic freedom of movement and no restrictions exist on unmarried women;

- The answer is "No" if permission, additional documentation, or the presence of a guardian is required in order to travel domestically;

- The answer is also "No" if an unmarried woman must justify her reasons for leaving the home to a guardian.

12b. Can a married woman travel outside her home in the same way as a married man?

- The answer is "Yes" if there are no restrictions on married women traveling alone domestically;

- The answer is also "Yes" if the Constitution establishes the right to domestic freedom of movement, or if men and women have the same rights inside of marriage, and no restrictions exist on married women's domestic travel;

- The answer is "No" if permission, additional documentation, or the presence of a guardian is required in order for a married woman to travel domestically;

- The answer is also "No" if a married woman must justify her reasons for leaving the home to her husband, or if leaving the home without a valid reason is considered disobedience with consequences under the law.

13a. Can an unmarried woman get a job or pursue a trade or profession in the same way as an unmarried man?

- The answer is "Yes" if no permission is needed for an unmarried woman to get a job or practice a trade or profession;

- The answer is also "Yes" if there is a nondiscrimination or equality provision in the Constitution or Gender Equality Act and no restriction in family or civil law regarding an unmarried woman's ability to work;

- The answer is "No" if permission or additional documentation is required, or if a guardian can stop an unmarried woman from working.

13b. Can a married woman get a job or pursue a trade or profession in the same way as a married man?

- The answer is "Yes" if no permission is needed for a married woman to get a job or practice a trade or profession;

- The answer is also "Yes" if there is a nondiscrimination or equality provision in the Constitution or Gender Equality Act and no restriction in family or civil law regarding a married woman's ability to work;

- The answer is also "Yes" if married women and married men have the same rights in marriage and there is no restriction in the family or civil law regarding a married woman's ability to work;

- The answer is "No" if husbands can prevent their wives from getting or keeping jobs or from pursuing a trade or profession;

- The answer is also "No" if permission or additional documentation is required for married women to get a job or if a married man can go to court to get his wife's employer to fire her from her job or force her to leave her profession;

- The answer is also "No" if it is considered a form of disobedience with legal ramifications for a wife to engage in employment contrary to her husband's wishes or the interests of the family.

14a. Can an unmarried woman sign any type of contract in the same way as an unmarried man?

- The answer is "Yes" if full legal capacity is obtained upon the age of majority and there are no restrictions on unmarried women signing legally binding contracts;

- The answer is "No" if unmarried women have limited legal capacity to sign a legally binding contract.

14b. Can a married woman sign any type of contract in the same way as a married man?

- The answer is "Yes" if full legal capacity is obtained upon the age of majority and there are no restrictions on married women signing legally binding contracts;

- The answer is "No" if married women have limited legal capacity to enter into contracts or if they need the signature, consent, or permission of their husbands in order to legally bind themselves; this question does not concern restrictions on married women signing contracts specifically related to marital property governed under the default marital property regime; these are covered under the Using property indicator.

15a. Can an unmarried woman register a business in the same way as an unmarried man?

- The answer is "Yes" if full legal capacity is obtained upon the age of majority and there are no restrictions on unmarried women registering businesses;

- The answer is "No" if unmarried women have limited legal capacity to register a business; this would include situations in which they may not legally bind themselves with a legal document.

15b. Can a married woman register a business in the same way as a married man?

- The answer is "Yes" if full legal capacity is obtained upon the age of majority and there are no restrictions on married women registering a business;

- The answer is "No" if married women have limited legal capacity to register a business; this would include if they may not legally bind themselves;

- The answer is also "No" if married women need the permission, signature, or consent of their husbands to register a business;

- The answer is also "No" if married women are required to provide information pertaining to their husbands during any stage of the incorporation process, but the requirement is not reciprocal.

16a. Can an unmarried woman open a bank account in the same way as an unmarried man?

- The answer is "Yes" if there are no restrictions on unmarried women opening bank accounts;

- The answer is "No" if there are specific provisions limiting the ability of unmarried women to open bank accounts; only provisions from the body of family laws are systematically counted; provisions that may exist in other types of law, such as banking regulations, are not included here.

16b. Can a married woman open a bank account in the same way as a married man?

- Only provisions from the body of family laws are systematically counted; provisions that may exist in other types of law are not;

- The answer is "Yes" if there are no restrictions on married women opening bank accounts;

- The answer is also "Yes" if explicit provisions exist stating that married women may open bank accounts, or that both spouses may open bank accounts in their own names;

- The answer is "No" if there are specific provisions limiting the ability of married women to open bank accounts. This includes provisions stating that married women who are separately employed from their husbands may open a bank account in their own name, as it implies that women without a separate income stream may not do so;

- The answer is also "No" if there are specific provisions limiting the legal capacity of married women and preventing them from opening a bank account in their own name.

17a. Can an unmarried woman choose where to live in the same way as an unmarried man?

- The answer is "Yes" if there are no restrictions on unmarried women choosing where to live; also "Yes" if there is a general constitutional provision stating that every person has the right to determine his or her own place of residence and where there are no restrictions on unmarried women choosing where to live;

- The answer is "No" if explicit restrictions exist on unmarried women choosing their place of residence.

17b. Can a married woman choose where to live in the same way as a married man?

- The answer is "Yes" if no explicit restrictions exist on a married woman choosing where her family may live;

- The answer is also "Yes" if there is a general constitutional provision stating that every person has the right to determine his or her own place of residence, or if the family law states that spouses have equal rights within marriage, and there are no restrictions on married women choosing where to live;

- The answer is "No" if the husband chooses the family residence, or has additional weight in determining where the family shall live.

18a. Can an unmarried woman confer citizenship on her children in the same way as an unmarried man?

- The answer is "Yes" if both mothers and fathers can convey citizenship to the child, regardless of where the child is born;

- The answer is also "Yes" if there are additional procedures that must be completed by men but not by women (e.g., providing proof of paternity);

- The answer is "No" if only fathers can convey citizenship to the child, wherever that child may be born;

- Where a citizenship law and the constitution conflict on the passage of citizenship to children or spouses, the answer is coded according to whichever came later in time.

18b. Can a married woman confer citizenship on her children in the same way as a married man?

- The answer is "Yes" if married mothers and fathers may both convey citizenship to their children, wherever the child is born; the answer is also "Yes" if there are additional procedures that must be completed by men but not by women (e.g., providing proof of paternity);

- The answer is "No" if only married fathers can convey citizenship to the child, wherever that child may be born;

- Where a citizenship law and the constitution conflict on the passage of citizenship to children or spouses, the answer is coded according to whichever came later in time.

19a. Can an unmarried woman be "head of household" or "head of family" in the same way as an unmarried man?

- The answer is "Yes" if head of household is codified and there are no explicit restrictions on unmarried women becoming "head of household" or "head of family;"

- The answer is "No" if there is an explicit restriction on unmarried women becoming "head of household" or "head of family;" e.g., a provision stating that only men can be "head of household" or "head of family" or that men "lead the family;"

- The answer is also "No" if a male is designated as the default family member who receives the family book or family book-type document which is mandatory or necessary for access to essential services;

- The answer is "N/A" if head of household is not codified.

19b. Can a married woman be "head of household" or "head of family" in the same way as a married man?

- The answer is "Yes" if head of household is codified and there are no explicit restrictions on married women becoming "head of household" or "head of family;"

- The answer is "No" if there is an explicit restriction on married women becoming "head of household" or "head of family;" e.g., a provision stating that only husbands can be "head of household" or "head of family" or that husbands "lead the family" or "represent the family;"

- The answer is also "No" if a male is designated as the default family member who receives the family book or family book-type document which is mandatory or necessary for access to essential services;

- The answer is "N/A" if head of household is not codified.

The data on the number of inequalities in Accessing institutions for unmarried women represent a count of the total number of "No" answers to the 11 questions applicable to unmarried women.

The data on the number of inequalities in Accessing institutions for married women represent a count of the total number of "No" answers to the 11 questions applicable to married women.

Division of responsibility within marriage

This sub-topic addresses potential legal inequalities that are only applicable to married women. It includes three questions as follows:

20. Can a woman convey citizenship to a non-national spouse in the same way as a man?

- This question compares the ability of an adult married woman to legally convey her citizenship to her non-national husband with that of an adult married man to do the same for his non-national wife;

- The answer is "Yes" if marriage to a national male or female equally confers some preference in naturalization to the non-national spouse;

- The answer is "Yes" if neither spouse may convey citizenship to the other, that is, if citizenship must be obtained through the general naturalization procedures with no preference of any sort given to the spouse of a national;

- The answer is "No" if a national husband can convey citizenship to his non-national wife, but if a national wife may not do so for her non-national husband;

- The answer is also "No" if the ability to convey citizenship to a spouse is procedurally differentiated by gender; e.g., if a woman married to a national receives automatic citizenship rights upon her marriage, but if a

man married to a national must wait a specific number of years to become a citizen.

21. Are married women required by law to obey their husbands?

- The answer is "Yes" if an explicit provision exists, stating that married women must obey their husbands;

- The answer is also "Yes" if there is a provision stating that disobedience towards her husband has legal ramifications for the wife, such as loss of maintenance;

- The answer is "No" in the absence of a provision stating that married women must obey their husbands.

22. Do married couples jointly share legal responsibility for financially maintaining the family's expenses?

- The answer is "Yes" if there is an explicit provision stating that spouses have joint or shared legal responsibility for financially maintaining their family's expenses;

- The answer is also "Yes" if spouses have equal rights and responsibilities within marriage;

- The answer is "Yes" if the law is silent on the matter;

- The answer is "No" in the case of provisions stating that husbands are solely responsible for the financial support of the family.

Using property

Assumptions

It is assumed that the woman:

- Resides in the economy's main business city;

- Has reached the legal age of majority and is capable of making decisions as an adult; if there is no legal age of majority, the woman is assumed to be 30 years old;

- Is sane, competent, in good health and has no criminal record;

- Is a lawful citizen of the economy being examined;

- Where the question assumes that the woman (or man) is unmarried, she (or he) has never been married;

- Where the question assumes that the woman (or man) is married, the marriage is monogamous and is registered with the authorities;

- Where the question assumes that the woman (or man) is married, the marital property regime she (or he) is married under is assumed to be the default marital property regime and it is also assumed that the marital property regime will not change during the course of the marriage;

- Where the answer differs according to the legal system applicable to the woman in question—as may be the case in economies where legal plurality exists—the answer used will be the one applicable to the majority of the population.

The answers to the questions below are based on codified law and not the implementation or practice of that law. Therefore, customary law is not taken into account unless the customary law has been codified.

The questions in the Using property indicator are designed to determine what the management and control of marital property looks like under the default marital property regime in each of the economies covered. For all questions concerning the ability of married women to carry out activities independently of their husbands, the key concern is reciprocity. Unequal treatment is counted only where a married man is able to carry out the activity and his wife cannot equally do so.

Marital property regime

The main areas of differentiation between women and men in exercising property rights lie in the rights granted to spouses under various marital property regimes, some of which grant spouses equal treatment for property ownership. Other regimes grant husbands administrative control over jointly owned marital property. Still others grant husbands administrative control over their wives' property. The marital property regime also determines ownership and administrative rights over property upon dissolution of marriage.

Women, Business and the Law summarizes the main characteristics of the default marital property regime by means of the following questions:

23. What is the default marital property regime?

- The default marital property regime is the set of rules that apply to the management of property within marriage when no prenuptial agreement exists, and also at the time of dissolution of the marriage through divorce. For the purposes of this question, the default marital property regimes are classified in the following categories:
    - **Separation of property**—under a separate property regime all property acquired by the spouses before they marry, as well as all property acquired during the marriage, remains the separate property of the acquiring spouse. This regime can also be referred to as "out of community property;"

- **Partial community of property**—whereby assets acquired prior to marriage are regarded as the separate property of the acquiring spouse, and assets and income acquired after marriage, with few exceptions provided for by law, are regarded as joint property of the couple. Also, whereby assets acquired prior to marriage and assets acquired during marriage are regarded as the separate property of the acquiring spouse, but the accrued value of the property acquired by any of the spouses is considered joint property. At the time of divorce, the common property is divided equally between the spouses;

- **Full community of property**—all assets and income brought into the marriage and acquired during the marriage become the joint property of the couple; it can also be referred to as "in community of property;" at the time of divorce, all property is divided equally between spouses;

- **Deferred full or partial community of property**—the rules of partial or full community of property apply at the time of dissolution of the marriage (divorce or death of one of the spouses); prior to that, separation of property applies;

- **Other**—in economies where there is a default property regime which does not fit any of the above four descriptions; this alternative also applies in economies where spouses must opt into the marital property regime of their choice—within the legal alternatives provided—before or at the time of marriage. In economies where there is no default marital property regime, the most common marital property regime is used instead.

24. Who legally administers marital property?

- The answer to this question assumes that the default marital property regime applies and is classified as follows:
    - **Original owner**—in this situation, each spouse retains administrative power over the property they brought to marriage, as well as the property they acquire during marriage. No consent is needed from the other spouse regarding separate property transactions. This administrative scheme is usually found in separation of property regimes and can also be found in deferred full or partial community regimes. This question does not cover special provisions concerning the marital home;
    - **Separate with spousal consent**—this choice implies that each spouse administers his or her separate property but, for major transactions, needs spousal

consent. This administrative scheme is mostly found in separation of property, but can also be found in deferred full or partial community, or in partial community regimes;

- **Both must agree**—both spouses have equal rights in joint property administration and transactions; they perform all acts of administration together and, if one of the spouses has been delegated administrative rights by the other, spousal consent is implied. This administrative scheme is mostly seen in full community and partial community regimes;

- **Husband**—the husband has administrative rights over all property, including his wife's separate property if applicable. This scheme has been found only in partial community regimes;

- **Other**—this alternative will apply in all cases in which the administrative scheme does not fit any of the above. It includes, for example, cases in which the law provides for both spouses to administer marital property but, in case of disagreement, either the husband is given the power to ultimately decide or other members of the family have a say on how the property is administered.

Protecting a wife's interests

This sub-topic focuses on two areas: 1) the existence of legal provisions establishing limits to transactions concerning major assets; and 2) the legal recognition of married women's contributions through non-remunerated efforts. The questions in this sub-topic measure the following:

25. If it is the husband who administers the property, does he need his wife's consent to undertake major transactions, such as selling or pledging the property as collateral?

- This question is designed to measure whether there is any legal provision establishing limits to the administrative rights granted to the husband over property, to prevent potential deterioration that may be detrimental to the wife.

- The answer is "Yes" where the law requires that the wife provide her consent when the husband is performing major transactions involving the property he administers;

- The answer is "No" where there is no legal requirement for the wife to consent to transactions performed by the husband involving the property he administers;

- The answer is "N/A" where the husband does not solely administer marital property.

26. Are there any special provisions governing transactions concerning the marital home, such as selling or pledging as collateral?

- This question is designed to measure specific legal protections concerning the marital home, regardless of the default marital property regime;

- The answer is "Yes" where a separate legal provision is included in the law regarding the administration of the marital home. Such provisions may require that both spouses agree to any major transaction involving the marital home or establish that the court will intervene in case of disagreement. Such provisions are particularly relevant in marriages where separation or deferred full or partial community are the default regimes;

- The answer is "No" if the general rule on transactions regarding property within marriage are followed.

27. Does the law provide for valuation of non-monetary contributions?[8]

- This question is designed to measure if, at the time of dissolution of marriage, the division of property benefits both spouses equally. The process of property division upon divorce is examined to identify whether caring for minor children, taking care of the family home, or any other non-monetized contribution from the non-working spouse is taken into consideration;

- The answer is "Yes" where an explicit legal provision recognizing such contributions is found;

- The answer is also "Yes" when the default marital property regime is full community, partial community or deferred full or partial community of property, as these regimes implicitly recognize non-monetary contributions at the time of property division and divide martial property equally, regardless of which spouse actually purchased it or is the title-holder.

- The answer is "No" where the default marital property regime is separation of property or other, and no explicit legal provision recognizing such contributions is found.

Property rights

This sub-topic focuses on property and measures the following two legal transactions:

28a. Do unmarried men and unmarried women have equal ownership rights to property?

- This question is designed to determine whether there are gender-based differences over property for unmarried men and unmarried women. Ownership rights as used here include the ability to manage, control, administer, access, encumber, receive, dispose of and transfer property;

- The answer is "Yes" when no specific legal restriction is applied to single women or men, based on gender, with regard to property;

- The answer is "No" when legal restrictions are applied to single women or men, based on gender, with regard to property.

28b. Do married men and married women have equal ownership rights to property?

- This question is designed to determine whether there are gender-based differences over property rights for married men and married women. Ownership rights as used here include the ability to manage, control, administer, access, encumber, receive, dispose of and transfer property. The answer to this question is based on whether husbands and wives married under the default property regime have equal ownership rights over property;

- The answer is "Yes" when no specific restriction or difference in legal treatment is applied to married women or men, based on gender;

- The answer is "No" when there are differences in the legal treatment of spouses regarding property based on gender, and broken down by marital status. For example, if husbands are granted administrative control over marital property, the answer is "No."

Inheritance rights

This sub-topic focuses on the applicable law in cases where there is no will. In economies where codified law is applicable only to individuals who have affirmatively renounced customary law, the presumption is that an affirmative renouncement has been made.

29. Do sons and daughters have equal inheritance rights to property from their parents?

- This question examines whether there are gender-based differences in the rules of intestate succession (that is, in the absence of a will) for property from parents to children;

- The answer is "Yes" where the law recognizes children as heirs without any restrictions based on gender with regard to property;

- The answer is "No" where there are gender-based differences between children recognized as heirs, on inheritance for property.

30. Do female and male surviving spouses have equal inheritance rights over property?

- For the purpose of this question, it is assumed that the deceased spouse left no children or any other heirs, other than the surviving spouse;

- This question examines whether both spouses have equal rank and rights when it comes to inheriting assets in the absence of a will;

- The answer is "Yes" where the law recognizes the same rights to surviving spouses, once his or her spouse is deceased;

- The answer is "No" where there are gender-based differences on inheritance.

Going to court

Assumptions

It is assumed that the woman:

- Resides in the economy's main business city;

- Has reached the legal age of majority and is capable of making decisions as an adult;

- Is sane, competent, in good health and has no criminal record;

- Where the question assumes that the woman (or man) is married, the marriage is monogamous and it is registered with the authorities;

- Where the question assumes that the woman (or man) is unmarried, she (or he) has never been married;

- Where the answer differs according to the legal system applicable to the woman in question—as may be the case in economies where legal plurality exists—the answer used will be the one applicable to the majority of the population.

The answers to the questions below are based on codified law and not the implementation or practice of that law. Therefore customary law is not taken into account unless the customary law has been codified.

This topic assesses both indirect and direct differentiation in the law regarding women's access to the judicial system. The first sub-topic on equality of access contains three questions examining the existence of courts adjudicating matters of customary or personal law and assessing the value of a woman's testimony in court relative to a man's.

Equality of access

31. Does the law recognize customary courts?[9]

- The answer is "Yes" if the constitution or the law establishes or recognizes the authority of a judicial body (e.g., a court or tribunal) that is competent to hear cases and apply the customary law, either codified or not.

32. Does the law recognize personal law courts?[10]

- The answer is "Yes" if the constitution or the law establishes or recognizes the authority of a judicial body (e.g., court or tribunal) that is competent to hear cases and apply the personal law, either codified or not.

33. Does a woman's testimony carry the same evidentiary weight in court as a man's?

- This question covers all types of court cases;
- The answer is "No" if the law establishes a differentiation between the evidentiary value of a woman's testimony and that of a man's testimony.

Efficacy of procedure

This sub-topic contains two questions examining the existence of small claim courts and the threshold for claims which they can adjudicate.

34. Is there a small-claims court or a fast-track procedure for small claims?

- Small-claims courts have limited jurisdiction and hear civil cases between private litigants involving relatively small amounts of money; though the names of such courts vary by jurisdiction, they share features that generally include relaxed rules of civil procedure, the appearance of adversaries without legal representation, the use of plain language and relaxed evidentiary rules. Fast-track procedures for small claims or simplified procedural rules for small claims operate in a similar way but function under the auspices of another court;
- If the answer is "Yes," there is either a small-claims court or a fast-track procedure for civil claims of small value;
- The answer is "No" if the small-claims court or fast-track procedures exist but are not competent in civil matters (e.g., commercial claims only).

35. If so, what is the maximum amount for a small claim (as a percentage of income per capita)?

- This indicates the highest amount for claims that can be heard in a small-claims court; when different amounts apply to civil and commercial cases, the amount applicable to civil cases was used;
- If the answer is N/A, the economy in question has no small-claims courts or fast-track procedures for civil claims of small value.

Equality of representation

This sub-topic contains three questions which look at women's representation on constitutional courts and other judicial institutions mandated with the control of legislative and executive acts and the interpretation of the Constitution.

36. How many justices are there on the Constitutional Court?[11]

- For the purposes of this question Constitutional Courts and the court-like institutions mandated with the constitutionality control of laws and regulations are examined.
- When the number of justices set by law is a minimum, a maximum or a range, the data reflect the actual number of justices;
- When the constitutional review is carried out by a separate chamber of the highest court, the question reflects the composition of this chamber.

37. Of those, how many are women?[12]

- This question reflects how many members of Constitutional Courts, or court-like institutions mandated with the constitutionality control of laws and regulations are women.

38. Is the Chief Justice a woman?[13]

- This question reflects if the Chief Justice of the Constitutional Court or the court-like body mandated with the constitutionality control of laws and regulations is a woman.

Getting a job

Assumptions

It is assumed that the woman:

- Resides in the economy's main business city;
- Has reached the legal age of majority and is capable of making decisions as an adult;
- For purposes of determining the retirement and pensionable ages, that she is currently 40 years old and started working at the age of 25;

- Is sane, competent, in good health and has no criminal record;

- Has been working long enough to accrue all benefits, including any maternity/parental or retirement benefits;

- If a question assumes that a woman is pregnant, it is her first pregnancy and a single uncomplicated birth is expected; The birth took place on or after January 1, 2011;

- Will be nursing until the child is 1 year old;

- For purposes of determining the retirement and pensionable ages, that she has raised one child only;

- Is an employee in a non-managerial post in the manufacturing sector in a firm of at least 50 employees.

It is assumed that the man:

- Resides in the country's main business city;

- Has reached the legal age of majority and is capable of making decisions as an adult;

- For purposes of determining the retirement and pensionable ages, that he is currently 40 years old and started working at the age of 25;

- Is sane, competent, in good health, and has no criminal record;

- Has been working long enough to accrue all benefits, including any paternity/parental or retirement benefits;

- If a question assumes that a man's wife is pregnant, that it is his first child and a single uncomplicated birth is expected and that the birth took place on or after January 1, 2011;

- Is an employee in a non-managerial post in the manufacturing sector in a firm of at least 50 employees;

- Has completed infant care training courses, which sometimes serve as a prerequisite for extended paternity leave.

In general, the answers to the questions in Getting a job are based on written law and not on collective bargaining agreements; however, the latter are taken into account when the following two conditions are met:

- They cover more than 50% of the work force in manufacturing;

- They apply to individuals who are not party to the original collective bargaining agreement.

Parental benefits

The sub-topic on parental benefits contains 19 questions on maternity, paternity and parental benefits. Maternity covers benefits applicable only to the mother, while paternity covers benefits applicable only to the father. Parental covers benefits applicable to both the mother and the father, even if the distribution of those benefits is unequal between the two parents.

39a. Does the law mandate paid or unpaid maternity leave?

- Here maternity leave can be paid or unpaid, as long as the government explicitly mandates some form of maternity leave;

- Maternity leave is defined as a leave available only to the mother; parental leave that is available to both parents is not included in maternity leave;

- Provisions for circumstantial leave by which an employee is entitled to a certain number of days of paid leave (usually fewer than five days) upon the birth of a child are considered paternity leave; even if the law is gender neutral, such leave is not considered maternity leave, provided maternity leave is covered elsewhere under the law. It is assumed that if the mother has an option to choose between two schemes of maternity leave, one being a shorter leave paid at 100% and the second being a longer leave paid at 80%, that she will choose the first at 100%.

39b. Does the law mandate paid or unpaid paternity leave?

- Here paternity leave can be paid or unpaid, as long as the government explicitly mandates some form of paternity leave;

- Paternity leave is defined as leave available only to the father; parental leave that is available to both parents is not included in paternity leave;

- Provisions for circumstantial leave in which an employee is entitled to a certain number of days of paid or unpaid leave (usually fewer than five days) upon the birth of a child are considered paternity leave; even if the law is gender neutral, such leave is not considered maternity leave, provided that maternity leave is covered elsewhere under the law. For example, if the labor code provides that a worker may take a "one-day leave for the birth of a child" as an unpaid justified absence, the term "worker" is gender neutral, and maternity leave is covered in another article of the code, in this case, the one-day unpaid justified absence is considered paternity leave.

39c. Does the law mandate paid or unpaid parental leave?

- Here parental leave can be paid or unpaid, as long as the government explicitly mandates some form of parental leave shared between both mother and father;

- Allowances for a fixed number of days per year to be applied towards family emergencies, or child-related responsibilities are not considered parental leave; the leave must be contiguous with the birth of the child and maternity or paternity leave.

40a. What is the mandatory minimum length of paid maternity leave (in calendar days)?

- This is the number of days of maternity leave that legally must be paid by the government, the employer or both;

- Maternity leave is defined as leave available only to the mother; parental leave that is available to both parents is not included in maternity leave;

- If paid leave not contiguous with the birth of a child is provided, this leave is not considered paid maternity leave, as it can be taken at any point after the birth of the child.

40b. What is the mandatory minimum length of paid paternity leave (in calendar days)?

- This is the number of days of paternity leave that legally must be paid by the government, the employer or both;

- Paternity leave is defined as leave available only to the father; parental leave available to both parents is not included in paternity leave;

- If a father can take paid paternity leave only if the mother does not take her maternity leave, the assumption is that the mother takes her full entitlement to maternity leave.

40c. What is the mandatory minimum length of paid parental leave (in calendar days)?

- This is the number of days of parental leave which by law must be paid by the government, the employer or both;

- If the law mandates that the length of parental leave is not a definite amount of time, but rather worded as "until the child reaches a *certain* age," then the number of post-natal maternity leave days is subtracted from the number of parental leave days;

- Parental leave is counted only if it is contiguous with maternity and paternity leaves;

- It is assumed that the mother and the father both take the full maternity and paternity leave available to them, before taking parental leave;

- If various parental leave schemes exist that the parents/family/mother can choose from, it is assumed that parents select the scheme with the highest pay.

41a. What is the mandatory minimum length of unpaid maternity leave (in calendar days)?

- This is the number of days of optional unpaid maternity leave that an employer must provide; parental leave that is optional for both parents is not included here;

- If leave is provided, but is not contiguous with the birth, this leave is not considered unpaid maternity leave, as it can be taken at any point after the birth of the child;

- The unpaid maternity leave is in addition to the paid maternity leave if such leave exists.

41b. What is the mandatory minimum length of unpaid paternity leave (in calendar days)?

- This is the number of days of optional unpaid paternity leave that an employer must provide; parental leave that is optional for both parents is not included here;

- If a father can take unpaid paternity leave only if the mother does not take her maternity leave, it is assumed that the mother takes her full entitlement to maternity leave;

- The unpaid paternity leave is in addition to the paid paternity leave if such leave exists.

41c. What is the mandatory minimum length of unpaid parental leave (in calendar days)?[14]

- This is the number of days of optional unpaid parental leave that an employer must provide;

- The unpaid parental leave is in addition to the paid parental leave if such leave exists.

42a. Who pays maternity leave benefits?

- This question covers whether maternity leave benefits are funded by the government, the employer or both; if only the employer funds maternity leave benefits, the employer bears the entire cost of the benefits and pays the employee directly;

- Employer contributions to government funds (such as Social Security) that pay maternity benefits are not considered to be employer payments of maternity benefits;

- If the answer is N/A, no paid maternity leave is available.

42b. Who pays paternity leave benefits?

- This question covers whether paternity leave benefits are funded by the government, the employer or both; if only the employer funds paternity leave benefits, the employer bears the entire cost of the benefits and pays the employee directly;

- Employer contributions to government funds (such as Social Security) that pay paternity benefits are not considered to be employer payments of paternity benefits;
- If the answer is N/A, no paid paternity leave is available.

42c. Who pays parental leave benefits?

- This question covers whether parental leave benefits are funded by the government, the employer or both; if only the employer funds parental leave benefits, the employer bears the entire cost of the benefits and pays the employee directly;
- Employer contributions to government funds (such as Social Security) that pay parental benefits are not considered to be employer payments of parental benefits;
- If the answer is N/A, no paid parental leave is available.

43a. What percentage of wages is paid during maternity leave?

- This is the total percentage of wages covered by all sources during paid maternity leave; when different percentages for wages are covered at different stages of maternity leave, a weighted average of this percentage is calculated; weights are proportional to the duration of those stages.

43b. What percentage of wages is paid during paternity leave?

- This is the total percentage of wages covered by all sources during paid paternity leave; when different percentages for wages are covered at different stages of paternity leave, a weighted average of this percentage is calculated; weights are proportional to the duration of those stages.

43c. What percentage of wages is paid during parental leave?

- This is the total percentage of wages covered by all sources during paid parental leave; when different percentages for wages are covered at different stages of parental leave, a weighted average of this percentage is calculated; weights are proportional to the duration of those stages.

44a. Where paid parental leave exists, what is the minimum amount which only the mother must take (in calendar days)?

- The question captures whether there is a minimum number of days which can be taken only by the mother and therefore cannot be shared with the father;
- If the answer is N/A, no paid parental leave is available.

44b. Where paid parental leave exists, what is the minimum amount which only the father must take (in calendar days)?

- The question captures whether there is a minimum number of days that can be taken only by the father and therefore cannot be shared with the mother. For example, if parental leave is 120 days, the mother must take 48 days and the father 10 days out of the 120; if neither mother nor father takes the parental leave days designated for them, they will lose those days; parents can decide how to divide the remaining 62 days between them or opt to allocate all 62 days to only one parent;
- If the answer is N/A, no paid parental leave is available.

45a. Where unpaid parental leave exists, what is the minimum amount which only the mother must take (in calendar days)?[15]

- The question captures whether there is a minimum number of days which can be taken only by the mother and therefore cannot be shared with the father;
- If the answer is N/A, no unpaid parental leave is available.

45b. Where unpaid parental leave exists, what is the minimum amount which only the father must take (in calendar days)?[16]

- The question captures whether there is a minimum number of days that can be taken only by the father and therefore cannot be shared with the mother;
- If the answer is N/A, no unpaid parental leave is available.

Retirement and pensions

This sub-topic includes six questions on retirement and pensions. Assumptions specific to this sub-topic include the following:

- If retirement is not governed by age, but by the number of years worked or the number of years in which contributions are made, or if there are transitional provisions increasing or decreasing the retirement age over a period of years, it is assumed that the worker is currently 40 years old and started working at age 25;
- Answers are rounded to the nearest year.

46a. What is the age at which a man can retire and receive full benefits?

- This is the age at which men working in the private sector can retire and receive full benefits;

- It is assumed that the retiree has completed all the necessary qualifications to retire at the retirement age;

- If there is no national law regarding retirement, this question is coded as N/A.

46b. What is the age at which a woman can retire and receive full benefits?

- This is the age at which women working in the private sector can retire and receive full benefits;

- It is assumed that the retiree has completed all the necessary qualifications to retire at the retirement age;

- If there is no national law regarding retirement, this question is coded as N/A.

47a. What is the age at which a man can retire and receive partial benefits?

- This is the age at which a man can retire and receive partial, not full, pension benefits, either because the man did not accumulate enough work experience, contributions or because he did not reach a certain age qualifying him for full pension benefits. This age is often called early pensionable age or early retirement age;

- If there is no age at which a man can retire and receive partial benefits, then the answer is the same as the age at which a man can retire and receive full benefits (see 46a above);

- If there is no national law regarding retirement, this question is coded as N/A.

47b. What is the age at which a woman can retire and receive partial benefits?

- This is the age at which a woman can retire and receive partial, not full, pension benefits, either because the woman did not accumulate enough work experience or contributions, or because she did not reach a certain age, qualifying her for full pension benefits. This age is often called early pensionable age or early retirement age;

- If there is no age at which a woman can retire and receive partial benefits, then the answer is the same as the age at which a woman can retire and receive full benefits (see 46b above);

- If there is no national law regarding retirement, this question is coded as N/A.

48a. What is the mandatory retirement age for men?

- N/A means there is no age at which a man is required to retire.

48b. What is the mandatory retirement age for women?

- N/A means there is no age at which a woman is required to retire.

Working hour and industry restrictions

This sub-topic includes ten questions and covers working hour and job-specific restrictions on women. For the purposes of this section, it is assumed the woman gave all necessary permissions, including written consent.

49. Can non-pregnant and non-nursing women do the same jobs as men?

- Restrictions which are specific to pregnant women or nursing mothers are not included in this question;

- This question is designed to determine if there are specific jobs in which women explicitly or implicitly cannot work, except in limited circumstances;

- Both partial and full restrictions on women's work are counted as restrictions. For example, if women are only allowed to work in certain jobs within the mining industry, e.g., as health care professionals within mines, but not as miners, this counts as a restriction;

- Explicit restrictions are examined regarding women doing certain jobs such as mining. Also examined are implicit restrictions stating that women cannot work in "hazardous" or "arduous" conditions;

- This includes jobs in which there is a limit on how many hours a woman can work, but no limit for men;

- This includes restrictions on night work for certain jobs, which do not apply to men;

- Where the law indicates that regulations restricting women's work in particular industries may be promulgated by the relevant minister or ministry, this is counted as a restriction.

Questions 50a-h below disaggregate the information collected in question 49, to determine in which job categories women face specific restrictions.

50a. Can non-pregnant and non-nursing women engage in [mining] in the same way as men?

- The answer is "Yes" if there is no restriction on women working in the mining industry;

- The answer is "No" if there is a full or partial restriction on women working in the mining industry.

50b. Can non-pregnant and non-nursing women engage in [construction] in the same way as men?

- The answer is "Yes" if there is no restriction on women working in construction;

- The answer is "No" if there is a full or partial restriction on women working in construction.

50c. Can non-pregnant and non-nursing women engage in [metal work] in the same way as men?

- The answer is "Yes" if there is no restriction on women working in metal work;

- The answer is "No" if there is a full or partial restriction on women working in metal work.

50d. Can non-pregnant and non-nursing women engage in [factory work] in the same way as men?

- The answer is "Yes" if there is no restriction on women working in factories;

- The answer is "No" if there is a full or partial restriction on women working in factories.

50e. Can non-pregnant and non-nursing women engage in [jobs requiring lifting weights above a threshold] in the same way as men?

- The answer is "Yes" if there is no restriction on women engaging in jobs with a minimum weight-lifting requirement;

- The answer is "No" if there is a full or partial restriction on women engaging in jobs with a minimum weight-lifting requirement.

- The answer is also "No" if women cannot perform work requiring heavy lifting, for example, if the law prohibits women from working in jobs which involve the loading and unloading of goods.

50f. Can non-pregnant and non-nursing women engage in [jobs deemed hazardous] in the same way as men?

- The answer is "Yes" if there are no jobs legally considered too hazardous for women, which are also not considered too hazardous for men;

- The answer is "No" if a certain category of jobs is deemed too hazardous for women, but are not deemed too hazardous for men. Work of a hazardous nature includes, for example, if the law prohibits women from working in jobs which could have a harmful effect or increased risk to their life or health, given women's psycho-physical qualities, or where such jobs are not deemed to have a harmful effect or increased risk to men's life or health given men's psycho-physical qualities.

50g. Can non-pregnant and non-nursing women engage in [jobs deemed arduous] in the same way as men?

- The answer is "Yes" if there are no jobs legally considered to be too arduous for women which are also not considered to be too arduous for men;

- The answer is "No" if a certain category of jobs are deemed too arduous for women, but are not deemed too arduous for men;

- Work of an arduous nature includes, for example, if the law prohibits women from working in jobs which involve particularly hard manual labor.

50h. Can non-pregnant and non-nursing women engage in [jobs which are considered morally inappropriate] in the same way as men?

- The answer is "Yes" if there are no jobs legally considered to be morally inappropriate for women which are also not considered to be morally inappropriate for men;

- The answer is "No" if a certain category of jobs is legally deemed morally inappropriate or socially harmful for women, but is not deemed morally inappropriate or socially harmful for men.

51. Can women work the same night hours as men?

- This question does not factor in night work restrictions on pregnant women or nursing mothers;

- Where the law indicates that regulations may be promulgated by the relevant minister or ministry, restricting women's work at night, this is counted as a restriction.

Workplace protections

This sub-topic includes seven questions examining women's legal rights in the workplace:

52. Does the law mandate equal remuneration for men and women for work of equal value?

- This question captures whether employers are legally obliged to remunerate equally male and female employees who do work of equal value.

53. Are there laws mandating nondiscrimination based on gender in hiring?

- This question is designed to determine whether the law specifically prevents and/or penalizes gender-based discrimination in the hiring process.

54. Is it illegal for an employer to ask about family status during a job interview?

- This question is designed to determine whether an employer is allowed to inquire about the family status of a prospective employee during a job interview; the law may prohibit discrimination based on this information, but remain silent as to whether employers are allowed to ask for it in the first place;

- Here, family status means whether the employee is married or not, and whether the employee has any minor children.

55. Are there laws penalizing or preventing the dismissal of pregnant women?

- This question is designed to determine whether pregnancy can serve as grounds for dismissal;

- The answer is "Yes" if the law explicitly prohibits and/or penalizes the dismissal of pregnant women.

56. Must employers give employees an equivalent position when they return from maternity leave?

- The question considers paid and unpaid leave and captures whether the employer has a legal obligation to reinstate the returning employee in an equivalent or better than the pre-leave position and salary;

- Where the maternity leave regime explicitly establishes a suspension of the employee's contract, the answer is assumed to be "Yes;"

- In economies which also have parental leave and the law guarantees the return to the same position or an equivalent position paid at the same rate after parental leave, but is silent about the guarantee to the same position after maternity leave, the answer is "Yes;"

- If the answer is N/A, no paid or unpaid maternity leave is available.

57. Are employers required to provide break time for nursing mothers?

- The answer is "Yes" if legal provisions specifically require firms and employers to provide break time for nursing mothers who express breast milk at work; such a legal requirement may depend on the size of the firm or the proportion of women it employs.

58. Do employees with minor children have rights to a flexible/part-time work schedule?

- The answer is "Yes" if the law offers employees with minor children easier access to flexible work schedule arrangements or part-time work in comparison with employees without minor children.

Building credit

The background information for this indicator comes from the depth of credit information index that forms part of the *Doing Business 2014* Getting credit indicator. That index measures rules affecting the scope, accessibility and quality of credit information available through private credit bureaus and public credit registries. It examines various features of private bureaus, public registries or both.

High-income economies are not included in the sample here, because microfinance institutions are far more prevalent in developing economies. In addition, traditional bank financing is, for the most part, widely available to women in high-income economies, making microfinance providers less critical to women's quest for capital. Four questions that could potentially have a large impact on women's ability to build credit were examined in detail.

59. What is the minimum loan amount covered in the private credit bureau or public credit registry (as a percentage of income per capita)?

- This number reflects the lowest minimum loan amount of any credit bureau or registry in the economy in question;

- If a credit bureau or registry collects data on loans worth less than 1% of income per capita, it is treated as if it collects data on loans of any value; thus an answer of 0 here means either that there is no minimum loan amount in at least one credit bureau or registry, or that at least one credit bureau or registry collects data on loans worth less than 1% of income per capita;

- The answer is N/A, if there is no credit bureau or registry in the economy.

60. Do microfinance institutions provide information to private credit bureaus or public credit registries?

- For the purposes of this question, it is sufficient that any one private credit bureau or public credit registry in the economy in question collects information from microfinance institutions;

- The answer is N/A, the economy in question is high-income;

- The answer is N/A if there is no private credit bureau or public credit registry;

- If the economy in question has no operational credit bureau or registry, or if these entities collect information for less than 0.1% of the adult population, the entities are treated as not collecting information from microfinance institutions.

61. Do retailers provide information to private credit bureaus or public credit registries?[17]

- For the purposes of this question, it is sufficient that any one private credit bureau or public credit registry in the economy in question collects information from any retailer;

- The answer is N/A if there is no private credit bureau or public credit registry.

62. Do utility companies provide information to private credit bureaus or public credit registries?[18]

- For the purposes of this question, it is sufficient that any one private credit bureau or public credit registry in the economy in question collects information from a utility company;

- The answer is N/A if there is no private credit bureau or public credit registry.

Providing incentives to work

Taxes and the provision of certain public services can make it easier or more difficult for women to participate in the labor force. This topic contains the following five questions:

Childcare and education

63. Are payments for childcare tax deductible?

- The answer is "Yes" if childcare expenses are listed as deductible items in the personal income tax code; for this purpose, childcare expenses cover various options: kindergartens or crèches, day-care centers, after-school centers, in-home care and child-minding arrangements.

64. Is there public provision of childcare for children under the age of primary education?

- For the purpose of this question, childcare may take several forms: kindergartens or crèches, day-care centers, after-school centers, in-home care and child-minding arrangements;

- The answer is "Yes" if public authorities/the government fund childcare facilities and services;

- The answer is "Yes" if public authorities/the government may also subsidize the use of private childcare facilities and services as well as the hiring of child-minders.

65. Does the law mandate free and compulsory primary education?

- The answer is "Yes" if primary or elementary education is made compulsory by the Constitution or another legal text and is publicly funded.

Personal income tax

66a. Are there specific tax deductions or tax credits that are applicable only to men?

- This question is designed to determine whether the personal income tax code differentiates between men and women on deductions and credits and includes instances where tax specific deductions and credits can only go to male heads of household;

- The answer is "Yes" if the personal income tax code includes a tax deduction or credit which applies only to male taxpayers;

- The answer is also "Yes" if the personal income tax code includes a tax deduction or credit which can only go to the head of household and only men can legally be the head of household.

66b. Are there specific tax deductions or tax credits that are only applicable to women?

- This question is designed to determine whether the personal income tax code differentiates between men and women on deductions and credits;

- The answer is "Yes" if the personal income tax code includes a tax credit or deduction which is applicable only to female tax payers.

Summary of methodology changes

As footnoted above there were several changes of methodology between *Women, Business and the Law 2012* and *Women, Business and the Law 2014*. For that reason, the data presented on the website were recomputed to match the new methodology. In all six of the topics there were changes of methodology as follows:

- **Accessing institutions**—The questions on customary and personal law within the constitutional system were disaggregated to examine customary and personal law separately. The questions concerning quotas on corporate boards, in local government and in parliament are new and a new question was also added on whether married and unmarried women can get a national ID card in the same way as men. Finally, the question on whether married and unmarried women can become head of household in the same way as men now incorporates whether men are designated as the default family member who receives the family book or family book-type documents that are mandatory or necessary for access to essential services. In economies where "head of household" is not a term with legal implications, the question is coded as N/A. For the question on whether a woman can confer citizenship to a non-national spouse in the same way as a man, instances where marriage does not confer a citizenship preference to the non-national spouse are coded as N/A. Because of the addition of a question asking whether there is a nondiscrimination clause in the constitution, the question on gender-based nondiscrimination clauses is now answered as N/A if there is no nondiscrimination clause.

- **Using property**—the questions in this topic are no longer disaggregated according to movable/immovable property, as there was previously no variation on movable property. The questions on joint titling, who is entitled to the marital home in case of dissolution, and whether there is a legal presumption of joint ownership between the husband and the wife were removed, as they previously clustered according to the default marital property regime. New questions were added to determine if the law provides for the valuation of nonmonetary contributions during marriage; if the husband administers property, does he need his wife's consent to undertake major transactions (such as selling or pledging the property as collateral); and are there special provisions governing transactions concerning the marital home. For the question of who legally administers joint marital property—in addition to the answer options: "both spouses," "the original owner" and "other"—two answer options were added: "separate with spousal consent" and "the husband."

- **Getting a job**—The previous question concerning whether there are laws or constitutional provisions mandating equal pay for equal work has been revised to reflect the ILO standard. The question now examines whether the law mandates equal remuneration for men and women for work of equal value. The question on industry restrictions for women's work has been disaggregated into eight specific areas, in which women face either a partial or a full employment ban: mining, construction, factory work, metalwork, work involving the lifting of weights above a certain threshold, work deemed too hazardous for women, work deemed too arduous for women and work considered morally or socially inappropriate for women. A question on the length of unpaid parental leave was added and the question formerly phrased "Where parental leave exists, what is the minimum amount which only the mother/father must take (in calendar days)?" was disaggregated into two separate questions for paid and unpaid parental leave. The wording of the question "What is the statutory retirement age in the private sector?" has been

changed to "What is the age at which one can retire and receive full benefits?" The wording of the question "What is the minimum pensionable age in the private sector?" has been changed to "What is the age at which one can retire and receive partial benefits?" The question "In the private sector, is it mandatory to retire at the statutory retirement age?" was rephrased to "What is the mandatory retirement age?" and disaggregated into two separate questions for men and women. The question on whether pregnant or nursing mothers can work the same number of hours as men or other women was removed. The questions on the presence of laws obligating the employer to give the employee the same job when he returns from paternity leave or when he or she returns from parental leave were also removed. The question on the presence of laws protecting employees from sexual harassment in the workplace has been moved from the Getting a job indicator to the new pilot indicator on Protecting women from violence, where sexual harassment is covered in greater depth.

- **Providing incentives to work**—The question on whether there are male specific tax deductions or credits now includes instances where men are heads of household either exclusively or by default and thereby receive specific tax deductions or credits attached to that status. Additionally, the previous two questions: "Does the law mandate compulsory primary education for children?" and "If the law does mandate compulsory primary education for children, is it provided by the state for free?" were combined into one question on "Does the law mandate free and compulsory primary education?"

- **Building credit**—Two new questions examine whether utility companies and retailers provide information to private credit bureaus or public credit registries.

- **Going to court**—Three new questions examine the number of justices seated on a constitutional court, the number of women among them, and whether the Chief Justice is a woman. Two questions were also added on whether the law recognizes customary courts and personal law courts. Finally, the questions on whether married/unmarried women need permission from their husbands or guardians in order to initiate proceedings in court were not retained due to lack of variation in the data.

Economy coverage and characteristics

The economies covered in this report are listed in table 7.1.

Gross national income (GNI) per capita

Women, Business and the Law uses 2012 income per capita as published in the World Bank's *World Development*

Data Notes

Indicators 2013. Income is calculated using the Atlas method (current U.S. dollars). For cost indicators expressed as a percentage of income per capita, 2012 GNI per capita in U.S. dollars is used as the denominator. GNI data were not available from the World Bank for the Islamic Republic of Iran, Kuwait, New Zealand, Oman, the Republic of Yemen, the Syrian Arab Republic, and West Bank and Gaza. In these cases GDP or GNP per capita data and growth rates from other sources such as the International Monetary Fund's World Economic Outlook database and the Economist Intelligence Unit were used.

Region and income group

Women, Business and the Law uses the World Bank regional and income group classifications, available at http://data.worldbank.org/about/country-classifications. The World Bank does not assign regional classifications to high-income economies. For the purpose of the *Women, Business and the Law* report, high-income OECD economies are assigned the "regional" classification *OECD high-income.* Figures and tables presenting regional averages include economies from all income groups (low-, lower-middle, upper-middle and high-income).

Female population and labor force participation rate

Women, Business and the Law reports mid-year 2012 female population data as published in the World Bank's *World Development Indicators 2013.* That publication was also used to obtain data on the female labor force participation rate, as percentage of the female population age 15–64.

Protecting women from violence

The pilot indicator on Protecting women from violence examines the existence and scope of laws covering domestic violence and sexual harassment in 100 economies.

Assumptions

It is assumed that the woman:

- Resides in the main business city of the economy being examined;

- Has reached the legal age of majority and is capable of making decisions as an adult. If there is no legal age of majority, the woman is assumed to be 30 years old;

- Is sane, competent, in good health, has no criminal record, and is a lawful citizen of the economy being examined.

The answers to the questions below are based on statutory or codified law for civil law systems, and on case law, i.e., law established by judicial decision in cases as binding precedent for common law systems. Therefore, customary law is not taken into account, unless it has been codified or upheld by case law, and the answers are based solely on the letter of the law and not the implementation or practice thereof.

| **TABLE 7.1** | **COVERAGE BY REGION** |

Region	Number of economies	Economies by region
East Asia & Pacific	14	Cambodia; China; Fiji; Hong Kong SAR, China; Indonesia; Lao PDR; Malaysia; Mongolia; Papua New Guinea; Philippines; Singapore; Taiwan, China; Thailand; Vietnam
Eastern Europe & Central Asia	23	Albania; Armenia; Azerbaijan; Belarus; Bosnia and Herzegovina; Bulgaria; Croatia; Georgia; Kazakhstan; Kosovo; Kyrgyz Republic; Latvia; Lithuania; FYR Macedonia; Moldova; Montenegro; Romania; Russian Federation; Serbia; Tajikistan; Turkey; Ukraine; Uzbekistan
OECD high-income	30	Australia; Austria; Belgium; Canada; Czech Republic; Denmark; Estonia; Finland; France; Germany; Greece; Hungary; Iceland; Ireland; Israel; Italy; Japan; Republic of Korea; Netherlands; New Zealand; Norway; Poland; Portugal; Slovak Republic; Slovenia; Spain; Sweden; Switzerland; United Kingdom; United States
Latin America & Caribbean	21	Argentina; Bolivia; Brazil; Chile; Colombia; Costa Rica; Dominican Republic; Ecuador; El Salvador; Guatemala; Haiti; Honduras; Jamaica; Mexico; Nicaragua; Panama; Paraguay; Peru; Puerto Rico (U.S.); Uruguay; Venezuela, RB
Middle East & North Africa	14	Algeria; Arab Republic of Egypt; Islamic Republic of Iran; Jordan; Kuwait; Lebanon; Morocco; Oman; Syrian Arab Republic; Tunisia; Saudi Arabia; United Arab Emirates; West Bank and Gaza; Republic of Yemen
South Asia	5	Bangladesh; India; Nepal; Pakistan; Sri Lanka
Sub-Saharan Africa	36	Angola; Benin; Botswana; Burkina Faso; Burundi; Cameroon; Chad; Democratic Republic of the Congo; Republic of Congo; Côte d'Ivoire; Ethiopia; Gabon; Ghana; Guinea; Kenya; Lesotho; Liberia; Madagascar; Malawi; Mali; Mauritania; Mauritius; Mozambique; Namibia; Niger; Nigeria; Rwanda; Sierra Leone; Senegal; South Africa; Sudan; Tanzania; Togo; Uganda; Zambia; Zimbabwe

The economies covered in the pilot indicator on Protecting women from violence are listed in table 7.2.

Domestic violence

This sub-topic covers the existence and scope of laws on domestic violence. *Domestic violence* is gender-specific violence commonly directed against women, occurring within the family and in intimate relationships. Intimate relationships can include both spouses and unmarried intimate partners. The violence can come in the form of physical, sexual, emotional or financial abuse. There are seven questions in this sub-topic as follows:

1. Is there legislation that specifically addresses domestic violence?

- The answer is "Yes" if there is a law or provision addressing domestic violence that includes criminal sanctions or provides for orders of protection for domestic violence (i.e., if domestic violence is only prohibited', the answer will be considered "No");

- The answer is "No" if there is no law or provision addressing domestic violence or if the law or provision only prohibits domestic violence but does not provide for sanctions or orders of protection;

- The answer is also "No" if the provision only protects a specific category of women (e.g., pregnant women) or defines the offence in connection to specific motives (e.g., violence against a person in connection with performing a professional or civil duty);

- Aggravated penalties for crimes committed between spouses or within the family will not be considered as legislation specifically addressing domestic violence; however, they are considered under the specific types of domestic violence offenses to which they are applicable.

2. Is there a specialized court or procedure for cases of domestic violence?

- The answer is "Yes" if the law establishes a court with exclusive jurisdiction on matters related to domestic violence;

- The answer is "Yes" if the law establishes revised rules of civil procedure, or the work of specially trained judges for matters related to domestic violence under the auspices of a non-specialized court;

- The answer is "Yes" if the law establishes special restraining order procedures for cases of domestic violence.

3. Does domestic violence legislation protect women in unmarried, intimate relationships?

- The answer is "Yes" if the law or provision addressing domestic violence clearly protects women in unmarried, intimate relationships, including co-habiting partners;

- The answer is "No" if the law or provision addressing domestic violence only covers married couples or spouses and does not protect women in unmarried, intimate relationships.

4a. Does domestic violence legislation include physical abuse?

- The answer is "Yes" if the term "physical" violence or abuse is clearly defined or stated in the law or provision as a form of domestic violence;

- The answer is also "Yes" if it includes language that can clearly be interpreted as physical violence or abuse as a form of domestic violence, including harassment if stated as affecting physical health;

- The answer is "No" if the domestic violence law or provision does not include the term "physical" violence or abuse or other language that can clearly be interpreted as physical violence or abuse.

4b. Does domestic violence legislation include sexual abuse?

- The answer is "Yes" if the term "sexual" violence or abuse is clearly defined or stated in the law or provision as a form of domestic violence;

- The answer is also "Yes" if it includes language that can clearly be interpreted as sexual violence or abuse as a form of domestic violence, including the offence of rape between spouses;

- The answer is also "Yes" where there is an aggravated penalty for crimes committed between spouses or within the family (e.g., where there is an increased penalty for forced sexual intercourse when committed between spouses or within a family);

- The answer is "No" if the domestic violence law or provision does not include the term "sexual" violence or abuse or other language that can clearly be interpreted as sexual violence or abuse;

- The answer is also "No" if the provision on sexual abuse is not classified as occurring within the context of domestic violence or if legislation only covers female genital mutilation.

4c. Does domestic violence legislation include emotional abuse?

- The answer is "Yes" if the term "psychological" or "emotional" violence or abuse is clearly defined or stated in the law or provision as a form of domestic violence;

- The answer is also "Yes" if it includes language that can clearly be interpreted as psychological or emotional violence or abuse as a form of domestic violence, including harassment, if stated as affecting mental health, and harm, if interpreted as emotional harm;

- The answer is "No" if the domestic violence law or provision does not include the term "psychological" or "emotional" violence or abuse or other language that can clearly be interpreted as psychological or emotional violence or abuse.

4d. Does domestic violence legislation include financial abuse?

- The answer is "Yes" if the term "financial" or "economic" violence or abuse is clearly defined or stated in the law or provision as a form of domestic violence;

- The answer is also "Yes" if it includes language that can clearly be interpreted as financial or economic violence or abuse;

- The answer is "No" if the domestic violence law or provision does not include the term "financial" or "economic" violence or abuse or other language that can clearly be interpreted as financial or economic violence or abuse.

Sexual harassment

This sub-topic covers the existence and scope of laws on sexual harassment. *Sexual harassment* is any unwelcome sexual advance, request for sexual favor, verbal or physical conduct or gesture of a sexual nature, or any other behavior of a sexual nature that might reasonably be expected or be perceived to cause offence or humiliation to another. Such harassment may be, but is not necessarily, of a form that interferes with work, is made a condition of employment, or creates an intimidating, hostile or offensive work environment. There are eight questions in this sub-topic as follows:

5. Is there legislation that specifically addresses sexual harassment?

- The answer is "Yes" if there is a law or provision specifically addressing and protecting from sexual harassment, including unwelcome sexual advances, requests for sexual favors, verbal or physical conducts or gestures of a sexual nature, annoyance, if understood to include harassment with sexual content, or any other behavior of a sexual nature that might reasonably be expected or be perceived to cause offence or humiliation to another;

- The answer is also "Yes" if sexual harassment is deemed as "discrimination" and the law or provision protects against discrimination;

- The answer is also "Yes" if there is a law or provision addressing and protecting from sexual harassment in employment, including compulsion to perform a sexual or indecent act coupled with financial or official dependence or authority, abuse of position or authority, or language that can be clearly interpreted to mean such dependence or abuse;

- The answer is "No" if there is no law or provision specifically addressing sexual harassment;

- The answer is also "No" if the act of sexual nature is performed by the use of "force" or "violence," which is understood to constitute a crime, e.g., sexual assault or abuse;

- The answer is also "No" if the law or provision only allows an employee to terminate an employment contract based on sexual harassment, but provides for no other protection;

- The answer is also "No" if the law or provision only protects a specific category of women or only protects in a specific area of employment, e.g., protection from sexual harassment in political functions.

6. Are there criminal sanctions for sexual harassment?

- The answer is "Yes" if the legislation includes criminal sanctions, including fines and imprisonment, for sexual harassment;

- The answer is "No" if there are no criminal sanctions for sexual harassment;

- The answer is also "No" if the law or provision on sexual harassment reverts to penalties for more serious offences in the criminal code, such as for sexual assault;

- The answer is also "No" if the law only "prohibits" sexual harassment in employment and sets forth that the employer should apply discretionary sanctions.

7. Is there a governmental office responsible for addressing sexual harassment?

- The answer is "Yes" if there is a governmental office or ombudsman that is responsible for addressing complaints or issues of sexual harassment, which is established by law or is part of the existing government structure;

- The answer is "No" if there is no governmental office or ombudsman that is responsible for addressing complaints or issues of sexual harassment.

8a. Is there legislation on sexual harassment in education?

- The answer is "Yes" if the law or provision specifically covers sexual harassment in education, including educational facilities, schools, between education professionals and pupils, or including language that can clearly be interpreted as sexual harassment in education;

- The answer is "No" if the law or provision does not specifically cover sexual harassment in education;

- The answer is also "No" if the law or provision covers sexual harassment only in public or private education, but not both.

8b. Is there legislation on sexual harassment in employment?

- The answer is "Yes" if there is a law or provision specifically addressing and protecting from sexual harassment in employment, including unwelcome sexual advances, requests for sexual favors, verbal or physical conduct or gestures of a sexual nature, annoyance if understood to include harassment with sexual content, or any other behavior of a sexual nature that might reasonably be expected or be perceived to cause offence or humiliation in connection with employment, including compulsion to perform a sexual or indecent act, coupled with financial or official dependence or authority, abuse of position or authority, or language that can be clearly interpreted to mean such dependence or abuse; the answer is also "Yes" if sexual harassment is deemed as "discrimination" in employment and the law or provision protects against discrimination;

- The answer is "No" if there is no law or provision specifically addressing sexual harassment in employment;

- The answer is also "No" if the act of sexual nature is performed through the use of "force" or "violence," which is understood as a crime, e.g., sexual assault or abuse;

- The answer is also "No" if the law or provision only allows the employee to terminate their employment contract based on sexual harassment, but provides for no other protection;

- The answer is also "No" if the law or provision covers only public or private sector employees, but not both;

- The answer is also "No" if the law or provision only protects a specific category of women or only protects in a specific area of employment, e.g., protection from sexual harassment in political functions.

8c. Is there legislation on sexual harassment in public places?

- The answer is "Yes" if the law or provision specifically covers sexual harassment in public places, including public spaces, in public, or in transportation;

- The answer is "No" if the law or provision does not cover sexual harassment in public places, public spaces, in public or in transportation.

8d. Is there legislation on sexual harassment in service provision?

TABLE 7.2 COVERAGE BY REGION FOR PILOT INDICATOR ON PROTECTING WOMEN FROM VIOLENCE

Region	Number of economies	Economies by region
East Asia & Pacific	9	Cambodia; China; Fiji; Indonesia; Malaysia; Mongolia; Philippines; Singapore; Thailand
Eastern Europe & Central Asia	15	Albania; Armenia; Azerbaijan; Bosnia and Herzegovina; Croatia; Kazakhstan; Latvia; Lithuania; FYR Macedonia; Romania; Russian Federation; Serbia; Turkey; Ukraine; Uzbekistan
OECD high-income	16	Australia; Canada; Denmark; Finland; France; Germany; Italy; Japan; Republic of Korea; Poland; Portugal; Spain; Sweden; Switzerland; United Kingdom; United States
Latin America & Caribbean	19	Argentina; Bolivia; Brazil; Chile; Colombia; Costa Rica; Ecuador; El Salvador; Guatemala; Haiti; Honduras; Jamaica; Mexico; Nicaragua; Panama; Paraguay; Peru; Uruguay; Venezuela, RB
Middle East & North Africa	10	Algeria; Arab Republic of Egypt; Islamic Republic of Iran; Jordan; Lebanon; Morocco; Saudi Arabia; Syrian Arab Republic; Tunisia; Republic of Yemen
South Asia	5	Bangladesh; India; Nepal; Pakistan; Sri Lanka
Sub-Saharan Africa	26	Angola; Benin; Burkina Faso; Cameroon; Democratic Republic of the Congo; Côte d'Ivoire; Ethiopia; Ghana; Kenya; Lesotho; Madagascar; Malawi; Mali; Mauritius; Mozambique; Namibia; Niger; Nigeria; Rwanda; Senegal; Sierra Leone; South Africa; Tanzania; Uganda; Zambia; Zimbabwe

- The answer is "Yes" if the law or provision specifically covers sexual harassment in the provision of services;

- The answer is "No" if the law or provision does not specifically cover sexual harassment in the provision of services.

9. Are there criminal sanctions for sexual harassment in employment?

- The answer is "Yes" if the legislation includes criminal sanctions, including fines and imprisonment for sexual harassment in employment;

- The answer is "No" if there are no criminal sanctions for sexual harassment in employment in the legislation;

- The answer is also "No" if the law or provision on sexual harassment reverts to penalties for more serious offences in the criminal code, such as for sexual assault;

- The answer is also "No" if the law only "prohibits" sexual harassment in employment and sets forth that the employer should apply discretionary sanctions.

Endnotes

1 There are 66 different questions, with subdivisions totaling 103 individual questions.

2 Case law systems are those developed by judges through decisions of courts, rather than through legislative statutes (Acts) or executive branch action (Decrees), creating binding precedent.

3 This is a new question.

4 This is a new question.

5 This is a new question.

6 This is a new question.

7 This is a new question.

8 This is a new question.

9 This is a new question.

10 This is a new question.

11 This is a new question.

12 This is a new question.

13 This is a new question.

14 This is a new question.

15 This is a new question.

16 This is a new question.

17 This is a new question.

18 This is a new question.

Economy Tables

Economy Tables

	ALBANIA		ALGERIA		ANGOLA	
REGION	Europe & Central Asia		Middle East & North Africa		Sub-Saharan Africa	
INCOME	Upper middle income		Upper middle income		Upper middle income	
FEMALE POPULATION	1,575,747		19,024,063		10,500,253	
FEMALE LABOR FORCE PARTICIPATION	56%		16%		64%	

ACCESSING INSTITUTIONS

Constitutional rights

	ALBANIA		ALGERIA		ANGOLA	
1. Is there a non-discrimination clause in the constitution?	Yes		Yes		Yes	
2. If there is a non-discrimination clause in the constitution, does it explicitly mention gender?	Yes		Yes		Yes	
3. Does the constitution guarantee equality before the law?	Yes		Yes		Yes	
	Customary	Personal	Customary	Personal	Customary	Personal
4. Is customary/personal law recognized as valid source of law under the constitution?	No	No	No	Yes	Yes	No
5. If so, is it invalid if it violates constitutional provisions on non-discrimination or equality?	N/A	N/A	N/A	No	Yes	N/A

Quotas

	ALBANIA	ALGERIA	ANGOLA
6. What are the legal quotas for women on corporate boards?	N/A	N/A	N/A
7. What are the legal quotas for women in parliament?	N/A	N/A	N/A
8. What are the legal quotas for women in local government?	N/A	N/A	N/A

Rights of married and unmarried women

	Unmarried	Married	Unmarried	Married	Unmarried	Married
9. Can a woman apply for a passport in the same way as a man?	Yes	Yes	Yes	Yes	Yes	Yes
10. Can a woman apply for a national ID card in the same way as a man?	Yes	Yes	Yes	Yes	Yes	Yes
11. Can a woman travel outside the country in the same way as a man?	Yes	Yes	Yes	Yes	Yes	Yes
12. Can a woman travel outside her home in the same way as a man?	Yes	Yes	Yes	Yes	Yes	Yes
13. Can a woman get a job or pursue a trade or profession in the same way as a man?	Yes	Yes	Yes	Yes	Yes	Yes
14. Can a woman sign a contract in the same way as a man?	Yes	Yes	Yes	Yes	Yes	Yes
15. Can a woman register a business in the same way as a man?	Yes	Yes	Yes	Yes	Yes	Yes
16. Can a woman open a bank account in the same way as a man?	Yes	Yes	Yes	Yes	Yes	Yes
17. Can a woman choose where to live in the same way as a man?	Yes	Yes	Yes	Yes	Yes	Yes
18. Can a woman confer citizenship on her children in the same way as a man?	Yes	Yes	Yes	Yes	Yes	Yes
19. Can a woman be "head of household" or "head of family" in the same way as a man?	Yes	Yes	N/A	N/A	Yes	Yes
Number of inequalities in accessing institutions	0	0	0	0	0	0

Division of responsibility within marriage

	ALBANIA	ALGERIA	ANGOLA
20. Can a woman convey citizenship to her non-national spouse in the same way as a man?	Yes	Yes	Yes
21. Are married women required by law to obey their husbands?	No	No	No
22. Do married couples jointly share legal responsibility for financially maintaining the family's expenses?	Yes	Yes	Yes

USING PROPERTY

Marital property regime

	ALBANIA	ALGERIA	ANGOLA
23. What is the default marital property regime?	Partial community of property	Separation of property	Partial community of property
24. Who legally administers property during marriage?	Both must agree	Original owner	Both must agree

Protecting a wife's interests

	ALBANIA	ALGERIA	ANGOLA
25. If it is the husband, does he need his wife's consent for major transactions	N/A	N/A	N/A
26. Are there special provisions governing the marital home?	Yes	No	No
27. Does the law provide for valuation of nonmonetary contributions during marriage?	Yes	No	Yes

Property rights

	Unmarried	Married	Unmarried	Married	Unmarried	Married
28. Do men and women have equal ownership rights to property?	Yes	Yes	Yes	Yes	Yes	Yes

Inheritance rights

	ALBANIA	ALGERIA	ANGOLA
29. Do sons and daughters have equal inheritance rights to property?	Yes	No	Yes
30. Do female and male surviving spouses have equal inheritance rights to property?	Yes	No	Yes

GOING TO COURT

Equality of access

	ALBANIA	ALGERIA	ANGOLA
31. Does the law recognize customary courts?	No	No	No
32. Does the law recognize personal law courts?	No	No	No
33. Does a woman's testimony carry the same evidentiary weight in court as a man's?	Yes	Yes	Yes

Efficiency of procedure

	ALBANIA	ALGERIA	ANGOLA
34. Is there a small claims court or a fast track procedure for small claims?	No	No	No
35. If so, what is the maximum amount for a small claim (as a percentage of income per capita)?	N/A	N/A	N/A

Judicial representation

	ALBANIA	ALGERIA	ANGOLA
36. How many justices are on the constitutional court?	9	9	11
37. Of those, how many are women?	2	2	4
38. Is the Chief Justice a woman?	No	No	No

	ALBANIA			ALGERIA			ANGOLA		

GETTING A JOB

Parental benefits	Maternity	Paternity	Parental	Maternity	Paternity	Parental	Maternity	Paternity	Parental
39. Does the law mandate paid or unpaid maternity/paternity/parental leave?	Yes	No	No	Yes	Yes	No	Yes	Yes	No
40. What is the mandatory minimum length of paid leave for maternity/paternity/parental leave (in calendar days)?	365	N/A	N/A	98	3	N/A	90	1	N/A
41. What is the mandatory minimum length of unpaid leave for maternity/paternity/parental leave (in calendar days)?	0	N/A	N/A	0	0	N/A	0	0	N/A
42. Who pays maternity/paternity/parental benefits?	Gov.	N/A	N/A	Gov.	Emp.	N/A	Gov.	Emp.	N/A
43. What percentage of wages are paid during maternity/paternity/parental leave?	65%	N/A	N/A	100%	100%	N/A	100%	0%	N/A

	Mother	Father		Mother	Father		Mother	Father	
44. Where **paid** parental leave exists, what is the minimum amount which only the mother/father must take (in calendar days)?	N/A	N/A		N/A	N/A		N/A	N/A	
45. Where **unpaid** parental leave exists, what is the minimum amount which only the mother/father must take (in calendar days)?	N/A	N/A		N/A	N/A		N/A	N/A	

Retirement & pensions	Women	Men		Women	Men		Women	Men	
46. What is the age at which one can retire and receive full benefits?	60	65		54	60		59	60	
47. What is the age at which one can retire and receive partial benefits?	60	62		45	50		59	60	
48. What is the mandatory retirement age?	N/A	N/A		54	60		N/A	N/A	

Working hours and industry restrictions									
49. Can non-pregnant and non-nursing women do the same jobs as men?	Yes			Yes			No		
50. Can non-pregnant and non-nursing women engage in the following occupations in the same way as men?									
a. Mining	Yes			Yes			Yes		
b. Construction	Yes			Yes			Yes		
c. Metalwork	Yes			Yes			Yes		
d. Factory work	Yes			Yes			Yes		
e. Jobs requiring lifting weights above a threshold	Yes			Yes			Yes		
f. Jobs deemed hazardous	Yes			Yes			No		
g. Jobs deemed arduous	Yes			Yes			Yes		
h. Jobs deemed morally or socially inappropriate	Yes			Yes			Yes		
51. Can non-pregnant and non-nursing women work the same night hours as men?	Yes			No			Yes		

Workplace protections									
52. Does the law mandate equal remuneration for men and women for work of equal value?	No			Yes			Yes		
53. Are there laws mandating non-discrimination based on gender in hiring?	Yes			No			Yes		
54. Is it illegal for an employer to ask about family status during a job interview?	No			No			No		
55. Are there laws penalizing or preventing the dismissal of pregnant women?	Yes			No			Yes		
56. Must employers give employees an equivalent position when they return from maternity leave?	No			Yes			No		
57. Are employers required to provide break time for nursing mothers?	Yes			No			Yes		
58. Do employees with minor children have rights to a flexible/part time schedule?	No			No			Yes		

BUILDING CREDIT

59. What is the minimum loan amount covered in the private credit bureau or public credit registry (as a percentage of income per capita)?	0%			0%			0%		
60. Do microfinance institutions provide information to private credit bureaus or public credit registries?	Yes			Yes			Yes		
61. Do utility companies provide information to private credit bureaus or public credit registries?	No			No			No		
62. Do retailers provide information to private credit bureaus or public credit registries?	No			No			No		

PROVIDING INCENTIVES TO WORK

Childcare									
63. Are payments for childcare tax deductible?	No			No			No		
64. Is there public provision of childcare for children under the age of primary education?	Yes			No			Yes		
65. Does the law mandate free and compulsory primary education?	Yes			Yes			Yes		

Personal income tax	Women	Men		Women	Men		Women	Men	
66. Are there specific tax deductions or credits that are applicable only to men/women?	No	No		No	No		No	No	

Economy Tables

	ARGENTINA		ARMENIA		AUSTRALIA	
REGION	Latin America & Caribbean		Europe & Central Asia		High income: OECD	
INCOME	Upper middle income		Lower middle income		High income	
FEMALE POPULATION	20,981,543		1,438,917		11,392,816	
FEMALE LABOR FORCE PARTICIPATION	55%		55%		70%	

ACCESSING INSTITUTIONS

Constitutional rights

	ARGENTINA		ARMENIA		AUSTRALIA	
1. Is there a non-discrimination clause in the constitution?	No		Yes		No	
2. If there is a non-discrimination clause in the constitution, does it explicitly mention gender?	N/A		Yes		N/A	
3. Does the constitution guarantee equality before the law?	Yes		Yes		No	

	Customary	Personal	Customary	Personal	Customary	Personal
4. Is customary/personal law recognized as valid source of law under the constitution?	No	No	No	No	No	No
5. If so, is it invalid if it violates constitutional provisions on non-discrimination or equality?	N/A	N/A	N/A	N/A	N/A	N/A

Quotas

	ARGENTINA	ARMENIA	AUSTRALIA
6. What are the legal quotas for women on corporate boards?	N/A	N/A	N/A
7. What are the legal quotas for women in parliament?	N/A	N/A	N/A
8. What are the legal quotas for women in local government?	N/A	N/A	N/A

Rights of married and unmarried women

	Unmarried	Married	Unmarried	Married	Unmarried	Married
9. Can a woman apply for a passport in the same way as a man?	Yes	Yes	Yes	Yes	Yes	Yes
10. Can a woman apply for a national ID card in the same way as a man?	Yes	Yes	Yes	Yes	N/A	N/A
11. Can a woman travel outside the country in the same way as a man?	Yes	Yes	Yes	Yes	Yes	Yes
12. Can a woman travel outside her home in the same way as a man?	Yes	Yes	Yes	Yes	Yes	Yes
13. Can a woman get a job or pursue a trade or profession in the same way as a man?	Yes	Yes	Yes	Yes	Yes	Yes
14. Can a woman sign a contract in the same way as a man?	Yes	Yes	Yes	Yes	Yes	Yes
15. Can a woman register a business in the same way as a man?	Yes	Yes	Yes	Yes	Yes	Yes
16. Can a woman open a bank account in the same way as a man?	Yes	Yes	Yes	Yes	Yes	Yes
17. Can a woman choose where to live in the same way as a man?	Yes	Yes	Yes	Yes	Yes	Yes
18. Can a woman confer citizenship on her children in the same way as a man?	Yes	Yes	Yes	Yes	Yes	Yes
19. Can a woman be "head of household" or "head of family" in the same way as a man?	Yes	Yes	N/A	N/A	N/A	N/A
Number of inequalities in accessing institutions	0	0	0	0	0	0

Division of responsibility within marriage

	ARGENTINA	ARMENIA	AUSTRALIA
20. Can a woman convey citizenship to her non-national spouse in the same way as a man?	Yes	Yes	Yes
21. Are married women required by law to obey their husbands?	No	No	No
22. Do married couples jointly share legal responsibility for financially maintaining the family's expenses?	Yes	Yes	Yes

USING PROPERTY

Marital property regime

	ARGENTINA	ARMENIA	AUSTRALIA
23. What is the default marital property regime?	Partial community of property	Partial community of property	Separation of property
24. Who legally administers property during marriage?	Separate with spousal consent	Both must agree	Original owner

Protecting a wife's interests

	ARGENTINA	ARMENIA	AUSTRALIA
25. If it is the husband, does he need his wife's consent for major transactions	N/A	N/A	N/A
26. Are there special provisions governing the marital home?	Yes	No	No
27. Does the law provide for valuation of nonmonetary contributions during marriage?	Yes	Yes	Yes

Property rights

	Unmarried	Married	Unmarried	Married	Unmarried	Married
28. Do men and women have equal ownership rights to property?	Yes	Yes	Yes	Yes	Yes	Yes

Inheritance rights

	ARGENTINA	ARMENIA	AUSTRALIA
29. Do sons and daughters have equal inheritance rights to property?	Yes	Yes	Yes
30. Do female and male surviving spouses have equal inheritance rights to property?	Yes	Yes	Yes

GOING TO COURT

Equality of access

	ARGENTINA	ARMENIA	AUSTRALIA
31. Does the law recognize customary courts?	No	No	No
32. Does the law recognize personal law courts?	No	No	No
33. Does a woman's testimony carry the same evidentiary weight in court as a man's?	Yes	Yes	Yes

Efficiency of procedure

	ARGENTINA	ARMENIA	AUSTRALIA
34. Is there a small claims court or a fast track procedure for small claims?	Yes	No	Yes
35. If so, what is the maximum amount for a small claim (as a percentage of income per capita)?	11%	N/A	16%

Judicial representation

	ARGENTINA	ARMENIA	AUSTRALIA
36. How many justices are on the constitutional court?	7	9	7
37. Of those, how many are women?	2	1	3
38. Is the Chief Justice a woman?	No	No	No

GETTING A JOB

	ARGENTINA			ARMENIA			AUSTRALIA		
Parental benefits	*Maternity*	*Paternity*	*Parental*	*Maternity*	*Paternity*	*Parental*	*Maternity*	*Paternity*	*Parental*
39. Does the law mandate paid or unpaid maternity/paternity/parental leave?	Yes	Yes	No	Yes	No	Yes	No	No	Yes
40. What is the mandatory minimum length of paid leave for maternity/paternity/parental leave (in calendar days)?	90	2	N/A	140	N/A	0	N/A	N/A	126
41. What is the mandatory minimum length of unpaid leave for maternity/paternity/parental leave (in calendar days)?	90	0	N/A	0	N/A	1025	N/A	N/A	0
42. Who pays maternity/paternity/parental benefits?	Gov.	Emp.	N/A	Gov.	N/A	N/A	N/A	N/A	Gov.
43. What percentage of wages are paid during maternity/paternity/parental leave?	100%	100%	N/A	100%	N/A	0%	N/A	N/A	Partially paid

	Mother	*Father*		*Mother*	*Father*		*Mother*	*Father*	
44. Where **paid** parental leave exists, what is the minimum amount which only the mother/father must take (in calendar days)?	N/A	N/A		N/A	N/A		0	0	
45. Where **unpaid** parental leave exists, what is the minimum amount which only the mother/father must take (in calendar days)?	N/A	N/A		0	0		N/A	N/A	

Retirement & pensions	*Women*	*Men*		*Women*	*Men*		*Women*	*Men*	
46. What is the age at which one can retire and receive full benefits?	60	65		63	63		67	67	
47. What is the age at which one can retire and receive partial benefits?	60	65		63	63		67	67	
48. What is the mandatory retirement age?	N/A	N/A		N/A	N/A		N/A	N/A	

Working hours and industry restrictions	ARGENTINA	ARMENIA	AUSTRALIA
49. Can non-pregnant and non-nursing women do the same jobs as men?	No	Yes	Yes
50. Can non-pregnant and non-nursing women engage in the following occupations in the same way as men?			
a. Mining	No	Yes	Yes
b. Construction	Yes	Yes	Yes
c. Metalwork	No	Yes	Yes
d. Factory work	No	Yes	Yes
e. Jobs requiring lifting weights above a threshold	No	Yes	Yes
f. Jobs deemed hazardous	No	Yes	Yes
g. Jobs deemed arduous	No	Yes	Yes
h. Jobs deemed morally or socially inappropriate	Yes	Yes	Yes
51. Can non-pregnant and non-nursing women work the same night hours as men?	Yes	Yes	Yes

Workplace protections	ARGENTINA	ARMENIA	AUSTRALIA
52. Does the law mandate equal remuneration for men and women for work of equal value?	Yes	Yes	Yes
53. Are there laws mandating non-discrimination based on gender in hiring?	Yes	No	Yes
54. Is it illegal for an employer to ask about family status during a job interview?	No	No	No
55. Are there laws penalizing or preventing the dismissal of pregnant women?	Yes	Yes	Yes
56. Must employers give employees an equivalent position when they return from maternity leave?	Yes	Yes	N/A
57. Are employers required to provide break time for nursing mothers?	Yes	Yes	No
58. Do employees with minor children have rights to a flexible/part time schedule?	No	Yes	Yes

BUILDING CREDIT

	ARGENTINA	ARMENIA	AUSTRALIA
59. What is the minimum loan amount covered in the private credit bureau or public credit registry (as a percentage of income per capita)?	0%	0%	0%
60. Do microfinance institutions provide information to private credit bureaus or public credit registries?	No	Yes	N/A
61. Do utility companies provide information to private credit bureaus or public credit registries?	No	Yes	Yes
62. Do retailers provide information to private credit bureaus or public credit registries?	No	No	Yes

PROVIDING INCENTIVES TO WORK

Childcare	ARGENTINA	ARMENIA	AUSTRALIA
63. Are payments for childcare tax deductible?	Yes	No	No
64. Is there public provision of childcare for children under the age of primary education?	Yes	Yes	Yes
65. Does the law mandate free and compulsory primary education?	Yes	Yes	Yes

Personal income tax	*Women*	*Men*		*Women*	*Men*		*Women*	*Men*	
66. Are there specific tax deductions or credits that are applicable only to men/women?	No	No		No	No		No	No	

Economy Tables

	AUSTRIA	AZERBAIJAN	BANGLADESH
REGION	High income: OECD	Europe & Central Asia	South Asia
INCOME	High income	Upper middle income	Low income
FEMALE POPULATION	4,333,829	4,680,102	76,348,446
FEMALE LABOR FORCE PARTICIPATION	69%	67%	60%

ACCESSING INSTITUTIONS

Constitutional rights

	AUSTRIA	AZERBAIJAN	BANGLADESH
1. Is there a non-discrimination clause in the constitution?	No	No	Yes
2. If there is a non-discrimination clause in the constitution, does it explicitly mention gender?	N/A	N/A	Yes
3. Does the constitution guarantee equality before the law?	Yes	Yes	Yes

	Customary	Personal	Customary	Personal	Customary	Personal
4. Is customary/personal law recognized as valid source of law under the constitution?	No	No	No	No	Yes	Yes
5. If so, is it invalid if it violates constitutional provisions on non-discrimination or equality?	N/A	N/A	N/A	N/A	Yes	Yes

Quotas

	AUSTRIA	AZERBAIJAN	BANGLADESH
6. What are the legal quotas for women on corporate boards?	N/A	N/A	N/A
7. What are the legal quotas for women in parliament?	N/A	N/A	14%
8. What are the legal quotas for women in local government?	N/A	N/A	21%

Rights of married and unmarried women

	Unmarried	Married	Unmarried	Married	Unmarried	Married
9. Can a woman apply for a passport in the same way as a man?	Yes	Yes	Yes	Yes	Yes	Yes
10. Can a woman apply for a national ID card in the same way as a man?	Yes	Yes	Yes	Yes	Yes	Yes
11. Can a woman travel outside the country in the same way as a man?	Yes	Yes	Yes	Yes	Yes	Yes
12. Can a woman travel outside her home in the same way as a man?	Yes	Yes	Yes	Yes	Yes	Yes
13. Can a woman get a job or pursue a trade or profession in the same way as a man?	Yes	Yes	Yes	Yes	Yes	Yes
14. Can a woman sign a contract in the same way as a man?	Yes	Yes	Yes	Yes	Yes	Yes
15. Can a woman register a business in the same way as a man?	Yes	Yes	Yes	Yes	Yes	Yes
16. Can a woman open a bank account in the same way as a man?	Yes	Yes	Yes	Yes	Yes	Yes
17. Can a woman choose where to live in the same way as a man?	Yes	Yes	Yes	Yes	Yes	Yes
18. Can a woman confer citizenship on her children in the same way as a man?	Yes	Yes	Yes	Yes	Yes	Yes
19. Can a woman be "head of household" or "head of family" in the same way as a man?	N/A	N/A	N/A	N/A	N/A	N/A
Number of inequalities in accessing institutions	0	0	0	0	0	0

Division of responsibility within marriage

	AUSTRIA	AZERBAIJAN	BANGLADESH
20. Can a woman convey citizenship to her non-national spouse in the same way as a man?	Yes	Yes	No
21. Are married women required by law to obey their husbands?	No	No	No
22. Do married couples jointly share legal responsibility for financially maintaining the family's expenses?	Yes	Yes	No

USING PROPERTY

Marital property regime

	AUSTRIA	AZERBAIJAN	BANGLADESH
23. What is the default marital property regime?	Deferred community of property	Partial community of property	Separation of property
24. Who legally administers property during marriage?	Original owner	Both must agree	Original owner

Protecting a wife's interests

	AUSTRIA	AZERBAIJAN	BANGLADESH
25. If it is the husband, does he need his wife's consent for major transactions	N/A	N/A	N/A
26. Are there special provisions governing the marital home?	No	No	No
27. Does the law provide for valuation of nonmonetary contributions during marriage?	Yes	Yes	No

Property rights

	Unmarried	Married	Unmarried	Married	Unmarried	Married
28. Do men and women have equal ownership rights to property?	Yes	Yes	Yes	Yes	Yes	Yes

Inheritance rights

	AUSTRIA	AZERBAIJAN	BANGLADESH
29. Do sons and daughters have equal inheritance rights to property?	Yes	Yes	No
30. Do female and male surviving spouses have equal inheritance rights to property?	Yes	Yes	No

GOING TO COURT

Equality of access

	AUSTRIA	AZERBAIJAN	BANGLADESH
31. Does the law recognize customary courts?	No	No	No
32. Does the law recognize personal law courts?	No	No	Yes
33. Does a woman's testimony carry the same evidentiary weight in court as a man's?	Yes	Yes	No

Efficiency of procedure

	AUSTRIA	AZERBAIJAN	BANGLADESH
34. Is there a small claims court or a fast track procedure for small claims?	Yes	No	Yes
35. If so, what is the maximum amount for a small claim (as a percentage of income per capita)?	42%	N/A	44%

Judicial representation

	AUSTRIA	AZERBAIJAN	BANGLADESH
36. How many justices are on the constitutional court?	12	9	9
37. Of those, how many are women?	5	2	1
38. Is the Chief Justice a woman?	No	No	No

GETTING A JOB

Parental benefits	AUSTRIA			AZERBAIJAN			BANGLADESH		
	Maternity	Paternity	Parental	Maternity	Paternity	Parental	Maternity	Paternity	Parental
39. Does the law mandate paid or unpaid maternity/paternity/parental leave?	Yes	No	Yes	Yes	Yes	Yes	Yes	No	No
40. What is the mandatory minimum length of paid leave for maternity/paternity/parental leave (in calendar days)?	112	N/A	232	126	0	1039	112	N/A	N/A
41. What is the mandatory minimum length of unpaid leave for maternity/paternity/parental leave (in calendar days)?	0	N/A	0	14	14	0	0	N/A	N/A
42. Who pays maternity/paternity/parental benefits?	Gov.	N/A	Gov.	Gov.	N/A	Gov.	Emp.	N/A	N/A
43. What percentage of wages are paid during maternity/paternity/parental leave?	100%	N/A	Partially paid	100%	0%	Partially paid	100%	N/A	N/A

	Mother	Father		Mother	Father		Mother	Father	
44. Where **paid** parental leave exists, what is the minimum amount which only the mother/father must take (in calendar days)?	172	60		0	0		N/A	N/A	
45. Where **unpaid** parental leave exists, what is the minimum amount which only the mother/father must take (in calendar days)?	N/A	N/A		N/A	N/A		N/A	N/A	

Retirement & pensions	Women	Men		Women	Men		Women	Men	
46. What is the age at which one can retire and receive full benefits?	65	65		58.5	63		60	60	
47. What is the age at which one can retire and receive partial benefits?	62	62		58.5	63		60	60	
48. What is the mandatory retirement age?	N/A	N/A		N/A	N/A		60	60	

Working hours and industry restrictions	AUSTRIA	AZERBAIJAN	BANGLADESH
49. Can non-pregnant and non-nursing women do the same jobs as men?	Yes	No	No
50. Can non-pregnant and non-nursing women engage in the following occupations in the same way as men?			
a. Mining	Yes	No	No
b. Construction	Yes	No	Yes
c. Metalwork	Yes	No	Yes
d. Factory work	Yes	No	No
e. Jobs requiring lifting weights above a threshold	Yes	No	Yes
f. Jobs deemed hazardous	Yes	No	No
g. Jobs deemed arduous	Yes	No	Yes
h. Jobs deemed morally or socially inappropriate	Yes	Yes	Yes
51. Can non-pregnant and non-nursing women work the same night hours as men?	Yes	No	Yes

Workplace protections	AUSTRIA	AZERBAIJAN	BANGLADESH
52. Does the law mandate equal remuneration for men and women for work of equal value?	No	Yes	Yes
53. Are there laws mandating non-discrimination based on gender in hiring?	No	Yes	No
54. Is it illegal for an employer to ask about family status during a job interview?	No	No	No
55. Are there laws penalizing or preventing the dismissal of pregnant women?	Yes	Yes	No
56. Must employers give employees an equivalent position when they return from maternity leave?	Yes	Yes	No
57. Are employers required to provide break time for nursing mothers?	Yes	Yes	No
58. Do employees with minor children have rights to a flexible/part time schedule?	Yes	Yes	No

BUILDING CREDIT

	AUSTRIA	AZERBAIJAN	BANGLADESH
59. What is the minimum loan amount covered in the private credit bureau or public credit registry (as a percentage of income per capita)?	1%	0%	87%
60. Do microfinance institutions provide information to private credit bureaus or public credit registries?	N/A	Yes	Yes
61. Do utility companies provide information to private credit bureaus or public credit registries?	No	No	No
62. Do retailers provide information to private credit bureaus or public credit registries?	No	No	No

PROVIDING INCENTIVES TO WORK

Childcare	AUSTRIA	AZERBAIJAN	BANGLADESH
63. Are payments for childcare tax deductible?	No	No	No
64. Is there public provision of childcare for children under the age of primary education?	Yes	Yes	No
65. Does the law mandate free and compulsory primary education?	Yes	Yes	Yes

Personal income tax	Women	Men		Women	Men		Women	Men	
66. Are there specific tax deductions or credits that are applicable only to men/women?	No	No		No	No		No	No	

Economy Tables

	BELARUS	BELGIUM	BENIN
REGION	Europe & Central Asia	High income: OECD	Sub-Saharan Africa
INCOME	Upper middle income	High income	Low income
FEMALE POPULATION	5,068,540	5,675,904	5,044,239
FEMALE LABOR FORCE PARTICIPATION	62%	62%	69%

ACCESSING INSTITUTIONS

Constitutional rights

	BELARUS	BELGIUM	BENIN
1. Is there a non-discrimination clause in the constitution?	Yes	No	No
2. If there is a non-discrimination clause in the constitution, does it explicitly mention gender?	No	N/A	N/A
3. Does the constitution guarantee equality before the law?	Yes	Yes	Yes

	Customary	Personal	Customary	Personal	Customary	Personal
4. Is customary/personal law recognized as valid source of law under the constitution?	No	No	No	No	Yes	No
5. If so, is it invalid if it violates constitutional provisions on non-discrimination or equality?	N/A	N/A	N/A	N/A	Yes	N/A

Quotas

	BELARUS	BELGIUM	BENIN
6. What are the legal quotas for women on corporate boards?	N/A	33%	N/A
7. What are the legal quotas for women in parliament?	N/A	N/A	N/A
8. What are the legal quotas for women in local government?	N/A	N/A	N/A

Rights of married and unmarried women

	Unmarried	Married	Unmarried	Married	Unmarried	Married
9. Can a woman apply for a passport in the same way as a man?	Yes	Yes	Yes	Yes	Yes	No
10. Can a woman apply for a national ID card in the same way as a man?	N/A	N/A	Yes	Yes	Yes	No
11. Can a woman travel outside the country in the same way as a man?	Yes	Yes	Yes	Yes	Yes	Yes
12. Can a woman travel outside her home in the same way as a man?	Yes	Yes	Yes	Yes	Yes	Yes
13. Can a woman get a job or pursue a trade or profession in the same way as a man?	Yes	Yes	Yes	Yes	Yes	Yes
14. Can a woman sign a contract in the same way as a man?	Yes	Yes	Yes	Yes	Yes	Yes
15. Can a woman register a business in the same way as a man?	Yes	Yes	Yes	Yes	Yes	Yes
16. Can a woman open a bank account in the same way as a man?	Yes	Yes	Yes	Yes	Yes	Yes
17. Can a woman choose where to live in the same way as a man?	Yes	Yes	Yes	Yes	Yes	No
18. Can a woman confer citizenship on her children in the same way as a man?	Yes	Yes	Yes	Yes	Yes	Yes
19. Can a woman be "head of household" or "head of family" in the same way as a man?	N/A	N/A	Yes	Yes	Yes	No
Number of inequalities in accessing institutions	0	0	0	0	0	4

Division of responsibility within marriage

	BELARUS	BELGIUM	BENIN
20. Can a woman convey citizenship to her non-national spouse in the same way as a man?	Yes	Yes	No
21. Are married women required by law to obey their husbands?	No	No	No
22. Do married couples jointly share legal responsibility for financially maintaining the family's expenses?	Yes	Yes	Yes

USING PROPERTY

Marital property regime

	BELARUS	BELGIUM	BENIN
23. What is the default marital property regime?	Partial community of property	Partial community of property	Separation of property
24. Who legally administers property during marriage?	Both must agree	Both must agree	Original owner

Protecting a wife's interests

	BELARUS	BELGIUM	BENIN
25. If it is the husband, does he need his wife's consent for major transactions	N/A	N/A	N/A
26. Are there special provisions governing the marital home?	No	Yes	Yes
27. Does the law provide for valuation of nonmonetary contributions during marriage?	Yes	Yes	Yes

Property rights

	Unmarried	Married	Unmarried	Married	Unmarried	Married
28. Do men and women have equal ownership rights to property?	Yes	Yes	Yes	Yes	Yes	Yes

Inheritance rights

	BELARUS	BELGIUM	BENIN
29. Do sons and daughters have equal inheritance rights to property?	Yes	Yes	Yes
30. Do female and male surviving spouses have equal inheritance rights to property?	Yes	Yes	Yes

GOING TO COURT

Equality of access

	BELARUS	BELGIUM	BENIN
31. Does the law recognize customary courts?	No	No	Yes
32. Does the law recognize personal law courts?	No	No	No
33. Does a woman's testimony carry the same evidentiary weight in court as a man's?	Yes	Yes	Yes

Efficiency of procedure

	BELARUS	BELGIUM	BENIN
34. Is there a small claims court or a fast track procedure for small claims?	Yes	Yes	No
35. If so, what is the maximum amount for a small claim (as a percentage of income per capita)?	36%	5%	N/A

Judicial representation

	BELARUS	BELGIUM	BENIN
36. How many justices are on the constitutional court?	12	12	7
37. Of those, how many are women?	4	1	2
38. Is the Chief Justice a woman?	No	No	No

	BELARUS			BELGIUM			BENIN		

GETTING A JOB

Parental benefits	Maternity	Paternity	Parental	Maternity	Paternity	Parental	Maternity	Paternity	Parental
39. Does the law mandate paid or unpaid maternity/paternity/parental leave?	Yes	No	Yes	Yes	Yes	Yes	Yes	Yes	No
40. What is the mandatory minimum length of paid leave for maternity/paternity/parental leave (in calendar days)?	126	N/A	1039	105	10	120	98	3	N/A
41. What is the mandatory minimum length of unpaid leave for maternity/paternity/parental leave (in calendar days)?	0	N/A	0	0	0	0	0	0	N/A
42. Who pays maternity/paternity/parental benefits?	Gov.	N/A	Gov.	Gov.	Emp. & Gov.	Gov.	Emp. & Gov.	Emp.	N/A
43. What percentage of wages are paid during maternity/paternity/parental leave?	100%	N/A	Partially paid	76%	87%	Partially paid	100%	100%	N/A

	Mother	Father		Mother	Father		Mother	Father	
44. Where **paid** parental leave exists, what is the minimum amount which only the mother/father must take (in calendar days)?	0	0		70	0		N/A	N/A	
45. Where **unpaid** parental leave exists, what is the minimum amount which only the mother/father must take (in calendar days)?	N/A	N/A		N/A	N/A		N/A	N/A	

Retirement & pensions	Women	Men		Women	Men		Women	Men	
46. What is the age at which one can retire and receive full benefits?	55	60		65	65		60	60	
47. What is the age at which one can retire and receive partial benefits?	55	60		62	62		55	55	
48. What is the mandatory retirement age?	N/A	N/A		N/A	N/A		N/A	N/A	

Working hours and industry restrictions	BELARUS	BELGIUM	BENIN
49. Can non-pregnant and non-nursing women do the same jobs as men?	No	Yes	No
50. Can non-pregnant and non-nursing women engage in the following occupations in the same way as men?			
a. Mining	No	Yes	No
b. Construction	No	Yes	No
c. Metalwork	No	Yes	No
d. Factory work	No	Yes	No
e. Jobs requiring lifting weights above a threshold	No	Yes	No
f. Jobs deemed hazardous	No	Yes	No
g. Jobs deemed arduous	No	Yes	No
h. Jobs deemed morally or socially inappropriate	Yes	Yes	Yes
51. Can non-pregnant and non-nursing women work the same night hours as men?	Yes	Yes	Yes

Workplace protections	BELARUS	BELGIUM	BENIN
52. Does the law mandate equal remuneration for men and women for work of equal value?	Yes	Yes	Yes
53. Are there laws mandating non-discrimination based on gender in hiring?	No	Yes	Yes
54. Is it illegal for an employer to ask about family status during a job interview?	No	No	No
55. Are there laws penalizing or preventing the dismissal of pregnant women?	Yes	Yes	Yes
56. Must employers give employees an equivalent position when they return from maternity leave?	Yes	Yes	No
57. Are employers required to provide break time for nursing mothers?	Yes	Yes	Yes
58. Do employees with minor children have rights to a flexible/part time schedule?	Yes	Yes	No

BUILDING CREDIT

	BELARUS	BELGIUM	BENIN
59. What is the minimum loan amount covered in the private credit bureau or public credit registry (as a percentage of income per capita)?	0%	1%	1323%
60. Do microfinance institutions provide information to private credit bureaus or public credit registries?	No	N/A	No
61. Do utility companies provide information to private credit bureaus or public credit registries?	No	No	No
62. Do retailers provide information to private credit bureaus or public credit registries?	No	No	No

PROVIDING INCENTIVES TO WORK

Childcare	BELARUS	BELGIUM	BENIN
63. Are payments for childcare tax deductible?	No	Yes	No
64. Is there public provision of childcare for children under the age of primary education?	Yes	Yes	Yes
65. Does the law mandate free and compulsory primary education?	Yes	Yes	Yes

Personal income tax	Women	Men	Women	Men	Women	Men
66. Are there specific tax deductions or credits that are applicable only to men/women?	No	No	No	No	No	Yes

Belarus-Benin

Economy Tables

	BOLIVIA	BOSNIA AND HERZEGOVINA	BOTSWANA
REGION	Latin America & Caribbean	Europe & Central Asia	Sub-Saharan Africa
INCOME	Lower middle income	Upper middle income	Upper middle income
FEMALE POPULATION	5,255,566	1,961,528	997,379
FEMALE LABOR FORCE PARTICIPATION	66%	42%	75%

ACCESSING INSTITUTIONS

Constitutional rights

	BOLIVIA	BOSNIA AND HERZEGOVINA	BOTSWANA
1. Is there a non-discrimination clause in the constitution?	Yes	Yes	Yes
2. If there is a non-discrimination clause in the constitution, does it explicitly mention gender?	Yes	Yes	Yes
3. Does the constitution guarantee equality before the law?	Yes	No	No

	Customary	Personal	Customary	Personal	Customary	Personal
4. Is customary/personal law recognized as valid source of law under the constitution?	Yes	No	No	No	Yes	No
5. If so, is it invalid if it violates constitutional provisions on non-discrimination or equality?	Yes	N/A	N/A	N/A	No	N/A

Quotas

	BOLIVIA	BOSNIA AND HERZEGOVINA	BOTSWANA
6. What are the legal quotas for women on corporate boards?	N/A	N/A	N/A
7. What are the legal quotas for women in parliament?	N/A	N/A	N/A
8. What are the legal quotas for women in local government?	N/A	N/A	N/A

Rights of married and unmarried women

	Unmarried	Married	Unmarried	Married	Unmarried	Married
9. Can a woman apply for a passport in the same way as a man?	Yes	Yes	Yes	Yes	Yes	No
10. Can a woman apply for a national ID card in the same way as a man?	Yes	Yes	Yes	Yes	Yes	Yes
11. Can a woman travel outside the country in the same way as a man?	Yes	Yes	Yes	Yes	Yes	Yes
12. Can a woman travel outside her home in the same way as a man?	Yes	Yes	Yes	Yes	Yes	Yes
13. Can a woman get a job or pursue a trade or profession in the same way as a man?	Yes	No	Yes	Yes	Yes	Yes
14. Can a woman sign a contract in the same way as a man?	Yes	Yes	Yes	Yes	Yes	Yes
15. Can a woman register a business in the same way as a man?	Yes	Yes	Yes	Yes	Yes	Yes
16. Can a woman open a bank account in the same way as a man?	Yes	Yes	Yes	Yes	Yes	Yes
17. Can a woman choose where to live in the same way as a man?	Yes	Yes	Yes	Yes	Yes	Yes
18. Can a woman confer citizenship on her children in the same way as a man?	Yes	Yes	Yes	Yes	Yes	Yes
19. Can a woman be "head of household" or "head of family" in the same way as a man?	N/A	N/A	N/A	N/A	N/A	N/A
Number of inequalities in accessing institutions	0	1	0	0	0	1

Division of responsibility within marriage

	BOLIVIA	BOSNIA AND HERZEGOVINA	BOTSWANA
20. Can a woman convey citizenship to her non-national spouse in the same way as a man?	Yes	Yes	Yes
21. Are married women required by law to obey their husbands?	No	No	No
22. Do married couples jointly share legal responsibility for financially maintaining the family's expenses?	Yes	Yes	Yes

USING PROPERTY

Marital property regime

	BOLIVIA	BOSNIA AND HERZEGOVINA	BOTSWANA
23. What is the default marital property regime?	Partial community of property	Partial community of property	Separation of property
24. Who legally administers property during marriage?	Both must agree	Both must agree	Original owner

Protecting a wife's interests

	BOLIVIA	BOSNIA AND HERZEGOVINA	BOTSWANA
25. If it is the husband, does he need his wife's consent for major transactions	N/A	N/A	N/A
26. Are there special provisions governing the marital home?	No	No	No
27. Does the law provide for valuation of nonmonetary contributions during marriage?	Yes	Yes	No

Property rights

	Unmarried	Married	Unmarried	Married	Unmarried	Married
28. Do men and women have equal ownership rights to property?	Yes	Yes	Yes	Yes	Yes	Yes

Inheritance rights

	BOLIVIA	BOSNIA AND HERZEGOVINA	BOTSWANA
29. Do sons and daughters have equal inheritance rights to property?	Yes	Yes	Yes
30. Do female and male surviving spouses have equal inheritance rights to property?	Yes	Yes	Yes

GOING TO COURT

Equality of access

	BOLIVIA	BOSNIA AND HERZEGOVINA	BOTSWANA
31. Does the law recognize customary courts?	No	No	Yes
32. Does the law recognize personal law courts?	No	No	No
33. Does a woman's testimony carry the same evidentiary weight in court as a man's?	Yes	Yes	Yes

Efficiency of procedure

	BOLIVIA	BOSNIA AND HERZEGOVINA	BOTSWANA
34. Is there a small claims court or a fast track procedure for small claims?	No	Yes	Yes
35. If so, what is the maximum amount for a small claim (as a percentage of income per capita)?	N/A	22%	17%

Judicial representation

	BOLIVIA	BOSNIA AND HERZEGOVINA	BOTSWANA
36. How many justices are on the constitutional court?	7	9	N/A
37. Of those, how many are women?	4	4	N/A
38. Is the Chief Justice a woman?	No	Yes	N/A

	BOLIVIA			BOSNIA AND HERZEGOVINA			BOTSWANA		

GETTING A JOB

Parental benefits	Maternity	Paternity	Parental	Maternity	Paternity	Parental	Maternity	Paternity	Parental
39. Does the law mandate paid or unpaid maternity/paternity/parental leave?	Yes	Yes	No	Yes	Yes	No	Yes	No	No
40. What is the mandatory minimum length of paid leave for maternity/paternity/parental leave (in calendar days)?	84	3	N/A	365	7	N/A	84	N/A	N/A
41. What is the mandatory minimum length of unpaid leave for maternity/paternity/parental leave (in calendar days)?	0	0	N/A	0	0	N/A	0	N/A	N/A
42. Who pays maternity/paternity/parental benefits?	Emp. & Gov.	Emp.	N/A	Gov.	Emp. & Gov.	N/A	Emp.	N/A	N/A
43. What percentage of wages are paid during maternity/paternity/parental leave?	83%	100%	N/A	60%	100%	N/A	50%	N/A	N/A

	Mother	Father		Mother	Father		Mother	Father	
44. Where **paid** parental leave exists, what is the minimum amount which only the mother/father must take (in calendar days)?	N/A	N/A		N/A	N/A		N/A	N/A	
45. Where **unpaid** parental leave exists, what is the minimum amount which only the mother/father must take (in calendar days)?	N/A	N/A		N/A	N/A		N/A	N/A	

Retirement & pensions	Women	Men		Women	Men		Women	Men	
46. What is the age at which one can retire and receive full benefits?	57	58		65	65		65	65	
47. What is the age at which one can retire and receive partial benefits?	49	55		55	60		65	65	
48. What is the mandatory retirement age?	N/A	N/A		65	65		N/A	N/A	

Working hours and industry restrictions									
49. Can non-pregnant and non-nursing women do the same jobs as men?	No			No			Yes		
50. Can non-pregnant and non-nursing women engage in the following occupations in the same way as men?									
a. Mining	Yes			No			Yes		
b. Construction	Yes			Yes			Yes		
c. Metalwork	Yes			Yes			Yes		
d. Factory work	Yes			Yes			Yes		
e. Jobs requiring lifting weights above a threshold	Yes			Yes			Yes		
f. Jobs deemed hazardous	No			No			Yes		
g. Jobs deemed arduous	No			No			Yes		
h. Jobs deemed morally or socially inappropriate	No			Yes			Yes		
51. Can non-pregnant and non-nursing women work the same night hours as men?	No			Yes			Yes		

Workplace protections									
52. Does the law mandate equal remuneration for men and women for work of equal value?	Yes			No			No		
53. Are there laws mandating non-discrimination based on gender in hiring?	No			Yes			No		
54. Is it illegal for an employer to ask about family status during a job interview?	No			No			No		
55. Are there laws penalizing or preventing the dismissal of pregnant women?	Yes			Yes			Yes		
56. Must employers give employees an equivalent position when they return from maternity leave?	Yes			Yes			No		
57. Are employers required to provide break time for nursing mothers?	Yes			Yes			Yes		
58. Do employees with minor children have rights to a flexible/part time schedule?	No			Yes			No		

BUILDING CREDIT

59. What is the minimum loan amount covered in the private credit bureau or public credit registry (as a percentage of income per capita)?	0%			0%			0%		
60. Do microfinance institutions provide information to private credit bureaus or public credit registries?	Yes			Yes			Yes		
61. Do utility companies provide information to private credit bureaus or public credit registries?	No			Yes			No		
62. Do retailers provide information to private credit bureaus or public credit registries?	Yes			No			Yes		

PROVIDING INCENTIVES TO WORK

Childcare									
63. Are payments for childcare tax deductible?	No			No			No		
64. Is there public provision of childcare for children under the age of primary education?	Yes			Yes			No		
65. Does the law mandate free and compulsory primary education?	Yes			Yes			No		

Personal income tax	Women	Men		Women	Men		Women	Men	
66. Are there specific tax deductions or credits that are applicable only to men/women?	No	No		No	No		No	No	

Economy Tables

	BRAZIL	BULGARIA	BURKINA FASO
REGION	Latin America & Caribbean	Europe & Central Asia	Sub-Saharan Africa
INCOME	Upper middle income	Upper middle income	Low income
FEMALE POPULATION	100,932,913	3,752,355	8,283,921
FEMALE LABOR FORCE PARTICIPATION	65%	63%	80%

ACCESSING INSTITUTIONS

Constitutional rights

	BRAZIL	BULGARIA	BURKINA FASO
1. Is there a non-discrimination clause in the constitution?	Yes	No	Yes
2. If there is a non-discrimination clause in the constitution, does it explicitly mention gender?	Yes	N/A	Yes
3. Does the constitution guarantee equality before the law?	Yes	Yes	Yes

	Customary	Personal	Customary	Personal	Customary	Personal
4. Is customary/personal law recognized as valid source of law under the constitution?	No	No	No	No	Yes	No
5. If so, is it invalid if it violates constitutional provisions on non-discrimination or equality?	N/A	N/A	N/A	N/A	Yes	N/A

Quotas

	BRAZIL	BULGARIA	BURKINA FASO
6. What are the legal quotas for women on corporate boards?	N/A	N/A	N/A
7. What are the legal quotas for women in parliament?	N/A	N/A	N/A
8. What are the legal quotas for women in local government?	N/A	N/A	N/A

Rights of married and unmarried women

	Unmarried	Married	Unmarried	Married	Unmarried	Married
9. Can a woman apply for a passport in the same way as a man?	Yes	Yes	Yes	Yes	Yes	Yes
10. Can a woman apply for a national ID card in the same way as a man?	Yes	Yes	Yes	Yes	Yes	Yes
11. Can a woman travel outside the country in the same way as a man?	Yes	Yes	Yes	Yes	Yes	Yes
12. Can a woman travel outside her home in the same way as a man?	Yes	Yes	Yes	Yes	Yes	Yes
13. Can a woman get a job or pursue a trade or profession in the same way as a man?	Yes	Yes	Yes	Yes	Yes	Yes
14. Can a woman sign a contract in the same way as a man?	Yes	Yes	Yes	Yes	Yes	Yes
15. Can a woman register a business in the same way as a man?	Yes	Yes	Yes	Yes	Yes	Yes
16. Can a woman open a bank account in the same way as a man?	Yes	Yes	Yes	Yes	Yes	Yes
17. Can a woman choose where to live in the same way as a man?	Yes	Yes	Yes	Yes	Yes	No
18. Can a woman confer citizenship on her children in the same way as a man?	Yes	Yes	Yes	Yes	Yes	Yes
19. Can a woman be "head of household" or "head of family" in the same way as a man?	N/A	N/A	N/A	N/A	N/A	N/A
Number of inequalities in accessing institutions	0	0	0	0	0	1

Division of responsibility within marriage

	BRAZIL	BULGARIA	BURKINA FASO
20. Can a woman convey citizenship to her non-national spouse in the same way as a man?	Yes	Yes	Yes
21. Are married women required by law to obey their husbands?	No	No	No
22. Do married couples jointly share legal responsibility for financially maintaining the family's expenses?	Yes	Yes	Yes

USING PROPERTY

Marital property regime

	BRAZIL	BULGARIA	BURKINA FASO
23. What is the default marital property regime?	Partial community of property	Partial community of property	Partial community of property
24. Who legally administers property during marriage?	Both must agree	Both must agree	Both must agree

Protecting a wife's interests

	BRAZIL	BULGARIA	BURKINA FASO
25. If it is the husband, does he need his wife's consent for major transactions	N/A	N/A	N/A
26. Are there special provisions governing the marital home?	No	Yes	Yes
27. Does the law provide for valuation of nonmonetary contributions during marriage?	Yes	Yes	Yes

Property rights

	Unmarried	Married	Unmarried	Married	Unmarried	Married
28. Do men and women have equal ownership rights to property?	Yes	Yes	Yes	Yes	Yes	Yes

Inheritance rights

	BRAZIL	BULGARIA	BURKINA FASO
29. Do sons and daughters have equal inheritance rights to property?	Yes	Yes	Yes
30. Do female and male surviving spouses have equal inheritance rights to property?	Yes	Yes	Yes

GOING TO COURT

Equality of access

	BRAZIL	BULGARIA	BURKINA FASO
31. Does the law recognize customary courts?	No	No	No
32. Does the law recognize personal law courts?	No	No	No
33. Does a woman's testimony carry the same evidentiary weight in court as a man's?	Yes	Yes	Yes

Efficiency of procedure

	BRAZIL	BULGARIA	BURKINA FASO
34. Is there a small claims court or a fast track procedure for small claims?	Yes	No	No
35. If so, what is the maximum amount for a small claim (as a percentage of income per capita)?	131%	N/A	N/A

Judicial representation

	BRAZIL	BULGARIA	BURKINA FASO
36. How many justices are on the constitutional court?	11	12	12
37. Of those, how many are women?	2	3	3
38. Is the Chief Justice a woman?	No	No	No

GETTING A JOB

Parental benefits	BRAZIL			BULGARIA			BURKINA FASO		
	Maternity	Paternity	Parental	Maternity	Paternity	Parental	Maternity	Paternity	Parental
39. Does the law mandate paid or unpaid maternity/paternity/parental leave?	Yes	Yes	No	Yes	Yes	Yes	Yes	Yes	No
40. What is the mandatory minimum length of paid leave for maternity/paternity/parental leave (in calendar days)?	120	5	N/A	410	15	547.5	98	3	N/A
41. What is the mandatory minimum length of unpaid leave for maternity/paternity/parental leave (in calendar days)?	0	0	N/A	0	0	0	0	0	N/A
42. Who pays maternity/paternity/parental benefits?	Gov.	Emp.	N/A	Gov.	Gov.	Gov.	Gov.	Emp.	N/A
43. What percentage of wages are paid during maternity/paternity/parental leave?	100%	100%	N/A	90%	90%	Partially paid	100%	100%	N/A

	Mother	Father		Mother	Father		Mother	Father	
44. Where **paid** parental leave exists, what is the minimum amount which only the mother/father must take (in calendar days)?	N/A	N/A		0	0		N/A	N/A	
45. Where **unpaid** parental leave exists, what is the minimum amount which only the mother/father must take (in calendar days)?	N/A	N/A		N/A	N/A		N/A	N/A	

Retirement & pensions	Women	Men		Women	Men		Women	Men	
46. What is the age at which one can retire and receive full benefits?	60	65		63	65		56	56	
47. What is the age at which one can retire and receive partial benefits?	48	53		63	65		56	56	
48. What is the mandatory retirement age?	N/A	N/A		N/A	N/A		N/A	N/A	

Working hours and industry restrictions	BRAZIL	BULGARIA	BURKINA FASO
49. Can non-pregnant and non-nursing women do the same jobs as men?	No	Yes	No
50. Can non-pregnant and non-nursing women engage in the following occupations in the same way as men?			
a. Mining	Yes	Yes	Yes
b. Construction	Yes	Yes	Yes
c. Metalwork	Yes	Yes	Yes
d. Factory work	Yes	Yes	Yes
e. Jobs requiring lifting weights above a threshold	No	Yes	Yes
f. Jobs deemed hazardous	Yes	Yes	No
g. Jobs deemed arduous	Yes	Yes	Yes
h. Jobs deemed morally or socially inappropriate	Yes	Yes	Yes
51. Can non-pregnant and non-nursing women work the same night hours as men?	Yes	Yes	Yes

Workplace protections	BRAZIL	BULGARIA	BURKINA FASO
52. Does the law mandate equal remuneration for men and women for work of equal value?	Yes	Yes	Yes
53. Are there laws mandating non-discrimination based on gender in hiring?	Yes	No	No
54. Is it illegal for an employer to ask about family status during a job interview?	No	Yes	No
55. Are there laws penalizing or preventing the dismissal of pregnant women?	Yes	Yes	Yes
56. Must employers give employees an equivalent position when they return from maternity leave?	Yes	No	No
57. Are employers required to provide break time for nursing mothers?	Yes	Yes	Yes
58. Do employees with minor children have rights to a flexible/part time schedule?	No	No	No

BUILDING CREDIT

	BRAZIL	BULGARIA	BURKINA FASO
59. What is the minimum loan amount covered in the private credit bureau or public credit registry (as a percentage of income per capita)?	0%	0%	1769%
60. Do microfinance institutions provide information to private credit bureaus or public credit registries?	Yes	No	No
61. Do utility companies provide information to private credit bureaus or public credit registries?	Yes	Yes	No
62. Do retailers provide information to private credit bureaus or public credit registries?	Yes	No	No

PROVIDING INCENTIVES TO WORK

Childcare	BRAZIL	BULGARIA	BURKINA FASO
63. Are payments for childcare tax deductible?	Yes	No	No
64. Is there public provision of childcare for children under the age of primary education?	Yes	Yes	Yes
65. Does the law mandate free and compulsory primary education?	Yes	Yes	Yes

Personal income tax	Women	Men		Women	Men		Women	Men	
66. Are there specific tax deductions or credits that are applicable only to men/women?	No	No		No	No		No	Yes	

Economy Tables

	BURUNDI		CAMBODIA		CAMEROON	
REGION	Sub-Saharan Africa		East Asia & Pacific		Sub-Saharan Africa	
INCOME	Low income		Low income		Lower middle income	
FEMALE POPULATION	4,985,172		7,614,222		10,853,507	
FEMALE LABOR FORCE PARTICIPATION	85%		82%		66%	

ACCESSING INSTITUTIONS

Constitutional rights

	BURUNDI		CAMBODIA		CAMEROON	
1. Is there a non-discrimination clause in the constitution?	Yes		Yes		No	
2. If there is a non-discrimination clause in the constitution, does it explicitly mention gender?	Yes		Yes		N/A	
3. Does the constitution guarantee equality before the law?	Yes		Yes		Yes	

	Customary	Personal	Customary	Personal	Customary	Personal
4. Is customary/personal law recognized as valid source of law under the constitution?	No	No	No	No	No	No
5. If so, is it invalid if it violates constitutional provisions on non-discrimination or equality?	N/A	N/A	N/A	N/A	N/A	N/A

Quotas

	BURUNDI	CAMBODIA	CAMEROON
6. What are the legal quotas for women on corporate boards?	N/A	N/A	N/A
7. What are the legal quotas for women in parliament?	30%	N/A	N/A
8. What are the legal quotas for women in local government?	30%	N/A	N/A

Rights of married and unmarried women

	Unmarried	Married	Unmarried	Married	Unmarried	Married
9. Can a woman apply for a passport in the same way as a man?	Yes	Yes	Yes	Yes	Yes	No
10. Can a woman apply for a national ID card in the same way as a man?	Yes	Yes	Yes	Yes	Yes	No
11. Can a woman travel outside the country in the same way as a man?	Yes	Yes	Yes	Yes	Yes	Yes
12. Can a woman travel outside her home in the same way as a man?	Yes	Yes	Yes	Yes	Yes	Yes
13. Can a woman get a job or pursue a trade or profession in the same way as a man?	Yes	Yes	Yes	Yes	Yes	No
14. Can a woman sign a contract in the same way as a man?	Yes	Yes	Yes	Yes	Yes	Yes
15. Can a woman register a business in the same way as a man?	Yes	Yes	Yes	Yes	Yes	Yes
16. Can a woman open a bank account in the same way as a man?	Yes	Yes	Yes	Yes	Yes	Yes
17. Can a woman choose where to live in the same way as a man?	Yes	Yes	Yes	Yes	Yes	No
18. Can a woman confer citizenship on her children in the same way as a man?	Yes	Yes	Yes	Yes	Yes	Yes
19. Can a woman be "head of household" or "head of family" in the same way as a man?	Yes	No	N/A	N/A	Yes	No
Number of inequalities in accessing institutions	0	1	0	0	0	5

Division of responsibility within marriage

	BURUNDI	CAMBODIA	CAMEROON
20. Can a woman convey citizenship to her non-national spouse in the same way as a man?	No	Yes	No
21. Are married women required by law to obey their husbands?	No	No	No
22. Do married couples jointly share legal responsibility for financially maintaining the family's expenses?	Yes	Yes	Yes

USING PROPERTY

Marital property regime

	BURUNDI	CAMBODIA	CAMEROON
23. What is the default marital property regime?	Full community of property	Partial community of property	Partial community of property
24. Who legally administers property during marriage?	Both must agree	Both must agree	Husband

Protecting a wife's interests

	BURUNDI	CAMBODIA	CAMEROON
25. If it is the husband, does he need his wife's consent for major transactions	N/A	N/A	No
26. Are there special provisions governing the marital home?	No	Yes	No
27. Does the law provide for valuation of nonmonetary contributions during marriage?	Yes	Yes	Yes

Property rights

	Unmarried	Married	Unmarried	Married	Unmarried	Married
28. Do men and women have equal ownership rights to property?	Yes	Yes	Yes	Yes	Yes	No

Inheritance rights

	BURUNDI	CAMBODIA	CAMEROON
29. Do sons and daughters have equal inheritance rights to property?	Yes	Yes	Yes
30. Do female and male surviving spouses have equal inheritance rights to property?	No	Yes	Yes

GOING TO COURT

Equality of access

	BURUNDI	CAMBODIA	CAMEROON
31. Does the law recognize customary courts?	No	No	Yes
32. Does the law recognize personal law courts?	No	No	No
33. Does a woman's testimony carry the same evidentiary weight in court as a man's?	Yes	Yes	Yes

Efficiency of procedure

	BURUNDI	CAMBODIA	CAMEROON
34. Is there a small claims court or a fast track procedure for small claims?	Yes	Yes	Yes
35. If so, what is the maximum amount for a small claim (as a percentage of income per capita)?	88%	29%	1683%

Judicial representation

	BURUNDI	CAMBODIA	CAMEROON
36. How many justices are on the constitutional court?	N/A	9	6
37. Of those, how many are women?	N/A	2	0
38. Is the Chief Justice a woman?	N/A	No	No

GETTING A JOB

Parental benefits	BURUNDI			CAMBODIA			CAMEROON		
	Maternity	Paternity	Parental	Maternity	Paternity	Parental	Maternity	Paternity	Parental
39. Does the law mandate paid or unpaid maternity/paternity/parental leave?	Yes	Yes	No	Yes	No	No	Yes	Yes	No
40. What is the mandatory minimum length of paid leave for maternity/paternity/parental leave (in calendar days)?	84	4	N/A	90	N/A	N/A	98	3	N/A
41. What is the mandatory minimum length of unpaid leave for maternity/paternity/parental leave (in calendar days)?	0	0	N/A	0	N/A	N/A	0	0	N/A
42. Who pays maternity/paternity/parental benefits?	Emp. & Gov.	Emp.	N/A	Emp.	N/A	N/A	Gov.	Emp.	N/A
43. What percentage of wages are paid during maternity/paternity/parental leave?	100%	100%	N/A	50%	N/A	N/A	100%	100%	N/A

	Mother	Father		Mother	Father		Mother	Father	
44. Where **paid** parental leave exists, what is the minimum amount which only the mother/father must take (in calendar days)?	N/A	N/A		N/A	N/A		N/A	N/A	
45. Where **unpaid** parental leave exists, what is the minimum amount which only the mother/father must take (in calendar days)?	N/A	N/A		N/A	N/A		N/A	N/A	

Retirement & pensions	Women	Men		Women	Men		Women	Men	
46. What is the age at which one can retire and receive full benefits?	60	60		55	55		60	60	
47. What is the age at which one can retire and receive partial benefits?	60	60		55	55		50	50	
48. What is the mandatory retirement age?	60	60		N/A	N/A		N/A	N/A	

Working hours and industry restrictions	BURUNDI	CAMBODIA	CAMEROON
49. Can non-pregnant and non-nursing women do the same jobs as men?	Yes	Yes	No
50. Can non-pregnant and non-nursing women engage in the following occupations in the same way as men?			
a. Mining	Yes	Yes	No
b. Construction	Yes	Yes	No
c. Metalwork	Yes	Yes	No
d. Factory work	Yes	Yes	No
e. Jobs requiring lifting weights above a threshold	Yes	Yes	No
f. Jobs deemed hazardous	Yes	Yes	No
g. Jobs deemed arduous	Yes	Yes	No
h. Jobs deemed morally or socially inappropriate	Yes	Yes	No
51. Can non-pregnant and non-nursing women work the same night hours as men?	Yes	Yes	No

Workplace protections	BURUNDI	CAMBODIA	CAMEROON
52. Does the law mandate equal remuneration for men and women for work of equal value?	Yes	Yes	No
53. Are there laws mandating non-discrimination based on gender in hiring?	Yes	Yes	No
54. Is it illegal for an employer to ask about family status during a job interview?	No	No	No
55. Are there laws penalizing or preventing the dismissal of pregnant women?	Yes	Yes	Yes
56. Must employers give employees an equivalent position when they return from maternity leave?	No	No	Yes
57. Are employers required to provide break time for nursing mothers?	Yes	Yes	Yes
58. Do employees with minor children have rights to a flexible/part time schedule?	No	No	No

BUILDING CREDIT

	BURUNDI	CAMBODIA	CAMEROON
59. What is the minimum loan amount covered in the private credit bureau or public credit registry (as a percentage of income per capita)?	293%	0%	0%
60. Do microfinance institutions provide information to private credit bureaus or public credit registries?	No	Yes	No
61. Do utility companies provide information to private credit bureaus or public credit registries?	No	No	No
62. Do retailers provide information to private credit bureaus or public credit registries?	No	No	No

PROVIDING INCENTIVES TO WORK

Childcare	BURUNDI	CAMBODIA	CAMEROON
63. Are payments for childcare tax deductible?	No	No	No
64. Is there public provision of childcare for children under the age of primary education?	No	Yes	Yes
65. Does the law mandate free and compulsory primary education?	Yes	Yes	Yes

Personal income tax	Women	Men		Women	Men		Women	Men	
66. Are there specific tax deductions or credits that are applicable only to men/women?	No	No		No	Yes		No	No	

Economy Tables

	CANADA	CHAD	CHILE
REGION	High income: OECD	Sub-Saharan Africa	High income: OECD
INCOME	High income	Low income	High income
FEMALE POPULATION	17,573,875	6,215,959	8,826,682
FEMALE LABOR FORCE PARTICIPATION	74%	65%	53%

ACCESSING INSTITUTIONS

Constitutional rights

	CANADA	CHAD	CHILE
1. Is there a non-discrimination clause in the constitution?	Yes	Yes	No
2. If there is a non-discrimination clause in the constitution, does it explicitly mention gender?	Yes	Yes	N/A
3. Does the constitution guarantee equality before the law?	Yes	Yes	Yes

	Customary	Personal	Customary	Personal	Customary	Personal
4. Is customary/personal law recognized as valid source of law under the constitution?	Yes	No	Yes	No	No	No
5. If so, is it invalid if it violates constitutional provisions on non-discrimination or equality?	Yes	N/A	No	N/A	N/A	N/A

Quotas

	CANADA	CHAD	CHILE
6. What are the legal quotas for women on corporate boards?	N/A	N/A	N/A
7. What are the legal quotas for women in parliament?	N/A	N/A	N/A
8. What are the legal quotas for women in local government?	N/A	N/A	N/A

Rights of married and unmarried women

	Unmarried	Married	Unmarried	Married	Unmarried	Married
9. Can a woman apply for a passport in the same way as a man?	Yes	Yes	Yes	Yes	Yes	Yes
10. Can a woman apply for a national ID card in the same way as a man?	Yes	Yes	..	..	Yes	Yes
11. Can a woman travel outside the country in the same way as a man?	Yes	Yes	Yes	Yes	Yes	Yes
12. Can a woman travel outside her home in the same way as a man?	Yes	Yes	Yes	Yes	Yes	Yes
13. Can a woman get a job or pursue a trade or profession in the same way as a man?	Yes	Yes	Yes	No	Yes	Yes
14. Can a woman sign a contract in the same way as a man?	Yes	Yes	Yes	Yes	Yes	Yes
15. Can a woman register a business in the same way as a man?	Yes	Yes	Yes	Yes	Yes	Yes
16. Can a woman open a bank account in the same way as a man?	Yes	Yes	Yes	Yes	Yes	Yes
17. Can a woman choose where to live in the same way as a man?	Yes	Yes	Yes	No	Yes	Yes
18. Can a woman confer citizenship on her children in the same way as a man?	Yes	Yes	Yes	Yes	Yes	Yes
19. Can a woman be "head of household" or "head of family" in the same way as a man?	N/A	N/A	Yes	No	Yes	No
Number of inequalities in accessing institutions	0	0	0	3	0	1

Division of responsibility within marriage

	CANADA	CHAD	CHILE
20. Can a woman convey citizenship to her non-national spouse in the same way as a man?	Yes	Yes	Yes
21. Are married women required by law to obey their husbands?	No	No	No
22. Do married couples jointly share legal responsibility for financially maintaining the family's expenses?	Yes	Yes	Yes

USING PROPERTY

Marital property regime

	CANADA	CHAD	CHILE
23. What is the default marital property regime?	Partial community of property	Partial community of property	Partial community of property
24. Who legally administers property during marriage?	Both must agree	Both must agree	Husband

Protecting a wife's interests

	CANADA	CHAD	CHILE
25. If it is the husband, does he need his wife's consent for major transactions	N/A	N/A	Yes
26. Are there special provisions governing the marital home?	Yes	No	No
27. Does the law provide for valuation of nonmonetary contributions during marriage?	Yes	Yes	Yes

Property rights

	Unmarried	Married	Unmarried	Married	Unmarried	Married
28. Do men and women have equal ownership rights to property?	Yes	Yes	Yes	Yes	Yes	No

Inheritance rights

	CANADA	CHAD	CHILE
29. Do sons and daughters have equal inheritance rights to property?	Yes	Yes	Yes
30. Do female and male surviving spouses have equal inheritance rights to property?	Yes	Yes	Yes

GOING TO COURT

Equality of access

	CANADA	CHAD	CHILE
31. Does the law recognize customary courts?	No	No	No
32. Does the law recognize personal law courts?	No	No	No
33. Does a woman's testimony carry the same evidentiary weight in court as a man's?	Yes	Yes	Yes

Efficiency of procedure

	CANADA	CHAD	CHILE
34. Is there a small claims court or a fast track procedure for small claims?	Yes	No	Yes
35. If so, what is the maximum amount for a small claim (as a percentage of income per capita)?	51%	N/A	308%

Judicial representation

	CANADA	CHAD	CHILE
36. How many justices are on the constitutional court?	9	6	10
37. Of those, how many are women?	3	1	1
38. Is the Chief Justice a woman?	Yes	No	No

GETTING A JOB

	CANADA			CHAD			CHILE		
Parental benefits	*Maternity*	*Paternity*	*Parental*	*Maternity*	*Paternity*	*Parental*	*Maternity*	*Paternity*	*Parental*
39. Does the law mandate paid or unpaid maternity/paternity/parental leave?	Yes	No	Yes	Yes	Yes	No	Yes	Yes	Yes
40. What is the mandatory minimum length of paid leave for maternity/paternity/parental leave (in calendar days)?	105	N/A	245	98	0	N/A	126	5	84
41. What is the mandatory minimum length of unpaid leave for maternity/paternity/parental leave (in calendar days)?	14	N/A	14	0	1	N/A	0	0	0
42. Who pays maternity/paternity/parental benefits?	Gov.	N/A	Gov.	Gov.	N/A	N/A	Gov.	Emp.	Gov.
43. What percentage of wages are paid during maternity/paternity/parental leave?	32%	N/A	Partially paid	50%	0%	N/A	100%	100%	100%

	Mother	*Father*		*Mother*	*Father*		*Mother*	*Father*	
44. Where **paid** parental leave exists, what is the minimum amount which only the mother/father must take (in calendar days)?	0	0		N/A	N/A		42	0	
45. Where **unpaid** parental leave exists, what is the minimum amount which only the mother/father must take (in calendar days)?	0	0		N/A	N/A		N/A	N/A	

Retirement & pensions	*Women*	*Men*		*Women*	*Men*		*Women*	*Men*	
46. What is the age at which one can retire and receive full benefits?	65	65		60	60		60	65	
47. What is the age at which one can retire and receive partial benefits?	55	55		55	55		0	0	
48. What is the mandatory retirement age?	0	N/A		N/A	N/A		N/A	N/A	

Working hours and industry restrictions	CANADA	CHAD	CHILE
49. Can non-pregnant and non-nursing women do the same jobs as men?	Yes	No	No
50. Can non-pregnant and non-nursing women engage in the following occupations in the same way as men?			
a. Mining	Yes	No	Yes
b. Construction	Yes	No	Yes
c. Metalwork	Yes	No	Yes
d. Factory work	Yes	No	Yes
e. Jobs requiring lifting weights above a threshold	Yes	Yes	No
f. Jobs deemed hazardous	Yes	No	Yes
g. Jobs deemed arduous	Yes	Yes	Yes
h. Jobs deemed morally or socially inappropriate	Yes	No	Yes
51. Can non-pregnant and non-nursing women work the same night hours as men?	Yes	No	Yes

Workplace protections	CANADA	CHAD	CHILE
52. Does the law mandate equal remuneration for men and women for work of equal value?	Yes	Yes	No
53. Are there laws mandating non-discrimination based on gender in hiring?	Yes	Yes	No
54. Is it illegal for an employer to ask about family status during a job interview?	Yes	No	No
55. Are there laws penalizing or preventing the dismissal of pregnant women?	Yes	Yes	Yes
56. Must employers give employees an equivalent position when they return from maternity leave?	Yes	Yes	Yes
57. Are employers required to provide break time for nursing mothers?	No	Yes	Yes
58. Do employees with minor children have rights to a flexible/part time schedule?	No	No	No

BUILDING CREDIT

	CANADA	CHAD	CHILE
59. What is the minimum loan amount covered in the private credit bureau or public credit registry (as a percentage of income per capita)?	0%	0%	0%
60. Do microfinance institutions provide information to private credit bureaus or public credit registries?	N/A	No	Yes
61. Do utility companies provide information to private credit bureaus or public credit registries?	No	No	No
62. Do retailers provide information to private credit bureaus or public credit registries?	No	No	Yes

PROVIDING INCENTIVES TO WORK

Childcare	CANADA	CHAD	CHILE
63. Are payments for childcare tax deductible?	Yes	No	No
64. Is there public provision of childcare for children under the age of primary education?	Yes	Yes	Yes
65. Does the law mandate free and compulsory primary education?	Yes	Yes	Yes

Personal income tax	*Women*	*Men*		*Women*	*Men*		*Women*	*Men*	
66. Are there specific tax deductions or credits that are applicable only to men/women?	No	No		No	No		No	No	

Economy Tables

	CHINA		COLOMBIA		CONGO, DEM. REP.	
REGION	East Asia & Pacific		Latin America & Caribbean		Sub-Saharan Africa	
INCOME	Upper middle income		Upper middle income		Low income	
FEMALE POPULATION	650,847,295		24,243,208		33,067,397	
FEMALE LABOR FORCE PARTICIPATION	75%		59%		71%	

ACCESSING INSTITUTIONS

Constitutional rights

	CHINA		COLOMBIA		CONGO, DEM. REP.	
1. Is there a non-discrimination clause in the constitution?	No		Yes		Yes	
2. If there is a non-discrimination clause in the constitution, does it explicitly mention gender?	N/A		Yes		Yes	
3. Does the constitution guarantee equality before the law?	Yes		Yes		Yes	
	Customary	Personal	Customary	Personal	Customary	Personal
4. Is customary/personal law recognized as valid source of law under the constitution?	No	No	Yes	No	Yes	No
5. If so, is it invalid if it violates constitutional provisions on non-discrimination or equality?	N/A	N/A	Yes	N/A	Yes	N/A

Quotas

	CHINA	COLOMBIA	CONGO, DEM. REP.
6. What are the legal quotas for women on corporate boards?	N/A	N/A	N/A
7. What are the legal quotas for women in parliament?	N/A	N/A	N/A
8. What are the legal quotas for women in local government?	N/A	30%	N/A

Rights of married and unmarried women

	Unmarried	Married	Unmarried	Married	Unmarried	Married
9. Can a woman apply for a passport in the same way as a man?	Yes	Yes	Yes	Yes	Yes	Yes
10. Can a woman apply for a national ID card in the same way as a man?	Yes	Yes	Yes	Yes	N/A	N/A
11. Can a woman travel outside the country in the same way as a man?	Yes	Yes	Yes	Yes	Yes	Yes
12. Can a woman travel outside her home in the same way as a man?	Yes	Yes	Yes	Yes	Yes	Yes
13. Can a woman get a job or pursue a trade or profession in the same way as a man?	Yes	Yes	Yes	Yes	Yes	No
14. Can a woman sign a contract in the same way as a man?	Yes	Yes	Yes	Yes	Yes	No
15. Can a woman register a business in the same way as a man?	Yes	Yes	Yes	Yes	Yes	No
16. Can a woman open a bank account in the same way as a man?	Yes	Yes	Yes	Yes	Yes	No
17. Can a woman choose where to live in the same way as a man?	Yes	Yes	Yes	Yes	Yes	No
18. Can a woman confer citizenship on her children in the same way as a man?	Yes	Yes	Yes	Yes	Yes	Yes
19. Can a woman be "head of household" or "head of family" in the same way as a man?	N/A	N/A	Yes	Yes	Yes	No
Number of inequalities in accessing institutions	0	0	0	0	0	6

Division of responsibility within marriage

	CHINA	COLOMBIA	CONGO, DEM. REP.
20. Can a woman convey citizenship to her non-national spouse in the same way as a man?	Yes	Yes	Yes
21. Are married women required by law to obey their husbands?	No	No	Yes
22. Do married couples jointly share legal responsibility for financially maintaining the family's expenses?	Yes	Yes	Yes

USING PROPERTY

Marital property regime

	CHINA	COLOMBIA	CONGO, DEM. REP.
23. What is the default marital property regime?	Partial community of property	Deferred community of property	Partial community of property
24. Who legally administers property during marriage?	Both must agree	Original owner	Husband

Protecting a wife's interests

	CHINA	COLOMBIA	CONGO, DEM. REP.
25. If it is the husband, does he need his wife's consent for major transactions	N/A	N/A	Yes
26. Are there special provisions governing the marital home?	No	No	No
27. Does the law provide for valuation of nonmonetary contributions during marriage?	Yes	Yes	Yes

Property rights

	Unmarried	Married	Unmarried	Married	Unmarried	Married
28. Do men and women have equal ownership rights to property?	Yes	Yes	Yes	Yes	Yes	No

Inheritance rights

	CHINA	COLOMBIA	CONGO, DEM. REP.
29. Do sons and daughters have equal inheritance rights to property?	Yes	Yes	Yes
30. Do female and male surviving spouses have equal inheritance rights to property?	Yes	Yes	Yes

GOING TO COURT

Equality of access

	CHINA	COLOMBIA	CONGO, DEM. REP.
31. Does the law recognize customary courts?	No	Yes	No
32. Does the law recognize personal law courts?	No	No	No
33. Does a woman's testimony carry the same evidentiary weight in court as a man's?	Yes	Yes	Yes

Efficiency of procedure

	CHINA	COLOMBIA	CONGO, DEM. REP.
34. Is there a small claims court or a fast track procedure for small claims?	No	Yes	No
35. If so, what is the maximum amount for a small claim (as a percentage of income per capita)?	N/A	71%	N/A

Judicial representation

	CHINA	COLOMBIA	CONGO, DEM. REP.
36. How many justices are on the constitutional court?	N/A	9	8
37. Of those, how many are women?	N/A	1	0
38. Is the Chief Justice a woman?	N/A	No	No

	CHINA			COLOMBIA			CONGO, DEM. REP.		
GETTING A JOB									
Parental benefits	*Maternity*	*Paternity*	*Parental*	*Maternity*	*Paternity*	*Parental*	*Maternity*	*Paternity*	*Parental*
39. Does the law mandate paid or unpaid maternity/paternity/parental leave?	Yes	Yes	No	Yes	Yes	No	Yes	Yes	No
40. What is the mandatory minimum length of paid leave for maternity/paternity/parental leave (in calendar days)?	98	3	N/A	98	10	N/A	98	2	N/A
41. What is the mandatory minimum length of unpaid leave for maternity/paternity/parental leave (in calendar days)?	0	0	N/A	0	0	N/A	0	0	N/A
42. Who pays maternity/paternity/parental benefits?	Emp. & Gov.	Emp.	N/A	Gov.	Gov.	N/A	Emp.	Emp.	N/A
43. What percentage of wages are paid during maternity/paternity/parental leave?	100%	100%	N/A	100%	100%	N/A	67%	100%	N/A
	Mother	*Father*		*Mother*	*Father*		*Mother*	*Father*	
44. Where **paid** parental leave exists, what is the minimum amount which only the mother/father must take (in calendar days)?	N/A	N/A		N/A	N/A		N/A	N/A	
45. Where **unpaid** parental leave exists, what is the minimum amount which only the mother/father must take (in calendar days)?	N/A	N/A		N/A	N/A		N/A	N/A	
Retirement & pensions	*Women*	*Men*		*Women*	*Men*		*Women*	*Men*	
46. What is the age at which one can retire and receive full benefits?	50	60		57	62		60	65	
47. What is the age at which one can retire and receive partial benefits?	50	60		57	62		60	65	
48. What is the mandatory retirement age?	N/A	N/A		N/A	N/A		60	65	
Working hours and industry restrictions									
49. Can non-pregnant and non-nursing women do the same jobs as men?	No			No			No		
50. Can non-pregnant and non-nursing women engage in the following occupations in the same way as men?									
a. Mining	No			No			Yes		
b. Construction	Yes			Yes			Yes		
c. Metalwork	Yes			Yes			Yes		
d. Factory work	Yes			Yes			Yes		
e. Jobs requiring lifting weights above a threshold	No			No			Yes		
f. Jobs deemed hazardous	Yes			No			Yes		
g. Jobs deemed arduous	No			No			No		
h. Jobs deemed morally or socially inappropriate	Yes			Yes			Yes		
51. Can non-pregnant and non-nursing women work the same night hours as men?	Yes			Yes			No		
Workplace protections									
52. Does the law mandate equal remuneration for men and women for work of equal value?	No			No			No		
53. Are there laws mandating non-discrimination based on gender in hiring?	Yes			No			No		
54. Is it illegal for an employer to ask about family status during a job interview?	No			No			No		
55. Are there laws penalizing or preventing the dismissal of pregnant women?	Yes			Yes			Yes		
56. Must employers give employees an equivalent position when they return from maternity leave?	No			Yes			No		
57. Are employers required to provide break time for nursing mothers?	Yes			Yes			Yes		
58. Do employees with minor children have rights to a flexible/part time schedule?	No			No			No		
BUILDING CREDIT									
59. What is the minimum loan amount covered in the private credit bureau or public credit registry (as a percentage of income per capita)?	N/A			103%			N/A		
60. Do microfinance institutions provide information to private credit bureaus or public credit registries?	Yes			Yes			N/A		
61. Do utility companies provide information to private credit bureaus or public credit registries?	No			Yes			N/A		
62. Do retailers provide information to private credit bureaus or public credit registries?	No			Yes			N/A		
PROVIDING INCENTIVES TO WORK									
Childcare									
63. Are payments for childcare tax deductible?	No			No			No		
64. Is there public provision of childcare for children under the age of primary education?	No			Yes			Yes		
65. Does the law mandate free and compulsory primary education?	Yes			Yes			Yes		
Personal income tax	*Women*	*Men*		*Women*	*Men*		*Women*	*Men*	
66. Are there specific tax deductions or credits that are applicable only to men/women?	No	No		No	No		No	No	

Economy Tables

	CONGO, REP.		COSTA RICA		CÔTE D'IVOIRE	
REGION	Sub-Saharan Africa		Latin America & Caribbean		Sub-Saharan Africa	
INCOME	Lower middle income		Upper middle income		Lower middle income	
FEMALE POPULATION	2,169,153		2,364,999		9,719,412	
FEMALE LABOR FORCE PARTICIPATION	70%		51%		53%	

ACCESSING INSTITUTIONS

Constitutional rights

	CONGO, REP.		COSTA RICA		CÔTE D'IVOIRE	
1. Is there a non-discrimination clause in the constitution?	Yes		Yes		No	
2. If there is a non-discrimination clause in the constitution, does it explicitly mention gender?	Yes		No		N/A	
3. Does the constitution guarantee equality before the law?	Yes		Yes		Yes	

	Customary	Personal	Customary	Personal	Customary	Personal
4. Is customary/personal law recognized as valid source of law under the constitution?	No	No	No	No	Yes	No
5. If so, is it invalid if it violates constitutional provisions on non-discrimination or equality?	N/A	N/A	N/A	N/A	Yes	N/A

Quotas

	CONGO, REP.		COSTA RICA		CÔTE D'IVOIRE	
6. What are the legal quotas for women on corporate boards?	N/A		N/A		N/A	
7. What are the legal quotas for women in parliament?	N/A		N/A		N/A	
8. What are the legal quotas for women in local government?	N/A		N/A		N/A	

Rights of married and unmarried women

	Unmarried	Married	Unmarried	Married	Unmarried	Married
9. Can a woman apply for a passport in the same way as a man?	Yes	No	Yes	Yes	Yes	Yes
10. Can a woman apply for a national ID card in the same way as a man?	Yes	Yes	Yes	Yes	Yes	Yes
11. Can a woman travel outside the country in the same way as a man?	Yes	Yes	Yes	Yes	Yes	Yes
12. Can a woman travel outside her home in the same way as a man?	Yes	Yes	Yes	Yes	Yes	Yes
13. Can a woman get a job or pursue a trade or profession in the same way as a man?	Yes	Yes	Yes	Yes	Yes	Yes
14. Can a woman sign a contract in the same way as a man?	Yes	Yes	Yes	Yes	Yes	Yes
15. Can a woman register a business in the same way as a man?	Yes	Yes	Yes	Yes	Yes	Yes
16. Can a woman open a bank account in the same way as a man?	Yes	Yes	Yes	Yes	Yes	Yes
17. Can a woman choose where to live in the same way as a man?	Yes	No	Yes	Yes	Yes	Yes
18. Can a woman confer citizenship on her children in the same way as a man?	Yes	Yes	Yes	Yes	Yes	Yes
19. Can a woman be "head of household" or "head of family" in the same way as a man?	Yes	No	N/A	N/A	N/A	N/A
Number of inequalities in accessing institutions	0	3	0	0	0	0

Division of responsibility within marriage

	CONGO, REP.		COSTA RICA		CÔTE D'IVOIRE	
20. Can a woman convey citizenship to her non-national spouse in the same way as a man?	No		Yes		Yes	
21. Are married women required by law to obey their husbands?	No		No		No	
22. Do married couples jointly share legal responsibility for financially maintaining the family's expenses?	Yes		Yes		Yes	

USING PROPERTY

Marital property regime

	CONGO, REP.		COSTA RICA		CÔTE D'IVOIRE	
23. What is the default marital property regime?	Partial community of property		Deferred community of property		Partial community of property	
24. Who legally administers property during marriage?	Husband		Original owner		Husband	

Protecting a wife's interests

	CONGO, REP.		COSTA RICA		CÔTE D'IVOIRE	
25. If it is the husband, does he need his wife's consent for major transactions	Yes		N/A		Yes	
26. Are there special provisions governing the marital home?	No		No		No	
27. Does the law provide for valuation of nonmonetary contributions during marriage?	Yes		Yes		Yes	

Property rights

	Unmarried	Married	Unmarried	Married	Unmarried	Married
28. Do men and women have equal ownership rights to property?	Yes	No	Yes	Yes	Yes	No

Inheritance rights

	CONGO, REP.		COSTA RICA		CÔTE D'IVOIRE	
29. Do sons and daughters have equal inheritance rights to property?	Yes		Yes		Yes	
30. Do female and male surviving spouses have equal inheritance rights to property?	Yes		Yes		Yes	

GOING TO COURT

Equality of access

	CONGO, REP.		COSTA RICA		CÔTE D'IVOIRE	
31. Does the law recognize customary courts?	No		No		No	
32. Does the law recognize personal law courts?	No		No		No	
33. Does a woman's testimony carry the same evidentiary weight in court as a man's?	Yes		Yes		Yes	

Efficiency of procedure

	CONGO, REP.		COSTA RICA		CÔTE D'IVOIRE	
34. Is there a small claims court or a fast track procedure for small claims?	No		Yes		No	
35. If so, what is the maximum amount for a small claim (as a percentage of income per capita)?	N/A		47%		N/A	

Judicial representation

	CONGO, REP.		COSTA RICA		CÔTE D'IVOIRE	
36. How many justices are on the constitutional court?	9		7		7	
37. Of those, how many are women?	1		1		2	
38. Is the Chief Justice a woman?	No		Yes		No	

GETTING A JOB

Parental benefits

	Maternity	Paternity	Parental	Maternity	Paternity	Parental	Maternity	Paternity	Parental
39. Does the law mandate paid or unpaid maternity/paternity/parental leave?	Yes	No	No	Yes	No	No	Yes	Yes	No
40. What is the mandatory minimum length of paid leave for maternity/paternity/parental leave (in calendar days)?	105	N/A	N/A	120	N/A	N/A	98	2	N/A
41. What is the mandatory minimum length of unpaid leave for maternity/paternity/parental leave (in calendar days)?	0	N/A	N/A	0	N/A	N/A	0	0	N/A
42. Who pays maternity/paternity/parental benefits?	Emp. & Gov.	N/A	N/A	Emp. & Gov.	N/A	N/A	Gov.	Emp.	N/A
43. What percentage of wages are paid during maternity/paternity/parental leave?	100%	N/A	N/A	100%	N/A	N/A	100%	100%	N/A

	Mother	Father		Mother	Father		Mother	Father	
44. Where **paid** parental leave exists, what is the minimum amount which only the mother/father must take (in calendar days)?	N/A	N/A		N/A	N/A		N/A	N/A	
45. Where **unpaid** parental leave exists, what is the minimum amount which only the mother/father must take (in calendar days)?	N/A	N/A		N/A	N/A		N/A	N/A	

Retirement & pensions

	Women	Men		Women	Men		Women	Men	
46. What is the age at which one can retire and receive full benefits?	65	65		65	65		55	55	
47. What is the age at which one can retire and receive partial benefits?	60	60		60	62		50	50	
48. What is the mandatory retirement age?	65	65		N/A	N/A		55	55	

Working hours and industry restrictions

	CONGO, REP.	COSTA RICA	CÔTE D'IVOIRE
49. Can non-pregnant and non-nursing women do the same jobs as men?	No	No	No
50. Can non-pregnant and non-nursing women engage in the following occupations in the same way as men?			
a. Mining	No	Yes	Yes
b. Construction	No	Yes	Yes
c. Metalwork	Yes	Yes	Yes
d. Factory work	No	Yes	Yes
e. Jobs requiring lifting weights above a threshold	Yes	Yes	Yes
f. Jobs deemed hazardous	Yes	No	Yes
g. Jobs deemed arduous	Yes	No	No
h. Jobs deemed morally or socially inappropriate	Yes	No	Yes
51. Can non-pregnant and non-nursing women work the same night hours as men?	No	No	Yes

Workplace protections

	CONGO, REP.	COSTA RICA	CÔTE D'IVOIRE
52. Does the law mandate equal remuneration for men and women for work of equal value?	No	No	No
53. Are there laws mandating non-discrimination based on gender in hiring?	No	Yes	Yes
54. Is it illegal for an employer to ask about family status during a job interview?	No	No	No
55. Are there laws penalizing or preventing the dismissal of pregnant women?	No	Yes	Yes
56. Must employers give employees an equivalent position when they return from maternity leave?	Yes	Yes	Yes
57. Are employers required to provide break time for nursing mothers?	Yes	Yes	Yes
58. Do employees with minor children have rights to a flexible/part time schedule?	No	No	Yes

BUILDING CREDIT

	CONGO, REP.	COSTA RICA	CÔTE D'IVOIRE
59. What is the minimum loan amount covered in the private credit bureau or public credit registry (as a percentage of income per capita)?	0%	0%	1846%
60. Do microfinance institutions provide information to private credit bureaus or public credit registries?	No	No	No
61. Do utility companies provide information to private credit bureaus or public credit registries?	No	No	No
62. Do retailers provide information to private credit bureaus or public credit registries?	No	No	No

PROVIDING INCENTIVES TO WORK

Childcare

	CONGO, REP.	COSTA RICA	CÔTE D'IVOIRE
63. Are payments for childcare tax deductible?	No	No	No
64. Is there public provision of childcare for children under the age of primary education?	Yes	Yes	No
65. Does the law mandate free and compulsory primary education?	Yes	Yes	No

Personal income tax

	Women	Men		Women	Men		Women	Men	
66. Are there specific tax deductions or credits that are applicable only to men/women?	No	Yes		No	No		No	No	

Economy Tables

	CROATIA		CZECH REPUBLIC		DENMARK	
REGION	Europe & Central Asia		High income: OECD		High income: OECD	
INCOME	High income		High income		High income	
FEMALE POPULATION	2,208,496		5,341,731		2,816,544	
FEMALE LABOR FORCE PARTICIPATION	59%		62%		76%	

ACCESSING INSTITUTIONS

Constitutional rights

	CROATIA		CZECH REPUBLIC		DENMARK	
1. Is there a non-discrimination clause in the constitution?	No		No		No	
2. If there is a non-discrimination clause in the constitution, does it explicitly mention gender?	N/A		N/A		N/A	
3. Does the constitution guarantee equality before the law?	Yes		No		No	

	Customary	Personal	Customary	Personal	Customary	Personal
4. Is customary/personal law recognized as valid source of law under the constitution?	No	No	No	No	No	No
5. If so, is it invalid if it violates constitutional provisions on non-discrimination or equality?	N/A	N/A	N/A	N/A	N/A	N/A

Quotas

	CROATIA	CZECH REPUBLIC	DENMARK
6. What are the legal quotas for women on corporate boards?	N/A	N/A	N/A
7. What are the legal quotas for women in parliament?	N/A	N/A	N/A
8. What are the legal quotas for women in local government?	N/A	N/A	N/A

Rights of married and unmarried women

	Unmarried	Married	Unmarried	Married	Unmarried	Married
9. Can a woman apply for a passport in the same way as a man?	Yes	Yes	Yes	Yes	Yes	Yes
10. Can a woman apply for a national ID card in the same way as a man?	Yes	Yes	Yes	Yes	Yes	Yes
11. Can a woman travel outside the country in the same way as a man?	Yes	Yes	Yes	Yes	Yes	Yes
12. Can a woman travel outside her home in the same way as a man?	Yes	Yes	Yes	Yes	Yes	Yes
13. Can a woman get a job or pursue a trade or profession in the same way as a man?	Yes	Yes	Yes	Yes	Yes	Yes
14. Can a woman sign a contract in the same way as a man?	Yes	Yes	Yes	Yes	Yes	Yes
15. Can a woman register a business in the same way as a man?	Yes	Yes	Yes	Yes	Yes	Yes
16. Can a woman open a bank account in the same way as a man?	Yes	Yes	Yes	Yes	Yes	Yes
17. Can a woman choose where to live in the same way as a man?	Yes	Yes	Yes	Yes	Yes	Yes
18. Can a woman confer citizenship on her children in the same way as a man?	Yes	Yes	Yes	Yes	Yes	Yes
19. Can a woman be "head of household" or "head of family" in the same way as a man?	N/A	N/A	N/A	N/A	N/A	N/A
Number of inequalities in accessing institutions	0	0	0	0	0	0

Division of responsibility within marriage

	CROATIA	CZECH REPUBLIC	DENMARK
20. Can a woman convey citizenship to her non-national spouse in the same way as a man?	Yes	Yes	Yes
21. Are married women required by law to obey their husbands?	No	No	No
22. Do married couples jointly share legal responsibility for financially maintaining the family's expenses?	Yes	Yes	Yes

USING PROPERTY

Marital property regime

	CROATIA	CZECH REPUBLIC	DENMARK
23. What is the default marital property regime?	Partial community of property	Partial community of property	Deferred community of property
24. Who legally administers property during marriage?	Both must agree	Both must agree	Original owner

Protecting a wife's interests

	CROATIA	CZECH REPUBLIC	DENMARK
25. If it is the husband, does he need his wife's consent for major transactions	N/A	N/A	N/A
26. Are there special provisions governing the marital home?	No	No	Yes
27. Does the law provide for valuation of nonmonetary contributions during marriage?	Yes	Yes	Yes

Property rights

	Unmarried	Married	Unmarried	Married	Unmarried	Married
28. Do men and women have equal ownership rights to property?	Yes	Yes	Yes	Yes	Yes	Yes

Inheritance rights

	CROATIA	CZECH REPUBLIC	DENMARK
29. Do sons and daughters have equal inheritance rights to property?	Yes	Yes	Yes
30. Do female and male surviving spouses have equal inheritance rights to property?	Yes	Yes	Yes

GOING TO COURT

Equality of access

	CROATIA	CZECH REPUBLIC	DENMARK
31. Does the law recognize customary courts?	No	No	No
32. Does the law recognize personal law courts?	No	No	No
33. Does a woman's testimony carry the same evidentiary weight in court as a man's?	Yes	Yes	Yes

Efficiency of procedure

	CROATIA	CZECH REPUBLIC	DENMARK
34. Is there a small claims court or a fast track procedure for small claims?	Yes	No	Yes
35. If so, what is the maximum amount for a small claim (as a percentage of income per capita)?	13%	N/A	15%

Judicial representation

	CROATIA	CZECH REPUBLIC	DENMARK
36. How many justices are on the constitutional court?	13	15	16
37. Of those, how many are women?	5	5	4
38. Is the Chief Justice a woman?	Yes	No	No

GETTING A JOB

Parental benefits

	CROATIA			CZECH REPUBLIC			DENMARK		
	Maternity	Paternity	Parental	Maternity	Paternity	Parental	Maternity	Paternity	Parental
39. Does the law mandate paid or unpaid maternity/paternity/parental leave?	Yes	No	Yes	Yes	No	Yes	Yes	Yes	Yes
40. What is the mandatory minimum length of paid leave for maternity/paternity/parental leave (in calendar days)?	208	N/A	180	196	N/A	1095	126	14	224
41. What is the mandatory minimum length of unpaid leave for maternity/paternity/parental leave (in calendar days)?	0	N/A	730	0	N/A	0	0	0	0
42. Who pays maternity/paternity/parental benefits?	Gov.	N/A	Gov.	Gov.	N/A	Gov.	Gov.	Gov.	Gov.
43. What percentage of wages are paid during maternity/paternity/parental leave?	100%	N/A	Partially paid	70%	N/A	Partially paid	50%	50%	Partially paid

	Mother	Father		Mother	Father		Mother	Father	
44. Where **paid** parental leave exists, what is the minimum amount which only the mother/father must take (in calendar days)?	90	90		0	0		0	0	
45. Where **unpaid** parental leave exists, what is the minimum amount which only the mother/father must take (in calendar days)?	0	0		N/A	N/A		N/A	N/A	

Retirement & pensions

	Women	Men		Women	Men		Women	Men	
46. What is the age at which one can retire and receive full benefits?	64.5	65		66	66		67	67	
47. What is the age at which one can retire and receive partial benefits?	59.5	60		61	61		67	67	
48. What is the mandatory retirement age?	N/A	N/A		N/A	N/A		N/A	N/A	

Working hours and industry restrictions

	CROATIA	CZECH REPUBLIC	DENMARK
49. Can non-pregnant and non-nursing women do the same jobs as men?	Yes	No	Yes
50. Can non-pregnant and non-nursing women engage in the following occupations in the same way as men?			
a. Mining	Yes	No	Yes
b. Construction	Yes	Yes	Yes
c. Metalwork	Yes	Yes	Yes
d. Factory work	Yes	Yes	Yes
e. Jobs requiring lifting weights above a threshold	Yes	No	Yes
f. Jobs deemed hazardous	Yes	Yes	Yes
g. Jobs deemed arduous	Yes	Yes	Yes
h. Jobs deemed morally or socially inappropriate	Yes	Yes	Yes
51. Can non-pregnant and non-nursing women work the same night hours as men?	Yes	Yes	Yes

Workplace protections

	CROATIA	CZECH REPUBLIC	DENMARK
52. Does the law mandate equal remuneration for men and women for work of equal value?	Yes	Yes	Yes
53. Are there laws mandating non-discrimination based on gender in hiring?	Yes	Yes	No
54. Is it illegal for an employer to ask about family status during a job interview?	Yes	Yes	No
55. Are there laws penalizing or preventing the dismissal of pregnant women?	Yes	Yes	Yes
56. Must employers give employees an equivalent position when they return from maternity leave?	Yes	Yes	Yes
57. Are employers required to provide break time for nursing mothers?	Yes	Yes	No
58. Do employees with minor children have rights to a flexible/part time schedule?	Yes	Yes	No

BUILDING CREDIT

	CROATIA	CZECH REPUBLIC	DENMARK
59. What is the minimum loan amount covered in the private credit bureau or public credit registry (as a percentage of income per capita)?	0%	0%	0%
60. Do microfinance institutions provide information to private credit bureaus or public credit registries?	N/A	N/A	N/A
61. Do utility companies provide information to private credit bureaus or public credit registries?	No	No	Yes
62. Do retailers provide information to private credit bureaus or public credit registries?	No	No	Yes

PROVIDING INCENTIVES TO WORK

Childcare

	CROATIA	CZECH REPUBLIC	DENMARK
63. Are payments for childcare tax deductible?	No	No	No
64. Is there public provision of childcare for children under the age of primary education?	Yes	Yes	Yes
65. Does the law mandate free and compulsory primary education?	Yes	Yes	Yes

Personal income tax

	Women	Men		Women	Men		Women	Men	
66. Are there specific tax deductions or credits that are applicable only to men/women?	No	No		No	No		No	No	

Economy Tables

	DOMINICAN REPUBLIC		ECUADOR		EGYPT, ARAB REP.	
REGION	Latin America & Caribbean		Latin America & Caribbean		Middle East & North Africa	
INCOME	Upper middle income		Upper middle income		Lower middle income	
FEMALE POPULATION	5,134,311		7,744,933		40,187,819	
FEMALE LABOR FORCE PARTICIPATION	55%		57%		26%	

ACCESSING INSTITUTIONS

Constitutional rights

	DOMINICAN REPUBLIC		ECUADOR		EGYPT, ARAB REP.	
1. Is there a non-discrimination clause in the constitution?	Yes		Yes		Yes	
2. If there is a non-discrimination clause in the constitution, does it explicitly mention gender?	Yes		Yes		No	
3. Does the constitution guarantee equality before the law?	Yes		Yes		Yes	

	Customary	Personal	Customary	Personal	Customary	Personal
4. Is customary/personal law recognized as valid source of law under the constitution?	No	No	Yes	No	No	Yes
5. If so, is it invalid if it violates constitutional provisions on non-discrimination or equality?	N/A	N/A	Yes	N/A	N/A	No

Quotas

	DOMINICAN REPUBLIC	ECUADOR	EGYPT, ARAB REP.
6. What are the legal quotas for women on corporate boards?	N/A	N/A	N/A
7. What are the legal quotas for women in parliament?	N/A	N/A	N/A
8. What are the legal quotas for women in local government?	N/A	N/A	N/A

Rights of married and unmarried women

	Unmarried	Married	Unmarried	Married	Unmarried	Married
9. Can a woman apply for a passport in the same way as a man?	Yes	Yes	Yes	Yes	Yes	No
10. Can a woman apply for a national ID card in the same way as a man?	Yes	Yes	Yes	Yes	No	No
11. Can a woman travel outside the country in the same way as a man?	Yes	Yes	Yes	Yes	Yes	Yes
12. Can a woman travel outside her home in the same way as a man?	Yes	Yes	Yes	Yes	Yes	Yes
13. Can a woman get a job or pursue a trade or profession in the same way as a man?	Yes	Yes	Yes	Yes	Yes	Yes
14. Can a woman sign a contract in the same way as a man?	Yes	Yes	Yes	Yes	Yes	Yes
15. Can a woman register a business in the same way as a man?	Yes	Yes	Yes	Yes	Yes	Yes
16. Can a woman open a bank account in the same way as a man?	Yes	Yes	Yes	Yes	Yes	Yes
17. Can a woman choose where to live in the same way as a man?	Yes	Yes	Yes	Yes	Yes	Yes
18. Can a woman confer citizenship on her children in the same way as a man?	Yes	Yes	Yes	Yes	Yes	Yes
19. Can a woman be "head of household" or "head of family" in the same way as a man?	N/A	N/A	N/A	N/A	N/A	N/A
Number of inequalities in accessing institutions	0	0	0	0	1	2

Division of responsibility within marriage

	DOMINICAN REPUBLIC	ECUADOR	EGYPT, ARAB REP.
20. Can a woman convey citizenship to her non-national spouse in the same way as a man?	Yes	Yes	No
21. Are married women required by law to obey their husbands?	No	No	Yes
22. Do married couples jointly share legal responsibility for financially maintaining the family's expenses?	Yes	Yes	No

USING PROPERTY

Marital property regime

	DOMINICAN REPUBLIC	ECUADOR	EGYPT, ARAB REP.
23. What is the default marital property regime?	Partial community of property	Partial community of property	Separation of property
24. Who legally administers property during marriage?	Both must agree	Other	Original owner

Protecting a wife's interests

	DOMINICAN REPUBLIC	ECUADOR	EGYPT, ARAB REP.
25. If it is the husband, does he need his wife's consent for major transactions	N/A	N/A	N/A
26. Are there special provisions governing the marital home?	No	No	No
27. Does the law provide for valuation of nonmonetary contributions during marriage?	Yes	Yes	No

Property rights

	Unmarried	Married	Unmarried	Married	Unmarried	Married
28. Do men and women have equal ownership rights to property?	Yes	Yes	Yes	No	Yes	Yes

Inheritance rights

	DOMINICAN REPUBLIC	ECUADOR	EGYPT, ARAB REP.
29. Do sons and daughters have equal inheritance rights to property?	Yes	Yes	No
30. Do female and male surviving spouses have equal inheritance rights to property?	Yes	Yes	No

GOING TO COURT

Equality of access

	DOMINICAN REPUBLIC	ECUADOR	EGYPT, ARAB REP.
31. Does the law recognize customary courts?	No	Yes	No
32. Does the law recognize personal law courts?	No	No	Yes
33. Does a woman's testimony carry the same evidentiary weight in court as a man's?	Yes	Yes	No

Efficiency of procedure

	DOMINICAN REPUBLIC	ECUADOR	EGYPT, ARAB REP.
34. Is there a small claims court or a fast track procedure for small claims?	Yes	No	Yes
35. If so, what is the maximum amount for a small claim (as a percentage of income per capita)?	2%	N/A	62%

Judicial representation

	DOMINICAN REPUBLIC	ECUADOR	EGYPT, ARAB REP.
36. How many justices are on the constitutional court?	13	9	11
37. Of those, how many are women?	3	4	0
38. Is the Chief Justice a woman?	No	No	No

GETTING A JOB

Parental benefits

	DOMINICAN REPUBLIC			ECUADOR			EGYPT, ARAB. REP.		
	Maternity	Paternity	Parental	Maternity	Paternity	Parental	Maternity	Paternity	Parental
39. Does the law mandate paid or unpaid maternity/paternity/parental leave?	Yes	Yes	No	Yes	Yes	No	Yes	No	No
40. What is the mandatory minimum length of paid leave for maternity/paternity/parental leave (in calendar days)?	84	2	N/A	84	12	N/A	90	N/A	N/A
41. What is the mandatory minimum length of unpaid leave for maternity/paternity/parental leave (in calendar days)?	0	0	N/A	0	0	N/A	730	N/A	N/A
42. Who pays maternity/paternity/parental benefits?	Emp. & Gov.	Emp.	N/A	Emp. & Gov.	Emp.	N/A	Emp. & Gov.	N/A	N/A
43. What percentage of wages are paid during maternity/paternity/parental leave?	100%	100%	N/A	100%	100%	N/A	100%	N/A	N/A

	Mother	Father		Mother	Father		Mother	Father	
44. Where **paid** parental leave exists, what is the minimum amount which only the mother/father must take (in calendar days)?	N/A	N/A		N/A	N/A		N/A	N/A	
45. Where **unpaid** parental leave exists, what is the minimum amount which only the mother/father must take (in calendar days)?	N/A	N/A		N/A	N/A		N/A	N/A	

Retirement & pensions

	Women	Men		Women	Men		Women	Men	
46. What is the age at which one can retire and receive full benefits?	60	60		60	60		60	60	
47. What is the age at which one can retire and receive partial benefits?	55	55		60	60		60	60	
48. What is the mandatory retirement age?	N/A	N/A		N/A	N/A		60	60	

Working hours and industry restrictions

	DOMINICAN REPUBLIC	ECUADOR	EGYPT, ARAB. REP.
49. Can non-pregnant and non-nursing women do the same jobs as men?	Yes	No	No
50. Can non-pregnant and non-nursing women engage in the following occupations in the same way as men?			
a. Mining	Yes	No	No
b. Construction	Yes	Yes	No
c. Metalwork	Yes	Yes	No
d. Factory work	Yes	Yes	No
e. Jobs requiring lifting weights above a threshold	Yes	No	No
f. Jobs deemed hazardous	Yes	Yes	No
g. Jobs deemed arduous	Yes	Yes	No
h. Jobs deemed morally or socially inappropriate	Yes	Yes	No
51. Can non-pregnant and non-nursing women work the same night hours as men?	Yes	Yes	No

Workplace protections

	DOMINICAN REPUBLIC	ECUADOR	EGYPT, ARAB. REP.
52. Does the law mandate equal remuneration for men and women for work of equal value?	No	Yes	No
53. Are there laws mandating non-discrimination based on gender in hiring?	No	Yes	No
54. Is it illegal for an employer to ask about family status during a job interview?	No	No	No
55. Are there laws penalizing or preventing the dismissal of pregnant women?	Yes	Yes	Yes
56. Must employers give employees an equivalent position when they return from maternity leave?	Yes	No	No
57. Are employers required to provide break time for nursing mothers?	Yes	Yes	Yes
58. Do employees with minor children have rights to a flexible/part time schedule?	No	No	No

BUILDING CREDIT

	DOMINICAN REPUBLIC	ECUADOR	EGYPT, ARAB. REP.
59. What is the minimum loan amount covered in the private credit bureau or public credit registry (as a percentage of income per capita)?	0%	0%	0%
60. Do microfinance institutions provide information to private credit bureaus or public credit registries?	Yes	Yes	Yes
61. Do utility companies provide information to private credit bureaus or public credit registries?	Yes	Yes	No
62. Do retailers provide information to private credit bureaus or public credit registries?	Yes	Yes	No

PROVIDING INCENTIVES TO WORK

Childcare

	DOMINICAN REPUBLIC	ECUADOR	EGYPT, ARAB. REP.
63. Are payments for childcare tax deductible?	No	No	No
64. Is there public provision of childcare for children under the age of primary education?	Yes	Yes	Yes
65. Does the law mandate free and compulsory primary education?	Yes	Yes	Yes

Personal income tax

	Women	Men		Women	Men		Women	Men	
66. Are there specific tax deductions or credits that are applicable only to men/women?	No	No		No	No		No	No	

Economy Tables

	EL SALVADOR		ESTONIA		ETHIOPIA	
REGION	Latin America & Caribbean		High income: OECD		Sub-Saharan Africa	
INCOME	Lower middle income		High income		Low income	
FEMALE POPULATION	3,310,287		718,214		45,842,030	
FEMALE LABOR FORCE PARTICIPATION	51%		72%		81%	

ACCESSING INSTITUTIONS

Constitutional rights

	EL SALVADOR		ESTONIA		ETHIOPIA	
1. Is there a non-discrimination clause in the constitution?	No		Yes		Yes	
2. If there is a non-discrimination clause in the constitution, does it explicitly mention gender?	N/A		Yes		Yes	
3. Does the constitution guarantee equality before the law?	Yes		Yes		Yes	

	Customary	Personal	Customary	Personal	Customary	Personal
4. Is customary/personal law recognized as valid source of law under the constitution?	No	No	No	No	Yes	Yes
5. If so, is it invalid if it violates constitutional provisions on non-discrimination or equality?	N/A	N/A	N/A	N/A	Yes	Yes

Quotas

	EL SALVADOR	ESTONIA	ETHIOPIA
6. What are the legal quotas for women on corporate boards?	N/A	N/A	N/A
7. What are the legal quotas for women in parliament?	N/A	N/A	N/A
8. What are the legal quotas for women in local government?	N/A	N/A	N/A

Rights of married and unmarried women

	Unmarried	Married	Unmarried	Married	Unmarried	Married
9. Can a woman apply for a passport in the same way as a man?	Yes	Yes	Yes	Yes	Yes	Yes
10. Can a woman apply for a national ID card in the same way as a man?	Yes	Yes	Yes	Yes	Yes	Yes
11. Can a woman travel outside the country in the same way as a man?	Yes	Yes	Yes	Yes	Yes	Yes
12. Can a woman travel outside her home in the same way as a man?	Yes	Yes	Yes	Yes	Yes	Yes
13. Can a woman get a job or pursue a trade or profession in the same way as a man?	Yes	Yes	Yes	Yes	Yes	Yes
14. Can a woman sign a contract in the same way as a man?	Yes	Yes	Yes	Yes	Yes	Yes
15. Can a woman register a business in the same way as a man?	Yes	Yes	Yes	Yes	Yes	Yes
16. Can a woman open a bank account in the same way as a man?	Yes	Yes	Yes	Yes	Yes	Yes
17. Can a woman choose where to live in the same way as a man?	Yes	Yes	Yes	Yes	Yes	Yes
18. Can a woman confer citizenship on her children in the same way as a man?	Yes	Yes	Yes	Yes	Yes	Yes
19. Can a woman be "head of household" or "head of family" in the same way as a man?	N/A	N/A	N/A	N/A	N/A	N/A
Number of inequalities in accessing institutions	0	0	0	0	0	0

Division of responsibility within marriage

	EL SALVADOR	ESTONIA	ETHIOPIA
20. Can a woman convey citizenship to her non-national spouse in the same way as a man?	Yes	Yes	Yes
21. Are married women required by law to obey their husbands?	No	No	No
22. Do married couples jointly share legal responsibility for financially maintaining the family's expenses?	Yes	Yes	Yes

USING PROPERTY

Marital property regime

	EL SALVADOR	ESTONIA	ETHIOPIA
23. What is the default marital property regime?	Deferred community of property	Partial community of property	Partial community of property
24. Who legally administers property during marriage?	Original owner	Both must agree	Both must agree

Protecting a wife's interests

	EL SALVADOR	ESTONIA	ETHIOPIA
25. If it is the husband, does he need his wife's consent for major transactions	N/A	N/A	N/A
26. Are there special provisions governing the marital home?	Yes	No	No
27. Does the law provide for valuation of nonmonetary contributions during marriage?	Yes	Yes	Yes

Property rights

	Unmarried	Married	Unmarried	Married	Unmarried	Married
28. Do men and women have equal ownership rights to property?	Yes	Yes	Yes	Yes	Yes	Yes

Inheritance rights

	EL SALVADOR	ESTONIA	ETHIOPIA
29. Do sons and daughters have equal inheritance rights to property?	Yes	Yes	Yes
30. Do female and male surviving spouses have equal inheritance rights to property?	Yes	Yes	Yes

GOING TO COURT

Equality of access

	EL SALVADOR	ESTONIA	ETHIOPIA
31. Does the law recognize customary courts?	No	No	Yes
32. Does the law recognize personal law courts?	No	No	Yes
33. Does a woman's testimony carry the same evidentiary weight in court as a man's?	Yes	Yes	Yes

Efficiency of procedure

	EL SALVADOR	ESTONIA	ETHIOPIA
34. Is there a small claims court or a fast track procedure for small claims?	Yes	Yes	Yes
35. If so, what is the maximum amount for a small claim (as a percentage of income per capita)?	694%	18%	83%

Judicial representation

	EL SALVADOR	ESTONIA	ETHIOPIA
36. How many justices are on the constitutional court?	5	9	N/A
37. Of those, how many are women?	0	1	N/A
38. Is the Chief Justice a woman?	No	No	N/A

GETTING A JOB

	EL SALVADOR			ESTONIA			ETHIOPIA		
Parental benefits	*Maternity*	*Paternity*	*Parental*	*Maternity*	*Paternity*	*Parental*	*Maternity*	*Paternity*	*Parental*
39. Does the law mandate paid or unpaid maternity/paternity/parental leave?	Yes	No	No	Yes	Yes	Yes	Yes	No	No
40. What is the mandatory minimum length of paid leave for maternity/paternity/parental leave (in calendar days)?	84	N/A	N/A	140	10	455	90	N/A	N/A
41. What is the mandatory minimum length of unpaid leave for maternity/paternity/parental leave (in calendar days)?	0	N/A	N/A	0	0	432	0	N/A	N/A
42. Who pays maternity/paternity/parental benefits?	Gov.	N/A	N/A	Gov.	Gov.	Gov.	Emp.	N/A	N/A
43. What percentage of wages are paid during maternity/paternity/parental leave?	100%	N/A	N/A	100%	100%	Partially paid	100%	N/A	N/A

	Mother	Father		Mother	Father		Mother	Father	
44. Where **paid** parental leave exists, what is the minimum amount which only the mother/father must take (in calendar days)?	N/A	N/A		70	0		N/A	N/A	
45. Where **unpaid** parental leave exists, what is the minimum amount which only the mother/father must take (in calendar days)?	N/A	N/A		0	0		N/A	N/A	

Retirement & pensions	Women	Men		Women	Men		Women	Men	
46. What is the age at which one can retire and receive full benefits?	55	60		63	63		60	60	
47. What is the age at which one can retire and receive partial benefits?	55	60		60	60		60	60	
48. What is the mandatory retirement age?	N/A	N/A		N/A	N/A		N/A	N/A	

Working hours and industry restrictions	EL SALVADOR			ESTONIA			ETHIOPIA		
49. Can non-pregnant and non-nursing women do the same jobs as men?	Yes			Yes			No		
50. Can non-pregnant and non-nursing women engage in the following occupations in the same way as men?									
a. Mining	Yes			Yes			Yes		
b. Construction	Yes			Yes			Yes		
c. Metalwork	Yes			Yes			Yes		
d. Factory work	Yes			Yes			Yes		
e. Jobs requiring lifting weights above a threshold	Yes			Yes			Yes		
f. Jobs deemed hazardous	Yes			Yes			No		
g. Jobs deemed arduous	Yes			Yes			No		
h. Jobs deemed morally or socially inappropriate	Yes			Yes			Yes		
51. Can non-pregnant and non-nursing women work the same night hours as men?	Yes			Yes			Yes		

Workplace protections									
52. Does the law mandate equal remuneration for men and women for work of equal value?	No			No			No		
53. Are there laws mandating non-discrimination based on gender in hiring?	Yes			Yes			No		
54. Is it illegal for an employer to ask about family status during a job interview?	No			Yes			No		
55. Are there laws penalizing or preventing the dismissal of pregnant women?	Yes			Yes			Yes		
56. Must employers give employees an equivalent position when they return from maternity leave?	Yes			Yes			No		
57. Are employers required to provide break time for nursing mothers?	Yes			Yes			No		
58. Do employees with minor children have rights to a flexible/part time schedule?	No			No			No		

BUILDING CREDIT

59. What is the minimum loan amount covered in the private credit bureau or public credit registry (as a percentage of income per capita)?	0%			0%			0%		
60. Do microfinance institutions provide information to private credit bureaus or public credit registries?	Yes			N/A			No		
61. Do utility companies provide information to private credit bureaus or public credit registries?	No			No			No		
62. Do retailers provide information to private credit bureaus or public credit registries?	Yes			No			No		

PROVIDING INCENTIVES TO WORK

Childcare									
63. Are payments for childcare tax deductible?	No			No			No		
64. Is there public provision of childcare for children under the age of primary education?	Yes			Yes			No		
65. Does the law mandate free and compulsory primary education?	Yes			Yes			No		

Personal income tax	Women	Men		Women	Men		Women	Men	
66. Are there specific tax deductions or credits that are applicable only to men/women?	No	No		No	No		No	No	

Economy Tables

	FIJI		FINLAND		FRANCE	
REGION	East Asia & Pacific		High income: OECD		High income: OECD	
INCOME	Upper middle income		High income		High income	
FEMALE POPULATION	428,801		2,755,168		33,903,771	
FEMALE LABOR FORCE PARTICIPATION	41%		73%		66%	

ACCESSING INSTITUTIONS

Constitutional rights

	FIJI	FINLAND	FRANCE
1. Is there a non-discrimination clause in the constitution?	Yes	No	No
2. If there is a non-discrimination clause in the constitution, does it explicitly mention gender?	Yes	N/A	N/A
3. Does the constitution guarantee equality before the law?	Yes	Yes	Yes

	Customary	Personal	Customary	Personal	Customary	Personal
4. Is customary/personal law recognized as valid source of law under the constitution?	Yes	No	No	No	No	No
5. If so, is it invalid if it violates constitutional provisions on non-discrimination or equality?	No	N/A	N/A	N/A	N/A	N/A

Quotas

	FIJI	FINLAND	FRANCE
6. What are the legal quotas for women on corporate boards?	N/A	N/A	20%
7. What are the legal quotas for women in parliament?	N/A	N/A	N/A
8. What are the legal quotas for women in local government?	N/A	N/A	N/A

Rights of married and unmarried women

	Unmarried	Married	Unmarried	Married	Unmarried	Married
9. Can a woman apply for a passport in the same way as a man?	Yes	No	Yes	Yes	Yes	Yes
10. Can a woman apply for a national ID card in the same way as a man?	N/A	N/A	Yes	Yes	Yes	Yes
11. Can a woman travel outside the country in the same way as a man?	Yes	Yes	Yes	Yes	Yes	Yes
12. Can a woman travel outside her home in the same way as a man?	Yes	Yes	Yes	Yes	Yes	Yes
13. Can a woman get a job or pursue a trade or profession in the same way as a man?	Yes	Yes	Yes	Yes	Yes	Yes
14. Can a woman sign a contract in the same way as a man?	Yes	Yes	Yes	Yes	Yes	Yes
15. Can a woman register a business in the same way as a man?	Yes	Yes	Yes	Yes	Yes	Yes
16. Can a woman open a bank account in the same way as a man?	Yes	Yes	Yes	Yes	Yes	Yes
17. Can a woman choose where to live in the same way as a man?	Yes	Yes	Yes	Yes	Yes	Yes
18. Can a woman confer citizenship on her children in the same way as a man?	Yes	Yes	Yes	Yes	Yes	Yes
19. Can a woman be "head of household" or "head of family" in the same way as a man?	N/A	N/A	N/A	N/A	N/A	N/A
Number of inequalities in accessing institutions	0	1	0	0	0	0

Division of responsibility within marriage

	FIJI	FINLAND	FRANCE
20. Can a woman convey citizenship to her non-national spouse in the same way as a man?	Yes	Yes	Yes
21. Are married women required by law to obey their husbands?	No	No	No
22. Do married couples jointly share legal responsibility for financially maintaining the family's expenses?	Yes	Yes	Yes

USING PROPERTY

Marital property regime

	FIJI	FINLAND	FRANCE
23. What is the default marital property regime?	Separation of property	Deferred community of property	Partial community of property
24. Who legally administers property during marriage?	Original owner	Original owner	Both must agree

Protecting a wife's interests

	FIJI	FINLAND	FRANCE
25. If it is the husband, does he need his wife's consent for major transactions	N/A	N/A	N/A
26. Are there special provisions governing the marital home?	No	Yes	Yes
27. Does the law provide for valuation of nonmonetary contributions during marriage?	No	Yes	Yes

Property rights

	Unmarried	Married	Unmarried	Married	Unmarried	Married
28. Do men and women have equal ownership rights to property?	Yes	Yes	Yes	Yes	Yes	Yes

Inheritance rights

	FIJI	FINLAND	FRANCE
29. Do sons and daughters have equal inheritance rights to property?	Yes	Yes	Yes
30. Do female and male surviving spouses have equal inheritance rights to property?	Yes	Yes	Yes

GOING TO COURT

Equality of access

	FIJI	FINLAND	FRANCE
31. Does the law recognize customary courts?	No	No	No
32. Does the law recognize personal law courts?	No	No	No
33. Does a woman's testimony carry the same evidentiary weight in court as a man's?	Yes	Yes	Yes

Efficiency of procedure

	FIJI	FINLAND	FRANCE
34. Is there a small claims court or a fast track procedure for small claims?	Yes	No	Yes
35. If so, what is the maximum amount for a small claim (as a percentage of income per capita)?	66%	N/A	13%

Judicial representation

	FIJI	FINLAND	FRANCE
36. How many justices are on the constitutional court?	N/A	N/A	12
37. Of those, how many are women?	N/A	N/A	3
38. Is the Chief Justice a woman?	N/A	N/A	No

GETTING A JOB

Parental benefits	FIJI			FINLAND			FRANCE		
	Maternity	Paternity	Parental	Maternity	Paternity	Parental	Maternity	Paternity	Parental
39. Does the law mandate paid or unpaid maternity/paternity/parental leave?	Yes	No	No	Yes	Yes	Yes	Yes	Yes	Yes
40. What is the mandatory minimum length of paid leave for maternity/paternity/parental leave (in calendar days)?	84	N/A	N/A	147	24	215	112	11	0
41. What is the mandatory minimum length of unpaid leave for maternity/paternity/parental leave (in calendar days)?	0	N/A	N/A	0	0	0	0	0	1025
42. Who pays maternity/paternity/parental benefits?	Emp.	N/A	N/A	Gov.	Gov.	Gov.	Gov.	Gov.	N/A
43. What percentage of wages are paid during maternity/paternity/parental leave?	100%	N/A	N/A	51%	51%	Partially paid	100%	100%	0%

	Mother	Father		Mother	Father		Mother	Father	
44. Where **paid** parental leave exists, what is the minimum amount which only the mother/father must take (in calendar days)?	N/A	N/A		0	0		N/A	N/A	
45. Where **unpaid** parental leave exists, what is the minimum amount which only the mother/father must take (in calendar days)?	N/A	N/A		N/A	N/A		0	0	

Retirement & pensions	Women	Men		Women	Men		Women	Men	
46. What is the age at which one can retire and receive full benefits?	55	55		63	63		67	67	
47. What is the age at which one can retire and receive partial benefits?	55	55		63	63		62	62	
48. What is the mandatory retirement age?	N/A	N/A		N/A	N/A		70	70	

Working hours and industry restrictions	FIJI	FINLAND	FRANCE
49. Can non-pregnant and non-nursing women do the same jobs as men?	No	Yes	No
50. Can non-pregnant and non-nursing women engage in the following occupations in the same way as men?			
a. Mining	No	Yes	Yes
b. Construction	Yes	Yes	Yes
c. Metalwork	Yes	Yes	Yes
d. Factory work	Yes	Yes	Yes
e. Jobs requiring lifting weights above a threshold	Yes	Yes	No
f. Jobs deemed hazardous	Yes	Yes	Yes
g. Jobs deemed arduous	Yes	Yes	Yes
h. Jobs deemed morally or socially inappropriate	Yes	Yes	Yes
51. Can non-pregnant and non-nursing women work the same night hours as men?	Yes	Yes	Yes

Workplace protections	FIJI	FINLAND	FRANCE
52. Does the law mandate equal remuneration for men and women for work of equal value?	Yes	No	No
53. Are there laws mandating non-discrimination based on gender in hiring?	Yes	No	Yes
54. Is it illegal for an employer to ask about family status during a job interview?	No	No	No
55. Are there laws penalizing or preventing the dismissal of pregnant women?	Yes	Yes	Yes
56. Must employers give employees an equivalent position when they return from maternity leave?	Yes	Yes	Yes
57. Are employers required to provide break time for nursing mothers?	No	No	Yes
58. Do employees with minor children have rights to a flexible/part time schedule?	No	Yes	No

BUILDING CREDIT

	FIJI	FINLAND	FRANCE
59. What is the minimum loan amount covered in the private credit bureau or public credit registry (as a percentage of income per capita)?	0%	0%	0%
60. Do microfinance institutions provide information to private credit bureaus or public credit registries?	Yes	N/A	N/A
61. Do utility companies provide information to private credit bureaus or public credit registries?	Yes	No	No
62. Do retailers provide information to private credit bureaus or public credit registries?	Yes	No	No

PROVIDING INCENTIVES TO WORK

Childcare	FIJI	FINLAND	FRANCE
63. Are payments for childcare tax deductible?	No	Yes	Yes
64. Is there public provision of childcare for children under the age of primary education?	No	Yes	Yes
65. Does the law mandate free and compulsory primary education?	No	Yes	Yes

Personal income tax	Women	Men		Women	Men		Women	Men	
66. Are there specific tax deductions or credits that are applicable only to men/women?	No	No		No	No		No	No	

Fiji-France

Economy Tables

	GABON		GEORGIA		GERMANY	
REGION	Sub-Saharan Africa		Europe & Central Asia		High income: OECD	
INCOME	Upper middle income		Lower middle income		High income	
FEMALE POPULATION	812,430		2,385,146		41,721,971	
FEMALE LABOR FORCE PARTICIPATION	57%		60%		71%	

ACCESSING INSTITUTIONS

Constitutional rights

	GABON		GEORGIA		GERMANY	
1. Is there a non-discrimination clause in the constitution?	No		No		No	
2. If there is a non-discrimination clause in the constitution, does it explicitly mention gender?	N/A		N/A		N/A	
3. Does the constitution guarantee equality before the law?	Yes		Yes		Yes	

	Customary	Personal	Customary	Personal	Customary	Personal
4. Is customary/personal law recognized as valid source of law under the constitution?	No	No	No	No	No	No
5. If so, is it invalid if it violates constitutional provisions on non-discrimination or equality?	N/A	N/A	N/A	N/A	N/A	N/A

Quotas

	GABON	GEORGIA	GERMANY
6. What are the legal quotas for women on corporate boards?	N/A	N/A	N/A
7. What are the legal quotas for women in parliament?	N/A	N/A	N/A
8. What are the legal quotas for women in local government?	N/A	N/A	N/A

Rights of married and unmarried women

	Unmarried	Married	Unmarried	Married	Unmarried	Married
9. Can a woman apply for a passport in the same way as a man?	Yes	No	Yes	Yes	Yes	Yes
10. Can a woman apply for a national ID card in the same way as a man?	Yes	Yes	Yes	Yes	Yes	Yes
11. Can a woman travel outside the country in the same way as a man?	Yes	Yes	Yes	Yes	Yes	Yes
12. Can a woman travel outside her home in the same way as a man?	Yes	Yes	Yes	Yes	Yes	Yes
13. Can a woman get a job or pursue a trade or profession in the same way as a man?	Yes	No	Yes	Yes	Yes	Yes
14. Can a woman sign a contract in the same way as a man?	Yes	Yes	Yes	Yes	Yes	Yes
15. Can a woman register a business in the same way as a man?	Yes	Yes	Yes	Yes	Yes	Yes
16. Can a woman open a bank account in the same way as a man?	Yes	Yes	Yes	Yes	Yes	Yes
17. Can a woman choose where to live in the same way as a man?	Yes	No	Yes	Yes	Yes	Yes
18. Can a woman confer citizenship on her children in the same way as a man?	Yes	Yes	Yes	Yes	Yes	Yes
19. Can a woman be "head of household" or "head of family" in the same way as a man?	Yes	No	N/A	N/A	N/A	N/A
Number of inequalities in accessing institutions	0	4	0	0	0	0

Division of responsibility within marriage

	GABON	GEORGIA	GERMANY
20. Can a woman convey citizenship to her non-national spouse in the same way as a man?	Yes	Yes	Yes
21. Are married women required by law to obey their husbands?	Yes	No	No
22. Do married couples jointly share legal responsibility for financially maintaining the family's expenses?	Yes	Yes	Yes

USING PROPERTY

Marital property regime

	GABON	GEORGIA	GERMANY
23. What is the default marital property regime?	Other	Partial community of property	Deferred community of property
24. Who legally administers property during marriage?	Other	Both must agree	Separate with spousal consent

Protecting a wife's interests

	GABON	GEORGIA	GERMANY
25. If it is the husband, does he need his wife's consent for major transactions	N/A	N/A	N/A
26. Are there special provisions governing the marital home?	Yes	No	No
27. Does the law provide for valuation of nonmonetary contributions during marriage?	No	Yes	Yes

Property rights

	Unmarried	Married	Unmarried	Married	Unmarried	Married
28. Do men and women have equal ownership rights to property?	Yes	No	Yes	Yes	Yes	Yes

Inheritance rights

	GABON	GEORGIA	GERMANY
29. Do sons and daughters have equal inheritance rights to property?	Yes	Yes	Yes
30. Do female and male surviving spouses have equal inheritance rights to property?	Yes	Yes	Yes

GOING TO COURT

Equality of access

	GABON	GEORGIA	GERMANY
31. Does the law recognize customary courts?	No	No	No
32. Does the law recognize personal law courts?	No	No	No
33. Does a woman's testimony carry the same evidentiary weight in court as a man's?	Yes	Yes	Yes

Efficiency of procedure

	GABON	GEORGIA	GERMANY
34. Is there a small claims court or a fast track procedure for small claims?	No	Yes	Yes
35. If so, what is the maximum amount for a small claim (as a percentage of income per capita)?	N/A	38%	2%

Judicial representation

	GABON	GEORGIA	GERMANY
36. How many justices are on the constitutional court?	9	9	16
37. Of those, how many are women?	4	3	5
38. Is the Chief Justice a woman?	Yes	No	No

GETTING A JOB

Parental benefits	Maternity	Paternity	Parental	Maternity	Paternity	Parental	Maternity	Paternity	Parental
39. Does the law mandate paid or unpaid maternity/paternity/parental leave?	Yes	No	No	Yes	No	No	Yes	No	Yes
40. What is the mandatory minimum length of paid leave for maternity/paternity/parental leave (in calendar days)?	98	N/A	N/A	126	N/A	N/A	98	N/A	360
41. What is the mandatory minimum length of unpaid leave for maternity/paternity/parental leave (in calendar days)?	0	N/A	N/A	351	N/A	N/A	0	N/A	1080
42. Who pays maternity/paternity/parental benefits?	Gov.	N/A	N/A	Gov.	N/A	N/A	Emp. & Gov.	N/A	Gov.
43. What percentage of wages are paid during maternity/paternity/parental leave?	100%	N/A	N/A	100%	N/A	N/A	100%	N/A	Partially paid

	Mother	Father		Mother	Father		Mother	Father	
44. Where **paid** parental leave exists, what is the minimum amount which only the mother/father must take (in calendar days)?	N/A	N/A		N/A	N/A		60	60	
45. Where **unpaid** parental leave exists, what is the minimum amount which only the mother/father must take (in calendar days)?	N/A	N/A		N/A	N/A		0	0	

Retirement & pensions	Women	Men		Women	Men		Women	Men	
46. What is the age at which one can retire and receive full benefits?	60	60		60	65		67	67	
47. What is the age at which one can retire and receive partial benefits?	60	60		60	65		63	63	
48. What is the mandatory retirement age?	60	60		N/A	N/A		N/A	N/A	

Working hours and industry restrictions	GABON	GEORGIA	GERMANY
49. Can non-pregnant and non-nursing women do the same jobs as men?	No	Yes	Yes
50. Can non-pregnant and non-nursing women engage in the following occupations in the same way as men?			
a. Mining	No	Yes	Yes
b. Construction	No	Yes	Yes
c. Metalwork	No	Yes	Yes
d. Factory work	No	Yes	Yes
e. Jobs requiring lifting weights above a threshold	Yes	Yes	Yes
f. Jobs deemed hazardous	Yes	Yes	Yes
g. Jobs deemed arduous	Yes	Yes	Yes
h. Jobs deemed morally or socially inappropriate	Yes	Yes	Yes
51. Can non-pregnant and non-nursing women work the same night hours as men?	No	Yes	Yes

Workplace protections	GABON	GEORGIA	GERMANY
52. Does the law mandate equal remuneration for men and women for work of equal value?	No	No	No
53. Are there laws mandating non-discrimination based on gender in hiring?	No	No	Yes
54. Is it illegal for an employer to ask about family status during a job interview?	No	No	No
55. Are there laws penalizing or preventing the dismissal of pregnant women?	Yes	No	Yes
56. Must employers give employees an equivalent position when they return from maternity leave?	Yes	No	No
57. Are employers required to provide break time for nursing mothers?	Yes	Yes	Yes
58. Do employees with minor children have rights to a flexible/part time schedule?	No	No	No

BUILDING CREDIT

	GABON	GEORGIA	GERMANY
59. What is the minimum loan amount covered in the private credit bureau or public credit registry (as a percentage of income per capita)?	0%	0%	0%
60. Do microfinance institutions provide information to private credit bureaus or public credit registries?	No	Yes	N/A
61. Do utility companies provide information to private credit bureaus or public credit registries?	No	Yes	No
62. Do retailers provide information to private credit bureaus or public credit registries?	No	Yes	No

PROVIDING INCENTIVES TO WORK

Childcare	GABON	GEORGIA	GERMANY
63. Are payments for childcare tax deductible?	No	No	No
64. Is there public provision of childcare for children under the age of primary education?	Yes	Yes	Yes
65. Does the law mandate free and compulsory primary education?	Yes	Yes	Yes

Personal income tax	Women	Men		Women	Men		Women	Men	
66. Are there specific tax deductions or credits that are applicable only to men/women?	No	No		No	No		No	No	

Economy Tables

	GHANA	GREECE	GUATEMALA
REGION	Sub-Saharan Africa	High income: OECD	Latin America & Caribbean
INCOME	Lower middle income	High income	Lower middle income
FEMALE POPULATION	12,804,293	5,715,117	7,729,269
FEMALE LABOR FORCE PARTICIPATION	69%	58%	51%

ACCESSING INSTITUTIONS

Constitutional rights

	GHANA	GREECE	GUATEMALA
1. Is there a non-discrimination clause in the constitution?	Yes	No	No
2. If there is a non-discrimination clause in the constitution, does it explicitly mention gender?	Yes	N/A	N/A
3. Does the constitution guarantee equality before the law?	Yes	Yes	Yes

	Customary	Personal	Customary	Personal	Customary	Personal
4. Is customary/personal law recognized as valid source of law under the constitution?	Yes	No	No	No	Yes	No
5. If so, is it invalid if it violates constitutional provisions on non-discrimination or equality?	No	N/A	N/A	N/A	Yes	N/A

Quotas

	GHANA	GREECE	GUATEMALA
6. What are the legal quotas for women on corporate boards?	N/A	N/A	N/A
7. What are the legal quotas for women in parliament?	N/A	N/A	N/A
8. What are the legal quotas for women in local government?	N/A	N/A	N/A

Rights of married and unmarried women

	Unmarried	Married	Unmarried	Married	Unmarried	Married
9. Can a woman apply for a passport in the same way as a man?	Yes	Yes	Yes	Yes	Yes	Yes
10. Can a woman apply for a national ID card in the same way as a man?	Yes	Yes	Yes	Yes	Yes	Yes
11. Can a woman travel outside the country in the same way as a man?	Yes	Yes	Yes	Yes	Yes	Yes
12. Can a woman travel outside her home in the same way as a man?	Yes	Yes	Yes	Yes	Yes	Yes
13. Can a woman get a job or pursue a trade or profession in the same way as a man?	Yes	Yes	Yes	Yes	Yes	Yes
14. Can a woman sign a contract in the same way as a man?	Yes	Yes	Yes	Yes	Yes	Yes
15. Can a woman register a business in the same way as a man?	Yes	Yes	Yes	Yes	Yes	Yes
16. Can a woman open a bank account in the same way as a man?	Yes	Yes	Yes	Yes	Yes	Yes
17. Can a woman choose where to live in the same way as a man?	Yes	Yes	Yes	Yes	Yes	Yes
18. Can a woman confer citizenship on her children in the same way as a man?	Yes	Yes	Yes	Yes	Yes	Yes
19. Can a woman be "head of household" or "head of family" in the same way as a man?	Yes	Yes	N/A	N/A	N/A	N/A
Number of inequalities in accessing institutions	0	0	0	0	0	0

Division of responsibility within marriage

	GHANA	GREECE	GUATEMALA
20. Can a woman convey citizenship to her non-national spouse in the same way as a man?	No	Yes	Yes
21. Are married women required by law to obey their husbands?	No	No	No
22. Do married couples jointly share legal responsibility for financially maintaining the family's expenses?	Yes	Yes	Yes

USING PROPERTY

Marital property regime

	GHANA	GREECE	GUATEMALA
23. What is the default marital property regime?	Separation of property	Deferred community of property	Partial community of property
24. Who legally administers property during marriage?	Original owner	Original owner	Both must agree

Protecting a wife's interests

	GHANA	GREECE	GUATEMALA
25. If it is the husband, does he need his wife's consent for major transactions	N/A	N/A	N/A
26. Are there special provisions governing the marital home?	No	No	No
27. Does the law provide for valuation of nonmonetary contributions during marriage?	No	Yes	Yes

Property rights

	Unmarried	Married	Unmarried	Married	Unmarried	Married
28. Do men and women have equal ownership rights to property?	Yes	Yes	Yes	Yes	Yes	Yes

Inheritance rights

	GHANA	GREECE	GUATEMALA
29. Do sons and daughters have equal inheritance rights to property?	Yes	Yes	Yes
30. Do female and male surviving spouses have equal inheritance rights to property?	Yes	Yes	Yes

GOING TO COURT

Equality of access

	GHANA	GREECE	GUATEMALA
31. Does the law recognize customary courts?	Yes	No	No
32. Does the law recognize personal law courts?	No	No	No
33. Does a woman's testimony carry the same evidentiary weight in court as a man's?	Yes	Yes	Yes

Efficiency of procedure

	GHANA	GREECE	GUATEMALA
34. Is there a small claims court or a fast track procedure for small claims?	No	Yes	Yes
35. If so, what is the maximum amount for a small claim (as a percentage of income per capita)?	N/A	8%	42%

Judicial representation

	GHANA	GREECE	GUATEMALA
36. How many justices are on the constitutional court?	14	N/A	5
37. Of those, how many are women?	5	N/A	1
38. Is the Chief Justice a woman?	Yes	N/A	No

GETTING A JOB

Parental benefits	GHANA Maternity	Paternity	Parental	GREECE Maternity	Paternity	Parental	GUATEMALA Maternity	Paternity	Parental
39. Does the law mandate paid or unpaid maternity/paternity/parental leave?	Yes	No	No	Yes	Yes	Yes	Yes	Yes	No
40. What is the mandatory minimum length of paid leave for maternity/paternity/parental leave (in calendar days)?	84	N/A	N/A	119	2	0	84	2	N/A
41. What is the mandatory minimum length of unpaid leave for maternity/paternity/parental leave (in calendar days)?	0	N/A	N/A	0	0	240	0	0	N/A
42. Who pays maternity/paternity/parental benefits?	Emp.	N/A	N/A	Gov.	Emp.	N/A	Emp. & Gov.	Emp.	N/A
43. What percentage of wages are paid during maternity/paternity/parental leave?	100%	N/A	N/A	100%	100%	0%	100%	100%	N/A

	Mother	Father		Mother	Father		Mother	Father	
44. Where **paid** parental leave exists, what is the minimum amount which only the mother/father must take (in calendar days)?	N/A	N/A		N/A	N/A		N/A	N/A	
45. Where **unpaid** parental leave exists, what is the minimum amount which only the mother/father must take (in calendar days)?	N/A	N/A		120	120		N/A	N/A	

Retirement & pensions	Women	Men		Women	Men		Women	Men	
46. What is the age at which one can retire and receive full benefits?	60	60		65	65		62	62	
47. What is the age at which one can retire and receive partial benefits?	55	55		60	60		62	62	
48. What is the mandatory retirement age?	N/A	N/A		N/A	N/A		N/A	N/A	

Working hours and industry restrictions	GHANA	GREECE	GUATEMALA
49. Can non-pregnant and non-nursing women do the same jobs as men?	Yes	Yes	Yes
50. Can non-pregnant and non-nursing women engage in the following occupations in the same way as men?			
a. Mining	Yes	Yes	Yes
b. Construction	Yes	Yes	Yes
c. Metalwork	Yes	Yes	Yes
d. Factory work	Yes	Yes	Yes
e. Jobs requiring lifting weights above a threshold	Yes	Yes	Yes
f. Jobs deemed hazardous	Yes	Yes	Yes
g. Jobs deemed arduous	Yes	Yes	Yes
h. Jobs deemed morally or socially inappropriate	Yes	Yes	Yes
51. Can non-pregnant and non-nursing women work the same night hours as men?	Yes	Yes	Yes

Workplace protections	GHANA	GREECE	GUATEMALA
52. Does the law mandate equal remuneration for men and women for work of equal value?	No	Yes	No
53. Are there laws mandating non-discrimination based on gender in hiring?	Yes	Yes	Yes
54. Is it illegal for an employer to ask about family status during a job interview?	No	No	No
55. Are there laws penalizing or preventing the dismissal of pregnant women?	Yes	Yes	Yes
56. Must employers give employees an equivalent position when they return from maternity leave?	No	Yes	Yes
57. Are employers required to provide break time for nursing mothers?	Yes	Yes	Yes
58. Do employees with minor children have rights to a flexible/part time schedule?	No	Yes	No

BUILDING CREDIT

	GHANA	GREECE	GUATEMALA
59. What is the minimum loan amount covered in the private credit bureau or public credit registry (as a percentage of income per capita)?	0%	0%	0%
60. Do microfinance institutions provide information to private credit bureaus or public credit registries?	Yes	N/A	No
61. Do utility companies provide information to private credit bureaus or public credit registries?	No	No	No
62. Do retailers provide information to private credit bureaus or public credit registries?	No	No	No

PROVIDING INCENTIVES TO WORK

Childcare	GHANA	GREECE	GUATEMALA
63. Are payments for childcare tax deductible?	No	No	No
64. Is there public provision of childcare for children under the age of primary education?	No	Yes	Yes
65. Does the law mandate free and compulsory primary education?	Yes	Yes	Yes

Personal income tax	Women	Men	Women	Men	Women	Men
66. Are there specific tax deductions or credits that are applicable only to men/women?	No	No	No	No	No	No

Economy Tables

	GUINEA	HAITI	HONDURAS
REGION	Sub-Saharan Africa	Latin America & Caribbean	Latin America & Caribbean
INCOME	Low income	Low income	Lower middle income
FEMALE POPULATION	5,717,115	5,146,946	3,966,425
FEMALE LABOR FORCE PARTICIPATION	67%	62%	44%

ACCESSING INSTITUTIONS

Constitutional rights

	GUINEA	HAITI	HONDURAS
1. Is there a non-discrimination clause in the constitution?	No	No	Yes
2. If there is a non-discrimination clause in the constitution, does it explicitly mention gender?	N/A	N/A	Yes
3. Does the constitution guarantee equality before the law?	Yes	Yes	Yes

	Customary	Personal	Customary	Personal	Customary	Personal
4. Is customary/personal law recognized as valid source of law under the constitution?	No	No	No	No	No	No
5. If so, is it invalid if it violates constitutional provisions on non-discrimination or equality?	N/A	N/A	N/A	N/A	N/A	N/A

Quotas

	GUINEA	HAITI	HONDURAS
6. What are the legal quotas for women on corporate boards?	N/A	N/A	N/A
7. What are the legal quotas for women in parliament?	N/A	N/A	N/A
8. What are the legal quotas for women in local government?	N/A	N/A	N/A

Rights of married and unmarried women

	Unmarried	Married	Unmarried	Married	Unmarried	Married
9. Can a woman apply for a passport in the same way as a man?	Yes	Yes	Yes	No	Yes	Yes
10. Can a woman apply for a national ID card in the same way as a man?	..	..	Yes	Yes	Yes	Yes
11. Can a woman travel outside the country in the same way as a man?	Yes	Yes	Yes	Yes	Yes	Yes
12. Can a woman travel outside her home in the same way as a man?	Yes	Yes	Yes	Yes	Yes	Yes
13. Can a woman get a job or pursue a trade or profession in the same way as a man?	Yes	No	Yes	Yes	Yes	Yes
14. Can a woman sign a contract in the same way as a man?	Yes	Yes	Yes	Yes	Yes	Yes
15. Can a woman register a business in the same way as a man?	Yes	Yes	Yes	Yes	Yes	Yes
16. Can a woman open a bank account in the same way as a man?	Yes	Yes	Yes	Yes	Yes	Yes
17. Can a woman choose where to live in the same way as a man?	Yes	No	Yes	No	Yes	Yes
18. Can a woman confer citizenship on her children in the same way as a man?	Yes	No	Yes	Yes	Yes	Yes
19. Can a woman be "head of household" or "head of family" in the same way as a man?	Yes	No	N/A	N/A	Yes	No
Number of inequalities in accessing institutions	0	4	0	2	0	1

Division of responsibility within marriage

	GUINEA	HAITI	HONDURAS
20. Can a woman convey citizenship to her non-national spouse in the same way as a man?	No	No	No
21. Are married women required by law to obey their husbands?	No	No	No
22. Do married couples jointly share legal responsibility for financially maintaining the family's expenses?	Yes	Yes	Yes

USING PROPERTY

Marital property regime

	GUINEA	HAITI	HONDURAS
23. What is the default marital property regime?	Separation of property	Partial community of property	Deferred community of property
24. Who legally administers property during marriage?	Original owner	Other	Original owner

Protecting a wife's interests

	GUINEA	HAITI	HONDURAS
25. If it is the husband, does he need his wife's consent for major transactions	N/A	N/A	N/A
26. Are there special provisions governing the marital home?	No	No	No
27. Does the law provide for valuation of nonmonetary contributions during marriage?	No	Yes	Yes

Property rights

	Unmarried	Married	Unmarried	Married	Unmarried	Married
28. Do men and women have equal ownership rights to property?	Yes	Yes	Yes	No	Yes	Yes

Inheritance rights

	GUINEA	HAITI	HONDURAS
29. Do sons and daughters have equal inheritance rights to property?	Yes	Yes	Yes
30. Do female and male surviving spouses have equal inheritance rights to property?	No	Yes	Yes

GOING TO COURT

Equality of access

	GUINEA	HAITI	HONDURAS
31. Does the law recognize customary courts?	No	No	No
32. Does the law recognize personal law courts?	No	No	No
33. Does a woman's testimony carry the same evidentiary weight in court as a man's?	Yes	Yes	Yes

Efficiency of procedure

	GUINEA	HAITI	HONDURAS
34. Is there a small claims court or a fast track procedure for small claims?	No	Yes	Yes
35. If so, what is the maximum amount for a small claim (as a percentage of income per capita)?	N/A	84%	126%

Judicial representation

	GUINEA	HAITI	HONDURAS
36. How many justices are on the constitutional court?	N/A	N/A	5
37. Of those, how many are women?	N/A	N/A	1
38. Is the Chief Justice a woman?	N/A	N/A	No

	GUINEA			HAITI			HONDURAS		

GETTING A JOB

Parental benefits

	Maternity	Paternity	Parental	Maternity	Paternity	Parental	Maternity	Paternity	Parental
39. Does the law mandate paid or unpaid maternity/paternity/parental leave?	Yes	No	No	Yes	No	No	Yes	No	No
40. What is the mandatory minimum length of paid leave for maternity/paternity/parental leave (in calendar days)?	98	N/A	N/A	42	N/A	N/A	84	N/A	N/A
41. What is the mandatory minimum length of unpaid leave for maternity/paternity/parental leave (in calendar days)?	270	N/A	N/A	0	N/A	N/A	0	N/A	N/A
42. Who pays maternity/paternity/parental benefits?	Emp. & Gov.	N/A	N/A	Emp.	N/A	N/A	Emp. & Gov.	N/A	N/A
43. What percentage of wages are paid during maternity/paternity/parental leave?	100%	N/A	N/A	100%	N/A	N/A	100%	N/A	N/A

	Mother	Father		Mother	Father		Mother	Father	
44. Where **paid** parental leave exists, what is the minimum amount which only the mother/father must take (in calendar days)?	N/A	N/A		N/A	N/A		N/A	N/A	
45. Where **unpaid** parental leave exists, what is the minimum amount which only the mother/father must take (in calendar days)?	N/A	N/A		N/A	N/A		N/A	N/A	

Retirement & pensions

	Women	Men		Women	Men		Women	Men	
46. What is the age at which one can retire and receive full benefits?	55	55		55	55		60	65	
47. What is the age at which one can retire and receive partial benefits?	55	55		55	55		60	65	
48. What is the mandatory retirement age?	N/A	N/A		N/A	N/A		N/A	N/A	

Working hours and industry restrictions

	GUINEA	HAITI	HONDURAS
49. Can non-pregnant and non-nursing women do the same jobs as men?	No	Yes	No
50. Can non-pregnant and non-nursing women engage in the following occupations in the same way as men?			
a. Mining	No	Yes	Yes
b. Construction	Yes	Yes	Yes
c. Metalwork	Yes	Yes	Yes
d. Factory work	Yes	Yes	Yes
e. Jobs requiring lifting weights above a threshold	Yes	Yes	Yes
f. Jobs deemed hazardous	No	Yes	No
g. Jobs deemed arduous	Yes	Yes	Yes
h. Jobs deemed morally or socially inappropriate	Yes	Yes	Yes
51. Can non-pregnant and non-nursing women work the same night hours as men?	No	Yes	Yes

Workplace protections

	GUINEA	HAITI	HONDURAS
52. Does the law mandate equal remuneration for men and women for work of equal value?	Yes	No	No
53. Are there laws mandating non-discrimination based on gender in hiring?	No	No	Yes
54. Is it illegal for an employer to ask about family status during a job interview?	No	No	No
55. Are there laws penalizing or preventing the dismissal of pregnant women?	Yes	Yes	Yes
56. Must employers give employees an equivalent position when they return from maternity leave?	Yes	Yes	Yes
57. Are employers required to provide break time for nursing mothers?	Yes	Yes	Yes
58. Do employees with minor children have rights to a flexible/part time schedule?	No	No	No

BUILDING CREDIT

	GUINEA	HAITI	HONDURAS
59. What is the minimum loan amount covered in the private credit bureau or public credit registry (as a percentage of income per capita)?	162%	252%	0%
60. Do microfinance institutions provide information to private credit bureaus or public credit registries?	No	No	Yes
61. Do utility companies provide information to private credit bureaus or public credit registries?	No	No	No
62. Do retailers provide information to private credit bureaus or public credit registries?	No	No	Yes

PROVIDING INCENTIVES TO WORK

Childcare

	GUINEA	HAITI	HONDURAS
63. Are payments for childcare tax deductible?	No	No	No
64. Is there public provision of childcare for children under the age of primary education?	No	No	Yes
65. Does the law mandate free and compulsory primary education?	No	Yes	Yes

Personal income tax

	Women	Men		Women	Men		Women	Men	
66. Are there specific tax deductions or credits that are applicable only to men/women?	No	Yes		No	No		No	No	

Economy Tables

	HONG KONG SAR, CHINA	HUNGARY	ICELAND
REGION	East Asia & Pacific	Europe & Central Asia	High income: OECD
INCOME	High income	Upper middle income	High income
FEMALE POPULATION	3,809,469	5,219,086	159,031
FEMALE LABOR FORCE PARTICIPATION	59%	57%	82%

ACCESSING INSTITUTIONS

Constitutional rights

	HONG KONG SAR, CHINA	HUNGARY	ICELAND
1. Is there a non-discrimination clause in the constitution?	No	Yes	No
2. If there is a non-discrimination clause in the constitution, does it explicitly mention gender?	N/A	Yes	N/A
3. Does the constitution guarantee equality before the law?	Yes	Yes	Yes

	Customary	Personal	Customary	Personal	Customary	Personal
4. Is customary/personal law recognized as valid source of law under the constitution?	Yes	No	No	No	No	No
5. If so, is it invalid if it violates constitutional provisions on non-discrimination or equality?	Yes	N/A	N/A	N/A	N/A	N/A

Quotas

	HONG KONG SAR, CHINA	HUNGARY	ICELAND
6. What are the legal quotas for women on corporate boards?	N/A	N/A	40%
7. What are the legal quotas for women in parliament?	N/A	N/A	N/A
8. What are the legal quotas for women in local government?	N/A	N/A	N/A

Rights of married and unmarried women

	Unmarried	Married	Unmarried	Married	Unmarried	Married
9. Can a woman apply for a passport in the same way as a man?	Yes	Yes	Yes	Yes	Yes	Yes
10. Can a woman apply for a national ID card in the same way as a man?	Yes	Yes	Yes	Yes	Yes	Yes
11. Can a woman travel outside the country in the same way as a man?	Yes	Yes	Yes	Yes	Yes	Yes
12. Can a woman travel outside her home in the same way as a man?	Yes	Yes	Yes	Yes	Yes	Yes
13. Can a woman get a job or pursue a trade or profession in the same way as a man?	Yes	Yes	Yes	Yes	Yes	Yes
14. Can a woman sign a contract in the same way as a man?	Yes	Yes	Yes	Yes	Yes	Yes
15. Can a woman register a business in the same way as a man?	Yes	Yes	Yes	Yes	Yes	Yes
16. Can a woman open a bank account in the same way as a man?	Yes	Yes	Yes	Yes	Yes	Yes
17. Can a woman choose where to live in the same way as a man?	Yes	Yes	Yes	Yes	Yes	Yes
18. Can a woman confer citizenship on her children in the same way as a man?	Yes	Yes	Yes	Yes	Yes	Yes
19. Can a woman be "head of household" or "head of family" in the same way as a man?	N/A	N/A	N/A	N/A	N/A	N/A
Number of inequalities in accessing institutions	0	0	0	0	0	0

Division of responsibility within marriage

	HONG KONG SAR, CHINA	HUNGARY	ICELAND
20. Can a woman convey citizenship to her non-national spouse in the same way as a man?	Yes	Yes	Yes
21. Are married women required by law to obey their husbands?	No	No	No
22. Do married couples jointly share legal responsibility for financially maintaining the family's expenses?	Yes	Yes	Yes

USING PROPERTY

Marital property regime

	HONG KONG SAR, CHINA	HUNGARY	ICELAND
23. What is the default marital property regime?	Separation of property	Partial community of property	Deferred community of property
24. Who legally administers property during marriage?	Original owner	Both must agree	Original owner

Protecting a wife's interests

	HONG KONG SAR, CHINA	HUNGARY	ICELAND
25. If it is the husband, does he need his wife's consent for major transactions	N/A	N/A	N/A
26. Are there special provisions governing the marital home?	No	No	Yes
27. Does the law provide for valuation of nonmonetary contributions during marriage?	Yes	Yes	Yes

Property rights

	Unmarried	Married	Unmarried	Married	Unmarried	Married
28. Do men and women have equal ownership rights to property?	Yes	Yes	Yes	Yes	Yes	Yes

Inheritance rights

	HONG KONG SAR, CHINA	HUNGARY	ICELAND
29. Do sons and daughters have equal inheritance rights to property?	Yes	Yes	Yes
30. Do female and male surviving spouses have equal inheritance rights to property?	Yes	Yes	Yes

GOING TO COURT

Equality of access

	HONG KONG SAR, CHINA	HUNGARY	ICELAND
31. Does the law recognize customary courts?	No	No	No
32. Does the law recognize personal law courts?	No	No	No
33. Does a woman's testimony carry the same evidentiary weight in court as a man's?	Yes	Yes	Yes

Efficiency of procedure

	HONG KONG SAR, CHINA	HUNGARY	ICELAND
34. Is there a small claims court or a fast track procedure for small claims?	Yes	Yes	No
35. If so, what is the maximum amount for a small claim (as a percentage of income per capita)?	18%	38%	N/A

Judicial representation

	HONG KONG SAR, CHINA	HUNGARY	ICELAND
36. How many justices are on the constitutional court?	4	15	12
37. Of those, how many are women?	0	1	2
38. Is the Chief Justice a woman?	No	No	No

	HONG KONG SAR, CHINA			HUNGARY			ICELAND		

GETTING A JOB

Parental benefits	Maternity	Paternity	Parental	Maternity	Paternity	Parental	Maternity	Paternity	Parental
39. Does the law mandate paid or unpaid maternity/paternity/parental leave?	Yes	No	No	Yes	Yes	Yes	Yes	Yes	Yes
40. What is the mandatory minimum length of paid leave for maternity/paternity/parental leave (in calendar days)?	70	N/A	N/A	168	5	1067	90	90	90
41. What is the mandatory minimum length of unpaid leave for maternity/paternity/parental leave (in calendar days)?	0	N/A	N/A	0	0	0	0	0	0
42. Who pays maternity/paternity/parental benefits?	Emp.	N/A	N/A	Gov.	Emp.	Gov.	Gov.	Gov.	Gov.
43. What percentage of wages are paid during maternity/paternity/parental leave?	80%	N/A	N/A	70%	100%	Partially paid	80%	80%	Partially paid

	Mother	Father		Mother	Father		Mother	Father	
44. Where **paid** parental leave exists, what is the minimum amount which only the mother/father must take (in calendar days)?	N/A	N/A		0	0		0	0	
45. Where **unpaid** parental leave exists, what is the minimum amount which only the mother/father must take (in calendar days)?	N/A	N/A		N/A	N/A		N/A	N/A	

Retirement & pensions	Women	Men		Women	Men		Women	Men	
46. What is the age at which one can retire and receive full benefits?	65	65		65	65		67	67	
47. What is the age at which one can retire and receive partial benefits?	60	60		65	65		67	67	
48. What is the mandatory retirement age?	N/A	N/A		N/A	N/A		N/A	N/A	

Working hours and industry restrictions									
49. Can non-pregnant and non-nursing women do the same jobs as men?	Yes			Yes			Yes		
50. Can non-pregnant and non-nursing women engage in the following occupations in the same way as men?									
a. Mining	Yes			Yes			Yes		
b. Construction	Yes			Yes			Yes		
c. Metalwork	Yes			Yes			Yes		
d. Factory work	Yes			Yes			Yes		
e. Jobs requiring lifting weights above a threshold	Yes			Yes			Yes		
f. Jobs deemed hazardous	Yes			Yes			Yes		
g. Jobs deemed arduous	Yes			Yes			Yes		
h. Jobs deemed morally or socially inappropriate	Yes			Yes			Yes		
51. Can non-pregnant and non-nursing women work the same night hours as men?	Yes			Yes			Yes		

Workplace protections									
52. Does the law mandate equal remuneration for men and women for work of equal value?	No			Yes			No		
53. Are there laws mandating non-discrimination based on gender in hiring?	Yes			Yes			No		
54. Is it illegal for an employer to ask about family status during a job interview?	No			No			No		
55. Are there laws penalizing or preventing the dismissal of pregnant women?	Yes			Yes			Yes		
56. Must employers give employees an equivalent position when they return from maternity leave?	No			Yes			Yes		
57. Are employers required to provide break time for nursing mothers?	No			Yes			No		
58. Do employees with minor children have rights to a flexible/part time schedule?	No			No			No		

BUILDING CREDIT

59. What is the minimum loan amount covered in the private credit bureau or public credit registry (as a percentage of income per capita)?	0%			0%			1%		
60. Do microfinance institutions provide information to private credit bureaus or public credit registries?	N/A			N/A			N/A		
61. Do utility companies provide information to private credit bureaus or public credit registries?	No			No			Yes		
62. Do retailers provide information to private credit bureaus or public credit registries?	No			No			Yes		

PROVIDING INCENTIVES TO WORK

Childcare									
63. Are payments for childcare tax deductible?	No			No			No		
64. Is there public provision of childcare for children under the age of primary education?	Yes			Yes			Yes		
65. Does the law mandate free and compulsory primary education?	Yes			Yes			Yes		

Personal income tax	Women	Men		Women	Men		Women	Men	
66. Are there specific tax deductions or credits that are applicable only to men/women?	No	No		No	No		No	No	

Economy Tables

	INDIA		INDONESIA		IRAN, ISLAMIC REP.	
REGION	South Asia		East Asia & Pacific		Middle East & North Africa	
INCOME	Lower middle income		Lower middle income		Upper middle income	
FEMALE POPULATION	597,121,072		122,658,460		37,928,548	
FEMALE LABOR FORCE PARTICIPATION	30%		53%		17%	

ACCESSING INSTITUTIONS

Constitutional rights

	INDIA		INDONESIA		IRAN, ISLAMIC REP.	
1. Is there a non-discrimination clause in the constitution?	Yes		Yes		No	
2. If there is a non-discrimination clause in the constitution, does it explicitly mention gender?	Yes		No		N/A	
3. Does the constitution guarantee equality before the law?	Yes		Yes		Yes	

	Customary	Personal	Customary	Personal	Customary	Personal
4. Is customary/personal law recognized as valid source of law under the constitution?	Yes	Yes	Yes	Yes	No	Yes
5. If so, is it invalid if it violates constitutional provisions on non-discrimination or equality?	No	No	Yes	No	N/A	No

Quotas

	INDIA		INDONESIA		IRAN, ISLAMIC REP.	
6. What are the legal quotas for women on corporate boards?	N/A		N/A		N/A	
7. What are the legal quotas for women in parliament?	N/A		N/A		N/A	
8. What are the legal quotas for women in local government?	N/A		N/A		N/A	

Rights of married and unmarried women	Unmarried	Married	Unmarried	Married	Unmarried	Married
9. Can a woman apply for a passport in the same way as a man?	Yes	Yes	Yes	Yes	Yes	No
10. Can a woman apply for a national ID card in the same way as a man?	N/A	N/A	Yes	Yes	Yes	Yes
11. Can a woman travel outside the country in the same way as a man?	Yes	Yes	Yes	Yes	Yes	Yes
12. Can a woman travel outside her home in the same way as a man?	Yes	Yes	Yes	Yes	Yes	No
13. Can a woman get a job or pursue a trade or profession in the same way as a man?	Yes	Yes	Yes	Yes	Yes	No
14. Can a woman sign a contract in the same way as a man?	Yes	Yes	Yes	Yes	Yes	Yes
15. Can a woman register a business in the same way as a man?	Yes	Yes	Yes	Yes	Yes	Yes
16. Can a woman open a bank account in the same way as a man?	Yes	Yes	Yes	Yes	Yes	Yes
17. Can a woman choose where to live in the same way as a man?	Yes	Yes	Yes	Yes	Yes	No
18. Can a woman confer citizenship on her children in the same way as a man?	Yes	Yes	Yes	Yes	No	No
19. Can a woman be "head of household" or "head of family" in the same way as a man?	N/A	N/A	Yes	No	Yes	No
Number of inequalities in accessing institutions	0	0	0	1	1	6

Division of responsibility within marriage

	INDIA		INDONESIA		IRAN, ISLAMIC REP.	
20. Can a woman convey citizenship to her non-national spouse in the same way as a man?	Yes		Yes		No	
21. Are married women required by law to obey their husbands?	No		No		Yes	
22. Do married couples jointly share legal responsibility for financially maintaining the family's expenses?	Yes		No		No	

USING PROPERTY

Marital property regime

	INDIA		INDONESIA		IRAN, ISLAMIC REP.	
23. What is the default marital property regime?	Separation of property		Partial community of property		Separation of property	
24. Who legally administers property during marriage?	Original owner		Both must agree		Original owner	

Protecting a wife's interests

	INDIA		INDONESIA		IRAN, ISLAMIC REP.	
25. If it is the husband, does he need his wife's consent for major transactions	N/A		N/A		N/A	
26. Are there special provisions governing the marital home?	No		No		No	
27. Does the law provide for valuation of nonmonetary contributions during marriage?	No		Yes		No	

Property rights	Unmarried	Married	Unmarried	Married	Unmarried	Married
28. Do men and women have equal ownership rights to property?	Yes	Yes	Yes	Yes	Yes	Yes

Inheritance rights

	INDIA		INDONESIA		IRAN, ISLAMIC REP.	
29. Do sons and daughters have equal inheritance rights to property?	Yes		No		No	
30. Do female and male surviving spouses have equal inheritance rights to property?	Yes		No		No	

GOING TO COURT

Equality of access

	INDIA		INDONESIA		IRAN, ISLAMIC REP.	
31. Does the law recognize customary courts?	No		No		No	
32. Does the law recognize personal law courts?	Yes		Yes		Yes	
33. Does a woman's testimony carry the same evidentiary weight in court as a man's?	Yes		Yes		No	

Efficiency of procedure

	INDIA		INDONESIA		IRAN, ISLAMIC REP.	
34. Is there a small claims court or a fast track procedure for small claims?	Yes		No		No	
35. If so, what is the maximum amount for a small claim (as a percentage of income per capita)?	3%		N/A		N/A	

Judicial representation

	INDIA		INDONESIA		IRAN, ISLAMIC REP.	
36. How many justices are on the constitutional court?	28		9		12	
37. Of those, how many are women?	2		1		0	
38. Is the Chief Justice a woman?	No		No		No	

GETTING A JOB

Parental benefits	INDIA			INDONESIA			IRAN, ISLAMIC REP.		
	Maternity	Paternity	Parental	Maternity	Paternity	Parental	Maternity	Paternity	Parental
39. Does the law mandate paid or unpaid maternity/paternity/parental leave?	Yes	No	No	Yes	Yes	No	Yes	No	No
40. What is the mandatory minimum length of paid leave for maternity/paternity/parental leave (in calendar days)?	84	N/A	N/A	90	2	N/A	90	N/A	N/A
41. What is the mandatory minimum length of unpaid leave for maternity/paternity/parental leave (in calendar days)?	0	N/A	N/A	0	0	N/A	0	N/A	N/A
42. Who pays maternity/paternity/parental benefits?	Emp.	N/A	N/A	Emp.	Emp.	N/A	Gov.	N/A	N/A
43. What percentage of wages are paid during maternity/paternity/parental leave?	100%	N/A	N/A	100%	100%	N/A	67%	N/A	N/A

	Mother	Father		Mother	Father		Mother	Father	
44. Where **paid** parental leave exists, what is the minimum amount which only the mother/father must take (in calendar days)?	N/A	N/A		N/A	N/A		N/A	N/A	
45. Where **unpaid** parental leave exists, what is the minimum amount which only the mother/father must take (in calendar days)?	N/A	N/A		N/A	N/A		N/A	N/A	

Retirement & pensions	Women	Men		Women	Men		Women	Men	
46. What is the age at which one can retire and receive full benefits?	58	58		55	55		55	60	
47. What is the age at which one can retire and receive partial benefits?	50	50		55	55		45	55	
48. What is the mandatory retirement age?	N/A	N/A		N/A	N/A		N/A	N/A	

Working hours and industry restrictions	INDIA	INDONESIA	IRAN, ISLAMIC REP.
49. Can non-pregnant and non-nursing women do the same jobs as men?	No	Yes	No
50. Can non-pregnant and non-nursing women engage in the following occupations in the same way as men?			
a. Mining	No	Yes	Yes
b. Construction	Yes	Yes	Yes
c. Metalwork	No	Yes	Yes
d. Factory work	No	Yes	Yes
e. Jobs requiring lifting weights above a threshold	No	Yes	No
f. Jobs deemed hazardous	No	Yes	No
g. Jobs deemed arduous	Yes	Yes	No
h. Jobs deemed morally or socially inappropriate	Yes	Yes	Yes
51. Can non-pregnant and non-nursing women work the same night hours as men?	No	Yes	Yes

Workplace protections	INDIA	INDONESIA	IRAN, ISLAMIC REP.
52. Does the law mandate equal remuneration for men and women for work of equal value?	No	No	No
53. Are there laws mandating non-discrimination based on gender in hiring?	Yes	No	No
54. Is it illegal for an employer to ask about family status during a job interview?	No	No	No
55. Are there laws penalizing or preventing the dismissal of pregnant women?	Yes	Yes	No
56. Must employers give employees an equivalent position when they return from maternity leave?	No	No	Yes
57. Are employers required to provide break time for nursing mothers?	Yes	Yes	Yes
58. Do employees with minor children have rights to a flexible/part time schedule?	No	No	No

BUILDING CREDIT

	INDIA	INDONESIA	IRAN, ISLAMIC REP.
59. What is the minimum loan amount covered in the private credit bureau or public credit registry (as a percentage of income per capita)?	0%	0%	0%
60. Do microfinance institutions provide information to private credit bureaus or public credit registries?	Yes	Yes	Yes
61. Do utility companies provide information to private credit bureaus or public credit registries?	No	No	No
62. Do retailers provide information to private credit bureaus or public credit registries?	No	No	No

PROVIDING INCENTIVES TO WORK

Childcare	INDIA	INDONESIA	IRAN, ISLAMIC REP.
63. Are payments for childcare tax deductible?	No	No	No
64. Is there public provision of childcare for children under the age of primary education?	No	No	No
65. Does the law mandate free and compulsory primary education?	Yes	Yes	No

Personal income tax	Women	Men		Women	Men		Women	Men	
66. Are there specific tax deductions or credits that are applicable only to men/women?	No	No		No	Yes		No	No	

Economy Tables

	IRELAND		ISRAEL		ITALY	
REGION	High income: OECD		High income: OECD		High income: OECD	
INCOME	High income		High income		High income	
FEMALE POPULATION	2,312,070		3,996,428		31,339,707	
FEMALE LABOR FORCE PARTICIPATION	62%		61%		51%	

ACCESSING INSTITUTIONS

Constitutional rights

	IRELAND		ISRAEL		ITALY	
1. Is there a non-discrimination clause in the constitution?	No		No		No	
2. If there is a non-discrimination clause in the constitution, does it explicitly mention gender?	N/A		N/A		N/A	
3. Does the constitution guarantee equality before the law?	Yes		No		Yes	

	Customary	Personal	Customary	Personal	Customary	Personal
4. Is customary/personal law recognized as valid source of law under the constitution?	No	No	No	Yes	No	No
5. If so, is it invalid if it violates constitutional provisions on non-discrimination or equality?	N/A	N/A	N/A	No	N/A	N/A

Quotas

	IRELAND	ISRAEL	ITALY
6. What are the legal quotas for women on corporate boards?	N/A	N/A	33%
7. What are the legal quotas for women in parliament?	N/A	N/A	N/A
8. What are the legal quotas for women in local government?	N/A	N/A	N/A

Rights of married and unmarried women

	Unmarried	Married	Unmarried	Married	Unmarried	Married
9. Can a woman apply for a passport in the same way as a man?	Yes	Yes	Yes	Yes	Yes	Yes
10. Can a woman apply for a national ID card in the same way as a man?	N/A	N/A	Yes	Yes	Yes	Yes
11. Can a woman travel outside the country in the same way as a man?	Yes	Yes	Yes	Yes	Yes	Yes
12. Can a woman travel outside her home in the same way as a man?	Yes	Yes	Yes	Yes	Yes	Yes
13. Can a woman get a job or pursue a trade or profession in the same way as a man?	Yes	Yes	Yes	Yes	Yes	Yes
14. Can a woman sign a contract in the same way as a man?	Yes	Yes	Yes	Yes	Yes	Yes
15. Can a woman register a business in the same way as a man?	Yes	Yes	Yes	Yes	Yes	Yes
16. Can a woman open a bank account in the same way as a man?	Yes	Yes	Yes	Yes	Yes	Yes
17. Can a woman choose where to live in the same way as a man?	Yes	Yes	Yes	Yes	Yes	Yes
18. Can a woman confer citizenship on her children in the same way as a man?	Yes	Yes	Yes	Yes	Yes	Yes
19. Can a woman be "head of household" or "head of family" in the same way as a man?	N/A	N/A	N/A	N/A	N/A	N/A
Number of inequalities in accessing institutions	0	0	0	0	0	0

Division of responsibility within marriage

	IRELAND	ISRAEL	ITALY
20. Can a woman convey citizenship to her non-national spouse in the same way as a man?	Yes	Yes	Yes
21. Are married women required by law to obey their husbands?	No	No	No
22. Do married couples jointly share legal responsibility for financially maintaining the family's expenses?	Yes	Yes	Yes

USING PROPERTY

Marital property regime

	IRELAND	ISRAEL	ITALY
23. What is the default marital property regime?	Separation of property	Deferred community of property	Partial community of property
24. Who legally administers property during marriage?	Original owner	Original owner	Both must agree

Protecting a wife's interests

	IRELAND	ISRAEL	ITALY
25. If it is the husband, does he need his wife's consent for major transactions	N/A	N/A	N/A
26. Are there special provisions governing the marital home?	Yes	No	No
27. Does the law provide for valuation of nonmonetary contributions during marriage?	Yes	Yes	Yes

Property rights

	Unmarried	Married	Unmarried	Married	Unmarried	Married
28. Do men and women have equal ownership rights to property?	Yes	Yes	Yes	Yes	Yes	Yes

Inheritance rights

	IRELAND	ISRAEL	ITALY
29. Do sons and daughters have equal inheritance rights to property?	Yes	Yes	Yes
30. Do female and male surviving spouses have equal inheritance rights to property?	Yes	Yes	Yes

GOING TO COURT

Equality of access

	IRELAND	ISRAEL	ITALY
31. Does the law recognize customary courts?	No	No	No
32. Does the law recognize personal law courts?	No	Yes	No
33. Does a woman's testimony carry the same evidentiary weight in court as a man's?	Yes	Yes	Yes

Efficiency of procedure

	IRELAND	ISRAEL	ITALY
34. Is there a small claims court or a fast track procedure for small claims?	Yes	Yes	Yes
35. If so, what is the maximum amount for a small claim (as a percentage of income per capita)?	7%	30%	19%

Judicial representation

	IRELAND	ISRAEL	ITALY
36. How many justices are on the constitutional court?	5	15	15
37. Of those, how many are women?	1	4	1
38. Is the Chief Justice a woman?	Yes	No	No

	IRELAND			ISRAEL			ITALY		

GETTING A JOB

Parental benefits	Maternity	Paternity	Parental	Maternity	Paternity	Parental	Maternity	Paternity	Parental
39. Does the law mandate paid or unpaid maternity/paternity/parental leave?	Yes	No	Yes	Yes	No	Yes	Yes	Yes	Yes
40. What is the mandatory minimum length of paid leave for maternity/paternity/parental leave (in calendar days)?	182	N/A	0	98	N/A	0	150	1	300
41. What is the mandatory minimum length of unpaid leave for maternity/paternity/parental leave (in calendar days)?	112	N/A	98	0	N/A	280	0	0	0
42. Who pays maternity/paternity/parental benefits?	Gov.	N/A	N/A	Gov.	N/A	N/A	Gov.	Gov.	Gov.
43. What percentage of wages are paid during maternity/paternity/parental leave?	41%	N/A	0%	100%	N/A	0%	80%	100%	Partially paid

	Mother	Father		Mother	Father		Mother	Father	
44. Where **paid** parental leave exists, what is the minimum amount which only the mother/father must take (in calendar days)?	N/A	N/A		N/A	N/A		0	0	
45. Where **unpaid** parental leave exists, what is the minimum amount which only the mother/father must take (in calendar days)?	0	0		0	0		N/A	N/A	

Retirement & pensions	Women	Men		Women	Men		Women	Men	
46. What is the age at which one can retire and receive full benefits?	68	68		64	67		66	66	
47. What is the age at which one can retire and receive partial benefits?	68	68		64	67		66	66	
48. What is the mandatory retirement age?	N/A	N/A		67	67		N/A	N/A	

Working hours and industry restrictions									
49. Can non-pregnant and non-nursing women do the same jobs as men?	Yes			No			Yes		
50. Can non-pregnant and non-nursing women engage in the following occupations in the same way as men?									
a. Mining	Yes			Yes			Yes		
b. Construction	Yes			Yes			Yes		
c. Metalwork	Yes			Yes			Yes		
d. Factory work	Yes			Yes			Yes		
e. Jobs requiring lifting weights above a threshold	Yes			Yes			Yes		
f. Jobs deemed hazardous	Yes			No			Yes		
g. Jobs deemed arduous	Yes			Yes			Yes		
h. Jobs deemed morally or socially inappropriate	Yes			Yes			Yes		
51. Can non-pregnant and non-nursing women work the same night hours as men?	Yes			Yes			Yes		

Workplace protections									
52. Does the law mandate equal remuneration for men and women for work of equal value?	Yes			No			Yes		
53. Are there laws mandating non-discrimination based on gender in hiring?	Yes			No			No		
54. Is it illegal for an employer to ask about family status during a job interview?	No			No			No		
55. Are there laws penalizing or preventing the dismissal of pregnant women?	Yes			Yes			Yes		
56. Must employers give employees an equivalent position when they return from maternity leave?	Yes			Yes			Yes		
57. Are employers required to provide break time for nursing mothers?	Yes			Yes			Yes		
58. Do employees with minor children have rights to a flexible/part time schedule?	No			No			No		

BUILDING CREDIT

59. What is the minimum loan amount covered in the private credit bureau or public credit registry (as a percentage of income per capita)?	1%			0%			0%		
60. Do microfinance institutions provide information to private credit bureaus or public credit registries?	N/A			N/A			N/A		
61. Do utility companies provide information to private credit bureaus or public credit registries?	No			Yes			No		
62. Do retailers provide information to private credit bureaus or public credit registries?	No			Yes			No		

PROVIDING INCENTIVES TO WORK

Childcare									
63. Are payments for childcare tax deductible?	No			No			Yes		
64. Is there public provision of childcare for children under the age of primary education?	Yes			Yes			Yes		
65. Does the law mandate free and compulsory primary education?	Yes			Yes			Yes		

Personal income tax	Women	Men		Women	Men		Women	Men	
66. Are there specific tax deductions or credits that are applicable only to men/women?	No	No		Yes	No		No	No	

Economy Tables

	JAMAICA		JAPAN		JORDAN	
REGION	Latin America & Caribbean		High income: OECD		Middle East & North Africa	
INCOME	Upper middle income		High income		Upper middle income	
FEMALE POPULATION	1,377,028		65,473,758		3,092,366	
FEMALE LABOR FORCE PARTICIPATION	61%		63%		17%	

ACCESSING INSTITUTIONS

Constitutional rights

	JAMAICA		JAPAN		JORDAN	
1. Is there a non-discrimination clause in the constitution?	Yes		Yes		Yes	
2. If there is a non-discrimination clause in the constitution, does it explicitly mention gender?	Yes		Yes		No	
3. Does the constitution guarantee equality before the law?	Yes		Yes		Yes	

	Customary	Personal	Customary	Personal	Customary	Personal
4. Is customary/personal law recognized as valid source of law under the constitution?	No	No	No	No	No	Yes
5. If so, is it invalid if it violates constitutional provisions on non-discrimination or equality?	N/A	N/A	N/A	N/A	N/A	No

Quotas

	JAMAICA	JAPAN	JORDAN
6. What are the legal quotas for women on corporate boards?	N/A	N/A	N/A
7. What are the legal quotas for women in parliament?	N/A	N/A	10%
8. What are the legal quotas for women in local government?	N/A	N/A	N/A

Rights of married and unmarried women

	Unmarried	Married	Unmarried	Married	Unmarried	Married
9. Can a woman apply for a passport in the same way as a man?	Yes	Yes	Yes	Yes	No	No
10. Can a woman apply for a national ID card in the same way as a man?	N/A	N/A	N/A	N/A	Yes	Yes
11. Can a woman travel outside the country in the same way as a man?	Yes	Yes	Yes	Yes	Yes	Yes
12. Can a woman travel outside her home in the same way as a man?	Yes	Yes	Yes	Yes	Yes	No
13. Can a woman get a job or pursue a trade or profession in the same way as a man?	Yes	Yes	Yes	Yes	Yes	No
14. Can a woman sign a contract in the same way as a man?	Yes	Yes	Yes	Yes	Yes	Yes
15. Can a woman register a business in the same way as a man?	Yes	Yes	Yes	Yes	Yes	Yes
16. Can a woman open a bank account in the same way as a man?	Yes	Yes	Yes	Yes	Yes	Yes
17. Can a woman choose where to live in the same way as a man?	Yes	Yes	Yes	Yes	Yes	No
18. Can a woman confer citizenship on her children in the same way as a man?	Yes	Yes	Yes	Yes	No	No
19. Can a woman be "head of household" or "head of family" in the same way as a man?	N/A	N/A	Yes	Yes	Yes	No
Number of inequalities in accessing institutions	0	0	0	0	2	6

Division of responsibility within marriage

	JAMAICA	JAPAN	JORDAN
20. Can a woman convey citizenship to her non-national spouse in the same way as a man?	Yes	Yes	No
21. Are married women required by law to obey their husbands?	No	No	No
22. Do married couples jointly share legal responsibility for financially maintaining the family's expenses?	Yes	Yes	No

USING PROPERTY

Marital property regime

	JAMAICA	JAPAN	JORDAN
23. What is the default marital property regime?	Separation of property	Other	Separation of property
24. Who legally administers property during marriage?	Original owner	Both must agree	Original owner

Protecting a wife's interests

	JAMAICA	JAPAN	JORDAN
25. If it is the husband, does he need his wife's consent for major transactions	N/A	N/A	N/A
26. Are there special provisions governing the marital home?	Yes	No	No
27. Does the law provide for valuation of nonmonetary contributions during marriage?	Yes	Yes	No

Property rights

	Unmarried	Married	Unmarried	Married	Unmarried	Married
28. Do men and women have equal ownership rights to property?	Yes	Yes	Yes	Yes	Yes	Yes

Inheritance rights

	JAMAICA	JAPAN	JORDAN
29. Do sons and daughters have equal inheritance rights to property?	Yes	Yes	No
30. Do female and male surviving spouses have equal inheritance rights to property?	Yes	Yes	No

GOING TO COURT

Equality of access

	JAMAICA	JAPAN	JORDAN
31. Does the law recognize customary courts?	No	No	No
32. Does the law recognize personal law courts?	No	No	Yes
33. Does a woman's testimony carry the same evidentiary weight in court as a man's?	Yes	Yes	No

Efficiency of procedure

	JAMAICA	JAPAN	JORDAN
34. Is there a small claims court or a fast track procedure for small claims?	Yes	Yes	No
35. If so, what is the maximum amount for a small claim (as a percentage of income per capita)?	11%	16%	N/A

Judicial representation

	JAMAICA	JAPAN	JORDAN
36. How many justices are on the constitutional court?	30	15	9
37. Of those, how many are women?	14	3	0
38. Is the Chief Justice a woman?	Yes	No	No

	JAMAICA			JAPAN			JORDAN		

GETTING A JOB

Parental benefits	Maternity	Paternity	Parental	Maternity	Paternity	Parental	Maternity	Paternity	Parental
39. Does the law mandate paid or unpaid maternity/paternity/parental leave?	Yes	No	No	Yes	No	Yes	Yes	No	No
40. What is the mandatory minimum length of paid leave for maternity/paternity/parental leave (in calendar days)?	56	N/A	N/A	98	N/A	209	70	N/A	N/A
41. What is the mandatory minimum length of unpaid leave for maternity/paternity/parental leave (in calendar days)?	28	N/A	N/A	0	N/A	0	0	N/A	N/A
42. Who pays maternity/paternity/parental benefits?	Emp.	N/A	N/A	Gov.	N/A	Gov.	Gov.	N/A	N/A
43. What percentage of wages are paid during maternity/paternity/parental leave?	100%	N/A	N/A	66%	N/A	Partially paid	100%	N/A	N/A

	Mother	Father		Mother	Father		Mother	Father	
44. Where **paid** parental leave exists, what is the minimum amount which only the mother/father must take (in calendar days)?	N/A	N/A		0	0		N/A	N/A	
45. Where **unpaid** parental leave exists, what is the minimum amount which only the mother/father must take (in calendar days)?	N/A	N/A		N/A	N/A		N/A	N/A	

Retirement & pensions	Women	Men		Women	Men		Women	Men	
46. What is the age at which one can retire and receive full benefits?	60	65		65	65		55	60	
47. What is the age at which one can retire and receive partial benefits?	60	65		60	60		50	50	
48. What is the mandatory retirement age?	N/A	N/A		N/A	N/A		N/A	N/A	

Working hours and industry restrictions	JAMAICA	JAPAN	JORDAN
49. Can non-pregnant and non-nursing women do the same jobs as men?	No	No	No
50. Can non-pregnant and non-nursing women engage in the following occupations in the same way as men?			
a. Mining	Yes	No	No
b. Construction	Yes	Yes	No
c. Metalwork	Yes	Yes	No
d. Factory work	No	Yes	No
e. Jobs requiring lifting weights above a threshold	Yes	Yes	No
f. Jobs deemed hazardous	Yes	Yes	Yes
g. Jobs deemed arduous	Yes	Yes	Yes
h. Jobs deemed morally or socially inappropriate	Yes	Yes	Yes
51. Can non-pregnant and non-nursing women work the same night hours as men?	No	Yes	No

Workplace protections	JAMAICA	JAPAN	JORDAN
52. Does the law mandate equal remuneration for men and women for work of equal value?	No	No	No
53. Are there laws mandating non-discrimination based on gender in hiring?	No	Yes	No
54. Is it illegal for an employer to ask about family status during a job interview?	No	No	No
55. Are there laws penalizing or preventing the dismissal of pregnant women?	Yes	Yes	Yes
56. Must employers give employees an equivalent position when they return from maternity leave?	Yes	No	Yes
57. Are employers required to provide break time for nursing mothers?	No	Yes	Yes
58. Do employees with minor children have rights to a flexible/part time schedule?	No	Yes	No

BUILDING CREDIT

	JAMAICA	JAPAN	JORDAN
59. What is the minimum loan amount covered in the private credit bureau or public credit registry (as a percentage of income per capita)?	N/A	0%	608%
60. Do microfinance institutions provide information to private credit bureaus or public credit registries?	N/A	N/A	Yes
61. Do utility companies provide information to private credit bureaus or public credit registries?	N/A	No	No
62. Do retailers provide information to private credit bureaus or public credit registries?	N/A	Yes	No

PROVIDING INCENTIVES TO WORK

Childcare	JAMAICA	JAPAN	JORDAN
63. Are payments for childcare tax deductible?	No	No	No
64. Is there public provision of childcare for children under the age of primary education?	Yes	No	Yes
65. Does the law mandate free and compulsory primary education?	Yes	Yes	Yes

Personal income tax	Women	Men		Women	Men		Women	Men	
66. Are there specific tax deductions or credits that are applicable only to men/women?	No	No		No	No		No	No	

Economy Tables

	KAZAKHSTAN	KENYA	KOREA, REP.
REGION	Europe & Central Asia	Sub-Saharan Africa	High income: OECD
INCOME	Upper middle income	Low income	High income
FEMALE POPULATION	8,704,910	21,633,197	25,136,292
FEMALE LABOR FORCE PARTICIPATION	74%	62%	54%

ACCESSING INSTITUTIONS

Constitutional rights

	KAZAKHSTAN	KENYA	KOREA, REP.
1. Is there a non-discrimination clause in the constitution?	Yes	Yes	Yes
2. If there is a non-discrimination clause in the constitution, does it explicitly mention gender?	Yes	Yes	Yes
3. Does the constitution guarantee equality before the law?	Yes	Yes	Yes

	Customary	Personal	Customary	Personal	Customary	Personal
4. Is customary/personal law recognized as valid source of law under the constitution?	No	No	Yes	Yes	No	No
5. If so, is it invalid if it violates constitutional provisions on non-discrimination or equality?	N/A	N/A	Yes	No	N/A	N/A

Quotas

	KAZAKHSTAN	KENYA	KOREA, REP.
6. What are the legal quotas for women on corporate boards?	N/A	N/A	N/A
7. What are the legal quotas for women in parliament?	N/A	33%	N/A
8. What are the legal quotas for women in local government?	N/A	33%	N/A

Rights of married and unmarried women

	Unmarried	Married	Unmarried	Married	Unmarried	Married
9. Can a woman apply for a passport in the same way as a man?	Yes	Yes	Yes	Yes	Yes	Yes
10. Can a woman apply for a national ID card in the same way as a man?	N/A	N/A	Yes	Yes	Yes	Yes
11. Can a woman travel outside the country in the same way as a man?	Yes	Yes	Yes	Yes	Yes	Yes
12. Can a woman travel outside her home in the same way as a man?	Yes	Yes	Yes	Yes	Yes	Yes
13. Can a woman get a job or pursue a trade or profession in the same way as a man?	Yes	Yes	Yes	Yes	Yes	Yes
14. Can a woman sign a contract in the same way as a man?	Yes	Yes	Yes	Yes	Yes	Yes
15. Can a woman register a business in the same way as a man?	Yes	Yes	Yes	Yes	Yes	Yes
16. Can a woman open a bank account in the same way as a man?	Yes	Yes	Yes	Yes	Yes	Yes
17. Can a woman choose where to live in the same way as a man?	Yes	Yes	Yes	Yes	Yes	Yes
18. Can a woman confer citizenship on her children in the same way as a man?	Yes	Yes	Yes	Yes	Yes	Yes
19. Can a woman be "head of household" or "head of family" in the same way as a man?	N/A	N/A	N/A	N/A	N/A	N/A
Number of inequalities in accessing institutions	0	0	0	0	0	0

Division of responsibility within marriage

	KAZAKHSTAN	KENYA	KOREA, REP.
20. Can a woman convey citizenship to her non-national spouse in the same way as a man?	Yes	Yes	Yes
21. Are married women required by law to obey their husbands?	No	No	No
22. Do married couples jointly share legal responsibility for financially maintaining the family's expenses?	Yes	Yes	Yes

USING PROPERTY

Marital property regime

	KAZAKHSTAN	KENYA	KOREA, REP.
23. What is the default marital property regime?	Partial community of property	Separation of property	Other
24. Who legally administers property during marriage?	Both must agree	Original owner	Both must agree

Protecting a wife's interests

	KAZAKHSTAN	KENYA	KOREA, REP.
25. If it is the husband, does he need his wife's consent for major transactions	N/A	N/A	N/A
26. Are there special provisions governing the marital home?	No	Yes	No
27. Does the law provide for valuation of nonmonetary contributions during marriage?	Yes	Yes	Yes

Property rights

	Unmarried	Married	Unmarried	Married	Unmarried	Married
28. Do men and women have equal ownership rights to property?	Yes	Yes	Yes	Yes	Yes	Yes

Inheritance rights

	KAZAKHSTAN	KENYA	KOREA, REP.
29. Do sons and daughters have equal inheritance rights to property?	Yes	Yes	Yes
30. Do female and male surviving spouses have equal inheritance rights to property?	Yes	Yes	Yes

GOING TO COURT

Equality of access

	KAZAKHSTAN	KENYA	KOREA, REP.
31. Does the law recognize customary courts?	No	Yes	No
32. Does the law recognize personal law courts?	No	Yes	No
33. Does a woman's testimony carry the same evidentiary weight in court as a man's?	Yes	Yes	Yes

Efficiency of procedure

	KAZAKHSTAN	KENYA	KOREA, REP.
34. Is there a small claims court or a fast track procedure for small claims?	No	Yes	Yes
35. If so, what is the maximum amount for a small claim (as a percentage of income per capita)?	N/A	70%	80%

Judicial representation

	KAZAKHSTAN	KENYA	KOREA, REP.
36. How many justices are on the constitutional court?	7	7	9
37. Of those, how many are women?	1	2	1
38. Is the Chief Justice a woman?	No	No	No

	KAZAKHSTAN			KENYA			KOREA, REP.		

GETTING A JOB

Parental benefits	Maternity	Paternity	Parental	Maternity	Paternity	Parental	Maternity	Paternity	Parental
39. Does the law mandate paid or unpaid maternity/paternity/parental leave?	Yes	No	Yes	Yes	Yes	No	Yes	Yes	No
40. What is the mandatory minimum length of paid leave for maternity/paternity/parental leave (in calendar days)?	126	N/A	0	90	14	N/A	90	0	N/A
41. What is the mandatory minimum length of unpaid leave for maternity/paternity/parental leave (in calendar days)?	0	N/A	1039	0	0	N/A	0	3	N/A
42. Who pays maternity/paternity/parental benefits?	Emp.	N/A	N/A	Emp.	Emp.	N/A	Emp. & Gov.	N/A	N/A
43. What percentage of wages are paid during maternity/paternity/parental leave?	100%	N/A	0%	100%	100%	N/A	100%	0%	N/A

	Mother	Father		Mother	Father		Mother	Father	
44. Where **paid** parental leave exists, what is the minimum amount which only the mother/father must take (in calendar days)?	N/A	N/A		N/A	N/A		N/A	N/A	
45. Where **unpaid** parental leave exists, what is the minimum amount which only the mother/father must take (in calendar days)?	0	0		N/A	N/A		N/A	N/A	

Retirement & pensions	Women	Men		Women	Men		Women	Men	
46. What is the age at which one can retire and receive full benefits?	58	63		55	55		60	60	
47. What is the age at which one can retire and receive partial benefits?	58	63		55	55		55	55	
48. What is the mandatory retirement age?	N/A	N/A		N/A	N/A		N/A	N/A	

Working hours and industry restrictions									
49. Can non-pregnant and non-nursing women do the same jobs as men?	No			No			No		
50. Can non-pregnant and non-nursing women engage in the following occupations in the same way as men?									
a. Mining	No			Yes			No		
b. Construction	No			Yes			Yes		
c. Metalwork	No			Yes			Yes		
d. Factory work	No			Yes			Yes		
e. Jobs requiring lifting weights above a threshold	No			Yes			Yes		
f. Jobs deemed hazardous	No			Yes			No		
g. Jobs deemed arduous	No			Yes			Yes		
h. Jobs deemed morally or socially inappropriate	Yes			Yes			Yes		
51. Can non-pregnant and non-nursing women work the same night hours as men?	Yes			Yes			Yes		

Workplace protections									
52. Does the law mandate equal remuneration for men and women for work of equal value?	No			Yes			Yes		
53. Are there laws mandating non-discrimination based on gender in hiring?	Yes			No			Yes		
54. Is it illegal for an employer to ask about family status during a job interview?	No			No			Yes		
55. Are there laws penalizing or preventing the dismissal of pregnant women?	Yes			Yes			Yes		
56. Must employers give employees an equivalent position when they return from maternity leave?	Yes			Yes			Yes		
57. Are employers required to provide break time for nursing mothers?	Yes			No			Yes		
58. Do employees with minor children have rights to a flexible/part time schedule?	Yes			No			Yes		

BUILDING CREDIT

59. What is the minimum loan amount covered in the private credit bureau or public credit registry (as a percentage of income per capita)?	0%			0%			0%		
60. Do microfinance institutions provide information to private credit bureaus or public credit registries?	Yes			Yes			N/A		
61. Do utility companies provide information to private credit bureaus or public credit registries?	No			No			No		
62. Do retailers provide information to private credit bureaus or public credit registries?	No			No			No		

PROVIDING INCENTIVES TO WORK

Childcare									
63. Are payments for childcare tax deductible?	No			No			Yes		
64. Is there public provision of childcare for children under the age of primary education?	Yes			No			Yes		
65. Does the law mandate free and compulsory primary education?	Yes			Yes			Yes		

Personal income tax	Women	Men		Women	Men		Women	Men	
66. Are there specific tax deductions or credits that are applicable only to men/women?	No	No		No	No		No	No	

Economy Tables

	KOSOVO	KUWAIT	KYRGYZ REPUBLIC
REGION	Europe & Central Asia	Middle East & North Africa	Europe & Central Asia
INCOME	Lower middle income	High income	Low income
FEMALE POPULATION	..	1,307,148	2,828,947
FEMALE LABOR FORCE PARTICIPATION	..	45%	59%

ACCESSING INSTITUTIONS

Constitutional rights

	KOSOVO	KUWAIT	KYRGYZ REPUBLIC
1. Is there a non-discrimination clause in the constitution?	Yes	No	Yes
2. If there is a non-discrimination clause in the constitution, does it explicitly mention gender?	Yes	N/A	Yes
3. Does the constitution guarantee equality before the law?	Yes	Yes	Yes

	Customary	Personal	Customary	Personal	Customary	Personal
4. Is customary/personal law recognized as valid source of law under the constitution?	No	No	No	Yes	No	No
5. If so, is it invalid if it violates constitutional provisions on non-discrimination or equality?	N/A	N/A	N/A	Yes	N/A	N/A

Quotas

	KOSOVO	KUWAIT	KYRGYZ REPUBLIC
6. What are the legal quotas for women on corporate boards?	N/A	N/A	N/A
7. What are the legal quotas for women in parliament?	N/A	N/A	N/A
8. What are the legal quotas for women in local government?	40%	N/A	N/A

Rights of married and unmarried women

	Unmarried	Married	Unmarried	Married	Unmarried	Married
9. Can a woman apply for a passport in the same way as a man?	Yes	Yes	Yes	No	Yes	Yes
10. Can a woman apply for a national ID card in the same way as a man?	Yes	Yes	Yes	Yes	Yes	Yes
11. Can a woman travel outside the country in the same way as a man?	Yes	Yes	Yes	Yes	Yes	Yes
12. Can a woman travel outside her home in the same way as a man?	Yes	Yes	Yes	No	Yes	Yes
13. Can a woman get a job or pursue a trade or profession in the same way as a man?	Yes	Yes	Yes	No	Yes	Yes
14. Can a woman sign a contract in the same way as a man?	Yes	Yes	Yes	Yes	Yes	Yes
15. Can a woman register a business in the same way as a man?	Yes	Yes	Yes	Yes	Yes	Yes
16. Can a woman open a bank account in the same way as a man?	Yes	Yes	Yes	Yes	Yes	Yes
17. Can a woman choose where to live in the same way as a man?	Yes	Yes	Yes	No	Yes	Yes
18. Can a woman confer citizenship on her children in the same way as a man?	Yes	Yes	No	No	Yes	Yes
19. Can a woman be "head of household" or "head of family" in the same way as a man?	N/A	N/A	N/A	N/A	N/A	N/A
Number of inequalities in accessing institutions	0	0	1	5	0	0

Division of responsibility within marriage

	KOSOVO	KUWAIT	KYRGYZ REPUBLIC
20. Can a woman convey citizenship to her non-national spouse in the same way as a man?	Yes	No	Yes
21. Are married women required by law to obey their husbands?	No	No	No
22. Do married couples jointly share legal responsibility for financially maintaining the family's expenses?	Yes	No	Yes

USING PROPERTY

Marital property regime

	KOSOVO	KUWAIT	KYRGYZ REPUBLIC
23. What is the default marital property regime?	Partial community of property	Separation of property	Partial community of property
24. Who legally administers property during marriage?	Both must agree	Original owner	Both must agree

Protecting a wife's interests

	KOSOVO	KUWAIT	KYRGYZ REPUBLIC
25. If it is the husband, does he need his wife's consent for major transactions	N/A	N/A	N/A
26. Are there special provisions governing the marital home?	No	No	No
27. Does the law provide for valuation of nonmonetary contributions during marriage?	Yes	No	Yes

Property rights

	Unmarried	Married	Unmarried	Married	Unmarried	Married
28. Do men and women have equal ownership rights to property?	Yes	Yes	Yes	Yes	Yes	Yes

Inheritance rights

	KOSOVO	KUWAIT	KYRGYZ REPUBLIC
29. Do sons and daughters have equal inheritance rights to property?	Yes	No	Yes
30. Do female and male surviving spouses have equal inheritance rights to property?	Yes	No	Yes

GOING TO COURT

Equality of access

	KOSOVO	KUWAIT	KYRGYZ REPUBLIC
31. Does the law recognize customary courts?	No	No	Yes
32. Does the law recognize personal law courts?	No	Yes	No
33. Does a woman's testimony carry the same evidentiary weight in court as a man's?	Yes	No	Yes

Efficiency of procedure

	KOSOVO	KUWAIT	KYRGYZ REPUBLIC
34. Is there a small claims court or a fast track procedure for small claims?	Yes	Yes	No
35. If so, what is the maximum amount for a small claim (as a percentage of income per capita)?	19%	38%	N/A

Judicial representation

	KOSOVO	KUWAIT	KYRGYZ REPUBLIC
36. How many justices are on the constitutional court?	9	5	9
37. Of those, how many are women?	2	0	5
38. Is the Chief Justice a woman?	No	No	No

	KOSOVO			KUWAIT			KYRGYZ REPUBLIC		

GETTING A JOB

Parental benefits	Maternity	Paternity	Parental	Maternity	Paternity	Parental	Maternity	Paternity	Parental
39. Does the law mandate paid or unpaid maternity/paternity/parental leave?	Yes	Yes	Yes	Yes	No	No	Yes	Yes	Yes
40. What is the mandatory minimum length of paid leave for maternity/paternity/parental leave (in calendar days)?	270	2	3	70	N/A	N/A	126	0	0
41. What is the mandatory minimum length of unpaid leave for maternity/paternity/parental leave (in calendar days)?	90	14	0	0	N/A	N/A	0	5	1039
42. Who pays maternity/paternity/parental benefits?	Emp. & Gov.	Emp.	Emp.	Emp.	N/A	N/A	Emp. & Gov.	N/A	N/A
43. What percentage of wages are paid during maternity/paternity/parental leave?	63%	100%	100%	100%	N/A	N/A	22%	0%	0%

	Mother	Father		Mother	Father		Mother	Father	
44. Where **paid** parental leave exists, what is the minimum amount which only the mother/father must take (in calendar days)?	0	0		N/A	N/A		N/A	N/A	
45. Where **unpaid** parental leave exists, what is the minimum amount which only the mother/father must take (in calendar days)?	N/A	N/A		N/A	N/A		0	0	

Retirement & pensions	Women	Men		Women	Men		Women	Men	
46. What is the age at which one can retire and receive full benefits?	65	65		N/A	N/A		58	63	
47. What is the age at which one can retire and receive partial benefits?	65	65		N/A	N/A		58	63	
48. What is the mandatory retirement age?	N/A	N/A		N/A	N/A		N/A	N/A	

Working hours and industry restrictions									
49. Can non-pregnant and non-nursing women do the same jobs as men?	Yes			No			No		
50. Can non-pregnant and non-nursing women engage in the following occupations in the same way as men?									
a. Mining	Yes			No			No		
b. Construction	Yes			No			No		
c. Metalwork	Yes			No			No		
d. Factory work	Yes			No			No		
e. Jobs requiring lifting weights above a threshold	Yes			Yes			No		
f. Jobs deemed hazardous	Yes			No			No		
g. Jobs deemed arduous	Yes			No			No		
h. Jobs deemed morally or socially inappropriate	Yes			No			Yes		
51. Can non-pregnant and non-nursing women work the same night hours as men?	Yes			No			Yes		

Workplace protections									
52. Does the law mandate equal remuneration for men and women for work of equal value?	Yes			No			Yes		
53. Are there laws mandating non-discrimination based on gender in hiring?	Yes			No			No		
54. Is it illegal for an employer to ask about family status during a job interview?	No			No			Yes		
55. Are there laws penalizing or preventing the dismissal of pregnant women?	Yes			No			Yes		
56. Must employers give employees an equivalent position when they return from maternity leave?	Yes			Yes			Yes		
57. Are employers required to provide break time for nursing mothers?	No			Yes			Yes		
58. Do employees with minor children have rights to a flexible/part time schedule?	No			No			Yes		

BUILDING CREDIT

59. What is the minimum loan amount covered in the private credit bureau or public credit registry (as a percentage of income per capita)?	0%			0%			0%		
60. Do microfinance institutions provide information to private credit bureaus or public credit registries?	Yes			N/A			Yes		
61. Do utility companies provide information to private credit bureaus or public credit registries?	No			No			No		
62. Do retailers provide information to private credit bureaus or public credit registries?	No			Yes			No		

PROVIDING INCENTIVES TO WORK

Childcare									
63. Are payments for childcare tax deductible?	No			No			No		
64. Is there public provision of childcare for children under the age of primary education?	Yes			Yes			Yes		
65. Does the law mandate free and compulsory primary education?	Yes			Yes			Yes		

Personal income tax	Women	Men		Women	Men		Women	Men	
66. Are there specific tax deductions or credits that are applicable only to men/women?	No	No		No	No		No	No	

Economy Tables

	LAO PDR		LATVIA		LEBANON	
REGION	East Asia & Pacific		Europe & Central Asia		Middle East & North Africa	
INCOME	Lower middle income		High income		Upper middle income	
FEMALE POPULATION	3,339,660		1,099,895		2,173,880	
FEMALE LABOR FORCE PARTICIPATION	80%		72%		25%	

ACCESSING INSTITUTIONS

Constitutional rights

	LAO PDR	LATVIA	LEBANON
1. Is there a non-discrimination clause in the constitution?	No	Yes	No
2. If there is a non-discrimination clause in the constitution, does it explicitly mention gender?	N/A	No	N/A
3. Does the constitution guarantee equality before the law?	Yes	Yes	Yes

	Customary	Personal	Customary	Personal	Customary	Personal
4. Is customary/personal law recognized as valid source of law under the constitution?	No	No	No	No	No	Yes
5. If so, is it invalid if it violates constitutional provisions on non-discrimination or equality?	N/A	N/A	N/A	N/A	N/A	No

Quotas

	LAO PDR	LATVIA	LEBANON
6. What are the legal quotas for women on corporate boards?	N/A	N/A	N/A
7. What are the legal quotas for women in parliament?	N/A	N/A	N/A
8. What are the legal quotas for women in local government?	N/A	N/A	N/A

Rights of married and unmarried women

	Unmarried	Married	Unmarried	Married	Unmarried	Married
9. Can a woman apply for a passport in the same way as a man?	Yes	Yes	Yes	Yes	Yes	Yes
10. Can a woman apply for a national ID card in the same way as a man?	Yes	Yes	N/A	N/A	Yes	Yes
11. Can a woman travel outside the country in the same way as a man?	Yes	Yes	Yes	Yes	Yes	Yes
12. Can a woman travel outside her home in the same way as a man?	Yes	Yes	Yes	Yes	Yes	Yes
13. Can a woman get a job or pursue a trade or profession in the same way as a man?	Yes	Yes	Yes	Yes	Yes	Yes
14. Can a woman sign a contract in the same way as a man?	Yes	Yes	Yes	Yes	Yes	Yes
15. Can a woman register a business in the same way as a man?	Yes	Yes	Yes	Yes	Yes	Yes
16. Can a woman open a bank account in the same way as a man?	Yes	Yes	Yes	Yes	Yes	Yes
17. Can a woman choose where to live in the same way as a man?	Yes	Yes	Yes	Yes	Yes	Yes
18. Can a woman confer citizenship on her children in the same way as a man?	Yes	Yes	Yes	Yes	No	No
19. Can a woman be "head of household" or "head of family" in the same way as a man?	Yes	Yes	N/A	N/A	N/A	N/A
Number of inequalities in accessing institutions	0	0	0	0	1	1

Division of responsibility within marriage

	LAO PDR	LATVIA	LEBANON
20. Can a woman convey citizenship to her non-national spouse in the same way as a man?	Yes	Yes	No
21. Are married women required by law to obey their husbands?	No	No	No
22. Do married couples jointly share legal responsibility for financially maintaining the family's expenses?	Yes	Yes	Yes

USING PROPERTY

Marital property regime

	LAO PDR	LATVIA	LEBANON
23. What is the default marital property regime?	Other	Other	Separation of property
24. Who legally administers property during marriage?	Both must agree	Both must agree	Original owner

Protecting a wife's interests

	LAO PDR	LATVIA	LEBANON
25. If it is the husband, does he need his wife's consent for major transactions	N/A	N/A	N/A
26. Are there special provisions governing the marital home?	No	No	No
27. Does the law provide for valuation of nonmonetary contributions during marriage?	Yes	Yes	No

Property rights

	Unmarried	Married	Unmarried	Married	Unmarried	Married
28. Do men and women have equal ownership rights to property?	Yes	Yes	Yes	Yes	Yes	Yes

Inheritance rights

	LAO PDR	LATVIA	LEBANON
29. Do sons and daughters have equal inheritance rights to property?	Yes	Yes	No
30. Do female and male surviving spouses have equal inheritance rights to property?	Yes	Yes	No

GOING TO COURT

Equality of access

	LAO PDR	LATVIA	LEBANON
31. Does the law recognize customary courts?	No	No	No
32. Does the law recognize personal law courts?	No	No	Yes
33. Does a woman's testimony carry the same evidentiary weight in court as a man's?	Yes	Yes	Yes

Efficiency of procedure

	LAO PDR	LATVIA	LEBANON
34. Is there a small claims court or a fast track procedure for small claims?	No	Yes	Yes
35. If so, what is the maximum amount for a small claim (as a percentage of income per capita)?	N/A	23%	7%

Judicial representation

	LAO PDR	LATVIA	LEBANON
36. How many justices are on the constitutional court?	N/A	7	10
37. Of those, how many are women?	N/A	4	0
38. Is the Chief Justice a woman?	N/A	No	No

GETTING A JOB

Parental benefits

	Maternity	Paternity	Parental	Maternity	Paternity	Parental	Maternity	Paternity	Parental
39. Does the law mandate paid or unpaid maternity/paternity/parental leave?	Yes	No	No	Yes	Yes	Yes	Yes	No	No
40. What is the mandatory minimum length of paid leave for maternity/paternity/parental leave (in calendar days)?	90	N/A	N/A	112	10	547.5	49	N/A	N/A
41. What is the mandatory minimum length of unpaid leave for maternity/paternity/parental leave (in calendar days)?	0	N/A	N/A	0	0	0	0	N/A	N/A
42. Who pays maternity/paternity/parental benefits?	Gov.	N/A	N/A	Gov.	Gov.	Gov.	Emp.	N/A	N/A
43. What percentage of wages are paid during maternity/paternity/parental leave?	100%	N/A	N/A	68%	68%	Partially paid	100%	N/A	N/A

	Mother	Father		Mother	Father		Mother	Father	
44. Where **paid** parental leave exists, what is the minimum amount which only the mother/father must take (in calendar days)?	N/A	N/A		0	0		N/A	N/A	
45. Where **unpaid** parental leave exists, what is the minimum amount which only the mother/father must take (in calendar days)?	N/A	N/A		N/A	N/A		N/A	N/A	

Retirement & pensions

	Women	Men		Women	Men		Women	Men	
46. What is the age at which one can retire and receive full benefits?	55	60		65	65		64	64	
47. What is the age at which one can retire and receive partial benefits?	55	60		65	65		60	60	
48. What is the mandatory retirement age?	N/A	N/A		N/A	N/A		64	64	

Working hours and industry restrictions

	LAO PDR	LATVIA	LEBANON
49. Can non-pregnant and non-nursing women do the same jobs as men?	Yes	Yes	No
50. Can non-pregnant and non-nursing women engage in the following occupations in the same way as men?			
a. Mining	Yes	Yes	No
b. Construction	Yes	Yes	Yes
c. Metalwork	Yes	Yes	No
d. Factory work	Yes	Yes	Yes
e. Jobs requiring lifting weights above a threshold	Yes	Yes	Yes
f. Jobs deemed hazardous	Yes	Yes	Yes
g. Jobs deemed arduous	Yes	Yes	Yes
h. Jobs deemed morally or socially inappropriate	Yes	Yes	Yes
51. Can non-pregnant and non-nursing women work the same night hours as men?	Yes	Yes	Yes

Workplace protections

	LAO PDR	LATVIA	LEBANON
52. Does the law mandate equal remuneration for men and women for work of equal value?	Yes	Yes	No
53. Are there laws mandating non-discrimination based on gender in hiring?	No	No	No
54. Is it illegal for an employer to ask about family status during a job interview?	No	Yes	No
55. Are there laws penalizing or preventing the dismissal of pregnant women?	Yes	Yes	Yes
56. Must employers give employees an equivalent position when they return from maternity leave?	No	Yes	No
57. Are employers required to provide break time for nursing mothers?	Yes	Yes	No
58. Do employees with minor children have rights to a flexible/part time schedule?	No	Yes	No

BUILDING CREDIT

	LAO PDR	LATVIA	LEBANON
59. What is the minimum loan amount covered in the private credit bureau or public credit registry (as a percentage of income per capita)?	507%	0%	49%
60. Do microfinance institutions provide information to private credit bureaus or public credit registries?	Yes	No	Yes
61. Do utility companies provide information to private credit bureaus or public credit registries?	No	No	No
62. Do retailers provide information to private credit bureaus or public credit registries?	No	No	No

PROVIDING INCENTIVES TO WORK

Childcare

	LAO PDR	LATVIA	LEBANON
63. Are payments for childcare tax deductible?	No	No	No
64. Is there public provision of childcare for children under the age of primary education?	No	Yes	No
65. Does the law mandate free and compulsory primary education?	Yes	Yes	Yes

Personal income tax

	Women	Men		Women	Men		Women	Men	
66. Are there specific tax deductions or credits that are applicable only to men/women?	No	No		No	No		No	Yes	

Lao PDR–Lebanon

Economy Tables

	LESOTHO		LIBERIA		LITHUANIA	
REGION	Sub-Saharan Africa		Sub-Saharan Africa		Europe & Central Asia	
INCOME	Lower middle income		Low income		High income	
FEMALE POPULATION	1,040,775		2,081,150		1,610,338	
FEMALE LABOR FORCE PARTICIPATION	60%		59%		69%	

ACCESSING INSTITUTIONS

Constitutional rights

	LESOTHO		LIBERIA		LITHUANIA	
1. Is there a non-discrimination clause in the constitution?	Yes		No		No	
2. If there is a non-discrimination clause in the constitution, does it explicitly mention gender?	Yes		N/A		N/A	
3. Does the constitution guarantee equality before the law?	Yes		Yes		Yes	

	Customary	Personal	Customary	Personal	Customary	Personal
4. Is customary/personal law recognized as valid source of law under the constitution?	Yes	No	Yes	No	No	No
5. If so, is it invalid if it violates constitutional provisions on non-discrimination or equality?	No	N/A	Yes	N/A	N/A	N/A

Quotas

	LESOTHO	LIBERIA	LITHUANIA
6. What are the legal quotas for women on corporate boards?	N/A	N/A	N/A
7. What are the legal quotas for women in parliament?	N/A	N/A	N/A
8. What are the legal quotas for women in local government?	33%	N/A	N/A

Rights of married and unmarried women

	Unmarried	Married	Unmarried	Married	Unmarried	Married
9. Can a woman apply for a passport in the same way as a man?	Yes	Yes	Yes	Yes	Yes	Yes
10. Can a woman apply for a national ID card in the same way as a man?	N/A	N/A	Yes	Yes	Yes	Yes
11. Can a woman travel outside the country in the same way as a man?	Yes	Yes	Yes	Yes	Yes	Yes
12. Can a woman travel outside her home in the same way as a man?	Yes	Yes	Yes	Yes	Yes	Yes
13. Can a woman get a job or pursue a trade or profession in the same way as a man?	Yes	Yes	Yes	Yes	Yes	Yes
14. Can a woman sign a contract in the same way as a man?	Yes	Yes	Yes	Yes	Yes	Yes
15. Can a woman register a business in the same way as a man?	Yes	Yes	Yes	Yes	Yes	Yes
16. Can a woman open a bank account in the same way as a man?	Yes	Yes	Yes	Yes	Yes	Yes
17. Can a woman choose where to live in the same way as a man?	Yes	Yes	Yes	Yes	Yes	Yes
18. Can a woman confer citizenship on her children in the same way as a man?	Yes	Yes	Yes	Yes	Yes	Yes
19. Can a woman be "head of household" or "head of family" in the same way as a man?	N/A	N/A	N/A	N/A	N/A	N/A
Number of inequalities in accessing institutions	0	0	0	0	0	0

Division of responsibility within marriage

	LESOTHO	LIBERIA	LITHUANIA
20. Can a woman convey citizenship to her non-national spouse in the same way as a man?	No	Yes	Yes
21. Are married women required by law to obey their husbands?	No	No	No
22. Do married couples jointly share legal responsibility for financially maintaining the family's expenses?	Yes	Yes	Yes

USING PROPERTY

Marital property regime

	LESOTHO	LIBERIA	LITHUANIA
23. What is the default marital property regime?	Partial community of property	Separation of property	Partial community of property
24. Who legally administers property during marriage?	Both must agree	Original owner	Both must agree

Protecting a wife's interests

	LESOTHO	LIBERIA	LITHUANIA
25. If it is the husband, does he need his wife's consent for major transactions	N/A	N/A	N/A
26. Are there special provisions governing the marital home?	No	No	Yes
27. Does the law provide for valuation of nonmonetary contributions during marriage?	Yes	No	Yes

Property rights

	Unmarried	Married	Unmarried	Married	Unmarried	Married
28. Do men and women have equal ownership rights to property?	Yes	Yes	Yes	Yes	Yes	Yes

Inheritance rights

	LESOTHO	LIBERIA	LITHUANIA
29. Do sons and daughters have equal inheritance rights to property?	No	Yes	Yes
30. Do female and male surviving spouses have equal inheritance rights to property?	Yes	Yes	Yes

GOING TO COURT

Equality of access

	LESOTHO	LIBERIA	LITHUANIA
31. Does the law recognize customary courts?	Yes	Yes	No
32. Does the law recognize personal law courts?	No	No	No
33. Does a woman's testimony carry the same evidentiary weight in court as a man's?	Yes	Yes	Yes

Efficiency of procedure

	LESOTHO	LIBERIA	LITHUANIA
34. Is there a small claims court or a fast track procedure for small claims?	Yes	No	Yes
35. If so, what is the maximum amount for a small claim (as a percentage of income per capita)?	103%	N/A	3%

Judicial representation

	LESOTHO	LIBERIA	LITHUANIA
36. How many justices are on the constitutional court?	N/A	5	9
37. Of those, how many are women?	N/A	2	2
38. Is the Chief Justice a woman?	N/A	No	No

GETTING A JOB

Parental benefits

	Maternity	Paternity	Parental	Maternity	Paternity	Parental	Maternity	Paternity	Parental
39. Does the law mandate paid or unpaid maternity/paternity/parental leave?	Yes	No	No	Yes	No	No	Yes	Yes	Yes
40. What is the mandatory minimum length of paid leave for maternity/paternity/parental leave (in calendar days)?	84	N/A	N/A	90	N/A	N/A	126	30	239
41. What is the mandatory minimum length of unpaid leave for maternity/paternity/parental leave (in calendar days)?	0	N/A	N/A	0	N/A	N/A	0	0	730
42. Who pays maternity/paternity/parental benefits?	Emp.	N/A	N/A	Emp.	N/A	N/A	Gov.	Gov.	Gov.
43. What percentage of wages are paid during maternity/paternity/parental leave?	100%	N/A	N/A	100%	N/A	N/A	100%	100%	100%

	Mother	Father		Mother	Father		Mother	Father	
44. Where **paid** parental leave exists, what is the minimum amount which only the mother/father must take (in calendar days)?	N/A	N/A		N/A	N/A		0	0	
45. Where **unpaid** parental leave exists, what is the minimum amount which only the mother/father must take (in calendar days)?	N/A	N/A		N/A	N/A		0	0	

Retirement & pensions

	Women	Men		Women	Men		Women	Men	
46. What is the age at which one can retire and receive full benefits?	70	70		60	60		65	65	
47. What is the age at which one can retire and receive partial benefits?	70	70		60	60		65	65	
48. What is the mandatory retirement age?	N/A	N/A		N/A	N/A		N/A	N/A	

Working hours and industry restrictions

	LESOTHO	LIBERIA	LITHUANIA
49. Can non-pregnant and non-nursing women do the same jobs as men?	No	Yes	Yes
50. Can non-pregnant and non-nursing women engage in the following occupations in the same way as men?			
a. Mining	No	Yes	Yes
b. Construction	Yes	Yes	Yes
c. Metalwork	Yes	Yes	Yes
d. Factory work	Yes	Yes	Yes
e. Jobs requiring lifting weights above a threshold	Yes	Yes	Yes
f. Jobs deemed hazardous	Yes	Yes	Yes
g. Jobs deemed arduous	Yes	Yes	Yes
h. Jobs deemed morally or socially inappropriate	Yes	Yes	Yes
51. Can non-pregnant and non-nursing women work the same night hours as men?	Yes	Yes	Yes

Workplace protections

	LESOTHO	LIBERIA	LITHUANIA
52. Does the law mandate equal remuneration for men and women for work of equal value?	Yes	No	No
53. Are there laws mandating non-discrimination based on gender in hiring?	No	No	No
54. Is it illegal for an employer to ask about family status during a job interview?	No	No	No
55. Are there laws penalizing or preventing the dismissal of pregnant women?	Yes	Yes	Yes
56. Must employers give employees an equivalent position when they return from maternity leave?	No	No	Yes
57. Are employers required to provide break time for nursing mothers?	Yes	No	Yes
58. Do employees with minor children have rights to a flexible/part time schedule?	No	No	Yes

BUILDING CREDIT

	LESOTHO	LIBERIA	LITHUANIA
59. What is the minimum loan amount covered in the private credit bureau or public credit registry (as a percentage of income per capita)?	N/A	0%	0%
60. Do microfinance institutions provide information to private credit bureaus or public credit registries?	N/A	No	Yes
61. Do utility companies provide information to private credit bureaus or public credit registries?	N/A	No	Yes
62. Do retailers provide information to private credit bureaus or public credit registries?	N/A	No	Yes

PROVIDING INCENTIVES TO WORK

Childcare

	LESOTHO	LIBERIA	LITHUANIA
63. Are payments for childcare tax deductible?	No	No	No
64. Is there public provision of childcare for children under the age of primary education?	No	Yes	Yes
65. Does the law mandate free and compulsory primary education?	Yes	Yes	Yes

Personal income tax

	Women	Men		Women	Men		Women	Men	
66. Are there specific tax deductions or credits that are applicable only to men/women?	No	No		No	No		No	No	

Economy Tables

	MACEDONIA, FYR	MADAGASCAR	MALAWI
REGION	Europe & Central Asia	Sub-Saharan Africa	Sub-Saharan Africa
INCOME	Upper middle income	Low income	Low income
FEMALE POPULATION	1,050,542	11,185,606	7,938,551
FEMALE LABOR FORCE PARTICIPATION	51%	85%	85%

ACCESSING INSTITUTIONS

Constitutional rights

	MACEDONIA, FYR	MADAGASCAR	MALAWI
1. Is there a non-discrimination clause in the constitution?	Yes	Yes	Yes
2. If there is a non-discrimination clause in the constitution, does it explicitly mention gender?	Yes	Yes	Yes
3. Does the constitution guarantee equality before the law?	Yes	Yes	Yes

	Customary	Personal	Customary	Personal	Customary	Personal
4. Is customary/personal law recognized as valid source of law under the constitution?	No	No	No	No	Yes	No
5. If so, is it invalid if it violates constitutional provisions on non-discrimination or equality?	N/A	N/A	N/A	N/A	Yes	N/A

Quotas

	MACEDONIA, FYR	MADAGASCAR	MALAWI
6. What are the legal quotas for women on corporate boards?	N/A	N/A	N/A
7. What are the legal quotas for women in parliament?	N/A	N/A	N/A
8. What are the legal quotas for women in local government?	N/A	N/A	N/A

Rights of married and unmarried women

	Unmarried	Married	Unmarried	Married	Unmarried	Married
9. Can a woman apply for a passport in the same way as a man?	Yes	Yes	Yes	Yes	Yes	No
10. Can a woman apply for a national ID card in the same way as a man?	Yes	Yes	Yes	Yes	N/A	N/A
11. Can a woman travel outside the country in the same way as a man?	Yes	Yes	Yes	Yes	Yes	Yes
12. Can a woman travel outside her home in the same way as a man?	Yes	Yes	Yes	Yes	Yes	Yes
13. Can a woman get a job or pursue a trade or profession in the same way as a man?	Yes	Yes	Yes	Yes	Yes	Yes
14. Can a woman sign a contract in the same way as a man?	Yes	Yes	Yes	Yes	Yes	Yes
15. Can a woman register a business in the same way as a man?	Yes	Yes	Yes	Yes	Yes	Yes
16. Can a woman open a bank account in the same way as a man?	Yes	Yes	Yes	Yes	Yes	Yes
17. Can a woman choose where to live in the same way as a man?	Yes	Yes	Yes	Yes	Yes	Yes
18. Can a woman confer citizenship on her children in the same way as a man?	Yes	Yes	Yes	No	Yes	Yes
19. Can a woman be "head of household" or "head of family" in the same way as a man?	N/A	N/A	Yes	No	N/A	N/A
Number of inequalities in accessing institutions	0	0	0	2	0	1

Division of responsibility within marriage

	MACEDONIA, FYR	MADAGASCAR	MALAWI
20. Can a woman convey citizenship to her non-national spouse in the same way as a man?	Yes	No	No
21. Are married women required by law to obey their husbands?	No	No	No
22. Do married couples jointly share legal responsibility for financially maintaining the family's expenses?	Yes	Yes	Yes

USING PROPERTY

Marital property regime

	MACEDONIA, FYR	MADAGASCAR	MALAWI
23. What is the default marital property regime?	Partial community of property	Partial community of property	Separation of property
24. Who legally administers property during marriage?	Both must agree	Both must agree	Original owner

Protecting a wife's interests

	MACEDONIA, FYR	MADAGASCAR	MALAWI
25. If it is the husband, does he need his wife's consent for major transactions	N/A	N/A	N/A
26. Are there special provisions governing the marital home?	No	No	No
27. Does the law provide for valuation of nonmonetary contributions during marriage?	Yes	Yes	No

Property rights

	Unmarried	Married	Unmarried	Married	Unmarried	Married
28. Do men and women have equal ownership rights to property?	Yes	Yes	Yes	Yes	Yes	Yes

Inheritance rights

	MACEDONIA, FYR	MADAGASCAR	MALAWI
29. Do sons and daughters have equal inheritance rights to property?	Yes	Yes	Yes
30. Do female and male surviving spouses have equal inheritance rights to property?	Yes	Yes	Yes

GOING TO COURT

Equality of access

	MACEDONIA, FYR	MADAGASCAR	MALAWI
31. Does the law recognize customary courts?	No	No	No
32. Does the law recognize personal law courts?	No	No	No
33. Does a woman's testimony carry the same evidentiary weight in court as a man's?	Yes	Yes	Yes

Efficiency of procedure

	MACEDONIA, FYR	MADAGASCAR	MALAWI
34. Is there a small claims court or a fast track procedure for small claims?	Yes	No	Yes
35. If so, what is the maximum amount for a small claim (as a percentage of income per capita)?	84%	N/A	9%

Judicial representation

	MACEDONIA, FYR	MADAGASCAR	MALAWI
36. How many justices are on the constitutional court?	9	9	N/A
37. Of those, how many are women?	3	3	N/A
38. Is the Chief Justice a woman?	No	No	N/A

GETTING A JOB

Parental benefits	MACEDONIA, FYR			MADAGASCAR			MALAWI		
	Maternity	Paternity	Parental	Maternity	Paternity	Parental	Maternity	Paternity	Parental
39. Does the law mandate paid or unpaid maternity/paternity/parental leave?	Yes	No	No	Yes	No	No	Yes	No	No
40. What is the mandatory minimum length of paid leave for maternity/paternity/parental leave (in calendar days)?	270	N/A	N/A	98	N/A	N/A	56	N/A	N/A
41. What is the mandatory minimum length of unpaid leave for maternity/paternity/parental leave (in calendar days)?	0	N/A	N/A	0	N/A	N/A	0	N/A	N/A
42. Who pays maternity/paternity/parental benefits?	Gov.	N/A	N/A	Emp. & Gov.	N/A	N/A	Emp.	N/A	N/A
43. What percentage of wages are paid during maternity/paternity/parental leave?	100%	N/A	N/A	100%	N/A	N/A	100%	N/A	N/A

	Mother	Father		Mother	Father		Mother	Father	
44. Where **paid** parental leave exists, what is the minimum amount which only the mother/father must take (in calendar days)?	N/A	N/A		N/A	N/A		N/A	N/A	
45. Where **unpaid** parental leave exists, what is the minimum amount which only the mother/father must take (in calendar days)?	N/A	N/A		N/A	N/A		N/A	N/A	

Retirement & pensions	Women	Men		Women	Men		Women	Men	
46. What is the age at which one can retire and receive full benefits?	62	64		55	60		50	50	
47. What is the age at which one can retire and receive partial benefits?	62	64		55	60		50	50	
48. What is the mandatory retirement age?	64	64		N/A	N/A		70	70	

Working hours and industry restrictions	MACEDONIA, FYR	MADAGASCAR	MALAWI
49. Can non-pregnant and non-nursing women do the same jobs as men?	No	No	Yes
50. Can non-pregnant and non-nursing women engage in the following occupations in the same way as men?			
a. Mining	No	No	Yes
b. Construction	No	No	Yes
c. Metalwork	No	No	Yes
d. Factory work	No	No	Yes
e. Jobs requiring lifting weights above a threshold	Yes	No	Yes
f. Jobs deemed hazardous	Yes	No	Yes
g. Jobs deemed arduous	Yes	Yes	Yes
h. Jobs deemed morally or socially inappropriate	Yes	Yes	Yes
51. Can non-pregnant and non-nursing women work the same night hours as men?	No	No	Yes

Workplace protections	MACEDONIA, FYR	MADAGASCAR	MALAWI
52. Does the law mandate equal remuneration for men and women for work of equal value?	No	Yes	Yes
53. Are there laws mandating non-discrimination based on gender in hiring?	Yes	No	Yes
54. Is it illegal for an employer to ask about family status during a job interview?	No	No	No
55. Are there laws penalizing or preventing the dismissal of pregnant women?	Yes	Yes	Yes
56. Must employers give employees an equivalent position when they return from maternity leave?	No	No	Yes
57. Are employers required to provide break time for nursing mothers?	Yes	Yes	No
58. Do employees with minor children have rights to a flexible/part time schedule?	No	No	No

BUILDING CREDIT

	MACEDONIA, FYR	MADAGASCAR	MALAWI
59. What is the minimum loan amount covered in the private credit bureau or public credit registry (as a percentage of income per capita)?	0%	0%	N/A
60. Do microfinance institutions provide information to private credit bureaus or public credit registries?	Yes	Yes	N/A
61. Do utility companies provide information to private credit bureaus or public credit registries?	Yes	No	N/A
62. Do retailers provide information to private credit bureaus or public credit registries?	No	No	N/A

PROVIDING INCENTIVES TO WORK

Childcare	MACEDONIA, FYR	MADAGASCAR	MALAWI
63. Are payments for childcare tax deductible?	No	No	No
64. Is there public provision of childcare for children under the age of primary education?	Yes	Yes	No
65. Does the law mandate free and compulsory primary education?	Yes	Yes	No

Personal income tax	Women	Men		Women	Men		Women	Men	
66. Are there specific tax deductions or credits that are applicable only to men/women?	No	No		No	No		No	No	

Economy Tables

	MALAYSIA		MALI		MAURITANIA	
REGION	East Asia & Pacific		Sub-Saharan Africa		Sub-Saharan Africa	
INCOME	Upper middle income		Low income		Lower middle income	
FEMALE POPULATION	15,055,845		7,369,773		1,884,706	
FEMALE LABOR FORCE PARTICIPATION	46%		38%		29%	

ACCESSING INSTITUTIONS

Constitutional rights

	MALAYSIA		MALI		MAURITANIA	
1. Is there a non-discrimination clause in the constitution?	Yes		Yes		No	
2. If there is a non-discrimination clause in the constitution, does it explicitly mention gender?	Yes		Yes		N/A	
3. Does the constitution guarantee equality before the law?	Yes		Yes		Yes	

	Customary	Personal	Customary	Personal	Customary	Personal
4. Is customary/personal law recognized as valid source of law under the constitution?	Yes	Yes	No	No	No	Yes
5. If so, is it invalid if it violates constitutional provisions on non-discrimination or equality?	No	No	N/A	N/A	N/A	No

Quotas

	MALAYSIA	MALI	MAURITANIA
6. What are the legal quotas for women on corporate boards?	N/A	N/A	N/A
7. What are the legal quotas for women in parliament?	N/A	N/A	N/A
8. What are the legal quotas for women in local government?	N/A	N/A	N/A

Rights of married and unmarried women	Unmarried	Married	Unmarried	Married	Unmarried	Married
9. Can a woman apply for a passport in the same way as a man?	Yes	Yes	Yes	Yes	Yes	Yes
10. Can a woman apply for a national ID card in the same way as a man?	Yes	Yes	..	..	Yes	Yes
11. Can a woman travel outside the country in the same way as a man?	Yes	Yes	Yes	Yes	Yes	Yes
12. Can a woman travel outside her home in the same way as a man?	Yes	No	Yes	Yes	Yes	Yes
13. Can a woman get a job or pursue a trade or profession in the same way as a man?	Yes	Yes	Yes	Yes	Yes	No
14. Can a woman sign a contract in the same way as a man?	Yes	Yes	Yes	Yes	Yes	Yes
15. Can a woman register a business in the same way as a man?	Yes	Yes	Yes	Yes	Yes	Yes
16. Can a woman open a bank account in the same way as a man?	Yes	Yes	Yes	Yes	Yes	Yes
17. Can a woman choose where to live in the same way as a man?	Yes	No	Yes	No	Yes	Yes
18. Can a woman confer citizenship on her children in the same way as a man?	No	No	Yes	No	No	No
19. Can a woman be "head of household" or "head of family" in the same way as a man?	N/A	N/A	Yes	No	Yes	No
Number of inequalities in accessing institutions	1	3	0	3	1	3

Division of responsibility within marriage

	MALAYSIA	MALI	MAURITANIA
20. Can a woman convey citizenship to her non-national spouse in the same way as a man?	No	No	No
21. Are married women required by law to obey their husbands?	Yes	Yes	No
22. Do married couples jointly share legal responsibility for financially maintaining the family's expenses?	No	No	No

USING PROPERTY

Marital property regime

	MALAYSIA	MALI	MAURITANIA
23. What is the default marital property regime?	Separation of property	Separation of property	Separation of property
24. Who legally administers property during marriage?	Original owner	Original owner	Other

Protecting a wife's interests

	MALAYSIA	MALI	MAURITANIA
25. If it is the husband, does he need his wife's consent for major transactions	N/A	N/A	N/A
26. Are there special provisions governing the marital home?	No	No	No
27. Does the law provide for valuation of nonmonetary contributions during marriage?	Yes	No	No

Property rights	Unmarried	Married	Unmarried	Married	Unmarried	Married
28. Do men and women have equal ownership rights to property?	Yes	Yes	Yes	Yes	Yes	No

Inheritance rights

	MALAYSIA	MALI	MAURITANIA
29. Do sons and daughters have equal inheritance rights to property?	No	No	No
30. Do female and male surviving spouses have equal inheritance rights to property?	No	Yes	No

GOING TO COURT

Equality of access

	MALAYSIA	MALI	MAURITANIA
31. Does the law recognize customary courts?	Yes	No	No
32. Does the law recognize personal law courts?	Yes	No	Yes
33. Does a woman's testimony carry the same evidentiary weight in court as a man's?	No	Yes	No

Efficiency of procedure

	MALAYSIA	MALI	MAURITANIA
34. Is there a small claims court or a fast track procedure for small claims?	Yes	No	No
35. If so, what is the maximum amount for a small claim (as a percentage of income per capita)?	17%	N/A	N/A

Judicial representation

	MALAYSIA	MALI	MAURITANIA
36. How many justices are on the constitutional court?	9	9	6
37. Of those, how many are women?	2	3	0
38. Is the Chief Justice a woman?	No	No	No

GETTING A JOB

Parental benefits	MALAYSIA			MALI			MAURITANIA		
	Maternity	Paternity	Parental	Maternity	Paternity	Parental	Maternity	Paternity	Parental
39. Does the law mandate paid or unpaid maternity/paternity/parental leave?	Yes	No	No	Yes	Yes	No	Yes	No	No
40. What is the mandatory minimum length of paid leave for maternity/paternity/parental leave (in calendar days)?	60	N/A	N/A	98	3	N/A	98	N/A	N/A
41. What is the mandatory minimum length of unpaid leave for maternity/paternity/parental leave (in calendar days)?	0	N/A	N/A	0	0	N/A	0	N/A	N/A
42. Who pays maternity/paternity/parental benefits?	Emp.	N/A	N/A	Gov.	Gov.	N/A	Gov.	N/A	N/A
43. What percentage of wages are paid during maternity/paternity/parental leave?	100%	N/A	N/A	100%	100%	N/A	100%	N/A	N/A

	Mother	Father		Mother	Father		Mother	Father	
44. Where **paid** parental leave exists, what is the minimum amount which only the mother/father must take (in calendar days)?	N/A	N/A		N/A	N/A		N/A	N/A	
45. Where **unpaid** parental leave exists, what is the minimum amount which only the mother/father must take (in calendar days)?	N/A	N/A		N/A	N/A		N/A	N/A	

Retirement & pensions	Women	Men		Women	Men		Women	Men	
46. What is the age at which one can retire and receive full benefits?	60	60		58	58		55	60	
47. What is the age at which one can retire and receive partial benefits?	55	55		53	53		55	60	
48. What is the mandatory retirement age?	N/A	N/A		N/A	N/A		55	60	

Working hours and industry restrictions	MALAYSIA	MALI	MAURITANIA
49. Can non-pregnant and non-nursing women do the same jobs as men?	No	No	No
50. Can non-pregnant and non-nursing women engage in the following occupations in the same way as men?			
a. Mining	No	No	No
b. Construction	Yes	No	No
c. Metalwork	Yes	No	Yes
d. Factory work	Yes	No	No
e. Jobs requiring lifting weights above a threshold	Yes	No	Yes
f. Jobs deemed hazardous	Yes	No	No
g. Jobs deemed arduous	Yes	No	No
h. Jobs deemed morally or socially inappropriate	Yes	No	No
51. Can non-pregnant and non-nursing women work the same night hours as men?	No	No	No

Workplace protections	MALAYSIA	MALI	MAURITANIA
52. Does the law mandate equal remuneration for men and women for work of equal value?	No	No	No
53. Are there laws mandating non-discrimination based on gender in hiring?	No	No	Yes
54. Is it illegal for an employer to ask about family status during a job interview?	No	No	No
55. Are there laws penalizing or preventing the dismissal of pregnant women?	Yes	Yes	Yes
56. Must employers give employees an equivalent position when they return from maternity leave?	No	Yes	Yes
57. Are employers required to provide break time for nursing mothers?	No	Yes	Yes
58. Do employees with minor children have rights to a flexible/part time schedule?	No	No	No

BUILDING CREDIT

	MALAYSIA	MALI	MAURITANIA
59. What is the minimum loan amount covered in the private credit bureau or public credit registry (as a percentage of income per capita)?	0%	1660%	164%
60. Do microfinance institutions provide information to private credit bureaus or public credit registries?	Yes	No	No
61. Do utility companies provide information to private credit bureaus or public credit registries?	Yes	No	No
62. Do retailers provide information to private credit bureaus or public credit registries?	Yes	No	No

PROVIDING INCENTIVES TO WORK

Childcare	MALAYSIA	MALI	MAURITANIA
63. Are payments for childcare tax deductible?	Yes	No	No
64. Is there public provision of childcare for children under the age of primary education?	Yes	Yes	No
65. Does the law mandate free and compulsory primary education?	Yes	Yes	Yes

Personal income tax	Women	Men		Women	Men		Women	Men	
66. Are there specific tax deductions or credits that are applicable only to men/women?	No	Yes		No	Yes		No	Yes	

Economy Tables

	MAURITIUS	MEXICO	MOLDOVA
REGION	Sub-Saharan Africa	Latin America & Caribbean	Europe & Central Asia
INCOME	Upper middle income	Upper middle income	Lower middle income
FEMALE POPULATION	653,620	62,313,207	1,872,099
FEMALE LABOR FORCE PARTICIPATION	49%	47%	45%

ACCESSING INSTITUTIONS

Constitutional rights

	MAURITIUS	MEXICO	MOLDOVA
1. Is there a non-discrimination clause in the constitution?	Yes	Yes	Yes
2. If there is a non-discrimination clause in the constitution, does it explicitly mention gender?	Yes	Yes	Yes
3. Does the constitution guarantee equality before the law?	Yes	Yes	Yes

	Customary	Personal	Customary	Personal	Customary	Personal
4. Is customary/personal law recognized as valid source of law under the constitution?	Yes	Yes	Yes	No	No	No
5. If so, is it invalid if it violates constitutional provisions on non-discrimination or equality?	No	No	Yes	N/A	N/A	N/A

Quotas

	MAURITIUS	MEXICO	MOLDOVA
6. What are the legal quotas for women on corporate boards?	N/A	N/A	N/A
7. What are the legal quotas for women in parliament?	N/A	N/A	N/A
8. What are the legal quotas for women in local government?	N/A	N/A	N/A

Rights of married and unmarried women

	Unmarried	Married	Unmarried	Married	Unmarried	Married
9. Can a woman apply for a passport in the same way as a man?	Yes	Yes	Yes	Yes	Yes	Yes
10. Can a woman apply for a national ID card in the same way as a man?	Yes	No	N/A	N/A	Yes	Yes
11. Can a woman travel outside the country in the same way as a man?	Yes	Yes	Yes	Yes	Yes	Yes
12. Can a woman travel outside her home in the same way as a man?	Yes	Yes	Yes	Yes	Yes	Yes
13. Can a woman get a job or pursue a trade or profession in the same way as a man?	Yes	Yes	Yes	Yes	Yes	Yes
14. Can a woman sign a contract in the same way as a man?	Yes	Yes	Yes	Yes	Yes	Yes
15. Can a woman register a business in the same way as a man?	Yes	Yes	Yes	Yes	Yes	Yes
16. Can a woman open a bank account in the same way as a man?	Yes	Yes	Yes	Yes	Yes	Yes
17. Can a woman choose where to live in the same way as a man?	Yes	Yes	Yes	Yes	Yes	Yes
18. Can a woman confer citizenship on her children in the same way as a man?	Yes	Yes	Yes	Yes	Yes	Yes
19. Can a woman be "head of household" or "head of family" in the same way as a man?	N/A	N/A	N/A	N/A	N/A	N/A
Number of inequalities in accessing institutions	0	1	0	0	0	0

Division of responsibility within marriage

	MAURITIUS	MEXICO	MOLDOVA
20. Can a woman convey citizenship to her non-national spouse in the same way as a man?	Yes	Yes	Yes
21. Are married women required by law to obey their husbands?	No	No	No
22. Do married couples jointly share legal responsibility for financially maintaining the family's expenses?	Yes	Yes	Yes

USING PROPERTY

Marital property regime

	MAURITIUS	MEXICO	MOLDOVA
23. What is the default marital property regime?	Partial community of property	Other	Partial community of property
24. Who legally administers property during marriage?	Both must agree	Other	Both must agree

Protecting a wife's interests

	MAURITIUS	MEXICO	MOLDOVA
25. If it is the husband, does he need his wife's consent for major transactions	N/A	N/A	N/A
26. Are there special provisions governing the marital home?	Yes	No	No
27. Does the law provide for valuation of nonmonetary contributions during marriage?	Yes	Yes	Yes

Property rights

	Unmarried	Married	Unmarried	Married	Unmarried	Married
28. Do men and women have equal ownership rights to property?	Yes	Yes	Yes	Yes	Yes	Yes

Inheritance rights

	MAURITIUS	MEXICO	MOLDOVA
29. Do sons and daughters have equal inheritance rights to property?	Yes	Yes	Yes
30. Do female and male surviving spouses have equal inheritance rights to property?	Yes	Yes	Yes

GOING TO COURT

Equality of access

	MAURITIUS	MEXICO	MOLDOVA
31. Does the law recognize customary courts?	No	No	No
32. Does the law recognize personal law courts?	No	No	No
33. Does a woman's testimony carry the same evidentiary weight in court as a man's?	Yes	Yes	Yes

Efficiency of procedure

	MAURITIUS	MEXICO	MOLDOVA
34. Is there a small claims court or a fast track procedure for small claims?	Yes	Yes	No
35. If so, what is the maximum amount for a small claim (as a percentage of income per capita)?	10%	422%	N/A

Judicial representation

	MAURITIUS	MEXICO	MOLDOVA
36. How many justices are on the constitutional court?	20	11	6
37. Of those, how many are women?	7	2	0
38. Is the Chief Justice a woman?	No	No	No

GETTING A JOB

Parental benefits	Maternity	Paternity	Parental	Maternity	Paternity	Parental	Maternity	Paternity	Parental
39. Does the law mandate paid or unpaid maternity/paternity/parental leave?	Yes	Yes	No	Yes	Yes	No	Yes	No	Yes
40. What is the mandatory minimum length of paid leave for maternity/paternity/parental leave (in calendar days)?	84	5	N/A	84	5	N/A	126	N/A	1095
41. What is the mandatory minimum length of unpaid leave for maternity/paternity/parental leave (in calendar days)?	0	0	N/A	0	0	N/A	0	N/A	1095
42. Who pays maternity/paternity/parental benefits?	Emp.	Emp.	N/A	Gov.	Emp.	N/A	Gov.	N/A	Gov.
43. What percentage of wages are paid during maternity/paternity/parental leave?	100%	100%	N/A	100%	100%	N/A	100%	N/A	Partially paid

	Mother	Father		Mother	Father		Mother	Father	
44. Where **paid** parental leave exists, what is the minimum amount which only the mother/father must take (in calendar days)?	N/A	N/A		N/A	N/A		0	0	
45. Where **unpaid** parental leave exists, what is the minimum amount which only the mother/father must take (in calendar days)?	N/A	N/A		N/A	N/A		0	0	

Retirement & pensions	Women	Men		Women	Men		Women	Men	
46. What is the age at which one can retire and receive full benefits?	60	60		65	65		57	62	
47. What is the age at which one can retire and receive partial benefits?	60	60		65	65		57	62	
48. What is the mandatory retirement age?	65	65		N/A	N/A		N/A	N/A	

Working hours and industry restrictions			
49. Can non-pregnant and non-nursing women do the same jobs as men?	Yes	Yes	No
50. Can non-pregnant and non-nursing women engage in the following occupations in the same way as men?			
a. Mining	Yes	Yes	No
b. Construction	Yes	Yes	No
c. Metalwork	Yes	Yes	No
d. Factory work	Yes	Yes	No
e. Jobs requiring lifting weights above a threshold	Yes	Yes	No
f. Jobs deemed hazardous	Yes	Yes	No
g. Jobs deemed arduous	Yes	Yes	No
h. Jobs deemed morally or socially inappropriate	Yes	Yes	Yes
51. Can non-pregnant and non-nursing women work the same night hours as men?	Yes	Yes	No

Workplace protections			
52. Does the law mandate equal remuneration for men and women for work of equal value?	Yes	No	Yes
53. Are there laws mandating non-discrimination based on gender in hiring?	Yes	Yes	Yes
54. Is it illegal for an employer to ask about family status during a job interview?	No	No	No
55. Are there laws penalizing or preventing the dismissal of pregnant women?	Yes	Yes	Yes
56. Must employers give employees an equivalent position when they return from maternity leave?	No	Yes	No
57. Are employers required to provide break time for nursing mothers?	Yes	Yes	No
58. Do employees with minor children have rights to a flexible/part time schedule?	No	No	Yes

BUILDING CREDIT

59. What is the minimum loan amount covered in the private credit bureau or public credit registry (as a percentage of income per capita)?	0%	0%	0%
60. Do microfinance institutions provide information to private credit bureaus or public credit registries?	Yes	Yes	No
61. Do utility companies provide information to private credit bureaus or public credit registries?	Yes	Yes	No
62. Do retailers provide information to private credit bureaus or public credit registries?	Yes	Yes	No

PROVIDING INCENTIVES TO WORK

Childcare			
63. Are payments for childcare tax deductible?	No	No	No
64. Is there public provision of childcare for children under the age of primary education?	No	Yes	Yes
65. Does the law mandate free and compulsory primary education?	Yes	Yes	Yes

Personal income tax	Women	Men		Women	Men		Women	Men	
66. Are there specific tax deductions or credits that are applicable only to men/women?	No	No		No	No		No	No	

Mauritius–Moldova

Economy Tables

	MONGOLIA		MONTENEGRO		MOROCCO	
REGION	East Asia & Pacific		Europe & Central Asia		Middle East & North Africa	
INCOME	Lower middle income		Upper middle income		Lower middle income	
FEMALE POPULATION	1,410,397		314,231		16,498,066	
FEMALE LABOR FORCE PARTICIPATION	57%		..		27%	

ACCESSING INSTITUTIONS

Constitutional rights

1. Is there a non-discrimination clause in the constitution?	Yes		Yes		No	
2. If there is a non-discrimination clause in the constitution, does it explicitly mention gender?	Yes		No		N/A	
3. Does the constitution guarantee equality before the law?	Yes		Yes		Yes	

	Customary	Personal	Customary	Personal	Customary	Personal
4. Is customary/personal law recognized as valid source of law under the constitution?	No	No	No	No	No	No
5. If so, is it invalid if it violates constitutional provisions on non-discrimination or equality?	N/A	N/A	N/A	N/A	N/A	N/A

Quotas

6. What are the legal quotas for women on corporate boards?	N/A		N/A		N/A	
7. What are the legal quotas for women in parliament?	N/A		N/A		N/A	
8. What are the legal quotas for women in local government?	40%		N/A		N/A	

Rights of married and unmarried women

	Unmarried	Married	Unmarried	Married	Unmarried	Married
9. Can a woman apply for a passport in the same way as a man?	Yes	Yes	Yes	Yes	Yes	Yes
10. Can a woman apply for a national ID card in the same way as a man?	Yes	Yes	Yes	Yes	Yes	Yes
11. Can a woman travel outside the country in the same way as a man?	Yes	Yes	Yes	Yes	Yes	Yes
12. Can a woman travel outside her home in the same way as a man?	Yes	Yes	Yes	Yes	Yes	Yes
13. Can a woman get a job or pursue a trade or profession in the same way as a man?	Yes	Yes	Yes	Yes	Yes	Yes
14. Can a woman sign a contract in the same way as a man?	Yes	Yes	Yes	Yes	Yes	Yes
15. Can a woman register a business in the same way as a man?	Yes	Yes	Yes	Yes	Yes	Yes
16. Can a woman open a bank account in the same way as a man?	Yes	Yes	Yes	Yes	Yes	Yes
17. Can a woman choose where to live in the same way as a man?	Yes	Yes	Yes	Yes	Yes	Yes
18. Can a woman confer citizenship on her children in the same way as a man?	Yes	Yes	Yes	Yes	Yes	Yes
19. Can a woman be "head of household" or "head of family" in the same way as a man?	N/A	N/A	N/A	N/A	Yes	No
Number of inequalities in accessing institutions	0	0	0	0	0	1

Division of responsibility within marriage

20. Can a woman convey citizenship to her non-national spouse in the same way as a man?	Yes		Yes		No	
21. Are married women required by law to obey their husbands?	No		No		No	
22. Do married couples jointly share legal responsibility for financially maintaining the family's expenses?	Yes		Yes		Yes	

USING PROPERTY

Marital property regime

23. What is the default marital property regime?	Other		Partial community of property		Separation of property	
24. Who legally administers property during marriage?	Other		Both must agree		Original owner	

Protecting a wife's interests

25. If it is the husband, does he need his wife's consent for major transactions	N/A		N/A		N/A	
26. Are there special provisions governing the marital home?	No		No		No	
27. Does the law provide for valuation of nonmonetary contributions during marriage?	Yes		Yes		No	

Property rights

	Unmarried	Married	Unmarried	Married	Unmarried	Married
28. Do men and women have equal ownership rights to property?	Yes	Yes	Yes	Yes	Yes	Yes

Inheritance rights

29. Do sons and daughters have equal inheritance rights to property?	Yes		Yes		No	
30. Do female and male surviving spouses have equal inheritance rights to property?	Yes		Yes		No	

GOING TO COURT

Equality of access

31. Does the law recognize customary courts?	No		No		No	
32. Does the law recognize personal law courts?	No		No		Yes	
33. Does a woman's testimony carry the same evidentiary weight in court as a man's?	Yes		Yes		Yes	

Efficiency of procedure

34. Is there a small claims court or a fast track procedure for small claims?	No		Yes		Yes	
35. If so, what is the maximum amount for a small claim (as a percentage of income per capita)?	N/A		10%		4%	

Judicial representation

36. How many justices are on the constitutional court?	9		7		12	
37. Of those, how many are women?	2		2		1	
38. Is the Chief Justice a woman?	No		No		No	

	MONGOLIA			MONTENEGRO			MOROCCO		

GETTING A JOB

Parental benefits

	Maternity	Paternity	Parental	Maternity	Paternity	Parental	Maternity	Paternity	Parental
39. Does the law mandate paid or unpaid maternity/paternity/parental leave?	Yes	No	No	Yes	No	Yes	Yes	Yes	No
40. What is the mandatory minimum length of paid leave for maternity/paternity/parental leave (in calendar days)?	120	N/A	N/A	45	N/A	365	98	3	N/A
41. What is the mandatory minimum length of unpaid leave for maternity/paternity/parental leave (in calendar days)?	0	N/A	N/A	0	N/A	730	90	0	N/A
42. Who pays maternity/paternity/parental benefits?	Gov.	N/A	N/A	Gov.	N/A	Gov.	Gov.	Gov.	N/A
43. What percentage of wages are paid during maternity/paternity/parental leave?	70%	N/A	N/A	100%	N/A	100%	67%	100%	N/A

	Mother	Father		Mother	Father		Mother	Father	
44. Where **paid** parental leave exists, what is the minimum amount which only the mother/father must take (in calendar days)?	N/A	N/A		45	0		N/A	N/A	
45. Where **unpaid** parental leave exists, what is the minimum amount which only the mother/father must take (in calendar days)?	N/A	N/A		0	0		N/A	N/A	

Retirement & pensions

	Women	Men		Women	Men		Women	Men	
46. What is the age at which one can retire and receive full benefits?	55	60		60	65		60	60	
47. What is the age at which one can retire and receive partial benefits?	55	60		60	62		60	60	
48. What is the mandatory retirement age?	N/A	N/A		67	67		60	60	

Working hours and industry restrictions

	MONGOLIA	MONTENEGRO	MOROCCO
49. Can non-pregnant and non-nursing women do the same jobs as men?	No	No	No
50. Can non-pregnant and non-nursing women engage in the following occupations in the same way as men?			
a. Mining	No	No	No
b. Construction	No	Yes	Yes
c. Metalwork	No	No	Yes
d. Factory work	Yes	No	Yes
e. Jobs requiring lifting weights above a threshold	No	Yes	Yes
f. Jobs deemed hazardous	Yes	No	No
g. Jobs deemed arduous	Yes	No	No
h. Jobs deemed morally or socially inappropriate	Yes	Yes	Yes
51. Can non-pregnant and non-nursing women work the same night hours as men?	Yes	No	No

Workplace protections

	MONGOLIA	MONTENEGRO	MOROCCO
52. Does the law mandate equal remuneration for men and women for work of equal value?	No	Yes	Yes
53. Are there laws mandating non-discrimination based on gender in hiring?	No	Yes	Yes
54. Is it illegal for an employer to ask about family status during a job interview?	Yes	Yes	No
55. Are there laws penalizing or preventing the dismissal of pregnant women?	Yes	Yes	Yes
56. Must employers give employees an equivalent position when they return from maternity leave?	Yes	Yes	Yes
57. Are employers required to provide break time for nursing mothers?	Yes	Yes	Yes
58. Do employees with minor children have rights to a flexible/part time schedule?	No	Yes	No

BUILDING CREDIT

	MONGOLIA	MONTENEGRO	MOROCCO
59. What is the minimum loan amount covered in the private credit bureau or public credit registry (as a percentage of income per capita)?	0%	0%	0%
60. Do microfinance institutions provide information to private credit bureaus or public credit registries?	Yes	Yes	Yes
61. Do utility companies provide information to private credit bureaus or public credit registries?	No	No	No
62. Do retailers provide information to private credit bureaus or public credit registries?	No	No	No

PROVIDING INCENTIVES TO WORK

Childcare

	MONGOLIA	MONTENEGRO	MOROCCO
63. Are payments for childcare tax deductible?	No	No	No
64. Is there public provision of childcare for children under the age of primary education?	Yes	Yes	Yes
65. Does the law mandate free and compulsory primary education?	Yes	Yes	Yes

Personal income tax

	Women	Men	Women	Men	Women	Men
66. Are there specific tax deductions or credits that are applicable only to men/women?	No	No	No	No	No	No

Economy Tables

	MOZAMBIQUE		NAMIBIA		NEPAL	
REGION	Sub-Saharan Africa		Sub-Saharan Africa		South Asia	
INCOME	Low income		Upper middle income		Low income	
FEMALE POPULATION	12,894,418		1,163,181		14,144,155	
FEMALE LABOR FORCE PARTICIPATION	87%		61%		83%	

ACCESSING INSTITUTIONS

Constitutional rights

	MOZAMBIQUE		NAMIBIA		NEPAL	
1. Is there a non-discrimination clause in the constitution?	No		Yes		Yes	
2. If there is a non-discrimination clause in the constitution, does it explicitly mention gender?	N/A		Yes		Yes	
3. Does the constitution guarantee equality before the law?	Yes		Yes		Yes	

	Customary	Personal	Customary	Personal	Customary	Personal
4. Is customary/personal law recognized as valid source of law under the constitution?	Yes	No	Yes	No	No	No
5. If so, is it invalid if it violates constitutional provisions on non-discrimination or equality?	Yes	N/A	Yes	N/A	N/A	N/A

Quotas

	MOZAMBIQUE	NAMIBIA	NEPAL
6. What are the legal quotas for women on corporate boards?	N/A	N/A	N/A
7. What are the legal quotas for women in parliament?	N/A	N/A	33%
8. What are the legal quotas for women in local government?	N/A	N/A	N/A

Rights of married and unmarried women

	Unmarried	Married	Unmarried	Married	Unmarried	Married
9. Can a woman apply for a passport in the same way as a man?	Yes	Yes	Yes	Yes	Yes	Yes
10. Can a woman apply for a national ID card in the same way as a man?	Yes	Yes	Yes	Yes	N/A	N/A
11. Can a woman travel outside the country in the same way as a man?	Yes	Yes	Yes	Yes	Yes	Yes
12. Can a woman travel outside her home in the same way as a man?	Yes	Yes	Yes	Yes	Yes	Yes
13. Can a woman get a job or pursue a trade or profession in the same way as a man?	Yes	Yes	Yes	Yes	Yes	Yes
14. Can a woman sign a contract in the same way as a man?	Yes	Yes	Yes	Yes	Yes	Yes
15. Can a woman register a business in the same way as a man?	Yes	Yes	Yes	Yes	Yes	Yes
16. Can a woman open a bank account in the same way as a man?	Yes	Yes	Yes	Yes	Yes	Yes
17. Can a woman choose where to live in the same way as a man?	Yes	Yes	Yes	Yes	Yes	Yes
18. Can a woman confer citizenship on her children in the same way as a man?	Yes	Yes	Yes	Yes	No	No
19. Can a woman be "head of household" or "head of family" in the same way as a man?	N/A	N/A	N/A	N/A	N/A	N/A
Number of inequalities in accessing institutions	0	0	0	0	1	1

Division of responsibility within marriage

	MOZAMBIQUE	NAMIBIA	NEPAL
20. Can a woman convey citizenship to her non-national spouse in the same way as a man?	Yes	Yes	No
21. Are married women required by law to obey their husbands?	No	No	No
22. Do married couples jointly share legal responsibility for financially maintaining the family's expenses?	Yes	Yes	No

USING PROPERTY

Marital property regime

	MOZAMBIQUE	NAMIBIA	NEPAL
23. What is the default marital property regime?	Partial community of property	Full community of property	Separation of property
24. Who legally administers property during marriage?	Both must agree	Both must agree	Original owner

Protecting a wife's interests

	MOZAMBIQUE	NAMIBIA	NEPAL
25. If it is the husband, does he need his wife's consent for major transactions	N/A	N/A	N/A
26. Are there special provisions governing the marital home?	No	No	No
27. Does the law provide for valuation of nonmonetary contributions during marriage?	Yes	Yes	No

Property rights

	Unmarried	Married	Unmarried	Married	Unmarried	Married
28. Do men and women have equal ownership rights to property?	Yes	Yes	Yes	Yes	Yes	Yes

Inheritance rights

	MOZAMBIQUE	NAMIBIA	NEPAL
29. Do sons and daughters have equal inheritance rights to property?	Yes	Yes	No
30. Do female and male surviving spouses have equal inheritance rights to property?	Yes	Yes	No

GOING TO COURT

Equality of access

	MOZAMBIQUE	NAMIBIA	NEPAL
31. Does the law recognize customary courts?	No	No	No
32. Does the law recognize personal law courts?	No	No	No
33. Does a woman's testimony carry the same evidentiary weight in court as a man's?	Yes	Yes	Yes

Efficiency of procedure

	MOZAMBIQUE	NAMIBIA	NEPAL
34. Is there a small claims court or a fast track procedure for small claims?	No	No	No
35. If so, what is the maximum amount for a small claim (as a percentage of income per capita)?	N/A	N/A	N/A

Judicial representation

	MOZAMBIQUE	NAMIBIA	NEPAL
36. How many justices are on the constitutional court?	7	N/A	11
37. Of those, how many are women?	1	N/A	1
38. Is the Chief Justice a woman?	No	N/A	No

	MOZAMBIQUE			NAMIBIA			NEPAL		

GETTING A JOB

Parental benefits	Maternity	Paternity	Parental	Maternity	Paternity	Parental	Maternity	Paternity	Parental
39. Does the law mandate paid or unpaid maternity/paternity/parental leave?	Yes	Yes	No	Yes	No	No	Yes	No	No
40. What is the mandatory minimum length of paid leave for maternity/paternity/parental leave (in calendar days)?	60	1	N/A	84	N/A	N/A	52	N/A	N/A
41. What is the mandatory minimum length of unpaid leave for maternity/paternity/parental leave (in calendar days)?	0	0	N/A	0	N/A	N/A	0	N/A	N/A
42. Who pays maternity/paternity/parental benefits?	Gov.	Emp.	N/A	Gov.	N/A	N/A	Emp.	N/A	N/A
43. What percentage of wages are paid during maternity/paternity/parental leave?	100%	100%	N/A	100%	N/A	N/A	100%	N/A	N/A

	Mother	Father		Mother	Father		Mother	Father	
44. Where **paid** parental leave exists, what is the minimum amount which only the mother/father must take (in calendar days)?	N/A	N/A		N/A	N/A		N/A	N/A	
45. Where **unpaid** parental leave exists, what is the minimum amount which only the mother/father must take (in calendar days)?	N/A	N/A		N/A	N/A		N/A	N/A	

Retirement & pensions	Women	Men		Women	Men		Women	Men	
46. What is the age at which one can retire and receive full benefits?	55	60		60	60		N/A	N/A	
47. What is the age at which one can retire and receive partial benefits?	55	60		60	60		N/A	N/A	
48. What is the mandatory retirement age?	55	60		N/A	N/A		55	55	

Working hours and industry restrictions									
49. Can non-pregnant and non-nursing women do the same jobs as men?	No			Yes			Yes		
50. Can non-pregnant and non-nursing women engage in the following occupations in the same way as men?									
a. Mining	Yes			Yes			Yes		
b. Construction	Yes			Yes			Yes		
c. Metalwork	Yes			Yes			Yes		
d. Factory work	Yes			Yes			Yes		
e. Jobs requiring lifting weights above a threshold	Yes			Yes			Yes		
f. Jobs deemed hazardous	No			Yes			Yes		
g. Jobs deemed arduous	Yes			Yes			Yes		
h. Jobs deemed morally or socially inappropriate	Yes			Yes			Yes		
51. Can non-pregnant and non-nursing women work the same night hours as men?	Yes			Yes			No		

Workplace protections									
52. Does the law mandate equal remuneration for men and women for work of equal value?	No			Yes			No		
53. Are there laws mandating non-discrimination based on gender in hiring?	No			Yes			No		
54. Is it illegal for an employer to ask about family status during a job interview?	No			No			No		
55. Are there laws penalizing or preventing the dismissal of pregnant women?	Yes			Yes			No		
56. Must employers give employees an equivalent position when they return from maternity leave?	No			No			No		
57. Are employers required to provide break time for nursing mothers?	Yes			No			Yes		
58. Do employees with minor children have rights to a flexible/part time schedule?	No			No			No		

BUILDING CREDIT

59. What is the minimum loan amount covered in the private credit bureau or public credit registry (as a percentage of income per capita)?	0%			0%			2232%		
60. Do microfinance institutions provide information to private credit bureaus or public credit registries?	Yes			Yes			No		
61. Do utility companies provide information to private credit bureaus or public credit registries?	No			No			No		
62. Do retailers provide information to private credit bureaus or public credit registries?	No			Yes			No		

PROVIDING INCENTIVES TO WORK

Childcare									
63. Are payments for childcare tax deductible?	No			No			No		
64. Is there public provision of childcare for children under the age of primary education?	Yes			No			No		
65. Does the law mandate free and compulsory primary education?	Yes			Yes			No		

Personal income tax	Women	Men		Women	Men		Women	Men	
66. Are there specific tax deductions or credits that are applicable only to men/women?	No	No		No	No		No	No	

Economy Tables

	NETHERLANDS	NEW ZEALAND	NICARAGUA
REGION	High income: OECD	High income: OECD	Latin America & Caribbean
INCOME	High income	High income	Lower middle income
FEMALE POPULATION	8,458,836	2,255,727	3,028,34 1
FEMALE LABOR FORCE PARTICIPATION	73%	72%	49%

ACCESSING INSTITUTIONS

Constitutional rights

	NETHERLANDS	NEW ZEALAND	NICARAGUA
1. Is there a non-discrimination clause in the constitution?	Yes	Yes	Yes
2. If there is a non-discrimination clause in the constitution, does it explicitly mention gender?	Yes	Yes	Yes
3. Does the constitution guarantee equality before the law?	Yes	No	Yes

	Customary	Personal	Customary	Personal	Customary	Personal
4. Is customary/personal law recognized as valid source of law under the constitution?	No	No	No	No	No	No
5. If so, is it invalid if it violates constitutional provisions on non-discrimination or equality?	N/A	N/A	N/A	N/A	N/A	N/A

Quotas

	NETHERLANDS	NEW ZEALAND	NICARAGUA
6. What are the legal quotas for women on corporate boards?	N/A	N/A	N/A
7. What are the legal quotas for women in parliament?	N/A	N/A	N/A
8. What are the legal quotas for women in local government?	N/A	N/A	N/A

Rights of married and unmarried women

	Unmarried	Married	Unmarried	Married	Unmarried	Married
9. Can a woman apply for a passport in the same way as a man?	Yes	Yes	Yes	Yes	Yes	Yes
10. Can a woman apply for a national ID card in the same way as a man?	Yes	Yes	N/A	N/A	Yes	Yes
11. Can a woman travel outside the country in the same way as a man?	Yes	Yes	Yes	Yes	Yes	Yes
12. Can a woman travel outside her home in the same way as a man?	Yes	Yes	Yes	Yes	Yes	Yes
13. Can a woman get a job or pursue a trade or profession in the same way as a man?	Yes	Yes	Yes	Yes	Yes	Yes
14. Can a woman sign a contract in the same way as a man?	Yes	Yes	Yes	Yes	Yes	Yes
15. Can a woman register a business in the same way as a man?	Yes	Yes	Yes	Yes	Yes	Yes
16. Can a woman open a bank account in the same way as a man?	Yes	Yes	Yes	Yes	Yes	Yes
17. Can a woman choose where to live in the same way as a man?	Yes	Yes	Yes	Yes	Yes	No
18. Can a woman confer citizenship on her children in the same way as a man?	Yes	Yes	Yes	Yes	Yes	Yes
19. Can a woman be "head of household" or "head of family" in the same way as a man?	N/A	N/A	N/A	N/A	Yes	No
Number of inequalities in accessing institutions	0	0	0	0	0	2

Division of responsibility within marriage

	NETHERLANDS	NEW ZEALAND	NICARAGUA
20. Can a woman convey citizenship to her non-national spouse in the same way as a man?	Yes	Yes	Yes
21. Are married women required by law to obey their husbands?	No	No	No
22. Do married couples jointly share legal responsibility for financially maintaining the family's expenses?	Yes	Yes	Yes

USING PROPERTY

Marital property regime

	NETHERLANDS	NEW ZEALAND	NICARAGUA
23. What is the default marital property regime?	Full community of property	Partial community of property	Other
24. Who legally administers property during marriage?	Both must agree	Both must agree	Original owner

Protecting a wife's interests

	NETHERLANDS	NEW ZEALAND	NICARAGUA
25. If it is the husband, does he need his wife's consent for major transactions	N/A	N/A	N/A
26. Are there special provisions governing the marital home?	Yes	No	No
27. Does the law provide for valuation of nonmonetary contributions during marriage?	Yes	Yes	Yes

Property rights

	Unmarried	Married	Unmarried	Married	Unmarried	Married
28. Do men and women have equal ownership rights to property?	Yes	Yes	Yes	Yes	Yes	Yes

Inheritance rights

	NETHERLANDS	NEW ZEALAND	NICARAGUA
29. Do sons and daughters have equal inheritance rights to property?	Yes	Yes	Yes
30. Do female and male surviving spouses have equal inheritance rights to property?	Yes	Yes	Yes

GOING TO COURT

Equality of access

	NETHERLANDS	NEW ZEALAND	NICARAGUA
31. Does the law recognize customary courts?	No	Yes	No
32. Does the law recognize personal law courts?	No	No	No
33. Does a woman's testimony carry the same evidentiary weight in court as a man's?	Yes	Yes	Yes

Efficiency of procedure

	NETHERLANDS	NEW ZEALAND	NICARAGUA
34. Is there a small claims court or a fast track procedure for small claims?	Yes	Yes	No
35. If so, what is the maximum amount for a small claim (as a percentage of income per capita)?	69%	32%	N/A

Judicial representation

	NETHERLANDS	NEW ZEALAND	NICARAGUA
36. How many justices are on the constitutional court?	N/A	5	5
37. Of those, how many are women?	N/A	2	1
38. Is the Chief Justice a woman?	N/A	Yes	No

GETTING A JOB

Parental benefits	NETHERLANDS			NEW ZEALAND			NICARAGUA		
	Maternity	Paternity	Parental	Maternity	Paternity	Parental	Maternity	Paternity	Parental
39. Does the law mandate paid or unpaid maternity/paternity/parental leave?	Yes	Yes	No	Yes	Yes	Yes	Yes	No	No
40. What is the mandatory minimum length of paid leave for maternity/paternity/parental leave (in calendar days)?	112	2	N/A	98	0	0	84	N/A	N/A
41. What is the mandatory minimum length of unpaid leave for maternity/paternity/parental leave (in calendar days)?	0	0	N/A	0	0	364	0	N/A	N/A
42. Who pays maternity/paternity/parental benefits?	Gov.	Emp.	N/A	Gov.	N/A	N/A	Emp. & Gov.	N/A	N/A
43. What percentage of wages are paid during maternity/paternity/parental leave?	100%	100%	N/A	100%	0%	0%	100%	N/A	N/A

	Mother	Father		Mother	Father		Mother	Father	
44. Where **paid** parental leave exists, what is the minimum amount which only the mother/father must take (in calendar days)?	N/A	N/A		N/A	N/A		N/A	N/A	
45. Where **unpaid** parental leave exists, what is the minimum amount which only the mother/father must take (in calendar days)?	N/A	N/A		0	0		N/A	N/A	

Retirement & pensions	Women	Men		Women	Men		Women	Men	
46. What is the age at which one can retire and receive full benefits?	67	67		65	65		60	60	
47. What is the age at which one can retire and receive partial benefits?	67	67		65	65		60	60	
48. What is the mandatory retirement age?	N/A	N/A		N/A	N/A		N/A	N/A	

Working hours and industry restrictions	NETHERLANDS	NEW ZEALAND	NICARAGUA
49. Can non-pregnant and non-nursing women do the same jobs as men?	Yes	Yes	No
50. Can non-pregnant and non-nursing women engage in the following occupations in the same way as men?			
a. Mining	Yes	Yes	Yes
b. Construction	Yes	Yes	Yes
c. Metalwork	Yes	Yes	Yes
d. Factory work	Yes	Yes	Yes
e. Jobs requiring lifting weights above a threshold	Yes	Yes	No
f. Jobs deemed hazardous	Yes	Yes	Yes
g. Jobs deemed arduous	Yes	Yes	Yes
h. Jobs deemed morally or socially inappropriate	Yes	Yes	Yes
51. Can non-pregnant and non-nursing women work the same night hours as men?	Yes	Yes	Yes

Workplace protections	NETHERLANDS	NEW ZEALAND	NICARAGUA
52. Does the law mandate equal remuneration for men and women for work of equal value?	Yes	No	No
53. Are there laws mandating non-discrimination based on gender in hiring?	Yes	Yes	Yes
54. Is it illegal for an employer to ask about family status during a job interview?	No	No	No
55. Are there laws penalizing or preventing the dismissal of pregnant women?	Yes	Yes	Yes
56. Must employers give employees an equivalent position when they return from maternity leave?	Yes	Yes	Yes
57. Are employers required to provide break time for nursing mothers?	Yes	Yes	Yes
58. Do employees with minor children have rights to a flexible/part time schedule?	No	Yes	No

BUILDING CREDIT

	NETHERLANDS	NEW ZEALAND	NICARAGUA
59. What is the minimum loan amount covered in the private credit bureau or public credit registry (as a percentage of income per capita)?	1%	0%	0%
60. Do microfinance institutions provide information to private credit bureaus or public credit registries?	N/A	N/A	Yes
61. Do utility companies provide information to private credit bureaus or public credit registries?	No	Yes	Yes
62. Do retailers provide information to private credit bureaus or public credit registries?	Yes	Yes	Yes

PROVIDING INCENTIVES TO WORK

Childcare	NETHERLANDS	NEW ZEALAND	NICARAGUA
63. Are payments for childcare tax deductible?	No	No	No
64. Is there public provision of childcare for children under the age of primary education?	Yes	Yes	Yes
65. Does the law mandate free and compulsory primary education?	Yes	Yes	Yes

Personal income tax	Women	Men		Women	Men		Women	Men	
66. Are there specific tax deductions or credits that are applicable only to men/women?	No	No		No	No		No	No	

Economy Tables

	NIGER	NIGERIA	NORWAY
REGION	Sub-Saharan Africa	Sub-Saharan Africa	High income: OECD
INCOME	Low income	Lower middle income	High income
FEMALE POPULATION	8,515,165	82,935,471	2,507,004
FEMALE LABOR FORCE PARTICIPATION	40%	48%	76%

ACCESSING INSTITUTIONS

Constitutional rights

	NIGER	NIGERIA	NORWAY
1. Is there a non-discrimination clause in the constitution?	Yes	Yes	No
2. If there is a non-discrimination clause in the constitution, does it explicitly mention gender?	Yes	Yes	N/A
3. Does the constitution guarantee equality before the law?	Yes	Yes	No

	Customary	Personal	Customary	Personal	Customary	Personal
4. Is customary/personal law recognized as valid source of law under the constitution?	Yes	No	Yes	Yes	No	No
5. If so, is it invalid if it violates constitutional provisions on non-discrimination or equality?	Yes	N/A	Yes	Yes	N/A	N/A

Quotas

	NIGER	NIGERIA	NORWAY
6. What are the legal quotas for women on corporate boards?	N/A	N/A	40%
7. What are the legal quotas for women in parliament?	10%	N/A	N/A
8. What are the legal quotas for women in local government?	N/A	N/A	N/A

Rights of married and unmarried women

	Unmarried	Married	Unmarried	Married	Unmarried	Married
9. Can a woman apply for a passport in the same way as a man?	Yes	Yes	Yes	Yes	Yes	Yes
10. Can a woman apply for a national ID card in the same way as a man?	..	..	Yes	Yes	N/A	N/A
11. Can a woman travel outside the country in the same way as a man?	Yes	Yes	Yes	Yes	Yes	Yes
12. Can a woman travel outside her home in the same way as a man?	Yes	Yes	Yes	Yes	Yes	Yes
13. Can a woman get a job or pursue a trade or profession in the same way as a man?	Yes	No	Yes	Yes	Yes	Yes
14. Can a woman sign a contract in the same way as a man?	Yes	Yes	Yes	Yes	Yes	Yes
15. Can a woman register a business in the same way as a man?	Yes	Yes	Yes	Yes	Yes	Yes
16. Can a woman open a bank account in the same way as a man?	Yes	No	Yes	Yes	Yes	Yes
17. Can a woman choose where to live in the same way as a man?	Yes	No	Yes	Yes	Yes	Yes
18. Can a woman confer citizenship on her children in the same way as a man?	Yes	Yes	Yes	Yes	Yes	Yes
19. Can a woman be "head of household" or "head of family" in the same way as a man?	Yes	No	N/A	N/A	N/A	N/A
Number of inequalities in accessing institutions	0	4	0	0	0	0

Division of responsibility within marriage

	NIGER	NIGERIA	NORWAY
20. Can a woman convey citizenship to her non-national spouse in the same way as a man?	No	No	Yes
21. Are married women required by law to obey their husbands?	No	No	No
22. Do married couples jointly share legal responsibility for financially maintaining the family's expenses?	Yes	Yes	Yes

USING PROPERTY

Marital property regime

	NIGER	NIGERIA	NORWAY
23. What is the default marital property regime?	Other	Separation of property	Deferred community of property
24. Who legally administers property during marriage?	Other	Original owner	Original owner

Protecting a wife's interests

	NIGER	NIGERIA	NORWAY
25. If it is the husband, does he need his wife's consent for major transactions	..	N/A	N/A
26. Are there special provisions governing the marital home?	..	No	Yes
27. Does the law provide for valuation of nonmonetary contributions during marriage?	..	No	Yes

Property rights

	Unmarried	Married	Unmarried	Married	Unmarried	Married
28. Do men and women have equal ownership rights to property?	..	..	Yes	Yes	Yes	Yes

Inheritance rights

	NIGER	NIGERIA	NORWAY
29. Do sons and daughters have equal inheritance rights to property?	..	Yes	Yes
30. Do female and male surviving spouses have equal inheritance rights to property?	..	Yes	Yes

GOING TO COURT

Equality of access

	NIGER	NIGERIA	NORWAY
31. Does the law recognize customary courts?	No	Yes	No
32. Does the law recognize personal law courts?	No	Yes	No
33. Does a woman's testimony carry the same evidentiary weight in court as a man's?	Yes	Yes	Yes

Efficiency of procedure

	NIGER	NIGERIA	NORWAY
34. Is there a small claims court or a fast track procedure for small claims?	No	No	Yes
35. If so, what is the maximum amount for a small claim (as a percentage of income per capita)?	N/A	N/A	22%

Judicial representation

	NIGER	NIGERIA	NORWAY
36. How many justices are on the constitutional court?	7	16	20
37. Of those, how many are women?	1	3	7
38. Is the Chief Justice a woman?	Yes	Yes	No

	NIGER			NIGERIA			NORWAY		

GETTING A JOB

Parental benefits	Maternity	Paternity	Parental	Maternity	Paternity	Parental	Maternity	Paternity	Parental
39. Does the law mandate paid or unpaid maternity/paternity/parental leave?	Yes	Yes	No	Yes	No	No	No	No	Yes
40. What is the mandatory minimum length of paid leave for maternity/paternity/parental leave (in calendar days)?	98	1	N/A	84	N/A	N/A	N/A	N/A	343
41. What is the mandatory minimum length of unpaid leave for maternity/paternity/parental leave (in calendar days)?	0	0	N/A	0	N/A	N/A	N/A	N/A	0
42. Who pays maternity/paternity/parental benefits?	Emp. & Gov.	Emp.	N/A	Emp.	N/A	N/A	N/A	N/A	Gov.
43. What percentage of wages are paid during maternity/paternity/parental leave?	100%	0%	N/A	50%	N/A	N/A	N/A	N/A	100%

	Mother	Father		Mother	Father		Mother	Father	
44. Where **paid** parental leave exists, what is the minimum amount which only the mother/father must take (in calendar days)?	N/A	N/A		N/A	N/A		98	98	
45. Where **unpaid** parental leave exists, what is the minimum amount which only the mother/father must take (in calendar days)?	N/A	N/A		N/A	N/A		N/A	N/A	

Retirement & pensions	Women	Men		Women	Men		Women	Men	
46. What is the age at which one can retire and receive full benefits?	60	60		50	50		67	67	
47. What is the age at which one can retire and receive partial benefits?	60	60		50	50		62	62	
48. What is the mandatory retirement age?	N/A	N/A		N/A	N/A		N/A	N/A	

Working hours and industry restrictions	NIGER	NIGERIA	NORWAY
49. Can non-pregnant and non-nursing women do the same jobs as men?	No	No	Yes
50. Can non-pregnant and non-nursing women engage in the following occupations in the same way as men?			
a. Mining	Yes	No	Yes
b. Construction	Yes	Yes	Yes
c. Metalwork	Yes	Yes	Yes
d. Factory work	Yes	Yes	Yes
e. Jobs requiring lifting weights above a threshold	Yes	Yes	Yes
f. Jobs deemed hazardous	No	Yes	Yes
g. Jobs deemed arduous	Yes	Yes	Yes
h. Jobs deemed morally or socially inappropriate	Yes	Yes	Yes
51. Can non-pregnant and non-nursing women work the same night hours as men?	Yes	No	Yes

Workplace protections	NIGER	NIGERIA	NORWAY
52. Does the law mandate equal remuneration for men and women for work of equal value?	Yes	No	Yes
53. Are there laws mandating non-discrimination based on gender in hiring?	Yes	No	Yes
54. Is it illegal for an employer to ask about family status during a job interview?	No	No	Yes
55. Are there laws penalizing or preventing the dismissal of pregnant women?	Yes	Yes	Yes
56. Must employers give employees an equivalent position when they return from maternity leave?	Yes	No	N/A
57. Are employers required to provide break time for nursing mothers?	Yes	Yes	Yes
58. Do employees with minor children have rights to a flexible/part time schedule?	No	No	No

BUILDING CREDIT

	NIGER	NIGERIA	NORWAY
59. What is the minimum loan amount covered in the private credit bureau or public credit registry (as a percentage of income per capita)?	2864%	0%	0%
60. Do microfinance institutions provide information to private credit bureaus or public credit registries?	No	Yes	N/A
61. Do utility companies provide information to private credit bureaus or public credit registries?	No	No	No
62. Do retailers provide information to private credit bureaus or public credit registries?	No	Yes	No

PROVIDING INCENTIVES TO WORK

Childcare	NIGER	NIGERIA	NORWAY
63. Are payments for childcare tax deductible?	No	No	Yes
64. Is there public provision of childcare for children under the age of primary education?	Yes	No	Yes
65. Does the law mandate free and compulsory primary education?	Yes	Yes	Yes

Personal income tax	Women	Men		Women	Men		Women	Men	
66. Are there specific tax deductions or credits that are applicable only to men/women?	No	Yes		No	No		No	No	

Economy Tables

	OMAN	PAKISTAN	PANAMA
REGION	Middle East & North Africa	South Asia	Latin America & Caribbean
INCOME	High income	Lower middle income	Upper middle income
FEMALE POPULATION	1,257,318	87,140,798	1,881,976
FEMALE LABOR FORCE PARTICIPATION	30%	23%	54%

ACCESSING INSTITUTIONS

Constitutional rights

	OMAN	PAKISTAN	PANAMA
1. Is there a non-discrimination clause in the constitution?	Yes	Yes	Yes
2. If there is a non-discrimination clause in the constitution, does it explicitly mention gender?	Yes	Yes	Yes
3. Does the constitution guarantee equality before the law?	Yes	Yes	No

	Customary	Personal	Customary	Personal	Customary	Personal
4. Is customary/personal law recognized as valid source of law under the constitution?	No	Yes	Yes	Yes	No	No
5. If so, is it invalid if it violates constitutional provisions on non-discrimination or equality?	N/A	Yes	Yes	No	N/A	N/A

Quotas

	OMAN	PAKISTAN	PANAMA
6. What are the legal quotas for women on corporate boards?	N/A	N/A	N/A
7. What are the legal quotas for women in parliament?	N/A	17.5%	N/A
8. What are the legal quotas for women in local government?	N/A	N/A	N/A

Rights of married and unmarried women

	Unmarried	Married	Unmarried	Married	Unmarried	Married
9. Can a woman apply for a passport in the same way as a man?	Yes	No	Yes	No	Yes	Yes
10. Can a woman apply for a national ID card in the same way as a man?	No	No	Yes	No	Yes	Yes
11. Can a woman travel outside the country in the same way as a man?	Yes	No	Yes	Yes	Yes	Yes
12. Can a woman travel outside her home in the same way as a man?	Yes	No	Yes	Yes	Yes	Yes
13. Can a woman get a job or pursue a trade or profession in the same way as a man?	Yes	Yes	Yes	Yes	Yes	Yes
14. Can a woman sign a contract in the same way as a man?	Yes	Yes	Yes	Yes	Yes	Yes
15. Can a woman register a business in the same way as a man?	Yes	Yes	Yes	No	Yes	Yes
16. Can a woman open a bank account in the same way as a man?	Yes	Yes	Yes	Yes	Yes	Yes
17. Can a woman choose where to live in the same way as a man?	Yes	No	Yes	Yes	Yes	Yes
18. Can a woman confer citizenship on her children in the same way as a man?	No	No	Yes	Yes	Yes	Yes
19. Can a woman be "head of household" or "head of family" in the same way as a man?	Yes	No	N/A	N/A	N/A	N/A
Number of inequalities in accessing institutions	2	7	0	3	0	0

Division of responsibility within marriage

	OMAN	PAKISTAN	PANAMA
20. Can a woman convey citizenship to her non-national spouse in the same way as a man?	No	No	Yes
21. Are married women required by law to obey their husbands?	No	No	No
22. Do married couples jointly share legal responsibility for financially maintaining the family's expenses?	No	No	Yes

USING PROPERTY

Marital property regime

	OMAN	PAKISTAN	PANAMA
23. What is the default marital property regime?	Separation of property	Separation of property	Deferred community of property
24. Who legally administers property during marriage?	Original owner	Original owner	Original owner

Protecting a wife's interests

	OMAN	PAKISTAN	PANAMA
25. If it is the husband, does he need his wife's consent for major transactions	N/A	N/A	N/A
26. Are there special provisions governing the marital home?	No	No	Yes
27. Does the law provide for valuation of nonmonetary contributions during marriage?	No	No	Yes

Property rights

	Unmarried	Married	Unmarried	Married	Unmarried	Married
28. Do men and women have equal ownership rights to property?	Yes	Yes	Yes	Yes	Yes	Yes

Inheritance rights

	OMAN	PAKISTAN	PANAMA
29. Do sons and daughters have equal inheritance rights to property?	No	No	Yes
30. Do female and male surviving spouses have equal inheritance rights to property?	No	No	Yes

GOING TO COURT

Equality of access

	OMAN	PAKISTAN	PANAMA
31. Does the law recognize customary courts?	No	No	No
32. Does the law recognize personal law courts?	Yes	Yes	No
33. Does a woman's testimony carry the same evidentiary weight in court as a man's?	No	No	Yes

Efficiency of procedure

	OMAN	PAKISTAN	PANAMA
34. Is there a small claims court or a fast track procedure for small claims?	Yes	Yes	Yes
35. If so, what is the maximum amount for a small claim (as a percentage of income per capita)?	167%	94%	12%

Judicial representation

	OMAN	PAKISTAN	PANAMA
36. How many justices are on the constitutional court?	N/A	16	9
37. Of those, how many are women?	N/A	0	0
38. Is the Chief Justice a woman?	N/A	No	No

	OMAN			PAKISTAN			PANAMA		

GETTING A JOB

Parental benefits	Maternity	Paternity	Parental	Maternity	Paternity	Parental	Maternity	Paternity	Parental
39. Does the law mandate paid or unpaid maternity/paternity/parental leave?	Yes	No	No	Yes	No	No	Yes	No	No
40. What is the mandatory minimum length of paid leave for maternity/ paternity/parental leave (in calendar days)?	42	N/A	N/A	84	N/A	N/A	98	N/A	N/A
41. What is the mandatory minimum length of unpaid leave for maternity/ paternity/parental leave (in calendar days)?	0	N/A	N/A	0	N/A	N/A	0	N/A	N/A
42. Who pays maternity/paternity/parental benefits?	Emp.	N/A	N/A	Emp.	N/A	N/A	Emp. & Gov.	N/A	N/A
43. What percentage of wages are paid during maternity/paternity/parental leave?	75%	N/A	N/A	100%	N/A	N/A	100%	N/A	N/A

	Mother	Father		Mother	Father		Mother	Father	
44. Where **paid** parental leave exists, what is the minimum amount which only the mother/father must take (in calendar days)?	N/A	N/A		N/A	N/A		N/A	N/A	
45. Where **unpaid** parental leave exists, what is the minimum amount which only the mother/father must take (in calendar days)?	N/A	N/A		N/A	N/A		N/A	N/A	

Retirement & pensions	Women	Men		Women	Men		Women	Men	
46. What is the age at which one can retire and receive full benefits?	55	60		55	60		57	62	
47. What is the age at which one can retire and receive partial benefits?	45	45		50	55		55	60	
48. What is the mandatory retirement age?	60	60		N/A	N/A		N/A	N/A	

Working hours and industry restrictions									
49. Can non-pregnant and non-nursing women do the same jobs as men?	No			No			No		
50. Can non-pregnant and non-nursing women engage in the following occupations in the same way as men?									
a. Mining	Yes			No			Yes		
b. Construction	Yes			Yes			Yes		
c. Metalwork	Yes			Yes			Yes		
d. Factory work	Yes			No			Yes		
e. Jobs requiring lifting weights above a threshold	Yes			No			Yes		
f. Jobs deemed hazardous	No			No			No		
g. Jobs deemed arduous	No			Yes			Yes		
h. Jobs deemed morally or socially inappropriate	Yes			Yes			Yes		
51. Can non-pregnant and non-nursing women work the same night hours as men?	No			No			Yes		

Workplace protections									
52. Does the law mandate equal remuneration for men and women for work of equal value?	No			No			No		
53. Are there laws mandating non-discrimination based on gender in hiring?	No			No			No		
54. Is it illegal for an employer to ask about family status during a job interview?	No			No			No		
55. Are there laws penalizing or preventing the dismissal of pregnant women?	Yes			Yes			Yes		
56. Must employers give employees an equivalent position when they return from maternity leave?	No			No			Yes		
57. Are employers required to provide break time for nursing mothers?	No			No			Yes		
58. Do employees with minor children have rights to a flexible/part time schedule?	No			No			No		

BUILDING CREDIT

59. What is the minimum loan amount covered in the private credit bureau or public credit registry (as a percentage of income per capita)?	0%			0%			0%		
60. Do microfinance institutions provide information to private credit bureaus or public credit registries?	N/A			Yes			Yes		
61. Do utility companies provide information to private credit bureaus or public credit registries?	No			No			Yes		
62. Do retailers provide information to private credit bureaus or public credit registries?	No			No			Yes		

PROVIDING INCENTIVES TO WORK

Childcare									
63. Are payments for childcare tax deductible?	No			No			No		
64. Is there public provision of childcare for children under the age of primary education?	No			No			Yes		
65. Does the law mandate free and compulsory primary education?	No			Yes			Yes		

Personal income tax	Women	Men		Women	Men		Women	Men	
66. Are there specific tax deductions or credits that are applicable only to men/women?	No	No		No	No		No	No	

Oman-Panama

Economy Tables

	PAPUA NEW GUINEA		PARAGUAY		PERU	
REGION	East Asia & Pacific		Latin America & Caribbean		Latin America & Caribbean	
INCOME	Lower middle income		Lower middle income		Upper middle income	
FEMALE POPULATION	3,510,923		3,315,398		14,959,737	
FEMALE LABOR FORCE PARTICIPATION	72%		61%		71%	

ACCESSING INSTITUTIONS

Constitutional rights

	PAPUA NEW GUINEA	PARAGUAY	PERU
1. Is there a non-discrimination clause in the constitution?	No	Yes	Yes
2. If there is a non-discrimination clause in the constitution, does it explicitly mention gender?	N/A	No	Yes
3. Does the constitution guarantee equality before the law?	Yes	Yes	Yes

	Customary	Personal	Customary	Personal	Customary	Personal
4. Is customary/personal law recognized as valid source of law under the constitution?	Yes	No	No	No	Yes	No
5. If so, is it invalid if it violates constitutional provisions on non-discrimination or equality?	Yes	N/A	N/A	N/A	Yes	N/A

Quotas

	PAPUA NEW GUINEA	PARAGUAY	PERU
6. What are the legal quotas for women on corporate boards?	N/A	N/A	N/A
7. What are the legal quotas for women in parliament?	N/A	N/A	N/A
8. What are the legal quotas for women in local government?	N/A	N/A	N/A

Rights of married and unmarried women

	Unmarried	Married	Unmarried	Married	Unmarried	Married
9. Can a woman apply for a passport in the same way as a man?	Yes	Yes	Yes	Yes	Yes	Yes
10. Can a woman apply for a national ID card in the same way as a man?	N/A	N/A	Yes	Yes	Yes	Yes
11. Can a woman travel outside the country in the same way as a man?	Yes	Yes	Yes	Yes	Yes	Yes
12. Can a woman travel outside her home in the same way as a man?	Yes	Yes	Yes	Yes	Yes	Yes
13. Can a woman get a job or pursue a trade or profession in the same way as a man?	Yes	Yes	Yes	Yes	Yes	Yes
14. Can a woman sign a contract in the same way as a man?	Yes	Yes	Yes	Yes	Yes	Yes
15. Can a woman register a business in the same way as a man?	Yes	Yes	Yes	Yes	Yes	Yes
16. Can a woman open a bank account in the same way as a man?	Yes	Yes	Yes	Yes	Yes	Yes
17. Can a woman choose where to live in the same way as a man?	Yes	Yes	Yes	Yes	Yes	Yes
18. Can a woman confer citizenship on her children in the same way as a man?	Yes	Yes	Yes	Yes	Yes	Yes
19. Can a woman be "head of household" or "head of family" in the same way as a man?	N/A	N/A	N/A	N/A	N/A	N/A
Number of inequalities in accessing institutions	0	0	0	0	0	0

Division of responsibility within marriage

	PAPUA NEW GUINEA	PARAGUAY	PERU
20. Can a woman convey citizenship to her non-national spouse in the same way as a man?	Yes	Yes	Yes
21. Are married women required by law to obey their husbands?	No	No	No
22. Do married couples jointly share legal responsibility for financially maintaining the family's expenses?	Yes	Yes	Yes

USING PROPERTY

Marital property regime

	PAPUA NEW GUINEA	PARAGUAY	PERU
23. What is the default marital property regime?	Separation of property	Partial community of property	Partial community of property
24. Who legally administers property during marriage?	Original owner	Both must agree	Both must agree

Protecting a wife's interests

	PAPUA NEW GUINEA	PARAGUAY	PERU
25. If it is the husband, does he need his wife's consent for major transactions	N/A	N/A	N/A
26. Are there special provisions governing the marital home?	No	No	No
27. Does the law provide for valuation of nonmonetary contributions during marriage?	No	Yes	Yes

Property rights

	Unmarried	Married	Unmarried	Married	Unmarried	Married
28. Do men and women have equal ownership rights to property?	Yes	Yes	Yes	Yes	Yes	Yes

Inheritance rights

	PAPUA NEW GUINEA	PARAGUAY	PERU
29. Do sons and daughters have equal inheritance rights to property?	Yes	Yes	Yes
30. Do female and male surviving spouses have equal inheritance rights to property?	Yes	Yes	Yes

GOING TO COURT

Equality of access

	PAPUA NEW GUINEA	PARAGUAY	PERU
31. Does the law recognize customary courts?	Yes	No	No
32. Does the law recognize personal law courts?	No	No	No
33. Does a woman's testimony carry the same evidentiary weight in court as a man's?	Yes	Yes	Yes

Efficiency of procedure

	PAPUA NEW GUINEA	PARAGUAY	PERU
34. Is there a small claims court or a fast track procedure for small claims?	No	Yes	Yes
35. If so, what is the maximum amount for a small claim (as a percentage of income per capita)?	N/A	129%	2272%

Judicial representation

	PAPUA NEW GUINEA	PARAGUAY	PERU
36. How many justices are on the constitutional court?	25	3	7
37. Of those, how many are women?	3	1	0
38. Is the Chief Justice a woman?	No	No	No

	PAPUA NEW GUINEA			PARAGUAY			PERU		

GETTING A JOB

Parental benefits	Maternity	Paternity	Parental	Maternity	Paternity	Parental	Maternity	Paternity	Parental
39. Does the law mandate paid or unpaid maternity/paternity/parental leave?	Yes	No	No	Yes	Yes	No	Yes	Yes	No
40. What is the mandatory minimum length of paid leave for maternity/paternity/parental leave (in calendar days)?	0	N/A	N/A	63	2	N/A	90	4	N/A
41. What is the mandatory minimum length of unpaid leave for maternity/paternity/parental leave (in calendar days)?	42	N/A	N/A	21	0	N/A	0	0	N/A
42. Who pays maternity/paternity/parental benefits?	N/A	N/A	N/A	Gov.	Emp.	N/A	Gov.	Emp.	N/A
43. What percentage of wages are paid during maternity/paternity/parental leave?	0%	N/A	N/A	50%	100%	N/A	100%	100%	N/A

	Mother	Father		Mother	Father		Mother	Father	
44. Where **paid** parental leave exists, what is the minimum amount which only the mother/father must take (in calendar days)?	N/A	N/A		N/A	N/A		N/A	N/A	
45. Where **unpaid** parental leave exists, what is the minimum amount which only the mother/father must take (in calendar days)?	N/A	N/A		N/A	N/A		N/A	N/A	

Retirement & pensions	Women	Men		Women	Men		Women	Men	
46. What is the age at which one can retire and receive full benefits?	55	55		60	60		65	65	
47. What is the age at which one can retire and receive partial benefits?	55	55		55	55		65	65	
48. What is the mandatory retirement age?	N/A	N/A		N/A	N/A		70	70	

Working hours and industry restrictions									
49. Can non-pregnant and non-nursing women do the same jobs as men?	No			Yes			Yes		
50. Can non-pregnant and non-nursing women engage in the following occupations in the same way as men?									
a. Mining	No			Yes			Yes		
b. Construction	Yes			Yes			Yes		
c. Metalwork	Yes			Yes			Yes		
d. Factory work	Yes			Yes			Yes		
e. Jobs requiring lifting weights above a threshold	Yes			Yes			Yes		
f. Jobs deemed hazardous	Yes			Yes			Yes		
g. Jobs deemed arduous	No			Yes			Yes		
h. Jobs deemed morally or socially inappropriate	Yes			Yes			Yes		
51. Can non-pregnant and non-nursing women work the same night hours as men?	No			Yes			Yes		

Workplace protections									
52. Does the law mandate equal remuneration for men and women for work of equal value?	No			Yes			No		
53. Are there laws mandating non-discrimination based on gender in hiring?	No			No			No		
54. Is it illegal for an employer to ask about family status during a job interview?	No			No			No		
55. Are there laws penalizing or preventing the dismissal of pregnant women?	Yes			Yes			Yes		
56. Must employers give employees an equivalent position when they return from maternity leave?	No			Yes			No		
57. Are employers required to provide break time for nursing mothers?	Yes			Yes			Yes		
58. Do employees with minor children have rights to a flexible/part time schedule?	No			No			No		

BUILDING CREDIT

59. What is the minimum loan amount covered in the private credit bureau or public credit registry (as a percentage of income per capita)?	0%			0%			0%		
60. Do microfinance institutions provide information to private credit bureaus or public credit registries?	Yes			Yes			Yes		
61. Do utility companies provide information to private credit bureaus or public credit registries?	No			Yes			Yes		
62. Do retailers provide information to private credit bureaus or public credit registries?	Yes			Yes			Yes		

PROVIDING INCENTIVES TO WORK

Childcare									
63. Are payments for childcare tax deductible?	No			No			No		
64. Is there public provision of childcare for children under the age of primary education?	No			Yes			Yes		
65. Does the law mandate free and compulsory primary education?	No			Yes			Yes		

Personal income tax	Women	Men		Women	Men		Women	Men	
66. Are there specific tax deductions or credits that are applicable only to men/women?	No	No		No	No		No	No	

Economy Tables

	PHILIPPINES		POLAND		PORTUGAL	
REGION	East Asia & Pacific		High income: OECD		High income: OECD	
INCOME	Lower middle income		High income		High income	
FEMALE POPULATION	48,253,375		19,933,894		5,428,403	
FEMALE LABOR FORCE PARTICIPATION	51%		59%		70%	

ACCESSING INSTITUTIONS

Constitutional rights

	PHILIPPINES		POLAND		PORTUGAL	
1. Is there a non-discrimination clause in the constitution?	No		Yes		Yes	
2. If there is a non-discrimination clause in the constitution, does it explicitly mention gender?	N/A		No		No	
3. Does the constitution guarantee equality before the law?	Yes		Yes		Yes	

	Customary	Personal	Customary	Personal	Customary	Personal
4. Is customary/personal law recognized as valid source of law under the constitution?	Yes	No	No	No	No	No
5. If so, is it invalid if it violates constitutional provisions on non-discrimination or equality?	Yes	N/A	N/A	N/A	N/A	N/A

Quotas

	PHILIPPINES	POLAND	PORTUGAL
6. What are the legal quotas for women on corporate boards?	N/A	N/A	N/A
7. What are the legal quotas for women in parliament?	N/A	N/A	N/A
8. What are the legal quotas for women in local government?	N/A	N/A	N/A

Rights of married and unmarried women

	Unmarried	Married	Unmarried	Married	Unmarried	Married
9. Can a woman apply for a passport in the same way as a man?	Yes	Yes	Yes	Yes	Yes	Yes
10. Can a woman apply for a national ID card in the same way as a man?	N/A	N/A	Yes	Yes	Yes	Yes
11. Can a woman travel outside the country in the same way as a man?	Yes	Yes	Yes	Yes	Yes	Yes
12. Can a woman travel outside her home in the same way as a man?	Yes	Yes	Yes	Yes	Yes	Yes
13. Can a woman get a job or pursue a trade or profession in the same way as a man?	Yes	Yes	Yes	Yes	Yes	Yes
14. Can a woman sign a contract in the same way as a man?	Yes	Yes	Yes	Yes	Yes	Yes
15. Can a woman register a business in the same way as a man?	Yes	Yes	Yes	Yes	Yes	Yes
16. Can a woman open a bank account in the same way as a man?	Yes	Yes	Yes	Yes	Yes	Yes
17. Can a woman choose where to live in the same way as a man?	Yes	Yes	Yes	Yes	Yes	Yes
18. Can a woman confer citizenship on her children in the same way as a man?	Yes	Yes	Yes	Yes	Yes	Yes
19. Can a woman be "head of household" or "head of family" in the same way as a man?	Yes	No	N/A	N/A	N/A	N/A
Number of inequalities in accessing institutions	0	1	0	0	0	0

Division of responsibility within marriage

	PHILIPPINES	POLAND	PORTUGAL
20. Can a woman convey citizenship to her non-national spouse in the same way as a man?	No	Yes	Yes
21. Are married women required by law to obey their husbands?	No	No	No
22. Do married couples jointly share legal responsibility for financially maintaining the family's expenses?	Yes	Yes	Yes

USING PROPERTY

Marital property regime

	PHILIPPINES	POLAND	PORTUGAL
23. What is the default marital property regime?	Full community of property	Partial community of property	Partial community of property
24. Who legally administers property during marriage?	Other	Both must agree	Both must agree

Protecting a wife's interests

	PHILIPPINES	POLAND	PORTUGAL
25. If it is the husband, does he need his wife's consent for major transactions	N/A	N/A	N/A
26. Are there special provisions governing the marital home?	No	No	No
27. Does the law provide for valuation of nonmonetary contributions during marriage?	Yes	Yes	Yes

Property rights

	Unmarried	Married	Unmarried	Married	Unmarried	Married
28. Do men and women have equal ownership rights to property?	Yes	No	Yes	Yes	Yes	Yes

Inheritance rights

	PHILIPPINES	POLAND	PORTUGAL
29. Do sons and daughters have equal inheritance rights to property?	Yes	Yes	Yes
30. Do female and male surviving spouses have equal inheritance rights to property?	Yes	Yes	Yes

GOING TO COURT

Equality of access

	PHILIPPINES	POLAND	PORTUGAL
31. Does the law recognize customary courts?	Yes	No	No
32. Does the law recognize personal law courts?	Yes	No	No
33. Does a woman's testimony carry the same evidentiary weight in court as a man's?	Yes	Yes	Yes

Efficiency of procedure

	PHILIPPINES	POLAND	PORTUGAL
34. Is there a small claims court or a fast track procedure for small claims?	Yes	Yes	Yes
35. If so, what is the maximum amount for a small claim (as a percentage of income per capita)?	97%	26%	32%

Judicial representation

	PHILIPPINES	POLAND	PORTUGAL
36. How many justices are on the constitutional court?	15	15	13
37. Of those, how many are women?	3	4	6
38. Is the Chief Justice a woman?	Yes	No	No

GETTING A JOB

Parental benefits	Maternity	Paternity	Parental	Maternity	Paternity	Parental	Maternity	Paternity	Parental
39. Does the law mandate paid or unpaid maternity/paternity/parental leave?	Yes	Yes	No	Yes	Yes	Yes	No	No	Yes
40. What is the mandatory minimum length of paid leave for maternity/paternity/parental leave (in calendar days)?	60	7	N/A	182	14	0	N/A	N/A	120
41. What is the mandatory minimum length of unpaid leave for maternity/paternity/parental leave (in calendar days)?	0	0	N/A	0	0	1278	N/A	N/A	0
42. Who pays maternity/paternity/parental benefits?	Gov.	Emp.	N/A	Gov.	Gov.	N/A	N/A	N/A	Gov.
43. What percentage of wages are paid during maternity/paternity/parental leave?	100%	100%	N/A	100%	100%	0%	N/A	N/A	100%

	Mother	Father		Mother	Father		Mother	Father	
44. Where **paid** parental leave exists, what is the minimum amount which only the mother/father must take (in calendar days)?	N/A	N/A		N/A	N/A		42	14	
45. Where **unpaid** parental leave exists, what is the minimum amount which only the mother/father must take (in calendar days)?	N/A	N/A		0	0		N/A	N/A	

Retirement & pensions	Women	Men		Women	Men		Women	Men	
46. What is the age at which one can retire and receive full benefits?	60	60		67	67		65	65	
47. What is the age at which one can retire and receive partial benefits?	60	60		62	65		65	65	
48. What is the mandatory retirement age?	65	65		N/A	N/A		N/A	N/A	

Working hours and industry restrictions	PHILIPPINES	POLAND	PORTUGAL
49. Can non-pregnant and non-nursing women do the same jobs as men?	Yes	No	Yes
50. Can non-pregnant and non-nursing women engage in the following occupations in the same way as men?			
a. Mining	Yes	No	Yes
b. Construction	Yes	Yes	Yes
c. Metalwork	Yes	Yes	Yes
d. Factory work	Yes	Yes	Yes
e. Jobs requiring lifting weights above a threshold	Yes	No	Yes
f. Jobs deemed hazardous	Yes	No	Yes
g. Jobs deemed arduous	Yes	No	Yes
h. Jobs deemed morally or socially inappropriate	Yes	Yes	Yes
51. Can non-pregnant and non-nursing women work the same night hours as men?	Yes	Yes	Yes

Workplace protections			
52. Does the law mandate equal remuneration for men and women for work of equal value?	Yes	Yes	Yes
53. Are there laws mandating non-discrimination based on gender in hiring?	No	No	Yes
54. Is it illegal for an employer to ask about family status during a job interview?	No	No	Yes
55. Are there laws penalizing or preventing the dismissal of pregnant women?	Yes	Yes	Yes
56. Must employers give employees an equivalent position when they return from maternity leave?	No	Yes	N/A
57. Are employers required to provide break time for nursing mothers?	Yes	Yes	Yes
58. Do employees with minor children have rights to a flexible/part time schedule?	No	No	Yes

BUILDING CREDIT

	PHILIPPINES	POLAND	PORTUGAL
59. What is the minimum loan amount covered in the private credit bureau or public credit registry (as a percentage of income per capita)?	0%	0%	0%
60. Do microfinance institutions provide information to private credit bureaus or public credit registries?	Yes	N/A	N/A
61. Do utility companies provide information to private credit bureaus or public credit registries?	No	No	No
62. Do retailers provide information to private credit bureaus or public credit registries?	No	No	No

PROVIDING INCENTIVES TO WORK

Childcare			
63. Are payments for childcare tax deductible?	No	No	Yes
64. Is there public provision of childcare for children under the age of primary education?	Yes	Yes	Yes
65. Does the law mandate free and compulsory primary education?	Yes	Yes	Yes

Personal income tax	Women	Men		Women	Men		Women	Men	
66. Are there specific tax deductions or credits that are applicable only to men/women?	No	Yes		No	No		No	No	

Economy Tables

	PUERTO RICO (U.S.)		ROMANIA		RUSSIAN FEDERATION	
REGION	Latin America & Caribbean		Europe & Central Asia		Europe & Central Asia	
INCOME	High income		Upper middle income		High income	
FEMALE POPULATION	1,904,022		10,936,646		77,287,344	
FEMALE LABOR FORCE PARTICIPATION	43%		57%		69%	

ACCESSING INSTITUTIONS

Constitutional rights

	PUERTO RICO		ROMANIA		RUSSIAN FEDERATION	
1. Is there a non-discrimination clause in the constitution?	Yes		Yes		No	
2. If there is a non-discrimination clause in the constitution, does it explicitly mention gender?	Yes		No		N/A	
3. Does the constitution guarantee equality before the law?	Yes		Yes		Yes	

	Customary	Personal	Customary	Personal	Customary	Personal
4. Is customary/personal law recognized as valid source of law under the constitution?	No	No	No	No	No	No
5. If so, is it invalid if it violates constitutional provisions on non-discrimination or equality?	N/A	N/A	N/A	No	N/A	N/A

Quotas

	PUERTO RICO	ROMANIA	RUSSIAN FEDERATION
6. What are the legal quotas for women on corporate boards?	N/A	N/A	N/A
7. What are the legal quotas for women in parliament?	N/A	N/A	N/A
8. What are the legal quotas for women in local government?	N/A	N/A	N/A

Rights of married and unmarried women

	Unmarried	Married	Unmarried	Married	Unmarried	Married
9. Can a woman apply for a passport in the same way as a man?	Yes	Yes	Yes	Yes	Yes	Yes
10. Can a woman apply for a national ID card in the same way as a man?	N/A	N/A	Yes	Yes	Yes	Yes
11. Can a woman travel outside the country in the same way as a man?	Yes	Yes	Yes	Yes	Yes	Yes
12. Can a woman travel outside her home in the same way as a man?	Yes	Yes	Yes	Yes	Yes	Yes
13. Can a woman get a job or pursue a trade or profession in the same way as a man?	Yes	Yes	Yes	Yes	Yes	Yes
14. Can a woman sign a contract in the same way as a man?	Yes	Yes	Yes	Yes	Yes	Yes
15. Can a woman register a business in the same way as a man?	Yes	Yes	Yes	Yes	Yes	Yes
16. Can a woman open a bank account in the same way as a man?	Yes	Yes	Yes	Yes	Yes	Yes
17. Can a woman choose where to live in the same way as a man?	Yes	Yes	Yes	Yes	Yes	Yes
18. Can a woman confer citizenship on her children in the same way as a man?	Yes	Yes	Yes	Yes	Yes	Yes
19. Can a woman be "head of household" or "head of family" in the same way as a man?	Yes	Yes	Yes	Yes	N/A	N/A
Number of inequalities in accessing institutions	0	0	0	0	0	0

Division of responsibility within marriage

	PUERTO RICO	ROMANIA	RUSSIAN FEDERATION
20. Can a woman convey citizenship to her non-national spouse in the same way as a man?	Yes	Yes	Yes
21. Are married women required by law to obey their husbands?	No	No	No
22. Do married couples jointly share legal responsibility for financially maintaining the family's expenses?	Yes	Yes	Yes

USING PROPERTY

Marital property regime

	PUERTO RICO	ROMANIA	RUSSIAN FEDERATION
23. What is the default marital property regime?	Partial community of property	Partial community of property	Partial community of property
24. Who legally administers property during marriage?	Both must agree	Both must agree	Both must agree

Protecting a wife's interests

	PUERTO RICO	ROMANIA	RUSSIAN FEDERATION
25. If it is the husband, does he need his wife's consent for major transactions	N/A	N/A	N/A
26. Are there special provisions governing the marital home?	No	Yes	No
27. Does the law provide for valuation of nonmonetary contributions during marriage?	Yes	Yes	Yes

Property rights

	Unmarried	Married	Unmarried	Married	Unmarried	Married
28. Do men and women have equal ownership rights to property?	Yes	Yes	Yes	Yes	Yes	Yes

Inheritance rights

	PUERTO RICO	ROMANIA	RUSSIAN FEDERATION
29. Do sons and daughters have equal inheritance rights to property?	Yes	Yes	Yes
30. Do female and male surviving spouses have equal inheritance rights to property?	Yes	Yes	Yes

GOING TO COURT

Equality of access

	PUERTO RICO	ROMANIA	RUSSIAN FEDERATION
31. Does the law recognize customary courts?	No	No	No
32. Does the law recognize personal law courts?	No	No	No
33. Does a woman's testimony carry the same evidentiary weight in court as a man's?	Yes	Yes	Yes

Efficiency of procedure

	PUERTO RICO	ROMANIA	RUSSIAN FEDERATION
34. Is there a small claims court or a fast track procedure for small claims?	Yes	Yes	Yes
35. If so, what is the maximum amount for a small claim (as a percentage of income per capita)?	85%	39%	14%

Judicial representation

	PUERTO RICO	ROMANIA	RUSSIAN FEDERATION
36. How many justices are on the constitutional court?	9	9	19
37. Of those, how many are women?	3	2	3
38. Is the Chief Justice a woman?	No	No	No

GETTING A JOB

Parental benefits	PUERTO RICO (U.S.)			ROMANIA			RUSSIAN FEDERATION		
	Maternity	Paternity	Parental	Maternity	Paternity	Parental	Maternity	Paternity	Parental
39. Does the law mandate paid or unpaid maternity/paternity/parental leave?	Yes	No	Yes	Yes	Yes	Yes	Yes	No	Yes
40. What is the mandatory minimum length of paid leave for maternity/paternity/parental leave (in calendar days)?	56	N/A	0	126	15	302	140	N/A	955
41. What is the mandatory minimum length of unpaid leave for maternity/paternity/parental leave (in calendar days)?	0	N/A	84	0	0	0	0	N/A	0
42. Who pays maternity/paternity/parental benefits?	Emp.	N/A	N/A	Gov.	Emp.	Gov.	Gov.	N/A	Gov.
43. What percentage of wages are paid during maternity/paternity/parental leave?	100%	N/A	0%	85%	100%	Partially paid	100%	N/A	Partially paid

	Mother	Father		Mother	Father		Mother	Father	
44. Where **paid** parental leave exists, what is the minimum amount which only the mother/father must take (in calendar days)?	N/A	N/A		0	0		0	0	
45. Where **unpaid** parental leave exists, what is the minimum amount which only the mother/father must take (in calendar days)?	0	0		N/A	N/A		N/A	N/A	

Retirement & pensions	Women	Men		Women	Men		Women	Men	
46. What is the age at which one can retire and receive full benefits?	67	67		63	65		55	60	
47. What is the age at which one can retire and receive partial benefits?	62	62		63	65		55	60	
48. What is the mandatory retirement age?	N/A	N/A		63	65		N/A	N/A	

Working hours and industry restrictions	PUERTO RICO (U.S.)	ROMANIA	RUSSIAN FEDERATION
49. Can non-pregnant and non-nursing women do the same jobs as men?	Yes	Yes	No
50. Can non-pregnant and non-nursing women engage in the following occupations in the same way as men?			
a. Mining	Yes	Yes	No
b. Construction	Yes	Yes	No
c. Metalwork	Yes	Yes	No
d. Factory work	Yes	Yes	No
e. Jobs requiring lifting weights above a threshold	Yes	Yes	No
f. Jobs deemed hazardous	Yes	Yes	No
g. Jobs deemed arduous	Yes	Yes	No
h. Jobs deemed morally or socially inappropriate	Yes	Yes	Yes
51. Can non-pregnant and non-nursing women work the same night hours as men?	Yes	Yes	Yes

Workplace protections	PUERTO RICO (U.S.)	ROMANIA	RUSSIAN FEDERATION
52. Does the law mandate equal remuneration for men and women for work of equal value?	No	No	No
53. Are there laws mandating non-discrimination based on gender in hiring?	Yes	Yes	No
54. Is it illegal for an employer to ask about family status during a job interview?	Yes	No	No
55. Are there laws penalizing or preventing the dismissal of pregnant women?	Yes	Yes	Yes
56. Must employers give employees an equivalent position when they return from maternity leave?	Yes	Yes	Yes
57. Are employers required to provide break time for nursing mothers?	Yes	Yes	Yes
58. Do employees with minor children have rights to a flexible/part time schedule?	No	No	Yes

BUILDING CREDIT

	PUERTO RICO (U.S.)	ROMANIA	RUSSIAN FEDERATION
59. What is the minimum loan amount covered in the private credit bureau or public credit registry (as a percentage of income per capita)?	0%	0%	0%
60. Do microfinance institutions provide information to private credit bureaus or public credit registries?	N/A	No	Yes
61. Do utility companies provide information to private credit bureaus or public credit registries?	Yes	No	No
62. Do retailers provide information to private credit bureaus or public credit registries?	Yes	No	No

PROVIDING INCENTIVES TO WORK

Childcare	PUERTO RICO (U.S.)	ROMANIA	RUSSIAN FEDERATION
63. Are payments for childcare tax deductible?	Yes	No	No
64. Is there public provision of childcare for children under the age of primary education?	No	Yes	Yes
65. Does the law mandate free and compulsory primary education?	Yes	Yes	Yes

Personal income tax	Women	Men		Women	Men		Women	Men	
66. Are there specific tax deductions or credits that are applicable only to men/women?	No	No		No	No		No	No	

Economy Tables

	RWANDA		SAUDI ARABIA		SENEGAL	
REGION	Sub-Saharan Africa		Middle East & North Africa		Sub-Saharan Africa	
INCOME	Low income		High income		Lower middle income	
FEMALE POPULATION	5,865,167		12,138,409		6,998,849	
FEMALE LABOR FORCE PARTICIPATION	88%		19%		67%	

ACCESSING INSTITUTIONS

Constitutional rights

	RWANDA		SAUDI ARABIA		SENEGAL	
1. Is there a non-discrimination clause in the constitution?	Yes		No		Yes	
2. If there is a non-discrimination clause in the constitution, does it explicitly mention gender?	Yes		N/A		No	
3. Does the constitution guarantee equality before the law?	Yes		No		Yes	

	Customary	Personal	Customary	Personal	Customary	Personal
4. Is customary/personal law recognized as valid source of law under the constitution?	Yes	No	No	Yes	No	No
5. If so, is it invalid if it violates constitutional provisions on non-discrimination or equality?	Yes	N/A	N/A	No	N/A	N/A

Quotas

	RWANDA	SAUDI ARABIA	SENEGAL
6. What are the legal quotas for women on corporate boards?	30%	N/A	N/A
7. What are the legal quotas for women in parliament?	30%	N/A	N/A
8. What are the legal quotas for women in local government?	30%	N/A	N/A

Rights of married and unmarried women

	Unmarried	Married	Unmarried	Married	Unmarried	Married
9. Can a woman apply for a passport in the same way as a man?	Yes	Yes	No	No	Yes	Yes
10. Can a woman apply for a national ID card in the same way as a man?	Yes	Yes	No	No	Yes	No
11. Can a woman travel outside the country in the same way as a man?	Yes	Yes	No	No	Yes	Yes
12. Can a woman travel outside her home in the same way as a man?	Yes	Yes	Yes	Yes	Yes	Yes
13. Can a woman get a job or pursue a trade or profession in the same way as a man?	Yes	Yes	Yes	Yes	Yes	Yes
14. Can a woman sign a contract in the same way as a man?	Yes	Yes	Yes	Yes	Yes	Yes
15. Can a woman register a business in the same way as a man?	Yes	Yes	Yes	Yes	Yes	Yes
16. Can a woman open a bank account in the same way as a man?	Yes	Yes	Yes	Yes	Yes	Yes
17. Can a woman choose where to live in the same way as a man?	Yes	No	Yes	No	Yes	No
18. Can a woman confer citizenship on her children in the same way as a man?	Yes	Yes	No	No	Yes	Yes
19. Can a woman be "head of household" or "head of family" in the same way as a man?	Yes	No	No	No	Yes	No
Number of inequalities in accessing institutions	0	2	5	6	0	3

Division of responsibility within marriage

	RWANDA	SAUDI ARABIA	SENEGAL
20. Can a woman convey citizenship to her non-national spouse in the same way as a man?	Yes	No	No
21. Are married women required by law to obey their husbands?	No	No	No
22. Do married couples jointly share legal responsibility for financially maintaining the family's expenses?	Yes	No	Yes

USING PROPERTY

Marital property regime

	RWANDA	SAUDI ARABIA	SENEGAL
23. What is the default marital property regime?	Full community of property.	Separation of property	Separation of property
24. Who legally administers property during marriage?	Both must agree	Original owner	Original owner

Protecting a wife's interests

	RWANDA	SAUDI ARABIA	SENEGAL
25. If it is the husband, does he need his wife's consent for major transactions	N/A	N/A	N/A
26. Are there special provisions governing the marital home?	No	No	No
27. Does the law provide for valuation of nonmonetary contributions during marriage?	Yes	No	No

Property rights

	Unmarried	Married	Unmarried	Married	Unmarried	Married
28. Do men and women have equal ownership rights to property?	Yes	Yes	Yes	Yes	Yes	Yes

Inheritance rights

	RWANDA	SAUDI ARABIA	SENEGAL
29. Do sons and daughters have equal inheritance rights to property?	Yes	No	No
30. Do female and male surviving spouses have equal inheritance rights to property?	Yes	No	No

GOING TO COURT

Equality of access

	RWANDA	SAUDI ARABIA	SENEGAL
31. Does the law recognize customary courts?	No	No	No
32. Does the law recognize personal law courts?	No	Yes	No
33. Does a woman's testimony carry the same evidentiary weight in court as a man's?	Yes	No	Yes

Efficiency of procedure

	RWANDA	SAUDI ARABIA	SENEGAL
34. Is there a small claims court or a fast track procedure for small claims?	No	Yes	No
35. If so, what is the maximum amount for a small claim (as a percentage of income per capita)?	N/A	13%	N/A

Judicial representation

	RWANDA	SAUDI ARABIA	SENEGAL
36. How many justices are on the constitutional court?	14	N/A	5
37. Of those, how many are women?	7	N/A	0
38. Is the Chief Justice a woman?	No	N/A	No

GETTING A JOB

Parental benefits	RWANDA			SAUDI ARABIA			SENEGAL		
	Maternity	Paternity	Parental	Maternity	Paternity	Parental	Maternity	Paternity	Parental
39. Does the law mandate paid or unpaid maternity/paternity/parental leave?	Yes	Yes	No	Yes	Yes	No	Yes	No	No
40. What is the mandatory minimum length of paid leave for maternity/paternity/parental leave (in calendar days)?	84	4	N/A	70	1	N/A	98	N/A	N/A
41. What is the mandatory minimum length of unpaid leave for maternity/paternity/parental leave (in calendar days)?	0	0	N/A	0	0	N/A	0	N/A	N/A
42. Who pays maternity/paternity/parental benefits?	Emp.	Emp.	N/A	Emp.	Emp.	N/A	Gov.	N/A	N/A
43. What percentage of wages are paid during maternity/paternity/parental leave?	60%	100%	N/A	100%	100%	N/A	100%	N/A	N/A

	Mother	Father		Mother	Father		Mother	Father	
44. Where **paid** parental leave exists, what is the minimum amount which only the mother/father must take (in calendar days)?	N/A	N/A		N/A	N/A		N/A	N/A	
45. Where **unpaid** parental leave exists, what is the minimum amount which only the mother/father must take (in calendar days)?	N/A	N/A		N/A	N/A		N/A	N/A	

Retirement & pensions	Women	Men		Women	Men		Women	Men	
46. What is the age at which one can retire and receive full benefits?	55	55		55	60		60	60	
47. What is the age at which one can retire and receive partial benefits?	55	55		55	50		53	53	
48. What is the mandatory retirement age?	65	65		55	60		60	60	

Working hours and industry restrictions	RWANDA	SAUDI ARABIA	SENEGAL
49. Can non-pregnant and non-nursing women do the same jobs as men?	Yes	No	No
50. Can non-pregnant and non-nursing women engage in the following occupations in the same way as men?			
a. Mining	Yes	No	No
b. Construction	Yes	No	No
c. Metalwork	Yes	No	No
d. Factory work	Yes	No	No
e. Jobs requiring lifting weights above a threshold	Yes	Yes	No
f. Jobs deemed hazardous	Yes	No	No
g. Jobs deemed arduous	Yes	Yes	No
h. Jobs deemed morally or socially inappropriate	Yes	Yes	No
51. Can non-pregnant and non-nursing women work the same night hours as men?	Yes	No	No

Workplace protections	RWANDA	SAUDI ARABIA	SENEGAL
52. Does the law mandate equal remuneration for men and women for work of equal value?	No	No	No
53. Are there laws mandating non-discrimination based on gender in hiring?	No	No	No
54. Is it illegal for an employer to ask about family status during a job interview?	No	No	No
55. Are there laws penalizing or preventing the dismissal of pregnant women?	Yes	No	No
56. Must employers give employees an equivalent position when they return from maternity leave?	Yes	No	Yes
57. Are employers required to provide break time for nursing mothers?	Yes	Yes	Yes
58. Do employees with minor children have rights to a flexible/part time schedule?	No	No	No

BUILDING CREDIT

	RWANDA	SAUDI ARABIA	SENEGAL
59. What is the minimum loan amount covered in the private credit bureau or public credit registry (as a percentage of income per capita)?	0%	0%	962%
60. Do microfinance institutions provide information to private credit bureaus or public credit registries?	Yes	N/A	No
61. Do utility companies provide information to private credit bureaus or public credit registries?	Yes	Yes	No
62. Do retailers provide information to private credit bureaus or public credit registries?	No	Yes	No

PROVIDING INCENTIVES TO WORK

Childcare	RWANDA	SAUDI ARABIA	SENEGAL
63. Are payments for childcare tax deductible?	No	No	No
64. Is there public provision of childcare for children under the age of primary education?	No	No	Yes
65. Does the law mandate free and compulsory primary education?	Yes	Yes	Yes

Personal income tax	Women	Men		Women	Men		Women	Men	
66. Are there specific tax deductions or credits that are applicable only to men/women?	No	No		No	No		No	No	

Economy Tables

	SERBIA	SIERRA LEONE	SINGAPORE
REGION	Europe & Central Asia	Sub-Saharan Africa	East Asia & Pacific
INCOME	Upper middle income	Low income	High income
FEMALE POPULATION	3,692,728	3,011,511	2,691,384
FEMALE LABOR FORCE PARTICIPATION	..	68%	63%

ACCESSING INSTITUTIONS

Constitutional rights

	SERBIA	SIERRA LEONE	SINGAPORE
1. Is there a non-discrimination clause in the constitution?	Yes	Yes	Yes
2. If there is a non-discrimination clause in the constitution, does it explicitly mention gender?	Yes	Yes	No
3. Does the constitution guarantee equality before the law?	Yes	Yes	Yes

	Customary	Personal	Customary	Personal	Customary	Personal
4. Is customary/personal law recognized as valid source of law under the constitution?	No	No	Yes	No	No	Yes
5. If so, is it invalid if it violates constitutional provisions on non-discrimination or equality?	N/A	N/A	No	N/A	No	No

Quotas

	SERBIA	SIERRA LEONE	SINGAPORE
6. What are the legal quotas for women on corporate boards?	N/A	N/A	N/A
7. What are the legal quotas for women in parliament?	N/A	N/A	N/A
8. What are the legal quotas for women in local government?	N/A	N/A	N/A

Rights of married and unmarried women

	Unmarried	Married	Unmarried	Married	Unmarried	Married
9. Can a woman apply for a passport in the same way as a man?	Yes	Yes	Yes	Yes	Yes	Yes
10. Can a woman apply for a national ID card in the same way as a man?	Yes	Yes	Yes	Yes	Yes	Yes
11. Can a woman travel outside the country in the same way as a man?	Yes	Yes	Yes	Yes	Yes	Yes
12. Can a woman travel outside her home in the same way as a man?	Yes	Yes	Yes	Yes	Yes	Yes
13. Can a woman get a job or pursue a trade or profession in the same way as a man?	Yes	Yes	Yes	Yes	Yes	Yes
14. Can a woman sign a contract in the same way as a man?	Yes	Yes	Yes	Yes	Yes	Yes
15. Can a woman register a business in the same way as a man?	Yes	Yes	Yes	Yes	Yes	Yes
16. Can a woman open a bank account in the same way as a man?	Yes	Yes	Yes	Yes	Yes	Yes
17. Can a woman choose where to live in the same way as a man?	Yes	Yes	Yes	Yes	Yes	Yes
18. Can a woman confer citizenship on her children in the same way as a man?	Yes	Yes	Yes	Yes	Yes	Yes
19. Can a woman be "head of household" or "head of family" in the same way as a man?	N/A	N/A	N/A	N/A	N/A	N/A
Number of inequalities in accessing institutions	0	0	0	0	0	0

Division of responsibility within marriage

	SERBIA	SIERRA LEONE	SINGAPORE
20. Can a woman convey citizenship to her non-national spouse in the same way as a man?	Yes	No	Yes
21. Are married women required by law to obey their husbands?	No	No	No
22. Do married couples jointly share legal responsibility for financially maintaining the family's expenses?	Yes	Yes	Yes

USING PROPERTY

Marital property regime

	SERBIA	SIERRA LEONE	SINGAPORE
23. What is the default marital property regime?	Partial community of property	Separation of property	Other
24. Who legally administers property during marriage?	Both must agree	Original owner	Original owner

Protecting a wife's interests

	SERBIA	SIERRA LEONE	SINGAPORE
25. If it is the husband, does he need his wife's consent for major transactions	N/A	N/A	N/A
26. Are there special provisions governing the marital home?	No	No	No
27. Does the law provide for valuation of nonmonetary contributions during marriage?	Yes	No	Yes

Property rights

	Unmarried	Married	Unmarried	Married	Unmarried	Married
28. Do men and women have equal ownership rights to property?	Yes	Yes	Yes	Yes	Yes	Yes

Inheritance rights

	SERBIA	SIERRA LEONE	SINGAPORE
29. Do sons and daughters have equal inheritance rights to property?	Yes	Yes	Yes
30. Do female and male surviving spouses have equal inheritance rights to property?	Yes	Yes	Yes

GOING TO COURT

Equality of access

	SERBIA	SIERRA LEONE	SINGAPORE
31. Does the law recognize customary courts?	No	Yes	No
32. Does the law recognize personal law courts?	No	No	Yes
33. Does a woman's testimony carry the same evidentiary weight in court as a man's?	Yes	Yes	Yes

Efficiency of procedure

	SERBIA	SIERRA LEONE	SINGAPORE
34. Is there a small claims court or a fast track procedure for small claims?	Yes	No	Yes
35. If so, what is the maximum amount for a small claim (as a percentage of income per capita)?	77%	N/A	16%

Judicial representation

	SERBIA	SIERRA LEONE	SINGAPORE
36. How many justices are on the constitutional court?	15	5	12
37. Of those, how many are women?	6	3	3
38. Is the Chief Justice a woman?	No	Yes	No

GETTING A JOB

Parental benefits	Maternity	Paternity	Parental	Maternity	Paternity	Parental	Maternity	Paternity	Parental
39. Does the law mandate paid or unpaid maternity/paternity/parental leave?	Yes	No	Yes	Yes	No	No	Yes	No	No
40. What is the mandatory minimum length of paid leave for maternity/ paternity/parental leave (in calendar days)?	135	N/A	230	84	N/A	N/A	112	N/A	N/A
41. What is the mandatory minimum length of unpaid leave for maternity/ paternity/parental leave (in calendar days)?	0	N/A	0	0	N/A	N/A	0	N/A	N/A
42. Who pays maternity/paternity/parental benefits?	Gov.	N/A	Gov.	Emp.	N/A	N/A	Gov.	N/A	N/A
43. What percentage of wages are paid during maternity/paternity/parental leave?	108%	N/A	100%	100%	N/A	N/A	100%	N/A	N/A

	Mother	Father		Mother	Father		Mother	Father	
44. Where **paid** parental leave exists, what is the minimum amount which only the mother/father must take (in calendar days)?	0	0		N/A	N/A		N/A	N/A	
45. Where **unpaid** parental leave exists, what is the minimum amount which only the mother/father must take (in calendar days)?	N/A	N/A		N/A	N/A		N/A	N/A	

Retirement & pensions	Women	Men		Women	Men		Women	Men	
46. What is the age at which one can retire and receive full benefits?	60	65		60	60		62	62	
47. What is the age at which one can retire and receive partial benefits?	60	65		55	55		62	62	
48. What is the mandatory retirement age?	65	65		N/A	N/A		67	67	

Working hours and industry restrictions									
49. Can non-pregnant and non-nursing women do the same jobs as men?	Yes			No			Yes		
50. Can non-pregnant and non-nursing women engage in the following occupations in the same way as men?									
a. Mining	Yes			No			Yes		
b. Construction	Yes			Yes			Yes		
c. Metalwork	Yes			Yes			Yes		
d. Factory work	Yes			Yes			Yes		
e. Jobs requiring lifting weights above a threshold	Yes			Yes			Yes		
f. Jobs deemed hazardous	Yes			Yes			Yes		
g. Jobs deemed arduous	Yes			Yes			Yes		
h. Jobs deemed morally or socially inappropriate	Yes			Yes			Yes		
51. Can non-pregnant and non-nursing women work the same night hours as men?	Yes			No			Yes		

Workplace protections									
52. Does the law mandate equal remuneration for men and women for work of equal value?	No			No			No		
53. Are there laws mandating non-discrimination based on gender in hiring?	Yes			No			No		
54. Is it illegal for an employer to ask about family status during a job interview?	No			No			No		
55. Are there laws penalizing or preventing the dismissal of pregnant women?	Yes			No			Yes		
56. Must employers give employees an equivalent position when they return from maternity leave?	No			No			No		
57. Are employers required to provide break time for nursing mothers?	No			No			No		
58. Do employees with minor children have rights to a flexible/part time schedule?	No			No			No		

BUILDING CREDIT

59. What is the minimum loan amount covered in the private credit bureau or public credit registry (as a percentage of income per capita)?	0%			0%			0%		
60. Do microfinance institutions provide information to private credit bureaus or public credit registries?	No			No			N/A		
61. Do utility companies provide information to private credit bureaus or public credit registries?	No			No			No		
62. Do retailers provide information to private credit bureaus or public credit registries?	No			No			No		

PROVIDING INCENTIVES TO WORK

Childcare									
63. Are payments for childcare tax deductible?	No			No			No		
64. Is there public provision of childcare for children under the age of primary education?	Yes			Yes			Yes		
65. Does the law mandate free and compulsory primary education?	Yes			Yes			Yes		

Personal income tax	Women	Men		Women	Men		Women	Men	
66. Are there specific tax deductions or credits that are applicable only to men/women?	No	No		No	No		Yes	No	

Economy Tables

	SLOVAK REPUBLIC		SLOVENIA		SOUTH AFRICA	
REGION	High income: OECD		High income: OECD		Sub-Saharan Africa	
INCOME	High income		High income		Upper middle income	
FEMALE POPULATION	2,779,386		1,035,245		26,356,891	
FEMALE LABOR FORCE PARTICIPATION	62%		67%		48%	

ACCESSING INSTITUTIONS

Constitutional rights

	SLOVAK REPUBLIC		SLOVENIA		SOUTH AFRICA	
1. Is there a non-discrimination clause in the constitution?	Yes		No		Yes	
2. If there is a non-discrimination clause in the constitution, does it explicitly mention gender?	Yes		N/A		Yes	
3. Does the constitution guarantee equality before the law?	Yes		Yes		Yes	

	Customary	Personal	Customary	Personal	Customary	Personal
4. Is customary/personal law recognized as valid source of law under the constitution?	No	No	No	No	Yes	No
5. If so, is it invalid if it violates constitutional provisions on non-discrimination or equality?	N/A	N/A	N/A	N/A	Yes	Yes

Quotas

	SLOVAK REPUBLIC	SLOVENIA	SOUTH AFRICA
6. What are the legal quotas for women on corporate boards?	N/A	N/A	N/A
7. What are the legal quotas for women in parliament?	N/A	N/A	N/A
8. What are the legal quotas for women in local government?	N/A	N/A	N/A

Rights of married and unmarried women

	Unmarried	Married	Unmarried	Married	Unmarried	Married
9. Can a woman apply for a passport in the same way as a man?	Yes	Yes	Yes	Yes	Yes	Yes
10. Can a woman apply for a national ID card in the same way as a man?	Yes	Yes	Yes	Yes	Yes	Yes
11. Can a woman travel outside the country in the same way as a man?	Yes	Yes	Yes	Yes	Yes	Yes
12. Can a woman travel outside her home in the same way as a man?	Yes	Yes	Yes	Yes	Yes	Yes
13. Can a woman get a job or pursue a trade or profession in the same way as a man?	Yes	Yes	Yes	Yes	Yes	Yes
14. Can a woman sign a contract in the same way as a man?	Yes	Yes	Yes	Yes	Yes	Yes
15. Can a woman register a business in the same way as a man?	Yes	Yes	Yes	Yes	Yes	Yes
16. Can a woman open a bank account in the same way as a man?	Yes	Yes	Yes	Yes	Yes	Yes
17. Can a woman choose where to live in the same way as a man?	Yes	Yes	Yes	Yes	Yes	Yes
18. Can a woman confer citizenship on her children in the same way as a man?	Yes	Yes	Yes	Yes	Yes	Yes
19. Can a woman be "head of household" or "head of family" in the same way as a man?	N/A	N/A	N/A	N/A	N/A	N/A
Number of inequalities in accessing institutions	0	0	0	0	0	0

Division of responsibility within marriage

	SLOVAK REPUBLIC	SLOVENIA	SOUTH AFRICA
20. Can a woman convey citizenship to her non-national spouse in the same way as a man?	Yes	Yes	Yes
21. Are married women required by law to obey their husbands?	No	No	No
22. Do married couples jointly share legal responsibility for financially maintaining the family's expenses?	Yes	Yes	Yes

USING PROPERTY

Marital property regime

	SLOVAK REPUBLIC	SLOVENIA	SOUTH AFRICA
23. What is the default marital property regime?	Partial community of property	Partial community of property	Full community of property
24. Who legally administers property during marriage?	Both must agree	Both must agree	Both must agree

Protecting a wife's interests

	SLOVAK REPUBLIC	SLOVENIA	SOUTH AFRICA
25. If it is the husband, does he need his wife's consent for major transactions	N/A	N/A	N/A
26. Are there special provisions governing the marital home?	No	No	No
27. Does the law provide for valuation of nonmonetary contributions during marriage?	Yes	Yes	Yes

Property rights	Unmarried	Married	Unmarried	Married	Unmarried	Married
28. Do men and women have equal ownership rights to property?	Yes	Yes	Yes	Yes	Yes	Yes

Inheritance rights

	SLOVAK REPUBLIC	SLOVENIA	SOUTH AFRICA
29. Do sons and daughters have equal inheritance rights to property?	Yes	Yes	Yes
30. Do female and male surviving spouses have equal inheritance rights to property?	Yes	Yes	Yes

GOING TO COURT

Equality of access

	SLOVAK REPUBLIC	SLOVENIA	SOUTH AFRICA
31. Does the law recognize customary courts?	No	No	Yes
32. Does the law recognize personal law courts?	No	No	No
33. Does a woman's testimony carry the same evidentiary weight in court as a man's?	Yes	Yes	Yes

Efficiency of procedure

	SLOVAK REPUBLIC	SLOVENIA	SOUTH AFRICA
34. Is there a small claims court or a fast track procedure for small claims?	Yes	Yes	Yes
35. If so, what is the maximum amount for a small claim (as a percentage of income per capita)?	9%	5%	12%

Judicial representation

	SLOVAK REPUBLIC	SLOVENIA	SOUTH AFRICA
36. How many justices are on the constitutional court?	13	9	11
37. Of those, how many are women?	3	5	2
38. Is the Chief Justice a woman?	Yes	No	No

GETTING A JOB

Parental benefits	Maternity	Paternity	Parental	Maternity	Paternity	Parental	Maternity	Paternity	Parental
39. Does the law mandate paid or unpaid maternity/paternity/parental leave?	Yes	No	Yes	Yes	Yes	Yes	Yes	Yes	No
40. What is the mandatory minimum length of paid leave for maternity/paternity/parental leave (in calendar days)?	238	N/A	1053	105	15	260	120	3	N/A
41. What is the mandatory minimum length of unpaid leave for maternity/paternity/parental leave (in calendar days)?	0	N/A	0	0	75	0	0	0	N/A
42. Who pays maternity/paternity/parental benefits?	Gov.	N/A	Gov.	Gov.	Gov.	Gov.	Gov.	Emp.	N/A
43. What percentage of wages are paid during maternity/paternity/parental leave?	65%	N/A	Partially paid	100%	100%	100%	38%	100%	N/A

	Mother	Father		Mother	Father		Mother	Father	
44. Where **paid** parental leave exists, what is the minimum amount which only the mother/father must take (in calendar days)?	0	0		0	0		N/A	N/A	
45. Where **unpaid** parental leave exists, what is the minimum amount which only the mother/father must take (in calendar days)?	N/A	N/A		N/A	N/A		N/A	N/A	

Retirement & pensions	Women	Men		Women	Men		Women	Men	
46. What is the age at which one can retire and receive full benefits?	62	62		65	65		N/A	N/A	
47. What is the age at which one can retire and receive partial benefits?	60	60		65	65		N/A	N/A	
48. What is the mandatory retirement age?	0	0		N/A	N/A		N/A	N/A	

Working hours and industry restrictions	SLOVAK REPUBLIC	SLOVENIA	SOUTH AFRICA
49. Can non-pregnant and non-nursing women do the same jobs as men?	Yes	No	Yes
50. Can non-pregnant and non-nursing women engage in the following occupations in the same way as men?			
a. Mining	Yes	No	Yes
b. Construction	Yes	Yes	Yes
c. Metalwork	Yes	Yes	Yes
d. Factory work	Yes	Yes	Yes
e. Jobs requiring lifting weights above a threshold	Yes	Yes	Yes
f. Jobs deemed hazardous	Yes	Yes	Yes
g. Jobs deemed arduous	Yes	Yes	Yes
h. Jobs deemed morally or socially inappropriate	Yes	Yes	Yes
51. Can non-pregnant and non-nursing women work the same night hours as men?	Yes	Yes	Yes

Workplace protections			
52. Does the law mandate equal remuneration for men and women for work of equal value?	No	No	No
53. Are there laws mandating non-discrimination based on gender in hiring?	Yes	Yes	No
54. Is it illegal for an employer to ask about family status during a job interview?	Yes	No	No
55. Are there laws penalizing or preventing the dismissal of pregnant women?	Yes	Yes	Yes
56. Must employers give employees an equivalent position when they return from maternity leave?	Yes	No	No
57. Are employers required to provide break time for nursing mothers?	Yes	Yes	No
58. Do employees with minor children have rights to a flexible/part time schedule?	Yes	Yes	No

BUILDING CREDIT

	SLOVAK REPUBLIC	SLOVENIA	SOUTH AFRICA
59. What is the minimum loan amount covered in the private credit bureau or public credit registry (as a percentage of income per capita)?	0%	0%	0%
60. Do microfinance institutions provide information to private credit bureaus or public credit registries?	N/A	N/A	Yes
61. Do utility companies provide information to private credit bureaus or public credit registries?	No	No	Yes
62. Do retailers provide information to private credit bureaus or public credit registries?	No	No	Yes

PROVIDING INCENTIVES TO WORK

Childcare			
63. Are payments for childcare tax deductible?	No	No	No
64. Is there public provision of childcare for children under the age of primary education?	Yes	Yes	No
65. Does the law mandate free and compulsory primary education?	Yes	Yes	No

Personal income tax	Women	Men		Women	Men		Women	Men	
66. Are there specific tax deductions or credits that are applicable only to men/women?	No	No		No	No		No	No	

Economy Tables

	SPAIN	SRI LANKA	SUDAN
REGION	High income: OECD	South Asia	Sub-Saharan Africa
INCOME	High income	Lower middle income	Lower middle income
FEMALE POPULATION	23,385,893	10,382,591	18,534,408
FEMALE LABOR FORCE PARTICIPATION	66%	38%	32%

ACCESSING INSTITUTIONS

Constitutional rights

	SPAIN		SRI LANKA		SUDAN	
1. Is there a non-discrimination clause in the constitution?	Yes		Yes		Yes	
2. If there is a non-discrimination clause in the constitution, does it explicitly mention gender?	Yes		Yes		Yes	
3. Does the constitution guarantee equality before the law?	Yes		Yes		Yes	

	Customary	Personal	Customary	Personal	Customary	Personal
4. Is customary/personal law recognized as valid source of law under the constitution?	No	No	Yes	Yes	No	Yes
5. If so, is it invalid if it violates constitutional provisions on non-discrimination or equality?	N/A	N/A	No	No	N/A	Yes

Quotas

	SPAIN	SRI LANKA	SUDAN
6. What are the legal quotas for women on corporate boards?	N/A	N/A	N/A
7. What are the legal quotas for women in parliament?	N/A	N/A	N/A
8. What are the legal quotas for women in local government?	N/A	N/A	N/A

Rights of married and unmarried women

	Unmarried	Married	Unmarried	Married	Unmarried	Married
9. Can a woman apply for a passport in the same way as a man?	Yes	Yes	Yes	Yes	Yes	No
10. Can a woman apply for a national ID card in the same way as a man?	Yes	Yes	Yes	Yes	Yes	Yes
11. Can a woman travel outside the country in the same way as a man?	Yes	Yes	Yes	Yes	No	No
12. Can a woman travel outside her home in the same way as a man?	Yes	Yes	Yes	Yes	Yes	No
13. Can a woman get a job or pursue a trade or profession in the same way as a man?	Yes	Yes	Yes	Yes	Yes	No
14. Can a woman sign a contract in the same way as a man?	Yes	Yes	Yes	Yes	Yes	Yes
15. Can a woman register a business in the same way as a man?	Yes	Yes	Yes	Yes	Yes	Yes
16. Can a woman open a bank account in the same way as a man?	Yes	Yes	Yes	Yes	Yes	Yes
17. Can a woman choose where to live in the same way as a man?	Yes	Yes	Yes	Yes	Yes	No
18. Can a woman confer citizenship on her children in the same way as a man?	Yes	Yes	Yes	Yes	No	No
19. Can a woman be "head of household" or "head of family" in the same way as a man?	N/A	N/A	N/A	N/A	No	No
Number of inequalities in accessing institutions	0	0	0	0	3	7

Division of responsibility within marriage

	SPAIN	SRI LANKA	SUDAN
20. Can a woman convey citizenship to her non-national spouse in the same way as a man?	Yes	Yes	No
21. Are married women required by law to obey their husbands?	No	No	Yes
22. Do married couples jointly share legal responsibility for financially maintaining the family's expenses?	Yes	Yes	No

USING PROPERTY

Marital property regime

	SPAIN	SRI LANKA	SUDAN
23. What is the default marital property regime?	Partial community of property	Separation of property	Separation of property
24. Who legally administers property during marriage?	Both must agree	Original owner	Original owner

Protecting a wife's interests

	SPAIN	SRI LANKA	SUDAN
25. If it is the husband, does he need his wife's consent for major transactions	N/A	N/A	N/A
26. Are there special provisions governing the marital home?	Yes	No	No
27. Does the law provide for valuation of nonmonetary contributions during marriage?	Yes	No	No

Property rights

	Unmarried	Married	Unmarried	Married	Unmarried	Married
28. Do men and women have equal ownership rights to property?	Yes	Yes	Yes	Yes	Yes	Yes

Inheritance rights

	SPAIN	SRI LANKA	SUDAN
29. Do sons and daughters have equal inheritance rights to property?	Yes	Yes	No
30. Do female and male surviving spouses have equal inheritance rights to property?	Yes	Yes	No

GOING TO COURT

Equality of access

	SPAIN	SRI LANKA	SUDAN
31. Does the law recognize customary courts?	Yes	No	No
32. Does the law recognize personal law courts?	No	Yes	Yes
33. Does a woman's testimony carry the same evidentiary weight in court as a man's?	Yes	Yes	No

Efficiency of procedure

	SPAIN	SRI LANKA	SUDAN
34. Is there a small claims court or a fast track procedure for small claims?	Yes	No	No
35. If so, what is the maximum amount for a small claim (as a percentage of income per capita)?	26%	N/A	N/A

Judicial representation

	SPAIN	SRI LANKA	SUDAN
36. How many justices are on the constitutional court?	12	11	9
37. Of those, how many are women?	2	3	1
38. Is the Chief Justice a woman?	No	No	No

GETTING A JOB

Parental benefits	Maternity	Paternity	Parental	Maternity	Paternity	Parental	Maternity	Paternity	Parental
39. Does the law mandate paid or unpaid maternity/paternity/parental leave?	Yes	Yes	Yes	Yes	No	No	Yes	No	No
40. What is the mandatory minimum length of paid leave for maternity/paternity/parental leave (in calendar days)?	112	13	0	84	N/A	N/A	56	N/A	N/A
41. What is the mandatory minimum length of unpaid leave for maternity/paternity/parental leave (in calendar days)?	0	0	1095	0	N/A	N/A	0	N/A	N/A
42. Who pays maternity/paternity/parental benefits?	Gov.	Gov.	N/A	Emp.	N/A	N/A	Emp.	N/A	N/A
43. What percentage of wages are paid during maternity/paternity/parental leave?	100%	100%	0%	100%	N/A	N/A	100%	N/A	N/A

	Mother	Father		Mother	Father		Mother	Father	
44. Where **paid** parental leave exists, what is the minimum amount which only the mother/father must take (in calendar days)?	N/A	N/A		N/A	N/A		N/A	N/A	
45. Where **unpaid** parental leave exists, what is the minimum amount which only the mother/father must take (in calendar days)?	0	0		N/A	N/A		N/A	N/A	

Retirement & pensions	Women	Men		Women	Men		Women	Men	
46. What is the age at which one can retire and receive full benefits?	65	65		50	55		60	60	
47. What is the age at which one can retire and receive partial benefits?	65	65		50	55		50	50	
48. What is the mandatory retirement age?	N/A	N/A		N/A	N/A		N/A	N/A	

Working hours and industry restrictions			
49. Can non-pregnant and non-nursing women do the same jobs as men?	Yes	No	No
50. Can non-pregnant and non-nursing women engage in the following occupations in the same way as men?			
a. Mining	Yes	No	No
b. Construction	Yes	Yes	Yes
c. Metalwork	Yes	Yes	Yes
d. Factory work	Yes	Yes	Yes
e. Jobs requiring lifting weights above a threshold	Yes	Yes	No
f. Jobs deemed hazardous	Yes	Yes	No
g. Jobs deemed arduous	Yes	Yes	No
h. Jobs deemed morally or socially inappropriate	Yes	Yes	Yes
51. Can non-pregnant and non-nursing women work the same night hours as men?	Yes	Yes	No

Workplace protections			
52. Does the law mandate equal remuneration for men and women for work of equal value?	Yes	No	No
53. Are there laws mandating non-discrimination based on gender in hiring?	Yes	No	No
54. Is it illegal for an employer to ask about family status during a job interview?	Yes	No	No
55. Are there laws penalizing or preventing the dismissal of pregnant women?	Yes	Yes	Yes
56. Must employers give employees an equivalent position when they return from maternity leave?	Yes	No	No
57. Are employers required to provide break time for nursing mothers?	Yes	Yes	Yes
58. Do employees with minor children have rights to a flexible/part time schedule?	Yes	No	No

BUILDING CREDIT

59. What is the minimum loan amount covered in the private credit bureau or public credit registry (as a percentage of income per capita)?	0%	0%	N/A
60. Do microfinance institutions provide information to private credit bureaus or public credit registries?	N/A	Yes	N/A
61. Do utility companies provide information to private credit bureaus or public credit registries?	No	No	N/A
62. Do retailers provide information to private credit bureaus or public credit registries?	Yes	No	N/A

PROVIDING INCENTIVES TO WORK

Childcare			
63. Are payments for childcare tax deductible?	No	No	No
64. Is there public provision of childcare for children under the age of primary education?	Yes	No	No
65. Does the law mandate free and compulsory primary education?	Yes	Yes	Yes

Personal income tax	Women	Men		Women	Men		Women	Men	
66. Are there specific tax deductions or credits that are applicable only to men/women?	Yes	No		No	No		No	No	

Economy Tables

	SWEDEN		SWITZERLAND		SYRIAN ARAB REPUBLIC	
REGION	High income: OECD		High income: OECD		Middle East & North Africa	
INCOME	High income		High income		Lower middle income	
FEMALE POPULATION	4,774,327		4,055,247		10,985,664	
FEMALE LABOR FORCE PARTICIPATION	77%		76%		14%	

ACCESSING INSTITUTIONS

Constitutional rights

	SWEDEN		SWITZERLAND		SYRIAN ARAB REPUBLIC	
1. Is there a non-discrimination clause in the constitution?	No		Yes		Yes	
2. If there is a non-discrimination clause in the constitution, does it explicitly mention gender?	N/A		Yes		Yes	
3. Does the constitution guarantee equality before the law?	Yes		Yes		Yes	

	Customary	Personal	Customary	Personal	Customary	Personal
4. Is customary/personal law recognized as valid source of law under the constitution?	No	No	No	No	No	Yes
5. If so, is it invalid if it violates constitutional provisions on non-discrimination or equality?	N/A	N/A	N/A	N/A	N/A	No

Quotas

	SWEDEN	SWITZERLAND	SYRIAN ARAB REPUBLIC
6. What are the legal quotas for women on corporate boards?	N/A	N/A	N/A
7. What are the legal quotas for women in parliament?	N/A	N/A	N/A
8. What are the legal quotas for women in local government?	N/A	N/A	N/A

Rights of married and unmarried women

	Unmarried	Married	Unmarried	Married	Unmarried	Married
9. Can a woman apply for a passport in the same way as a man?	Yes	Yes	Yes	Yes	Yes	Yes
10. Can a woman apply for a national ID card in the same way as a man?	Yes	Yes	Yes	Yes	Yes	Yes
11. Can a woman travel outside the country in the same way as a man?	Yes	Yes	Yes	Yes	Yes	No
12. Can a woman travel outside her home in the same way as a man?	Yes	Yes	Yes	Yes	Yes	No
13. Can a woman get a job or pursue a trade or profession in the same way as a man?	Yes	Yes	Yes	Yes	Yes	No
14. Can a woman sign a contract in the same way as a man?	Yes	Yes	Yes	Yes	Yes	Yes
15. Can a woman register a business in the same way as a man?	Yes	Yes	Yes	Yes	Yes	Yes
16. Can a woman open a bank account in the same way as a man?	Yes	Yes	Yes	Yes	Yes	Yes
17. Can a woman choose where to live in the same way as a man?	Yes	Yes	Yes	Yes	Yes	No
18. Can a woman confer citizenship on her children in the same way as a man?	Yes	Yes	Yes	Yes	No	No
19. Can a woman be "head of household" or "head of family" in the same way as a man?	N/A	N/A	N/A	N/A	N/A	N/A
Number of inequalities in accessing institutions	0	0	0	0	1	5

Division of responsibility within marriage

	SWEDEN	SWITZERLAND	SYRIAN ARAB REPUBLIC
20. Can a woman convey citizenship to her non-national spouse in the same way as a man?	Yes	Yes	No
21. Are married women required by law to obey their husbands?	No	No	No
22. Do married couples jointly share legal responsibility for financially maintaining the family's expenses?	Yes	Yes	No

USING PROPERTY

Marital property regime

	SWEDEN	SWITZERLAND	SYRIAN ARAB REPUBLIC
23. What is the default marital property regime?	Deferred community of property	Deferred community of property	Separation of property
24. Who legally administers property during marriage?	Original owner	Original owner	Original owner

Protecting a wife's interests

	SWEDEN	SWITZERLAND	SYRIAN ARAB REPUBLIC
25. If it is the husband, does he need his wife's consent for major transactions	N/A	N/A	N/A
26. Are there special provisions governing the marital home?	Yes	No	No
27. Does the law provide for valuation of nonmonetary contributions during marriage?	Yes	Yes	No

Property rights

	Unmarried	Married	Unmarried	Married	Unmarried	Married
28. Do men and women have equal ownership rights to property?	Yes	Yes	Yes	Yes	Yes	Yes

Inheritance rights

	SWEDEN	SWITZERLAND	SYRIAN ARAB REPUBLIC
29. Do sons and daughters have equal inheritance rights to property?	Yes	Yes	No
30. Do female and male surviving spouses have equal inheritance rights to property?	Yes	Yes	No

GOING TO COURT

Equality of access

	SWEDEN	SWITZERLAND	SYRIAN ARAB REPUBLIC
31. Does the law recognize customary courts?	No	No	No
32. Does the law recognize personal law courts?	No	No	Yes
33. Does a woman's testimony carry the same evidentiary weight in court as a man's?	Yes	Yes	No

Efficiency of procedure

	SWEDEN	SWITZERLAND	SYRIAN ARAB REPUBLIC
34. Is there a small claims court or a fast track procedure for small claims?	Yes	Yes	Yes
35. If so, what is the maximum amount for a small claim (as a percentage of income per capita)?	6%	39%	8%

Judicial representation

	SWEDEN	SWITZERLAND	SYRIAN ARAB REPUBLIC
36. How many justices are on the constitutional court?	N/A	N/A	7
37. Of those, how many are women?	N/A	N/A	1
38. Is the Chief Justice a woman?	N/A	N/A	No

GETTING A JOB

Parental benefits	SWEDEN			SWITZERLAND			SYRIAN ARAB REPUBLIC		
	Maternity	Paternity	Parental	Maternity	Paternity	Parental	Maternity	Paternity	Parental
39. Does the law mandate paid or unpaid maternity/paternity/parental leave?	Yes	Yes	Yes	Yes	No	No	Yes	No	No
40. What is the mandatory minimum length of paid leave for maternity/paternity/parental leave (in calendar days)?	0	10	480	98	N/A	N/A	120	N/A	N/A
41. What is the mandatory minimum length of unpaid leave for maternity/paternity/parental leave (in calendar days)?	98	0	491	14	N/A	N/A	30	N/A	N/A
42. Who pays maternity/paternity/parental benefits?	N/A	Gov.	Gov.	Gov.	N/A	N/A	Emp.	N/A	N/A
43. What percentage of wages are paid during maternity/paternity/parental leave?	0%	80%	Partially paid	80%	N/A	N/A	100%	N/A	N/A

	Mother	Father		Mother	Father		Mother	Father	
44. Where **paid** parental leave exists, what is the minimum amount which only the mother/father must take (in calendar days)?	60	60		N/A	N/A		N/A	N/A	
45. Where **unpaid** parental leave exists, what is the minimum amount which only the mother/father must take (in calendar days)?	0	0		N/A	N/A		N/A	N/A	

Retirement & pensions	Women	Men		Women	Men		Women	Men	
46. What is the age at which one can retire and receive full benefits?	65	65		64	65		60	60	
47. What is the age at which one can retire and receive partial benefits?	61	61		62	63		60	60	
48. What is the mandatory retirement age?	67	67		69	70		65	65	

Working hours and industry restrictions

	SWEDEN	SWITZERLAND	SYRIAN ARAB REPUBLIC
49. Can non-pregnant and non-nursing women do the same jobs as men?	Yes	Yes	No
50. Can non-pregnant and non-nursing women engage in the following occupations in the same way as men?			
a. Mining	Yes	Yes	No
b. Construction	Yes	Yes	No
c. Metalwork	Yes	Yes	No
d. Factory work	Yes	Yes	No
e. Jobs requiring lifting weights above a threshold	Yes	Yes	No
f. Jobs deemed hazardous	Yes	Yes	No
g. Jobs deemed arduous	Yes	Yes	No
h. Jobs deemed morally or socially inappropriate	Yes	Yes	No
51. Can non-pregnant and non-nursing women work the same night hours as men?	Yes	Yes	No

Workplace protections

	SWEDEN	SWITZERLAND	SYRIAN ARAB REPUBLIC
52. Does the law mandate equal remuneration for men and women for work of equal value?	No	No	No
53. Are there laws mandating non-discrimination based on gender in hiring?	Yes	Yes	No
54. Is it illegal for an employer to ask about family status during a job interview?	No	No	No
55. Are there laws penalizing or preventing the dismissal of pregnant women?	Yes	Yes	No
56. Must employers give employees an equivalent position when they return from maternity leave?	Yes	No	No
57. Are employers required to provide break time for nursing mothers?	Yes	Yes	Yes
58. Do employees with minor children have rights to a flexible/part time schedule?	Yes	No	No

BUILDING CREDIT

	SWEDEN	SWITZERLAND	SYRIAN ARAB REPUBLIC
59. What is the minimum loan amount covered in the private credit bureau or public credit registry (as a percentage of income per capita)?	0%	1%	0%
60. Do microfinance institutions provide information to private credit bureaus or public credit registries?	N/A	N/A	Yes
61. Do utility companies provide information to private credit bureaus or public credit registries?	No	No	No
62. Do retailers provide information to private credit bureaus or public credit registries?	No	Yes	No

PROVIDING INCENTIVES TO WORK

Childcare

	SWEDEN	SWITZERLAND	SYRIAN ARAB REPUBLIC
63. Are payments for childcare tax deductible?	No	No	No
64. Is there public provision of childcare for children under the age of primary education?	Yes	Yes	Yes
65. Does the law mandate free and compulsory primary education?	Yes	Yes	Yes

Personal income tax	Women	Men	Women	Men	Women	Men
66. Are there specific tax deductions or credits that are applicable only to men/women?	No	No	No	No	No	No

Economy Tables

	TAIWAN, CHINA	TAJIKISTAN	TANZANIA
REGION	East Asia & Pacific	Europe & Central Asia	Sub-Saharan Africa
INCOME	High income	Low income	Low income
FEMALE POPULATION	..	3,985,542	23,892,647
FEMALE LABOR FORCE PARTICIPATION	..	61%	90%

ACCESSING INSTITUTIONS

Constitutional rights

	TAIWAN, CHINA	TAJIKISTAN	TANZANIA
1. Is there a non-discrimination clause in the constitution?	No	No	Yes
2. If there is a non-discrimination clause in the constitution, does it explicitly mention gender?	N/A	N/A	Yes
3. Does the constitution guarantee equality before the law?	Yes	Yes	Yes

	Customary	Personal	Customary	Personal	Customary	Personal
4. Is customary/personal law recognized as valid source of law under the constitution?	No	No	No	No	No	No
5. If so, is it invalid if it violates constitutional provisions on non-discrimination or equality?	N/A	N/A	N/A	N/A	N/A	N/A

Quotas

	TAIWAN, CHINA	TAJIKISTAN	TANZANIA
6. What are the legal quotas for women on corporate boards?	N/A	N/A	N/A
7. What are the legal quotas for women in parliament?	10%	N/A	30%
8. What are the legal quotas for women in local government?	25%	N/A	N/A

Rights of married and unmarried women

	Unmarried	Married	Unmarried	Married	Unmarried	Married
9. Can a woman apply for a passport in the same way as a man?	Yes	Yes	Yes	Yes	Yes	Yes
10. Can a woman apply for a national ID card in the same way as a man?	Yes	Yes	Yes	Yes	N/A	N/A
11. Can a woman travel outside the country in the same way as a man?	Yes	Yes	Yes	Yes	Yes	Yes
12. Can a woman travel outside her home in the same way as a man?	Yes	Yes	Yes	Yes	Yes	Yes
13. Can a woman get a job or pursue a trade or profession in the same way as a man?	Yes	Yes	Yes	Yes	Yes	Yes
14. Can a woman sign a contract in the same way as a man?	Yes	Yes	Yes	Yes	Yes	Yes
15. Can a woman register a business in the same way as a man?	Yes	Yes	Yes	Yes	Yes	Yes
16. Can a woman open a bank account in the same way as a man?	Yes	Yes	Yes	Yes	Yes	Yes
17. Can a woman choose where to live in the same way as a man?	Yes	Yes	Yes	Yes	Yes	Yes
18. Can a woman confer citizenship on her children in the same way as a man?	Yes	Yes	Yes	Yes	Yes	Yes
19. Can a woman be "head of household" or "head of family" in the same way as a man?	Yes	Yes	N/A	N/A	N/A	N/A
Number of inequalities in accessing institutions	0	0	0	0	0	0

Division of responsibility within marriage

	TAIWAN, CHINA	TAJIKISTAN	TANZANIA
20. Can a woman convey citizenship to her non-national spouse in the same way as a man?	Yes	Yes	No
21. Are married women required by law to obey their husbands?	No	No	No
22. Do married couples jointly share legal responsibility for financially maintaining the family's expenses?	Yes	Yes	No

USING PROPERTY

Marital property regime

	TAIWAN, CHINA	TAJIKISTAN	TANZANIA
23. What is the default marital property regime?	Deferred community of property	Partial community of property	Separation of property
24. Who legally administers property during marriage?	Original owner	Both must agree	Original owner

Protecting a wife's interests

	TAIWAN, CHINA	TAJIKISTAN	TANZANIA
25. If it is the husband, does he need his wife's consent for major transactions	N/A	N/A	N/A
26. Are there special provisions governing the marital home?	No	No	Yes
27. Does the law provide for valuation of nonmonetary contributions during marriage?	Yes	Yes	Yes

Property rights

	Unmarried	Married	Unmarried	Married	Unmarried	Married
28. Do men and women have equal ownership rights to property?	Yes	Yes	Yes	Yes	Yes	Yes

Inheritance rights

	TAIWAN, CHINA	TAJIKISTAN	TANZANIA
29. Do sons and daughters have equal inheritance rights to property?	Yes	Yes	No
30. Do female and male surviving spouses have equal inheritance rights to property?	Yes	Yes	No

GOING TO COURT

Equality of access

	TAIWAN, CHINA	TAJIKISTAN	TANZANIA
31. Does the law recognize customary courts?	No	No	Yes
32. Does the law recognize personal law courts?	No	No	Yes
33. Does a woman's testimony carry the same evidentiary weight in court as a man's?	Yes	Yes	Yes

Efficiency of procedure

	TAIWAN, CHINA	TAJIKISTAN	TANZANIA
34. Is there a small claims court or a fast track procedure for small claims?	Yes	Yes	No
35. If so, what is the maximum amount for a small claim (as a percentage of income per capita)?	16%	9%	N/A

Judicial representation

	TAIWAN, CHINA	TAJIKISTAN	TANZANIA
36. How many justices are on the constitutional court?	15	7	15
37. Of those, how many are women?	2	1	4
38. Is the Chief Justice a woman?	No	No	No

GETTING A JOB

Parental benefits	Maternity	Paternity	Parental	Maternity	Paternity	Parental	Maternity	Paternity	Parental
39. Does the law mandate paid or unpaid maternity/paternity/parental leave?	Yes	Yes	Yes	Yes	No	Yes	Yes	Yes	No
40. What is the mandatory minimum length of paid leave for maternity/paternity/parental leave (in calendar days)?	56	3	180	140	N/A	477.5	84	3	N/A
41. What is the mandatory minimum length of unpaid leave for maternity/paternity/parental leave (in calendar days)?	0	0	0	0	N/A	547.5	0	0	N/A
42. Who pays maternity/paternity/parental benefits?	Emp.	Emp.	Gov.	Gov.	N/A	Gov.	Emp.	Emp.	N/A
43. What percentage of wages are paid during maternity/paternity/parental leave?	100%	100%	Partially paid	100%	N/A	Partially paid	100%	100%	N/A

	Mother	Father		Mother	Father		Mother	Father	
44. Where **paid** parental leave exists, what is the minimum amount which only the mother/father must take (in calendar days)?	0	0		0	0		N/A	N/A	
45. Where **unpaid** parental leave exists, what is the minimum amount which only the mother/father must take (in calendar days)?	N/A	N/A		0	0		N/A	N/A	

Retirement & pensions	Women	Men		Women	Men		Women	Men	
46. What is the age at which one can retire and receive full benefits?	65	65		58	63		60	60	
47. What is the age at which one can retire and receive partial benefits?	60	60		58	63		55	55	
48. What is the mandatory retirement age?	65	65		N/A	N/A		N/A	N/A	

Working hours and industry restrictions			
49. Can non-pregnant and non-nursing women do the same jobs as men?	No	No	Yes
50. Can non-pregnant and non-nursing women engage in the following occupations in the same way as men?			
a. Mining	No	No	Yes
b. Construction	Yes	No	Yes
c. Metalwork	Yes	No	Yes
d. Factory work	Yes	No	Yes
e. Jobs requiring lifting weights above a threshold	No	No	Yes
f. Jobs deemed hazardous	No	No	Yes
g. Jobs deemed arduous	Yes	No	Yes
h. Jobs deemed morally or socially inappropriate	Yes	Yes	Yes
51. Can non-pregnant and non-nursing women work the same night hours as men?	No	No	Yes

Workplace protections			
52. Does the law mandate equal remuneration for men and women for work of equal value?	Yes	Yes	Yes
53. Are there laws mandating non-discrimination based on gender in hiring?	Yes	Yes	Yes
54. Is it illegal for an employer to ask about family status during a job interview?	No	No	No
55. Are there laws penalizing or preventing the dismissal of pregnant women?	Yes	Yes	Yes
56. Must employers give employees an equivalent position when they return from maternity leave?	No	Yes	Yes
57. Are employers required to provide break time for nursing mothers?	Yes	Yes	Yes
58. Do employees with minor children have rights to a flexible/part time schedule?	Yes	Yes	No

BUILDING CREDIT

59. What is the minimum loan amount covered in the private credit bureau or public credit registry (as a percentage of income per capita)?	0%	0%	N/A
60. Do microfinance institutions provide information to private credit bureaus or public credit registries?	N/A	Yes	N/A
61. Do utility companies provide information to private credit bureaus or public credit registries?	No	No	N/A
62. Do retailers provide information to private credit bureaus or public credit registries?	No	No	N/A

PROVIDING INCENTIVES TO WORK

Childcare			
63. Are payments for childcare tax deductible?	No	No	No
64. Is there public provision of childcare for children under the age of primary education?	Yes	No	No
65. Does the law mandate free and compulsory primary education?	Yes	Yes	No

Personal income tax	Women	Men		Women	Men		Women	Men	
66. Are there specific tax deductions or credits that are applicable only to men/women?	No	No		No	No		No	No	

Economy Tables

	THAILAND	TOGO	TUNISIA
REGION	East Asia & Pacific	Sub-Saharan Africa	Middle East & North Africa
INCOME	Upper middle income	Low income	Upper middle income
FEMALE POPULATION	34,065,346	3,368,782	5,431,418
FEMALE LABOR FORCE PARTICIPATION	70%	82%	28%

ACCESSING INSTITUTIONS

Constitutional rights

	THAILAND	TOGO	TUNISIA
1. Is there a non-discrimination clause in the constitution?	Yes	No	No
2. If there is a non-discrimination clause in the constitution, does it explicitly mention gender?	Yes	N/A	N/A
3. Does the constitution guarantee equality before the law?	Yes	Yes	Yes

	Customary	Personal	Customary	Personal	Customary	Personal
4. Is customary/personal law recognized as valid source of law under the constitution?	No	No	Yes	No	No	No
5. If so, is it invalid if it violates constitutional provisions on non-discrimination or equality?	N/A	N/A	Yes	N/A	N/A	N/A

Quotas

	THAILAND	TOGO	TUNISIA
6. What are the legal quotas for women on corporate boards?	N/A	N/A	N/A
7. What are the legal quotas for women in parliament?	N/A	N/A	N/A
8. What are the legal quotas for women in local government?	N/A	N/A	N/A

Rights of married and unmarried women

	Unmarried	Married	Unmarried	Married	Unmarried	Married
9. Can a woman apply for a passport in the same way as a man?	Yes	Yes	Yes	Yes	Yes	Yes
10. Can a woman apply for a national ID card in the same way as a man?	Yes	Yes	Yes	No	Yes	Yes
11. Can a woman travel outside the country in the same way as a man?	Yes	Yes	Yes	Yes	Yes	Yes
12. Can a woman travel outside her home in the same way as a man?	Yes	Yes	Yes	Yes	Yes	Yes
13. Can a woman get a job or pursue a trade or profession in the same way as a man?	Yes	Yes	Yes	Yes	Yes	Yes
14. Can a woman sign a contract in the same way as a man?	Yes	Yes	Yes	Yes	Yes	Yes
15. Can a woman register a business in the same way as a man?	Yes	Yes	Yes	Yes	Yes	Yes
16. Can a woman open a bank account in the same way as a man?	Yes	Yes	Yes	Yes	Yes	Yes
17. Can a woman choose where to live in the same way as a man?	Yes	Yes	Yes	Yes	Yes	Yes
18. Can a woman confer citizenship on her children in the same way as a man?	Yes	Yes	Yes	Yes	Yes	Yes
19. Can a woman be "head of household" or "head of family" in the same way as a man?	N/A	N/A	Yes	No	Yes	No
Number of inequalities in accessing institutions	0	0	0	2	0	1

Division of responsibility within marriage

	THAILAND	TOGO	TUNISIA
20. Can a woman convey citizenship to her non-national spouse in the same way as a man?	No	No	No
21. Are married women required by law to obey their husbands?	No	No	No
22. Do married couples jointly share legal responsibility for financially maintaining the family's expenses?	Yes	Yes	Yes

USING PROPERTY

Marital property regime

	THAILAND	TOGO	TUNISIA
23. What is the default marital property regime?	Partial community of property	Separation of property	Separation of property
24. Who legally administers property during marriage?	Both must agree	Original owner	Original owner

Protecting a wife's interests

	THAILAND	TOGO	TUNISIA
25. If it is the husband, does he need his wife's consent for major transactions	N/A	N/A	N/A
26. Are there special provisions governing the marital home?	No	No	No
27. Does the law provide for valuation of nonmonetary contributions during marriage?	Yes	No	No

Property rights

	Unmarried	Married	Unmarried	Married	Unmarried	Married
28. Do men and women have equal ownership rights to property?	Yes	Yes	Yes	Yes	Yes	Yes

Inheritance rights

	THAILAND	TOGO	TUNISIA
29. Do sons and daughters have equal inheritance rights to property?	Yes	Yes	No
30. Do female and male surviving spouses have equal inheritance rights to property?	Yes	Yes	No

GOING TO COURT

Equality of access

	THAILAND	TOGO	TUNISIA
31. Does the law recognize customary courts?	No	No	No
32. Does the law recognize personal law courts?	No	No	No
33. Does a woman's testimony carry the same evidentiary weight in court as a man's?	Yes	Yes	Yes

Efficiency of procedure

	THAILAND	TOGO	TUNISIA
34. Is there a small claims court or a fast track procedure for small claims?	Yes	No	Yes
35. If so, what is the maximum amount for a small claim (as a percentage of income per capita)?	205%	N/A	120%

Judicial representation

	THAILAND	TOGO	TUNISIA
36. How many justices are on the constitutional court?	9	9	N/A
37. Of those, how many are women?	0	1	N/A
38. Is the Chief Justice a woman?	No	No	N/A

GETTING A JOB

Parental benefits

	Maternity	Paternity	Parental	Maternity	Paternity	Parental	Maternity	Paternity	Parental
39. Does the law mandate paid or unpaid maternity/paternity/parental leave?	Yes	No	No	Yes	Yes	No	Yes	Yes	No
40. What is the mandatory minimum length of paid leave for maternity/paternity/parental leave (in calendar days)?	45	N/A	N/A	98	2	N/A	30	1	N/A
41. What is the mandatory minimum length of unpaid leave for maternity/paternity/parental leave (in calendar days)?	0	N/A	N/A	0	0	N/A	0	0	N/A
42. Who pays maternity/paternity/parental benefits?	Emp. & Gov.	N/A	N/A	Emp. & Gov.	Emp.	N/A	Gov.	Gov.	N/A
43. What percentage of wages are paid during maternity/paternity/parental leave?	75%	N/A	N/A	100%	100%	N/A	67%	100%	N/A

	Mother	Father		Mother	Father		Mother	Father	
44. Where **paid** parental leave exists, what is the minimum amount which only the mother/father must take (in calendar days)?	N/A	N/A		N/A	N/A		N/A	N/A	
45. Where **unpaid** parental leave exists, what is the minimum amount which only the mother/father must take (in calendar days)?	N/A	N/A		N/A	N/A		N/A	N/A	

Retirement & pensions

	Women	Men		Women	Men		Women	Men	
46. What is the age at which one can retire and receive full benefits?	50	50		60	60		60	60	
47. What is the age at which one can retire and receive partial benefits?	50	50		60	60		55	55	
48. What is the mandatory retirement age?	N/A	N/A		N/A	N/A		N/A	N/A	

Working hours and industry restrictions

	THAILAND	TOGO	TUNISIA
49. Can non-pregnant and non-nursing women do the same jobs as men?	No	Yes	No
50. Can non-pregnant and non-nursing women engage in the following occupations in the same way as men?			
a. Mining	No	Yes	No
b. Construction	No	Yes	Yes
c. Metalwork	Yes	Yes	No
d. Factory work	Yes	Yes	Yes
e. Jobs requiring lifting weights above a threshold	Yes	Yes	Yes
f. Jobs deemed hazardous	No	Yes	Yes
g. Jobs deemed arduous	Yes	Yes	Yes
h. Jobs deemed morally or socially inappropriate	Yes	Yes	Yes
51. Can non-pregnant and non-nursing women work the same night hours as men?	Yes	Yes	No

Workplace protections

	THAILAND	TOGO	TUNISIA
52. Does the law mandate equal remuneration for men and women for work of equal value?	No	Yes	No
53. Are there laws mandating non-discrimination based on gender in hiring?	No	Yes	No
54. Is it illegal for an employer to ask about family status during a job interview?	No	No	No
55. Are there laws penalizing or preventing the dismissal of pregnant women?	Yes	Yes	Yes
56. Must employers give employees an equivalent position when they return from maternity leave?	No	Yes	No
57. Are employers required to provide break time for nursing mothers?	No	Yes	Yes
58. Do employees with minor children have rights to a flexible/part time schedule?	No	No	No

BUILDING CREDIT

	THAILAND	TOGO	TUNISIA
59. What is the minimum loan amount covered in the private credit bureau or public credit registry (as a percentage of income per capita)?	0%	1828%	0%
60. Do microfinance institutions provide information to private credit bureaus or public credit registries?	Yes	No	Yes
61. Do utility companies provide information to private credit bureaus or public credit registries?	No	No	No
62. Do retailers provide information to private credit bureaus or public credit registries?	No	No	No

PROVIDING INCENTIVES TO WORK

Childcare

	THAILAND	TOGO	TUNISIA
63. Are payments for childcare tax deductible?	No	No	No
64. Is there public provision of childcare for children under the age of primary education?	No	No	Yes
65. Does the law mandate free and compulsory primary education?	Yes	Yes	Yes

Personal income tax

	Women	Men		Women	Men		Women	Men	
66. Are there specific tax deductions or credits that are applicable only to men/women?	No	No		No	Yes		No	No	

Economy Tables

	TURKEY	UGANDA	UKRAINE
REGION	Europe & Central Asia	Sub-Saharan Africa	Europe & Central Asia
INCOME	Upper middle income	Low income	Lower middle income
FEMALE POPULATION	37,655,879	18,124,684	24,576,360
FEMALE LABOR FORCE PARTICIPATION	30%	77%	63%

ACCESSING INSTITUTIONS

Constitutional rights

	TURKEY	UGANDA	UKRAINE
1. Is there a non-discrimination clause in the constitution?	Yes	Yes	No
2. If there is a non-discrimination clause in the constitution, does it explicitly mention gender?	Yes	Yes	N/A
3. Does the constitution guarantee equality before the law?	Yes	Yes	Yes

	Customary	Personal	Customary	Personal	Customary	Personal
4. Is customary/personal law recognized as valid source of law under the constitution?	No	No	Yes	Yes	No	No
5. If so, is it invalid if it violates constitutional provisions on non-discrimination or equality?	N/A	N/A	Yes	Yes	N/A	N/A

Quotas

	TURKEY	UGANDA	UKRAINE
6. What are the legal quotas for women on corporate boards?	N/A	N/A	N/A
7. What are the legal quotas for women in parliament?	N/A	29%	N/A
8. What are the legal quotas for women in local government?	N/A	33%	N/A

Rights of married and unmarried women

	Unmarried	Married	Unmarried	Married	Unmarried	Married
9. Can a woman apply for a passport in the same way as a man?	Yes	Yes	Yes	No	Yes	Yes
10. Can a woman apply for a national ID card in the same way as a man?	Yes	Yes	N/A	N/A	Yes	Yes
11. Can a woman travel outside the country in the same way as a man?	Yes	Yes	Yes	Yes	Yes	Yes
12. Can a woman travel outside her home in the same way as a man?	Yes	Yes	Yes	Yes	Yes	Yes
13. Can a woman get a job or pursue a trade or profession in the same way as a man?	Yes	Yes	Yes	Yes	Yes	Yes
14. Can a woman sign a contract in the same way as a man?	Yes	Yes	Yes	Yes	Yes	Yes
15. Can a woman register a business in the same way as a man?	Yes	Yes	Yes	Yes	Yes	Yes
16. Can a woman open a bank account in the same way as a man?	Yes	Yes	Yes	Yes	Yes	Yes
17. Can a woman choose where to live in the same way as a man?	Yes	Yes	Yes	Yes	Yes	Yes
18. Can a woman confer citizenship on her children in the same way as a man?	Yes	Yes	Yes	Yes	Yes	Yes
19. Can a woman be "head of household" or "head of family" in the same way as a man?	N/A	N/A	N/A	N/A	N/A	N/A
Number of inequalities in accessing institutions	0	0	0	1	0	0

Division of responsibility within marriage

	TURKEY	UGANDA	UKRAINE
20. Can a woman convey citizenship to her non-national spouse in the same way as a man?	Yes	Yes	Yes
21. Are married women required by law to obey their husbands?	No	No	No
22. Do married couples jointly share legal responsibility for financially maintaining the family's expenses?	Yes	Yes	Yes

USING PROPERTY

Marital property regime

	TURKEY	UGANDA	UKRAINE
23. What is the default marital property regime?	Partial community of property	Separation of property	Partial community of property
24. Who legally administers property during marriage?	Both must agree	Original owner	Both must agree

Protecting a wife's interests

	TURKEY	UGANDA	UKRAINE
25. If it is the husband, does he need his wife's consent for major transactions	N/A	N/A	N/A
26. Are there special provisions governing the marital home?	Yes	Yes	No
27. Does the law provide for valuation of nonmonetary contributions during marriage?	Yes	No	Yes

Property rights

	Unmarried	Married	Unmarried	Married	Unmarried	Married
28. Do men and women have equal ownership rights to property?	Yes	Yes	Yes	Yes	Yes	Yes

Inheritance rights

	TURKEY	UGANDA	UKRAINE
29. Do sons and daughters have equal inheritance rights to property?	Yes	No	Yes
30. Do female and male surviving spouses have equal inheritance rights to property?	Yes	No	Yes

GOING TO COURT

Equality of access

	TURKEY	UGANDA	UKRAINE
31. Does the law recognize customary courts?	No	Yes	No
32. Does the law recognize personal law courts?	No	No	No
33. Does a woman's testimony carry the same evidentiary weight in court as a man's?	Yes	Yes	Yes

Efficiency of procedure

	TURKEY	UGANDA	UKRAINE
34. Is there a small claims court or a fast track procedure for small claims?	No	Yes	No
35. If so, what is the maximum amount for a small claim (as a percentage of income per capita)?	N/A	897%	N/A

Judicial representation

	TURKEY	UGANDA	UKRAINE
36. How many justices are on the constitutional court?	17	7	18
37. Of those, how many are women?	1	3	2
38. Is the Chief Justice a woman?	No	No	No

	TURKEY			UGANDA			UKRAINE		

GETTING A JOB

Parental benefits	Maternity	Paternity	Parental	Maternity	Paternity	Parental	Maternity	Paternity	Parental
39. Does the law mandate paid or unpaid maternity/paternity/parental leave?	Yes	No	No	Yes	Yes	No	Yes	No	Yes
40. What is the mandatory minimum length of paid leave for maternity/paternity/parental leave (in calendar days)?	112	N/A	N/A	60	4	N/A	126	N/A	969
41. What is the mandatory minimum length of unpaid leave for maternity/paternity/parental leave (in calendar days)?	180	N/A	N/A	0	0	N/A	0	N/A	0
42. Who pays maternity/paternity/parental benefits?	Gov.	N/A	N/A	Emp.	Emp.	N/A	Gov.	N/A	Gov.
43. What percentage of wages are paid during maternity/paternity/parental leave?	66.6%	N/A	N/A	100%	100%	N/A	100%	N/A	Partially paid

	Mother	Father		Mother	Father		Mother	Father	
44. Where **paid** parental leave exists, what is the minimum amount which only the mother/father must take (in calendar days)?	N/A	N/A		N/A	N/A		0	0	
45. Where **unpaid** parental leave exists, what is the minimum amount which only the mother/father must take (in calendar days)?	N/A	N/A		N/A	N/A		N/A	N/A	

Retirement & pensions	Women	Men		Women	Men		Women	Men	
46. What is the age at which one can retire and receive full benefits?	58	60		55	55		60	60	
47. What is the age at which one can retire and receive partial benefits?	58	60		50	50		60	60	
48. What is the mandatory retirement age?	N/A	N/A		N/A	N/A		N/A	N/A	

Working hours and industry restrictions	TURKEY			UGANDA			UKRAINE		
49. Can non-pregnant and non-nursing women do the same jobs as men?	No			Yes			No		
50. Can non-pregnant and non-nursing women engage in the following occupations in the same way as men?									
a. Mining	No			Yes			No		
b. Construction	Yes			Yes			No		
c. Metalwork	Yes			Yes			No		
d. Factory work	Yes			Yes			No		
e. Jobs requiring lifting weights above a threshold	Yes			Yes			No		
f. Jobs deemed hazardous	Yes			Yes			No		
g. Jobs deemed arduous	Yes			Yes			No		
h. Jobs deemed morally or socially inappropriate	Yes			Yes			Yes		
51. Can non-pregnant and non-nursing women work the same night hours as men?	No			Yes			No		

Workplace protections									
52. Does the law mandate equal remuneration for men and women for work of equal value?	No			Yes			No		
53. Are there laws mandating non-discrimination based on gender in hiring?	No			No			Yes		
54. Is it illegal for an employer to ask about family status during a job interview?	No			No			No		
55. Are there laws penalizing or preventing the dismissal of pregnant women?	Yes			Yes			Yes		
56. Must employers give employees an equivalent position when they return from maternity leave?	No			Yes			Yes		
57. Are employers required to provide break time for nursing mothers?	Yes			No			Yes		
58. Do employees with minor children have rights to a flexible/part time schedule?	No			No			Yes		

BUILDING CREDIT

59. What is the minimum loan amount covered in the private credit bureau or public credit registry (as a percentage of income per capita)?	0%			0%			0%		
60. Do microfinance institutions provide information to private credit bureaus or public credit registries?	No			No			Yes		
61. Do utility companies provide information to private credit bureaus or public credit registries?	No			No			No		
62. Do retailers provide information to private credit bureaus or public credit registries?	No			No			No		

PROVIDING INCENTIVES TO WORK

Childcare									
63. Are payments for childcare tax deductible?	No			No			No		
64. Is there public provision of childcare for children under the age of primary education?	No			No			Yes		
65. Does the law mandate free and compulsory primary education?	Yes			Yes			Yes		

Personal income tax	Women	Men		Women	Men		Women	Men	
66. Are there specific tax deductions or credits that are applicable only to men/women?	No	No		No	No		No	No	

	UNITED ARAB EMIRATES		UNITED KINGDOM		UNITED STATES	
REGION	Middle East & North Africa		High income: OECD		High income: OECD	
INCOME	High income		High income		High income	
FEMALE POPULATION	2,729,352		32,089,974		159,488,496	
FEMALE LABOR FORCE PARTICIPATION	44%		70%		67%	

ACCESSING INSTITUTIONS

Constitutional rights

	UAE		UK		US	
1. Is there a non-discrimination clause in the constitution?	No		No		No	
2. If there is a non-discrimination clause in the constitution, does it explicitly mention gender?	N/A		N/A		N/A	
3. Does the constitution guarantee equality before the law?	Yes		No		Yes	

	Customary	Personal	Customary	Personal	Customary	Personal
4. Is customary/personal law recognized as valid source of law under the constitution?	No	Yes	No	No	No	No
5. If so, is it invalid if it violates constitutional provisions on non-discrimination or equality?	N/A	No	N/A	N/A	N/A	N/A

Quotas

	UAE	UK	US
6. What are the legal quotas for women on corporate boards?	N/A	N/A	N/A
7. What are the legal quotas for women in parliament?	N/A	N/A	N/A
8. What are the legal quotas for women in local government?	N/A	N/A	N/A

Rights of married and unmarried women

	Unmarried	Married	Unmarried	Married	Unmarried	Married
9. Can a woman apply for a passport in the same way as a man?	Yes	No	Yes	Yes	Yes	Yes
10. Can a woman apply for a national ID card in the same way as a man?	Yes	Yes	N/A	N/A	N/A	N/A
11. Can a woman travel outside the country in the same way as a man?	Yes	Yes	Yes	Yes	Yes	Yes
12. Can a woman travel outside her home in the same way as a man?	Yes	Yes	Yes	Yes	Yes	Yes
13. Can a woman get a job or pursue a trade or profession in the same way as a man?	Yes	No	Yes	Yes	Yes	Yes
14. Can a woman sign a contract in the same way as a man?	Yes	Yes	Yes	Yes	Yes	Yes
15. Can a woman register a business in the same way as a man?	Yes	Yes	Yes	Yes	Yes	Yes
16. Can a woman open a bank account in the same way as a man?	Yes	Yes	Yes	Yes	Yes	Yes
17. Can a woman choose where to live in the same way as a man?	Yes	No	Yes	Yes	Yes	Yes
18. Can a woman confer citizenship on her children in the same way as a man?	Yes	No	Yes	Yes	Yes	Yes
19. Can a woman be "head of household" or "head of family" in the same way as a man?	Yes	No	N/A	N/A	Yes	Yes
Number of inequalities in accessing institutions	0	5	0	0	0	0

Division of responsibility within marriage

	UAE	UK	US
20. Can a woman convey citizenship to her non-national spouse in the same way as a man?	No	Yes	Yes
21. Are married women required by law to obey their husbands?	Yes	No	No
22. Do married couples jointly share legal responsibility for financially maintaining the family's expenses?	No	Yes	Yes

USING PROPERTY

Marital property regime

	UAE	UK	US
23. What is the default marital property regime?	Separation of property	Separation of property	Separation of property
24. Who legally administers property during marriage?	Original owner	Original owner	Original owner

Protecting a wife's interests

	UAE	UK	US
25. If it is the husband, does he need his wife's consent for major transactions	N/A	N/A	N/A
26. Are there special provisions governing the marital home?	No	Yes	No
27. Does the law provide for valuation of nonmonetary contributions during marriage?	No	Yes	Yes

Property rights

	Unmarried	Married	Unmarried	Married	Unmarried	Married
28. Do men and women have equal ownership rights to property?	Yes	Yes	Yes	Yes	Yes	Yes

Inheritance rights

	UAE	UK	US
29. Do sons and daughters have equal inheritance rights to property?	No	Yes	Yes
30. Do female and male surviving spouses have equal inheritance rights to property?	No	Yes	Yes

GOING TO COURT

Equality of access

	UAE	UK	US
31. Does the law recognize customary courts?	No	No	No
32. Does the law recognize personal law courts?	Yes	No	No
33. Does a woman's testimony carry the same evidentiary weight in court as a man's?	No	Yes	Yes

Efficiency of procedure

	UAE	UK	US
34. Is there a small claims court or a fast track procedure for small claims?	Yes	Yes	Yes
35. If so, what is the maximum amount for a small claim (as a percentage of income per capita)?	60%	41%	10%

Judicial representation

	UAE	UK	US
36. How many justices are on the constitutional court?	5	12	9
37. Of those, how many are women?	0	1	3
38. Is the Chief Justice a woman?	No	No	No

	UNITED ARAB EMIRATES			UNITED KINGDOM			UNITED STATES		

GETTING A JOB

Parental benefits	*Maternity*	*Paternity*	*Parental*	*Maternity*	*Paternity*	*Parental*	*Maternity*	*Paternity*	*Parental*
39. Does the law mandate paid or unpaid maternity/paternity/parental leave?	Yes	No	No	Yes	Yes	No	No	No	Yes
40. What is the mandatory minimum length of paid leave for maternity/paternity/parental leave (in calendar days)?	45	N/A	N/A	273	14	N/A	N/A	N/A	0
41. What is the mandatory minimum length of unpaid leave for maternity/paternity/parental leave (in calendar days)?	0	N/A	N/A	91	0	N/A	N/A	N/A	84
42. Who pays maternity/paternity/parental benefits?	Emp.	N/A	N/A	Emp. & Gov.	Emp. & Gov.	N/A	N/A	N/A	N/A
43. What percentage of wages are paid during maternity/paternity/parental leave?	100%	N/A	N/A	29%	18%	N/A	N/A	N/A	0%

	Mother	*Father*		*Mother*	*Father*		*Mother*	*Father*	
44. Where **paid** parental leave exists, what is the minimum amount which only the mother/father must take (in calendar days)?	N/A	N/A		N/A	N/A		N/A	N/A	
45. Where **unpaid** parental leave exists, what is the minimum amount which only the mother/father must take (in calendar days)?	N/A	N/A		N/A	N/A		0	0	

Retirement & pensions	*Women*	*Men*		*Women*	*Men*		*Women*	*Men*	
46. What is the age at which one can retire and receive full benefits?	60	60		67	67		67	67	
47. What is the age at which one can retire and receive partial benefits?	50	55		N/A	N/A		62	62	
48. What is the mandatory retirement age?	N/A	N/A		N/A	N/A		N/A	N/A	

Working hours and industry restrictions									
49. Can non-pregnant and non-nursing women do the same jobs as men?	No			Yes			Yes		
50. Can non-pregnant and non-nursing women engage in the following occupations in the same way as men?									
a. Mining	No			Yes			Yes		
b. Construction	No			Yes			Yes		
c. Metalwork	No			Yes			Yes		
d. Factory work	No			Yes			Yes		
e. Jobs requiring lifting weights above a threshold	No			Yes			Yes		
f. Jobs deemed hazardous	No			Yes			Yes		
g. Jobs deemed arduous	No			Yes			Yes		
h. Jobs deemed morally or socially inappropriate	No			Yes			Yes		
51. Can non-pregnant and non-nursing women work the same night hours as men?	No			Yes			Yes		

Workplace protections									
52. Does the law mandate equal remuneration for men and women for work of equal value?	No			Yes			Yes		
53. Are there laws mandating non-discrimination based on gender in hiring?	No			Yes			Yes		
54. Is it illegal for an employer to ask about family status during a job interview?	No			No			Yes		
55. Are there laws penalizing or preventing the dismissal of pregnant women?	No			Yes			Yes		
56. Must employers give employees an equivalent position when they return from maternity leave?	No			Yes			N/A		
57. Are employers required to provide break time for nursing mothers?	Yes			No			Yes		
58. Do employees with minor children have rights to a flexible/part time schedule?	No			Yes			No		

BUILDING CREDIT

59. What is the minimum loan amount covered in the private credit bureau or public credit registry (as a percentage of income per capita)?	0%			0%			0%		
60. Do microfinance institutions provide information to private credit bureaus or public credit registries?	N/A			N/A			N/A		
61. Do utility companies provide information to private credit bureaus or public credit registries?	No			Yes			No		
62. Do retailers provide information to private credit bureaus or public credit registries?	No			Yes			No		

PROVIDING INCENTIVES TO WORK

Childcare									
63. Are payments for childcare tax deductible?	No			Yes			Yes		
64. Is there public provision of childcare for children under the age of primary education?	No			Yes			No		
65. Does the law mandate free and compulsory primary education?	Yes			Yes			Yes		

Personal income tax	*Women*	*Men*		*Women*	*Men*		*Women*	*Men*	
66. Are there specific tax deductions or credits that are applicable only to men/women?	No	No		No	No		No	No	

Economy Tables

	URUGUAY	UZBEKISTAN	VENEZUELA, RB
REGION	Latin America & Caribbean	Europe & Central Asia	Latin America & Caribbean
INCOME	High income	Lower middle income	Upper middle income
FEMALE POPULATION	1,755,689	14,965,539	14,930,889
FEMALE LABOR FORCE PARTICIPATION	67%	51%	56%

ACCESSING INSTITUTIONS

Constitutional rights

	URUGUAY	UZBEKISTAN	VENEZUELA, RB
1. Is there a non-discrimination clause in the constitution?	No	Yes	Yes
2. If there is a non-discrimination clause in the constitution, does it explicitly mention gender?	N/A	Yes	Yes
3. Does the constitution guarantee equality before the law?	Yes	Yes	Yes

	Customary	Personal	Customary	Personal	Customary	Personal
4. Is customary/personal law recognized as valid source of law under the constitution?	No	No	No	No	No	No
5. If so, is it invalid if it violates constitutional provisions on non-discrimination or equality?	N/A	N/A	N/A	N/A	N/A	N/A

Quotas

	URUGUAY	UZBEKISTAN	VENEZUELA, RB
6. What are the legal quotas for women on corporate boards?	N/A	N/A	N/A
7. What are the legal quotas for women in parliament?	N/A	N/A	N/A
8. What are the legal quotas for women in local government?	N/A	N/A	N/A

Rights of married and unmarried women

	Unmarried	Married	Unmarried	Married	Unmarried	Married
9. Can a woman apply for a passport in the same way as a man?	Yes	Yes	Yes	Yes	Yes	Yes
10. Can a woman apply for a national ID card in the same way as a man?	Yes	Yes	N/A	N/A	Yes	Yes
11. Can a woman travel outside the country in the same way as a man?	Yes	Yes	Yes	Yes	Yes	Yes
12. Can a woman travel outside her home in the same way as a man?	Yes	Yes	Yes	Yes	Yes	Yes
13. Can a woman get a job or pursue a trade or profession in the same way as a man?	Yes	Yes	Yes	Yes	Yes	Yes
14. Can a woman sign a contract in the same way as a man?	Yes	Yes	Yes	Yes	Yes	Yes
15. Can a woman register a business in the same way as a man?	Yes	Yes	Yes	Yes	Yes	Yes
16. Can a woman open a bank account in the same way as a man?	Yes	Yes	Yes	Yes	Yes	Yes
17. Can a woman choose where to live in the same way as a man?	Yes	Yes	Yes	Yes	Yes	Yes
18. Can a woman confer citizenship on her children in the same way as a man?	Yes	Yes	Yes	Yes	Yes	Yes
19. Can a woman be "head of household" or "head of family" in the same way as a man?	N/A	N/A	N/A	N/A	N/A	N/A
Number of inequalities in accessing institutions	0	0	0	0	0	0

Division of responsibility within marriage

	URUGUAY	UZBEKISTAN	VENEZUELA, RB
20. Can a woman convey citizenship to her non-national spouse in the same way as a man?	Yes	Yes	Yes
21. Are married women required by law to obey their husbands?	No	No	No
22. Do married couples jointly share legal responsibility for financially maintaining the family's expenses?	Yes	Yes	Yes

USING PROPERTY

Marital property regime

	URUGUAY	UZBEKISTAN	VENEZUELA, RB
23. What is the default marital property regime?	Partial community of property	Partial community of property	Partial community of property
24. Who legally administers property during marriage?	Both must agree	Both must agree	Separate with spousal consent

Protecting a wife's interests

	URUGUAY	UZBEKISTAN	VENEZUELA, RB
25. If it is the husband, does he need his wife's consent for major transactions	N/A	N/A	N/A
26. Are there special provisions governing the marital home?	No	No	No
27. Does the law provide for valuation of nonmonetary contributions during marriage?	Yes	Yes	Yes

Property rights

	Unmarried	Married	Unmarried	Married	Unmarried	Married
28. Do men and women have equal ownership rights to property?	Yes	Yes	Yes	Yes	Yes	Yes

Inheritance rights

	URUGUAY	UZBEKISTAN	VENEZUELA, RB
29. Do sons and daughters have equal inheritance rights to property?	Yes	Yes	Yes
30. Do female and male surviving spouses have equal inheritance rights to property?	Yes	Yes	Yes

GOING TO COURT

Equality of access

	URUGUAY	UZBEKISTAN	VENEZUELA, RB
31. Does the law recognize customary courts?	No	No	No
32. Does the law recognize personal law courts?	No	No	No
33. Does a woman's testimony carry the same evidentiary weight in court as a man's?	Yes	Yes	Yes

Efficiency of procedure

	URUGUAY	UZBEKISTAN	VENEZUELA, RB
34. Is there a small claims court or a fast track procedure for small claims?	Yes	No	Yes
35. If so, what is the maximum amount for a small claim (as a percentage of income per capita)?	127%	N/A	352%

Judicial representation

	URUGUAY	UZBEKISTAN	VENEZUELA, RB
36. How many justices are on the constitutional court?	5	7	7
37. Of those, how many are women?	0	1	3
38. Is the Chief Justice a woman?	No	No	Yes

	URUGUAY			UZBEKISTAN			VENEZUELA, RB		

GETTING A JOB

Parental benefits	Maternity	Paternity	Parental	Maternity	Paternity	Parental	Maternity	Paternity	Parental
39. Does the law mandate paid or unpaid maternity/paternity/parental leave?	Yes	Yes	No	Yes	No	Yes	Yes	Yes	No
40. What is the mandatory minimum length of paid leave for maternity/paternity/parental leave (in calendar days)?	84	3	N/A	126	N/A	674	182	14	N/A
41. What is the mandatory minimum length of unpaid leave for maternity/paternity/parental leave (in calendar days)?	0	0	N/A	0	N/A	0	0	0	N/A
42. Who pays maternity/paternity/parental benefits?	Gov.	Emp.	N/A	Gov.	N/A	Emp.	Emp. & Gov.	Emp. & Gov.	N/A
43. What percentage of wages are paid during maternity/paternity/parental leave?	100%	100%	N/A	100%	N/A	Partially paid	100%	100%	N/A

	Mother	Father		Mother	Father		Mother	Father	
44. Where **paid** parental leave exists, what is the minimum amount which only the mother/father must take (in calendar days)?	N/A	N/A		0	0		N/A	N/A	
45. Where **unpaid** parental leave exists, what is the minimum amount which only the mother/father must take (in calendar days)?	N/A	N/A		N/A	N/A		N/A	N/A	

Retirement & pensions	Women	Men		Women	Men		Women	Men	
46. What is the age at which one can retire and receive full benefits?	60	60		55	60		55	60	
47. What is the age at which one can retire and receive partial benefits?	60	60		55	60		55	60	
48. What is the mandatory retirement age?	N/A	N/A		55	60		N/A	N/A	

Working hours and industry restrictions	URUGUAY	UZBEKISTAN	VENEZUELA, RB
49. Can non-pregnant and non-nursing women do the same jobs as men?	Yes	No	Yes
50. Can non-pregnant and non-nursing women engage in the following occupations in the same way as men?			
a. Mining	Yes	No	Yes
b. Construction	Yes	No	Yes
c. Metalwork	Yes	No	Yes
d. Factory work	Yes	No	Yes
e. Jobs requiring lifting weights above a threshold	Yes	No	Yes
f. Jobs deemed hazardous	Yes	No	Yes
g. Jobs deemed arduous	Yes	Yes	Yes
h. Jobs deemed morally or socially inappropriate	Yes	Yes	Yes
51. Can non-pregnant and non-nursing women work the same night hours as men?	Yes	Yes	Yes

Workplace protections	URUGUAY	UZBEKISTAN	VENEZUELA, RB
52. Does the law mandate equal remuneration for men and women for work of equal value?	Yes	No	No
53. Are there laws mandating non-discrimination based on gender in hiring?	Yes	No	Yes
54. Is it illegal for an employer to ask about family status during a job interview?	No	No	No
55. Are there laws penalizing or preventing the dismissal of pregnant women?	Yes	Yes	Yes
56. Must employers give employees an equivalent position when they return from maternity leave?	Yes	Yes	Yes
57. Are employers required to provide break time for nursing mothers?	Yes	Yes	Yes
58. Do employees with minor children have rights to a flexible/part time schedule?	No	Yes	No

BUILDING CREDIT

	URUGUAY	UZBEKISTAN	VENEZUELA, RB
59. What is the minimum loan amount covered in the private credit bureau or public credit registry (as a percentage of income per capita)?	0%	0%	0%
60. Do microfinance institutions provide information to private credit bureaus or public credit registries?	Yes	Yes	Yes
61. Do utility companies provide information to private credit bureaus or public credit registries?	Yes	No	No
62. Do retailers provide information to private credit bureaus or public credit registries?	Yes	No	Yes

PROVIDING INCENTIVES TO WORK

Childcare	URUGUAY	UZBEKISTAN	VENEZUELA, RB
63. Are payments for childcare tax deductible?	No	No	No
64. Is there public provision of childcare for children under the age of primary education?	Yes	Yes	Yes
65. Does the law mandate free and compulsory primary education?	Yes	Yes	Yes

Personal income tax	Women	Men	Women	Men	Women	Men
66. Are there specific tax deductions or credits that are applicable only to men/women?	No	No	No	No	No	No

Economy Tables

	VIETNAM	WEST BANK AND GAZA	YEMEN, REP.
REGION	East Asia & Pacific	Middle East & North Africa	Middle East & North Africa
INCOME	Lower middle income	Lower middle income	Lower middle income
FEMALE POPULATION	44,912,843	1,993,055	11,826,409
FEMALE LABOR FORCE PARTICIPATION	78%	16%	26%

ACCESSING INSTITUTIONS

Constitutional rights

	VIETNAM	WEST BANK AND GAZA	YEMEN, REP.
1. Is there a non-discrimination clause in the constitution?	Yes	Yes	No
2. If there is a non-discrimination clause in the constitution, does it explicitly mention gender?	Yes	Yes	N/A
3. Does the constitution guarantee equality before the law?	Yes	Yes	Yes

	Customary	Personal	Customary	Personal	Customary	Personal
4. Is customary/personal law recognized as valid source of law under the constitution?	No	No	No	Yes	No	Yes
5. If so, is it invalid if it violates constitutional provisions on non-discrimination or equality?	N/A	N/A	N/A	Yes	N/A	No

Quotas

	VIETNAM	WEST BANK AND GAZA	YEMEN, REP.
6. What are the legal quotas for women on corporate boards?	N/A	N/A	N/A
7. What are the legal quotas for women in parliament?	N/A	N/A	N/A
8. What are the legal quotas for women in local government?	N/A	N/A	N/A

Rights of married and unmarried women

	Unmarried	Married	Unmarried	Married	Unmarried	Married
9. Can a woman apply for a passport in the same way as a man?	Yes	Yes	Yes	Yes	Yes	No
10. Can a woman apply for a national ID card in the same way as a man?	Yes	Yes	Yes	Yes	Yes	Yes
11. Can a woman travel outside the country in the same way as a man?	Yes	Yes	Yes	Yes	Yes	Yes
12. Can a woman travel outside her home in the same way as a man?	Yes	Yes	Yes	No	Yes	No
13. Can a woman get a job or pursue a trade or profession in the same way as a man?	Yes	Yes	Yes	No	Yes	Yes
14. Can a woman sign a contract in the same way as a man?	Yes	Yes	Yes	Yes	Yes	Yes
15. Can a woman register a business in the same way as a man?	Yes	Yes	Yes	Yes	Yes	Yes
16. Can a woman open a bank account in the same way as a man?	Yes	Yes	Yes	Yes	Yes	Yes
17. Can a woman choose where to live in the same way as a man?	Yes	Yes	Yes	No	Yes	No
18. Can a woman confer citizenship on her children in the same way as a man?	Yes	Yes	No	No	Yes	Yes
19. Can a woman be "head of household" or "head of family" in the same way as a man?	Yes	Yes	N/A	N/A	Yes	No
Number of inequalities in accessing institutions	0	0	1	4	0	4

Division of responsibility within marriage

	VIETNAM	WEST BANK AND GAZA	YEMEN, REP.
20. Can a woman convey citizenship to her non-national spouse in the same way as a man?	Yes	No	No
21. Are married women required by law to obey their husbands?	No	Yes	Yes
22. Do married couples jointly share legal responsibility for financially maintaining the family's expenses?	Yes	No	No

USING PROPERTY

Marital property regime

	VIETNAM	WEST BANK AND GAZA	YEMEN, REP.
23. What is the default marital property regime?	Partial community of property	Separation of property	Separation of property
24. Who legally administers property during marriage?	Both must agree	Original owner	Original owner

Protecting a wife's interests

	VIETNAM	WEST BANK AND GAZA	YEMEN, REP.
25. If it is the husband, does he need his wife's consent for major transactions	N/A	N/A	N/A
26. Are there special provisions governing the marital home?	No	No	No
27. Does the law provide for valuation of nonmonetary contributions during marriage?	Yes	No	No

Property rights

	Unmarried	Married	Unmarried	Married	Unmarried	Married
28. Do men and women have equal ownership rights to property?	Yes	Yes	Yes	Yes	Yes	Yes

Inheritance rights

	VIETNAM	WEST BANK AND GAZA	YEMEN, REP.
29. Do sons and daughters have equal inheritance rights to property?	Yes	No	No
30. Do female and male surviving spouses have equal inheritance rights to property?	Yes	No	No

GOING TO COURT

Equality of access

	VIETNAM	WEST BANK AND GAZA	YEMEN, REP.
31. Does the law recognize customary courts?	No	No	No
32. Does the law recognize personal law courts?	No	Yes	Yes
33. Does a woman's testimony carry the same evidentiary weight in court as a man's?	Yes	No	No

Efficiency of procedure

	VIETNAM	WEST BANK AND GAZA	YEMEN, REP.
34. Is there a small claims court or a fast track procedure for small claims?	No	Yes	No
35. If so, what is the maximum amount for a small claim (as a percentage of income per capita)?	N/A	165%	N/A

Judicial representation

	VIETNAM	WEST BANK AND GAZA	YEMEN, REP.
36. How many justices are on the constitutional court?	N/A	9	7
37. Of those, how many are women?	N/A	1	0
38. Is the Chief Justice a woman?	N/A	No	No

GETTING A JOB

Parental benefits	Maternity	Paternity	Parental	Maternity	Paternity	Parental	Maternity	Paternity	Parental
39. Does the law mandate paid or unpaid maternity/paternity/parental leave?	Yes	No	No	Yes	No	No	Yes	No	No
40. What is the mandatory minimum length of paid leave for maternity/paternity/parental leave (in calendar days)?	180	N/A	N/A	70	N/A	N/A	70	N/A	N/A
41. What is the mandatory minimum length of unpaid leave for maternity/paternity/parental leave (in calendar days)?	0	N/A	N/A	0	N/A	N/A	0	N/A	N/A
42. Who pays maternity/paternity/parental benefits?	Gov.	N/A	N/A	Emp.	N/A	N/A	Emp.	N/A	N/A
43. What percentage of wages are paid during maternity/paternity/parental leave?	100%	N/A	N/A	100%	N/A	N/A	100%	N/A	N/A

	Mother	Father		Mother	Father		Mother	Father	
44. Where **paid** parental leave exists, what is the minimum amount which only the mother/father must take (in calendar days)?	N/A	N/A		N/A	N/A		N/A	N/A	
45. Where **unpaid** parental leave exists, what is the minimum amount which only the mother/father must take (in calendar days)?	N/A	N/A		N/A	N/A		N/A	N/A	

Retirement & pensions	Women	Men		Women	Men		Women	Men	
46. What is the age at which one can retire and receive full benefits?	55	60		N/A	N/A		55	60	
47. What is the age at which one can retire and receive partial benefits?	55	60		N/A	N/A		46	50	
48. What is the mandatory retirement age?	60	65		N/A	N/A		60	60	

Working hours and industry restrictions									
49. Can non-pregnant and non-nursing women do the same jobs as men?	No			No			No		
50. Can non-pregnant and non-nursing women engage in the following occupations in the same way as men?									
a. Mining	No			No			Yes		
b. Construction	No			Yes			Yes		
c. Metalwork	No			No			Yes		
d. Factory work	Yes			Yes			Yes		
e. Jobs requiring lifting weights above a threshold	No			Yes			Yes		
f. Jobs deemed hazardous	No			No			No		
g. Jobs deemed arduous	No			No			No		
h. Jobs deemed morally or socially inappropriate	Yes			Yes			No		
51. Can non-pregnant and non-nursing women work the same night hours as men?	Yes			No			No		

Workplace protections									
52. Does the law mandate equal remuneration for men and women for work of equal value?	Yes			No			No		
53. Are there laws mandating non-discrimination based on gender in hiring?	Yes			No			No		
54. Is it illegal for an employer to ask about family status during a job interview?	No			No			No		
55. Are there laws penalizing or preventing the dismissal of pregnant women?	Yes			Yes			No		
56. Must employers give employees an equivalent position when they return from maternity leave?	Yes			No			No		
57. Are employers required to provide break time for nursing mothers?	Yes			Yes			Yes		
58. Do employees with minor children have rights to a flexible/part time schedule?	No			No			No		

BUILDING CREDIT

59. What is the minimum loan amount covered in the private credit bureau or public credit registry (as a percentage of income per capita)?	0%			0%			0%		
60. Do microfinance institutions provide information to private credit bureaus or public credit registries?	Yes			Yes			No		
61. Do utility companies provide information to private credit bureaus or public credit registries?	No			No			No		
62. Do retailers provide information to private credit bureaus or public credit registries?	No			No			No		

PROVIDING INCENTIVES TO WORK

Childcare									
63. Are payments for childcare tax deductible?	No			No			No		
64. Is there public provision of childcare for children under the age of primary education?	Yes			No			No		
65. Does the law mandate free and compulsory primary education?	Yes			Yes			Yes		

Personal income tax	Women	Men		Women	Men		Women	Men	
66. Are there specific tax deductions or credits that are applicable only to men/women?	No	No		No	No		No	No	

Economy Tables

	ZAMBIA	ZIMBABWE
REGION	Sub-Saharan Africa	Sub-Saharan Africa
INCOME	Lower middle income	Low income
FEMALE POPULATION	7,052,869	6,956,156
FEMALE LABOR FORCE PARTICIPATION	73%	84%

ACCESSING INSTITUTIONS

Constitutional rights

	ZAMBIA	ZIMBABWE
1. Is there a non-discrimination clause in the constitution?	Yes	Yes
2. If there is a non-discrimination clause in the constitution, does it explicitly mention gender?	Yes	Yes
3. Does the constitution guarantee equality before the law?	Yes	Yes

	Customary	Personal	Customary	Personal
4. Is customary/personal law recognized as valid source of law under the constitution?	Yes	No	Yes	No
5. If so, is it invalid if it violates constitutional provisions on non-discrimination or equality?	No	N/A	Yes	N/A

Quotas

	ZAMBIA	ZIMBABWE
6. What are the legal quotas for women on corporate boards?	N/A	N/A
7. What are the legal quotas for women in parliament?	N/A	22%
8. What are the legal quotas for women in local government?	N/A	N/A

Rights of married and unmarried women

	Unmarried	Married	Unmarried	Married
9. Can a woman apply for a passport in the same way as a man?	Yes	Yes	Yes	Yes
10. Can a woman apply for a national ID card in the same way as a man?	Yes	Yes	Yes	Yes
11. Can a woman travel outside the country in the same way as a man?	Yes	Yes	Yes	Yes
12. Can a woman travel outside her home in the same way as a man?	Yes	Yes	Yes	Yes
13. Can a woman get a job or pursue a trade or profession in the same way as a man?	Yes	Yes	Yes	Yes
14. Can a woman sign a contract in the same way as a man?	Yes	Yes	Yes	Yes
15. Can a woman register a business in the same way as a man?	Yes	Yes	Yes	Yes
16. Can a woman open a bank account in the same way as a man?	Yes	Yes	Yes	Yes
17. Can a woman choose where to live in the same way as a man?	Yes	Yes	Yes	Yes
18. Can a woman confer citizenship on her children in the same way as a man?	Yes	Yes	Yes	Yes
19. Can a woman be "head of household" or "head of family" in the same way as a man?	N/A	N/A	N/A	N/A
Number of inequalities in accessing institutions	0	0	0	0

Division of responsibility within marriage

	ZAMBIA	ZIMBABWE
20. Can a woman convey citizenship to her non-national spouse in the same way as a man?	Yes	Yes
21. Are married women required by law to obey their husbands?	No	No
22. Do married couples jointly share legal responsibility for financially maintaining the family's expenses?	Yes	Yes

USING PROPERTY

Marital property regime

	ZAMBIA	ZIMBABWE
23. What is the default marital property regime?	Separation of property	Separation of property
24. Who legally administers property during marriage?	Original owner	Original owner

Protecting a wife's interests

	ZAMBIA	ZIMBABWE
25. If it is the husband, does he need his wife's consent for major transactions	N/A	N/A
26. Are there special provisions governing the marital home?	No	No
27. Does the law provide for valuation of nonmonetary contributions during marriage?	Yes	No

Property rights

	Unmarried	Married	Unmarried	Married
28. Do men and women have equal ownership rights to property?	Yes	Yes	Yes	Yes

Inheritance rights

	ZAMBIA	ZIMBABWE
29. Do sons and daughters have equal inheritance rights to property?	Yes	Yes
30. Do female and male surviving spouses have equal inheritance rights to property?	Yes	Yes

GOING TO COURT

Equality of access

	ZAMBIA	ZIMBABWE
31. Does the law recognize customary courts?	Yes	Yes
32. Does the law recognize personal law courts?	No	No
33. Does a woman's testimony carry the same evidentiary weight in court as a man's?	Yes	Yes

Efficiency of procedure

	ZAMBIA	ZIMBABWE
34. Is there a small claims court or a fast track procedure for small claims?	Yes	Yes
35. If so, what is the maximum amount for a small claim (as a percentage of income per capita)?	314%	5213%

Judicial representation

	ZAMBIA	ZIMBABWE
36. How many justices are on the constitutional court?	9	9
37. Of those, how many are women?	5	3
38. Is the Chief Justice a woman?	Yes	No

GETTING A JOB

Parental benefits

	Maternity	Paternity	Parental	Maternity	Paternity	Parental
39. Does the law mandate paid or unpaid maternity/paternity/parental leave?	Yes	No	No	Yes	No	No
40. What is the mandatory minimum length of paid leave for maternity/paternity/parental leave (in calendar days)?	84	N/A	N/A	98	N/A	N/A
41. What is the mandatory minimum length of unpaid leave for maternity/paternity/parental leave (in calendar days)?	0	N/A	N/A	0	N/A	N/A
42. Who pays maternity/paternity/parental benefits?	Emp.	N/A	N/A	Emp.	N/A	N/A
43. What percentage of wages are paid during maternity/paternity/parental leave?	100%	N/A	N/A	100%	N/A	N/A

	Mother	Father		Mother	Father	
44. Where **paid** parental leave exists, what is the minimum amount which only the mother/father must take (in calendar days)?	N/A	N/A		N/A	N/A	
45. Where **unpaid** parental leave exists, what is the minimum amount which only the mother/father must take (in calendar days)?	N/A	N/A		N/A	N/A	

Retirement & pensions

	Women	Men		Women	Men	
46. What is the age at which one can retire and receive full benefits?	55	55		60	60	
47. What is the age at which one can retire and receive partial benefits?	50	50		60	60	
48. What is the mandatory retirement age?	N/A	N/A		N/A	N/A	

Working hours and industry restrictions

	ZAMBIA	ZIMBABWE
49. Can non-pregnant and non-nursing women do the same jobs as men?	Yes	No
50. Can non-pregnant and non-nursing women engage in the following occupations in the same way as men?		
a. Mining	Yes	No
b. Construction	Yes	No
c. Metalwork	Yes	No
d. Factory work	Yes	No
e. Jobs requiring lifting weights above a threshold	Yes	No
f. Jobs deemed hazardous	Yes	Yes
g. Jobs deemed arduous	Yes	Yes
h. Jobs deemed morally or socially inappropriate	Yes	Yes
51. Can non-pregnant and non-nursing women work the same night hours as men?	Yes	No

Workplace protections

	ZAMBIA	ZIMBABWE
52. Does the law mandate equal remuneration for men and women for work of equal value?	No	Yes
53. Are there laws mandating non-discrimination based on gender in hiring?	No	Yes
54. Is it illegal for an employer to ask about family status during a job interview?	No	No
55. Are there laws penalizing or preventing the dismissal of pregnant women?	Yes	No
56. Must employers give employees an equivalent position when they return from maternity leave?	No	Yes
57. Are employers required to provide break time for nursing mothers?	No	Yes
58. Do employees with minor children have rights to a flexible/part time schedule?	No	No

BUILDING CREDIT

	ZAMBIA	ZIMBABWE
59. What is the minimum loan amount covered in the private credit bureau or public credit registry (as a percentage of income per capita)?	0%	23%
60. Do microfinance institutions provide information to private credit bureaus or public credit registries?	Yes	Yes
61. Do utility companies provide information to private credit bureaus or public credit registries?	Yes	No
62. Do retailers provide information to private credit bureaus or public credit registries?	Yes	Yes

PROVIDING INCENTIVES TO WORK

Childcare

	ZAMBIA	ZIMBABWE
63. Are payments for childcare tax deductible?	No	No
64. Is there public provision of childcare for children under the age of primary education?	Yes	No
65. Does the law mandate free and compulsory primary education?	Yes	Yes

Personal income tax

	Women	Men		Women	Men	
66. Are there specific tax deductions or credits that are applicable only to men/women?	No	No		No	No	

Pilot data on Protecting women from violence

Pilot data on Protecting women from violence

DOMESTIC VIOLENCE	ALBANIA				ALGERIA			
1. Is there legislation that specifically addresses domestic violence?	Yes				No			
2. Is there a specialized court or procedure for cases of domestic violence?	Yes				No			
3. Does domestic violence legislation protect women in unmarried intimate relationships?	Yes				No			
	Emotional	Financial	Physical	Sexual	Emotional	Financial	Physical	Sexual
4. Does domestic violence legislation include the following types of abuse:	Yes	Yes	Yes	Yes	No	No	No	No

SEXUAL HARASSMENT								
5. Is there legislation that specifically addresses sexual harassment?	Yes				Yes			
6. Are there criminal sanctions for sexual harassment?	Yes				Yes			
7. Is there a governmental office tasked with addressing sexual harassment?	No				No			
	Education	Employment	Public Places	Service Provision	Education	Employment	Public Places	Service Provision
8. Is there legislation on sexual harassment in:	Yes	Yes	No	No	No	Yes	No	No
9. Are there criminal sanctions for sexual harassment in employment?	Yes				Yes			

DOMESTIC VIOLENCE	ANGOLA				ARGENTINA			
1. Is there legislation that specifically addresses domestic violence?	Yes				Yes			
2. Is there a specialized court or procedure for cases of domestic violence?	No				Yes			
3. Does domestic violence legislation protect women in unmarried intimate relationships?	No				Yes			
	Emotional	Financial	Physical	Sexual	Emotional	Financial	Physical	Sexual
4. Does domestic violence legislation include the following types of abuse:	Yes	Yes	Yes	Yes	Yes	Yes	Yes	Yes

SEXUAL HARASSMENT								
5. Is there legislation that specifically addresses sexual harassment?	Yes				Yes			
6. Are there criminal sanctions for sexual harassment?	Yes				No			
7. Is there a governmental office tasked with addressing sexual harassment?	No				No			
	Education	Employment	Public Places	Service Provision	Education	Employment	Public Places	Service Provision
8. Is there legislation on sexual harassment in:	No	Yes	No	No	Yes	No	No	No
9. Are there criminal sanctions for sexual harassment in employment?	Yes				No			

DOMESTIC VIOLENCE	ARMENIA				AUSTRALIA			
1. Is there legislation that specifically addresses domestic violence?	No				Yes			
2. Is there a specialized court or procedure for cases of domestic violence?	No				Yes			
3. Does domestic violence legislation protect women in unmarried intimate relationships?	No				Yes			
	Emotional	Financial	Physical	Sexual	Emotional	Financial	Physical	Sexual
4. Does domestic violence legislation include the following types of abuse:	No	No	No	No	Yes	Yes	Yes	Yes

SEXUAL HARASSMENT								
5. Is there legislation that specifically addresses sexual harassment?	Yes				Yes			
6. Are there criminal sanctions for sexual harassment?	No				No			
7. Is there a governmental office tasked with addressing sexual harassment?	Yes				Yes			
	Education	Employment	Public Places	Service Provision	Education	Employment	Public Places	Service Provision
8. Is there legislation on sexual harassment in:	No	Yes	No	No	Yes	Yes	No	Yes
9. Are there criminal sanctions for sexual harassment in employment?	No				No			

DOMESTIC VIOLENCE	AZERBAIJAN				BANGLADESH			
1. Is there legislation that specifically addresses domestic violence?	Yes				Yes			
2. Is there a specialized court or procedure for cases of domestic violence?	Yes				Yes			
3. Does domestic violence legislation protect women in unmarried intimate relationships?	Yes				Yes			
	Emotional	Financial	Physical	Sexual	Emotional	Financial	Physical	Sexual
4. Does domestic violence legislation include the following types of abuse:	Yes	Yes	Yes	Yes	Yes	Yes	Yes	Yes

SEXUAL HARASSMENT								
5. Is there legislation that specifically addresses sexual harassment?	Yes				Yes			
6. Are there criminal sanctions for sexual harassment?	No				Yes			
7. Is there a governmental office tasked with addressing sexual harassment?	Yes				No			
	Education	Employment	Public Places	Service Provision	Education	Employment	Public Places	Service Provision
8. Is there legislation on sexual harassment in:	No	Yes	No	No	Yes	Yes	Yes	No
9. Are there criminal sanctions for sexual harassment in employment?	No				No			

DOMESTIC VIOLENCE	BENIN				BOLIVIA			
1. Is there legislation that specifically addresses domestic violence?	Yes				Yes			
2. Is there a specialized court or procedure for cases of domestic violence?	Yes				Yes			
3. Does domestic violence legislation protect women in unmarried intimate relationships?	Yes				Yes			
	Emotional	Financial	Physical	Sexual	Emotional	Financial	Physical	Sexual
4. Does domestic violence legislation include the following types of abuse:	Yes	Yes	Yes	Yes	Yes	Yes	Yes	Yes
SEXUAL HARASSMENT								
5. Is there legislation that specifically addresses sexual harassment?	Yes				Yes			
6. Are there criminal sanctions for sexual harassment?	Yes				Yes			
7. Is there a governmental office tasked with addressing sexual harassment?	Yes				No			
	Education	Employment	Public Places	Service Provision	Education	Employment	Public Places	Service Provision
8. Is there legislation on sexual harassment in:	Yes	Yes	Yes	No	Yes	Yes	No	No
9. Are there criminal sanctions for sexual harassment in employment?	Yes				Yes			

DOMESTIC VIOLENCE	BOSNIA AND HERZEGOVINA				BRAZIL			
1. Is there legislation that specifically addresses domestic violence?	Yes				Yes			
2. Is there a specialized court or procedure for cases of domestic violence?	Yes				Yes			
3. Does domestic violence legislation protect women in unmarried intimate relationships?	Yes				Yes			
4. Does domestic violence legislation include the following types of abuse:	Emotional	Financial	Physical	Sexual	Emotional	Financial	Physical	Sexual
	Yes	Yes	Yes	Yes	Yes	Yes	Yes	Yes
SEXUAL HARASSMENT								
5. Is there legislation that specifically addresses sexual harassment?	Yes				Yes			
6. Are there criminal sanctions for sexual harassment?	Yes				Yes			
7. Is there a governmental office tasked with addressing sexual harassment?	Yes				Yes			
	Education	Employment	Public Places	Service Provision	Education	Employment	Public Places	Service Provision
8. Is there legislation on sexual harassment in:	Yes	Yes	No	No	No	Yes	No	No
9. Are there criminal sanctions for sexual harassment in employment?	Yes				Yes			

DOMESTIC VIOLENCE	BURKINA FASO				CAMBODIA			
1. Is there legislation that specifically addresses domestic violence?	No				Yes			
2. Is there a specialized court or procedure for cases of domestic violence?	No				No			
3. Does domestic violence legislation protect women in unmarried intimate relationships?	No				Yes			
	Emotional	Financial	Physical	Sexual	Emotional	Financial	Physical	Sexual
4. Does domestic violence legislation include the following types of abuse:	No	No	No	No	Yes	No	Yes	Yes
SEXUAL HARASSMENT								
5. Is there legislation that specifically addresses sexual harassment?	Yes				Yes			
6. Are there criminal sanctions for sexual harassment?	Yes				Yes			
7. Is there a governmental office tasked with addressing sexual harassment?	No				No			
	Education	Employment	Public Places	Service Provision	Education	Employment	Public Places	Service Provision
8. Is there legislation on sexual harassment in:	No	Yes	No	No	No	Yes	No	No
9. Are there criminal sanctions for sexual harassment in employment?	Yes				Yes			

DOMESTIC VIOLENCE	CAMEROON				CANADA			
1. Is there legislation that specifically addresses domestic violence?	No				No			
2. Is there a specialized court or procedure for cases of domestic violence?	No				Yes			
3. Does domestic violence legislation protect women in unmarried intimate relationships?	No				No			
	Emotional	Financial	Physical	Sexual	Emotional	Financial	Physical	Sexual
4. Does domestic violence legislation include the following types of abuse:	No	No	No	No	No	No	No	No
SEXUAL HARASSMENT								
5. Is there legislation that specifically addresses sexual harassment?	No				Yes			
6. Are there criminal sanctions for sexual harassment?	No				No			
7. Is there a governmental office tasked with addressing sexual harassment?	No				Yes			
	Education	Employment	Public Places	Service Provision	Education	Employment	Public Places	Service Provision
8. Is there legislation on sexual harassment in:	No	No	No	No	No	Yes	Yes	Yes
9. Are there criminal sanctions for sexual harassment in employment?	No				No			

Pilot data on Protecting women from violence

DOMESTIC VIOLENCE	CHILE				CHINA			
1. Is there legislation that specifically addresses domestic violence?	Yes				Yes			
2. Is there a specialized court or procedure for cases of domestic violence?	Yes				No			
3. Does domestic violence legislation protect women in unmarried intimate relationships?	Yes				Yes			
	Emotional	Financial	Physical	Sexual	Emotional	Financial	Physical	Sexual
4. Does domestic violence legislation include the following types of abuse:	Yes	No	Yes	No	Yes	No	Yes	No
SEXUAL HARASSMENT								
5. Is there legislation that specifically addresses sexual harassment?	Yes				Yes			
6. Are there criminal sanctions for sexual harassment?	No				No			
7. Is there a governmental office tasked with addressing sexual harassment?	Yes				No			
	Education	Employment	Public Places	Service Provision	Education	Employment	Public Places	Service Provision
8. Is there legislation on sexual harassment in:	No	Yes	No	No	No	Yes	No	No
9. Are there criminal sanctions for sexual harassment in employment?	No				No			

DOMESTIC VIOLENCE	COLOMBIA				CONGO, DEM. REP.			
1. Is there legislation that specifically addresses domestic violence?	Yes				No			
2. Is there a specialized court or procedure for cases of domestic violence?	Yes				No			
3. Does domestic violence legislation protect women in unmarried intimate relationships?	Yes				No			
	Emotional	Financial	Physical	Sexual	Emotional	Financial	Physical	Sexual
4. Does domestic violence legislation include the following types of abuse:	Yes	Yes	Yes	Yes	No	No	No	No
SEXUAL HARASSMENT								
5. Is there legislation that specifically addresses sexual harassment?	Yes				Yes			
6. Are there criminal sanctions for sexual harassment?	Yes				Yes			
7. Is there a governmental office tasked with addressing sexual harassment?	Yes				No			
	Education	Employment	Public Places	Service Provision	Education	Employment	Public Places	Service Provision
8. Is there legislation on sexual harassment in:	No	Yes	No	No	No	Yes	No	No
9. Are there criminal sanctions for sexual harassment in employment?	Yes				Yes			

DOMESTIC VIOLENCE	COSTA RICA				CÔTE D'IVOIRE			
1. Is there legislation that specifically addresses domestic violence?	Yes				No			
2. Is there a specialized court or procedure for cases of domestic violence?	Yes				No			
3. Does domestic violence legislation protect women in unmarried intimate relationships?	Yes				No			
	Emotional	Financial	Physical	Sexual	Emotional	Financial	Physical	Sexual
4. Does domestic violence legislation include the following types of abuse:	Yes	Yes	Yes	Yes	No	No	No	No
SEXUAL HARASSMENT								
5. Is there legislation that specifically addresses sexual harassment?	Yes				Yes			
6. Are there criminal sanctions for sexual harassment?	No				Yes			
7. Is there a governmental office tasked with addressing sexual harassment?	Yes				No			
	Education	Employment	Public Places	Service Provision	Education	Employment	Public Places	Service Provision
8. Is there legislation on sexual harassment in:	Yes	Yes	No	No	No	Yes	No	No
9. Are there criminal sanctions for sexual harassment in employment?	No				Yes			

DOMESTIC VIOLENCE	CROATIA				DENMARK			
1. Is there legislation that specifically addresses domestic violence?	Yes				Yes			
2. Is there a specialized court or procedure for cases of domestic violence?	Yes				No			
3. Does domestic violence legislation protect women in unmarried intimate relationships?	Yes				No			
	Emotional	Financial	Physical	Sexual	Emotional	Financial	Physical	Sexual
4. Does domestic violence legislation include the following types of abuse:	Yes	Yes	Yes	Yes	No	No	Yes	No
SEXUAL HARASSMENT								
5. Is there legislation that specifically addresses sexual harassment?	Yes				Yes			
6. Are there criminal sanctions for sexual harassment?	Yes				No			
7. Is there a governmental office tasked with addressing sexual harassment?	Yes				Yes			
	Education	Employment	Public Places	Service Provision	Education	Employment	Public Places	Service Provision
8. Is there legislation on sexual harassment in:	Yes	Yes	No	No	No	Yes	No	No
9. Are there criminal sanctions for sexual harassment in employment?	No				No			

DOMESTIC VIOLENCE	ECUADOR				EGYPT, ARAB REP.			
1. Is there legislation that specifically addresses domestic violence?	Yes				No			
2. Is there a specialized court or procedure for cases of domestic violence?	Yes				No			
3. Does domestic violence legislation protect women in unmarried intimate relationships?	Yes				No			
	Emotional	Financial	Physical	Sexual	Emotional	Financial	Physical	Sexual
4. Does domestic violence legislation include the following types of abuse:	Yes	No	Yes	Yes	No	No	No	No
SEXUAL HARASSMENT								
5. Is there legislation that specifically addresses sexual harassment?	Yes				No			
6. Are there criminal sanctions for sexual harassment?	Yes				No			
7. Is there a governmental office tasked with addressing sexual harassment?	Yes				No			
	Education	Employment	Public Places	Service Provision	Education	Employment	Public Places	Service Provision
8. Is there legislation on sexual harassment in:	Yes	Yes	Yes	No	No	No	No	No
9. Are there criminal sanctions for sexual harassment in employment?	Yes				No			

DOMESTIC VIOLENCE	EL SALVADOR				ETHIOPIA			
1. Is there legislation that specifically addresses domestic violence?	Yes				Yes			
2. Is there a specialized court or procedure for cases of domestic violence?	Yes				No			
3. Does domestic violence legislation protect women in unmarried intimate relationships?	Yes				Yes			
	Emotional	Financial	Physical	Sexual	Emotional	Financial	Physical	Sexual
4. Does domestic violence legislation include the following types of abuse:	Yes	No	Yes	Yes	Yes	No	Yes	No
SEXUAL HARASSMENT								
5. Is there legislation that specifically addresses sexual harassment?	Yes				Yes			
6. Are there criminal sanctions for sexual harassment?	Yes				Yes			
7. Is there a governmental office tasked with addressing sexual harassment?	No				No			
	Education	Employment	Public Places	Service Provision	Education	Employment	Public Places	Service Provision
8. Is there legislation on sexual harassment in:	Yes	Yes	No	No	Yes	Yes	Yes	No
9. Are there criminal sanctions for sexual harassment in employment?	Yes				Yes			

DOMESTIC VIOLENCE	FIJI				FINLAND			
1. Is there legislation that specifically addresses domestic violence?	Yes				Yes			
2. Is there a specialized court or procedure for cases of domestic violence?	Yes				Yes			
3. Does domestic violence legislation protect women in unmarried intimate relationships?	Yes				Yes			
	Emotional	Financial	Physical	Sexual	Emotional	Financial	Physical	Sexual
4. Does domestic violence legislation include the following types of abuse:	Yes	Yes	Yes	Yes	No	No	Yes	No
SEXUAL HARASSMENT								
5. Is there legislation that specifically addresses sexual harassment?	Yes				Yes			
6. Are there criminal sanctions for sexual harassment?	No				Yes			
7. Is there a governmental office tasked with addressing sexual harassment?	Yes				Yes			
	Education	Employment	Public Places	Service Provision	Education	Employment	Public Places	Service Provision
8. Is there legislation on sexual harassment in:	Yes	Yes	Yes	Yes	Yes	Yes	No	No
9. Are there criminal sanctions for sexual harassment in employment?	No				Yes			

DOMESTIC VIOLENCE	FRANCE				GERMANY			
1. Is there legislation that specifically addresses domestic violence?	Yes				Yes			
2. Is there a specialized court or procedure for cases of domestic violence?	Yes				Yes			
3. Does domestic violence legislation protect women in unmarried intimate relationships?	Yes				Yes			
	Emotional	Financial	Physical	Sexual	Emotional	Financial	Physical	Sexual
4. Does domestic violence legislation include the following types of abuse:	Yes	No	Yes	Yes	No	No	Yes	No
SEXUAL HARASSMENT								
5. Is there legislation that specifically addresses sexual harassment?	Yes				Yes			
6. Are there criminal sanctions for sexual harassment?	Yes				No			
7. Is there a governmental office tasked with addressing sexual harassment?	Yes				Yes			
	Education	Employment	Public Places	Service Provision	Education	Employment	Public Places	Service Provision
8. Is there legislation on sexual harassment in:	No	Yes	No	No	No	Yes	No	No
9. Are there criminal sanctions for sexual harassment in employment?	Yes				No			

Pilot data on Protecting women from violence

DOMESTIC VIOLENCE

	GHANA	GUATEMALA
1. Is there legislation that specifically addresses domestic violence?	Yes	Yes
2. Is there a specialized court or procedure for cases of domestic violence?	Yes	Yes
3. Does domestic violence legislation protect women in unmarried intimate relationships?	Yes	Yes

4. Does domestic violence legislation include the following types of abuse:	Emotional	Financial	Physical	Sexual	Emotional	Financial	Physical	Sexual
	Yes	Yes	Yes	Yes	Yes	Yes	Yes	Yes

SEXUAL HARASSMENT

	GHANA	GUATEMALA
5. Is there legislation that specifically addresses sexual harassment?	No	No
6. Are there criminal sanctions for sexual harassment?	No	No
7. Is there a governmental office tasked with addressing sexual harassment?	No	No

8. Is there legislation on sexual harassment in:	Education	Employment	Public Places	Service Provision	Education	Employment	Public Places	Service Provision
	No	No	No	No	No	No	No	No

9. Are there criminal sanctions for sexual harassment in employment?	No	No

DOMESTIC VIOLENCE

	HAITI	HONDURAS
1. Is there legislation that specifically addresses domestic violence?	No	Yes
2. Is there a specialized court or procedure for cases of domestic violence?	No	Yes
3. Does domestic violence legislation protect women in unmarried intimate relationships?	No	Yes

4. Does domestic violence legislation include the following types of abuse:	Emotional	Financial	Physical	Sexual	Emotional	Financial	Physical	Sexual
	No	No	No	No	Yes	Yes	Yes	Yes

SEXUAL HARASSMENT

	HAITI	HONDURAS
5. Is there legislation that specifically addresses sexual harassment?	No	Yes
6. Are there criminal sanctions for sexual harassment?	No	Yes
7. Is there a governmental office tasked with addressing sexual harassment?	No	Yes

8. Is there legislation on sexual harassment in:	Education	Employment	Public Places	Service Provision	Education	Employment	Public Places	Service Provision
	No	No	No	No	Yes	Yes	No	No

9. Are there criminal sanctions for sexual harassment in employment?	No	Yes

DOMESTIC VIOLENCE

	INDIA	INDONESIA
1. Is there legislation that specifically addresses domestic violence?	Yes	Yes
2. Is there a specialized court or procedure for cases of domestic violence?	Yes	Yes
3. Does domestic violence legislation protect women in unmarried intimate relationships?	Yes	Yes

4. Does domestic violence legislation include the following types of abuse:	Emotional	Financial	Physical	Sexual	Emotional	Financial	Physical	Sexual
	Yes	Yes	Yes	Yes	Yes	Yes	Yes	Yes

SEXUAL HARASSMENT

	INDIA	INDONESIA
5. Is there legislation that specifically addresses sexual harassment?	Yes	No
6. Are there criminal sanctions for sexual harassment?	Yes	No
7. Is there a governmental office tasked with addressing sexual harassment?	Yes	No

8. Is there legislation on sexual harassment in:	Education	Employment	Public Places	Service Provision	Education	Employment	Public Places	Service Provision
	No	Yes	No	No	No	No	No	No

9. Are there criminal sanctions for sexual harassment in employment?	Yes	No

DOMESTIC VIOLENCE

	IRAN, ISLAMIC REP.	ITALY
1. Is there legislation that specifically addresses domestic violence?	No	Yes
2. Is there a specialized court or procedure for cases of domestic violence?	Yes	No
3. Does domestic violence legislation protect women in unmarried intimate relationships?	No	Yes

4. Does domestic violence legislation include the following types of abuse:	Emotional	Financial	Physical	Sexual	Emotional	Financial	Physical	Sexual
	No	No	No	No	Yes	No	Yes	Yes

SEXUAL HARASSMENT

	IRAN, ISLAMIC REP.	ITALY
5. Is there legislation that specifically addresses sexual harassment?	No	Yes
6. Are there criminal sanctions for sexual harassment?	No	No
7. Is there a governmental office tasked with addressing sexual harassment?	No	Yes

8. Is there legislation on sexual harassment in:	Education	Employment	Public Places	Service Provision	Education	Employment	Public Places	Service Provision
	No	No	No	No	No	Yes	No	No

9. Are there criminal sanctions for sexual harassment in employment?	No	No

DOMESTIC VIOLENCE	JAMAICA				JAPAN			
1. Is there legislation that specifically addresses domestic violence?	Yes				Yes			
2. Is there a specialized court or procedure for cases of domestic violence?	No				Yes			
3. Does domestic violence legislation protect women in unmarried intimate relationships?	Yes				Yes			
	Emotional	Financial	Physical	Sexual	Emotional	Financial	Physical	Sexual
4. Does domestic violence legislation include the following types of abuse:	Yes	Yes	Yes	No	Yes	No	Yes	No

SEXUAL HARASSMENT								
5. Is there legislation that specifically addresses sexual harassment?	No				No			
6. Are there criminal sanctions for sexual harassment?	No				No			
7. Is there a governmental office tasked with addressing sexual harassment?	No				No			
	Education	Employment	Public Places	Service Provision	Education	Employment	Public Places	Service Provision
8. Is there legislation on sexual harassment in:	No	No	No	No	No	No	No	No
9. Are there criminal sanctions for sexual harassment in employment?	No				No			

DOMESTIC VIOLENCE	JORDAN				KAZAKHSTAN			
1. Is there legislation that specifically addresses domestic violence?	Yes				Yes			
2. Is there a specialized court or procedure for cases of domestic violence?	No				Yes			
3. Does domestic violence legislation protect women in unmarried intimate relationships?	No				Yes			
	Emotional	Financial	Physical	Sexual	Emotional	Financial	Physical	Sexual
4. Does domestic violence legislation include the following types of abuse:	No	No	No	No	Yes	Yes	Yes	Yes

SEXUAL HARASSMENT								
5. Is there legislation that specifically addresses sexual harassment?	Yes				No			
6. Are there criminal sanctions for sexual harassment?	Yes				No			
7. Is there a governmental office tasked with addressing sexual harassment?	No				No			
	Education	Employment	Public Places	Service Provision	Education	Employment	Public Places	Service Provision
8. Is there legislation on sexual harassment in:	No	No	No	No	No	No	No	No
9. Are there criminal sanctions for sexual harassment in employment?	No				No			

DOMESTIC VIOLENCE	KENYA				KOREA, REP.			
1. Is there legislation that specifically addresses domestic violence?	No				Yes			
2. Is there a specialized court or procedure for cases of domestic violence?	No				Yes			
3. Does domestic violence legislation protect women in unmarried intimate relationships?	No				Yes			
	Emotional	Financial	Physical	Sexual	Emotional	Financial	Physical	Sexual
4. Does domestic violence legislation include the following types of abuse:	No	No	No	No	Yes	Yes	Yes	No

SEXUAL HARASSMENT								
5. Is there legislation that specifically addresses sexual harassment?	Yes				Yes			
6. Are there criminal sanctions for sexual harassment?	Yes				Yes			
7. Is there a governmental office tasked with addressing sexual harassment?	No				Yes			
	Education	Employment	Public Places	Service Provision	Education	Employment	Public Places	Service Provision
8. Is there legislation on sexual harassment in:	Yes	Yes	No	No	Yes	Yes	No	No
9. Are there criminal sanctions for sexual harassment in employment?	Yes				Yes			

DOMESTIC VIOLENCE	LATVIA				LEBANON			
1. Is there legislation that specifically addresses domestic violence?	No				No			
2. Is there a specialized court or procedure for cases of domestic violence?	No				No			
3. Does domestic violence legislation protect women in unmarried intimate relationships?	No				No			
	Emotional	Financial	Physical	Sexual	Emotional	Financial	Physical	Sexual
4. Does domestic violence legislation include the following types of abuse:	No	No	No	No	No	No	No	No

SEXUAL HARASSMENT								
5. Is there legislation that specifically addresses sexual harassment?	Yes				No			
6. Are there criminal sanctions for sexual harassment?	No				No			
7. Is there a governmental office tasked with addressing sexual harassment?	Yes				No			
	Education	Employment	Public Places	Service Provision	Education	Employment	Public Places	Service Provision
8. Is there legislation on sexual harassment in:	No	Yes	No	No	No	No	No	No
9. Are there criminal sanctions for sexual harassment in employment?	No				No			

DOMESTIC VIOLENCE	LESOTHO				LITHUANIA			
1. Is there legislation that specifically addresses domestic violence?	No				Yes			
2. Is there a specialized court or procedure for cases of domestic violence?	No				Yes			
3. Does domestic violence legislation protect women in unmarried intimate relationships?	No				Yes			
	Emotional	Financial	Physical	Sexual	Emotional	Financial	Physical	Sexual
4. Does domestic violence legislation include the following types of abuse:	No	No	No	No	Yes	Yes	Yes	Yes

SEXUAL HARASSMENT								
5. Is there legislation that specifically addresses sexual harassment?	Yes				Yes			
6. Are there criminal sanctions for sexual harassment?	Yes				Yes			
7. Is there a governmental office tasked with addressing sexual harassment?	No				Yes			
	Education	Employment	Public Places	Service Provision	Education	Employment	Public Places	Service Provision
8. Is there legislation on sexual harassment in:	No	Yes	No	No	No	Yes	No	No
9. Are there criminal sanctions for sexual harassment in employment?	Yes				Yes			

DOMESTIC VIOLENCE	MACEDONIA, FYR				MADAGASCAR			
1. Is there legislation that specifically addresses domestic violence?	Yes				Yes			
2. Is there a specialized court or procedure for cases of domestic violence?	No				No			
3. Does domestic violence legislation protect women in unmarried intimate relationships?	Yes				No			
	Emotional	Financial	Physical	Sexual	Emotional	Financial	Physical	Sexual
4. Does domestic violence legislation include the following types of abuse:	Yes	No	Yes	Yes	No	No	Yes	No

SEXUAL HARASSMENT								
5. Is there legislation that specifically addresses sexual harassment?	Yes				Yes			
6. Are there criminal sanctions for sexual harassment?	Yes				Yes			
7. Is there a governmental office tasked with addressing sexual harassment?	Yes				No			
	Education	Employment	Public Places	Service Provision	Education	Employment	Public Places	Service Provision
8. Is there legislation on sexual harassment in:	Yes	Yes	No	No	No	Yes	No	No
9. Are there criminal sanctions for sexual harassment in employment?	Yes				Yes			

DOMESTIC VIOLENCE	MALAWI				MALAYSIA			
1. Is there legislation that specifically addresses domestic violence?	Yes				Yes			
2. Is there a specialized court or procedure for cases of domestic violence?	No				No			
3. Does domestic violence legislation protect women in unmarried intimate relationships?	Yes				Yes			
	Emotional	Financial	Physical	Sexual	Emotional	Financial	Physical	Sexual
4. Does domestic violence legislation include the following types of abuse:	Yes	Yes	Yes	Yes	Yes	Yes	Yes	Yes

SEXUAL HARASSMENT								
5. Is there legislation that specifically addresses sexual harassment?	Yes				Yes			
6. Are there criminal sanctions for sexual harassment?	Yes				Yes			
7. Is there a governmental office tasked with addressing sexual harassment?	Yes				Yes			
8. Is there legislation on sexual harassment in:	Education	Employment	Public Places	Service Provision	Education	Employment	Public Places	Service Provision
	No	Yes	No	No	No	Yes	No	No
9. Are there criminal sanctions for sexual harassment in employment?	No				Yes			

DOMESTIC VIOLENCE	MALI				MAURITIUS			
1. Is there legislation that specifically addresses domestic violence?	No				Yes			
2. Is there a specialized court or procedure for cases of domestic violence?	No				Yes			
3. Does domestic violence legislation protect women in unmarried intimate relationships?	No				Yes			
4. Does domestic violence legislation include the following types of abuse:	Emotional	Financial	Physical	Sexual	Emotional	Financial	Physical	Sexual
	No	No	No	No	Yes	Yes	Yes	Yes

SEXUAL HARASSMENT								
5. Is there legislation that specifically addresses sexual harassment?	No				Yes			
6. Are there criminal sanctions for sexual harassment?	No				Yes			
7. Is there a governmental office tasked with addressing sexual harassment?	No				Yes			
	Education	Employment	Public Places	Service Provision	Education	Employment	Public Places	Service Provision
8. Is there legislation on sexual harassment in:	No	No	No	No	Yes	Yes	No	Yes
9. Are there criminal sanctions for sexual harassment in employment?	No				Yes			

DOMESTIC VIOLENCE	MEXICO				MONGOLIA			
1. Is there legislation that specifically addresses domestic violence?	Yes				Yes			
2. Is there a specialized court or procedure for cases of domestic violence?	Yes				Yes			
3. Does domestic violence legislation protect women in unmarried intimate relationships?	Yes				Yes			
	Emotional	Financial	Physical	Sexual	Emotional	Financial	Physical	Sexual
4. Does domestic violence legislation include the following types of abuse:	Yes	Yes	Yes	Yes	Yes	Yes	Yes	Yes

SEXUAL HARASSMENT

5. Is there legislation that specifically addresses sexual harassment?	Yes				Yes			
6. Are there criminal sanctions for sexual harassment?	Yes				No			
7. Is there a governmental office tasked with addressing sexual harassment?	Yes				Yes			
	Education	Employment	Public Places	Service Provision	Education	Employment	Public Places	Service Provision
8. Is there legislation on sexual harassment in:	Yes	Yes	No	No	No	Yes	No	No
9. Are there criminal sanctions for sexual harassment in employment?	Yes				No			

DOMESTIC VIOLENCE	MOROCCO				MOZAMBIQUE			
1. Is there legislation that specifically addresses domestic violence?	Yes				Yes			
2. Is there a specialized court or procedure for cases of domestic violence?	Yes				No			
3. Does domestic violence legislation protect women in unmarried intimate relationships?	No				Yes			
	Emotional	Financial	Physical	Sexual	Emotional	Financial	Physical	Sexual
4. Does domestic violence legislation include the following types of abuse:	No	No	Yes	No	Yes	Yes	Yes	Yes

SEXUAL HARASSMENT

5. Is there legislation that specifically addresses sexual harassment?	Yes				Yes			
6. Are there criminal sanctions for sexual harassment?	Yes				Yes			
7. Is there a governmental office tasked with addressing sexual harassment?	No				No			
	Education	Employment	Public Places	Service Provision	Education	Employment	Public Places	Service Provision
8. Is there legislation on sexual harassment in:	No	Yes	No	No	No	Yes	No	No
9. Are there criminal sanctions for sexual harassment in employment?	Yes				No			

DOMESTIC VIOLENCE	NAMIBIA				NEPAL			
1. Is there legislation that specifically addresses domestic violence?	Yes				Yes			
2. Is there a specialized court or procedure for cases of domestic violence?	No				Yes			
3. Does domestic violence legislation protect women in unmarried intimate relationships?	Yes				Yes			
	Emotional	Financial	Physical	Sexual	Emotional	Financial	Physical	Sexual
4. Does domestic violence legislation include the following types of abuse:	Yes	Yes	Yes	Yes	Yes	Yes	Yes	Yes

SEXUAL HARASSMENT

5. Is there legislation that specifically addresses sexual harassment?	Yes				Yes			
6. Are there criminal sanctions for sexual harassment?	No				Yes			
7. Is there a governmental office tasked with addressing sexual harassment?	Yes				Yes			
8. Is there legislation on sexual harassment in:	Education	Employment	Public Places	Service Provision	Education	Employment	Public Places	Service Provision
	No	Yes	No	No	No	No	No	No
9. Are there criminal sanctions for sexual harassment in employment?	No				No			

DOMESTIC VIOLENCE	NICARAGUA				NIGER			
1. Is there legislation that specifically addresses domestic violence?	Yes				No			
2. Is there a specialized court or procedure for cases of domestic violence?	Yes				No			
3. Does domestic violence legislation protect women in unmarried intimate relationships?	Yes				No			
	Emotional	Financial	Physical	Sexual	Emotional	Financial	Physical	Sexual
4. Does domestic violence legislation include the following types of abuse:	Yes	Yes	Yes	Yes	No	No	No	No

SEXUAL HARASSMENT

5. Is there legislation that specifically addresses sexual harassment?	Yes				Yes			
6. Are there criminal sanctions for sexual harassment?	Yes				Yes			
7. Is there a governmental office tasked with addressing sexual harassment?	Yes				No			
	Education	Employment	Public Places	Service Provision	Education	Employment	Public Places	Service Provision
8. Is there legislation on sexual harassment in:	Yes	Yes	No	No	No	Yes	No	No
9. Are there criminal sanctions for sexual harassment in employment?	Yes				Yes			

Pilot data on Protecting women from violence

NIGERIA / PAKISTAN

DOMESTIC VIOLENCE	NIGERIA	PAKISTAN
1. Is there legislation that specifically addresses domestic violence?	Yes	No
2. Is there a specialized court or procedure for cases of domestic violence?	No	No
3. Does domestic violence legislation protect women in unmarried intimate relationships?	Yes	No

	Emotional	Financial	Physical	Sexual	Emotional	Financial	Physical	Sexual
4. Does domestic violence legislation include the following types of abuse:	Yes	Yes	Yes	Yes	No	No	No	No

SEXUAL HARASSMENT	NIGERIA	PAKISTAN
5. Is there legislation that specifically addresses sexual harassment?	No	Yes
6. Are there criminal sanctions for sexual harassment?	No	Yes
7. Is there a governmental office tasked with addressing sexual harassment?	No	Yes

	Education	Employment	Public Places	Service Provision	Education	Employment	Public Places	Service Provision
8. Is there legislation on sexual harassment in:	No	No	No	No	No	Yes	Yes	No
9. Are there criminal sanctions for sexual harassment in employment?	No				Yes			

PANAMA / PARAGUAY

DOMESTIC VIOLENCE	PANAMA	PARAGUAY
1. Is there legislation that specifically addresses domestic violence?	Yes	Yes
2. Is there a specialized court or procedure for cases of domestic violence?	Yes	Yes
3. Does domestic violence legislation protect women in unmarried intimate relationships?	Yes	Yes

	Emotional	Financial	Physical	Sexual	Emotional	Financial	Physical	Sexual
4. Does domestic violence legislation include the following types of abuse:	Yes	Yes	Yes	Yes	Yes	No	Yes	Yes

SEXUAL HARASSMENT	PANAMA	PARAGUAY
5. Is there legislation that specifically addresses sexual harassment?	Yes	Yes
6. Are there criminal sanctions for sexual harassment?	No	Yes
7. Is there a governmental office tasked with addressing sexual harassment?	Yes	Yes

	Education	Employment	Public Places	Service Provision	Education	Employment	Public Places	Service Provision
8. Is there legislation on sexual harassment in:	No	Yes	No	No	No	Yes	No	No
9. Are there criminal sanctions for sexual harassment in employment?	No				Yes			

PERU / PHILIPPINES

DOMESTIC VIOLENCE	PERU	PHILIPPINES
1. Is there legislation that specifically addresses domestic violence?	Yes	Yes
2. Is there a specialized court or procedure for cases of domestic violence?	Yes	Yes
3. Does domestic violence legislation protect women in unmarried intimate relationships?	Yes	Yes

	Emotional	Financial	Physical	Sexual	Emotional	Financial	Physical	Sexual
4. Does domestic violence legislation include the following types of abuse:	Yes	No	Yes	No	Yes	Yes	Yes	Yes

SEXUAL HARASSMENT	PERU	PHILIPPINES
5. Is there legislation that specifically addresses sexual harassment?	Yes	Yes
6. Are there criminal sanctions for sexual harassment?	No	Yes
7. Is there a governmental office tasked with addressing sexual harassment?	Yes	Yes

	Education	Employment	Public Places	Service Provision	Education	Employment	Public Places	Service Provision
8. Is there legislation on sexual harassment in:	Yes	Yes	No	No	Yes	Yes	No	No
9. Are there criminal sanctions for sexual harassment in employment?	No				Yes			

POLAND / PORTUGAL

DOMESTIC VIOLENCE	POLAND	PORTUGAL
1. Is there legislation that specifically addresses domestic violence?	Yes	Yes
2. Is there a specialized court or procedure for cases of domestic violence?	No	Yes
3. Does domestic violence legislation protect women in unmarried intimate relationships?	Yes	Yes

	Emotional	Financial	Physical	Sexual	Emotional	Financial	Physical	Sexual
4. Does domestic violence legislation include the following types of abuse:	Yes	Yes	Yes	Yes	Yes	Yes	Yes	No

SEXUAL HARASSMENT	POLAND	PORTUGAL
5. Is there legislation that specifically addresses sexual harassment?	Yes	Yes
6. Are there criminal sanctions for sexual harassment?	Yes	Yes
7. Is there a governmental office tasked with addressing sexual harassment?	Yes	No

	Education	Employment	Public Places	Service Provision	Education	Employment	Public Places	Service Provision
8. Is there legislation on sexual harassment in:	Yes	Yes	No	No	No	Yes	No	No
9. Are there criminal sanctions for sexual harassment in employment?	Yes				Yes			

DOMESTIC VIOLENCE	ROMANIA				RUSSIAN FEDERATION			
1. Is there legislation that specifically addresses domestic violence?	Yes				No			
2. Is there a specialized court or procedure for cases of domestic violence?	Yes				No			
3. Does domestic violence legislation protect women in unmarried intimate relationships?	Yes				No			
	Emotional	Financial	Physical	Sexual	Emotional	Financial	Physical	Sexual
4. Does domestic violence legislation include the following types of abuse:	Yes	No	Yes	Yes	No	No	No	No
SEXUAL HARASSMENT								
5. Is there legislation that specifically addresses sexual harassment?	Yes				Yes			
6. Are there criminal sanctions for sexual harassment?	Yes				Yes			
7. Is there a governmental office tasked with addressing sexual harassment?	Yes				No			
	Education	Employment	Public Places	Service Provision	Education	Employment	Public Places	Service Provision
8. Is there legislation on sexual harassment in:	No	Yes	No	No	No	Yes	No	No
9. Are there criminal sanctions for sexual harassment in employment?	Yes				Yes			

DOMESTIC VIOLENCE	RWANDA				SAUDI ARABIA			
1. Is there legislation that specifically addresses domestic violence?	Yes				No			
2. Is there a specialized court or procedure for cases of domestic violence?	Yes				No			
3. Does domestic violence legislation protect women in unmarried intimate relationships?	No				No			
	Emotional	Financial	Physical	Sexual	Emotional	Financial	Physical	Sexual
4. Does domestic violence legislation include the following types of abuse:	Yes	Yes	Yes	Yes	No	No	No	No
SEXUAL HARASSMENT								
5. Is there legislation that specifically addresses sexual harassment?	Yes				No			
6. Are there criminal sanctions for sexual harassment?	Yes				No			
7. Is there a governmental office tasked with addressing sexual harassment?	Yes				No			
	Education	Employment	Public Places	Service Provision	Education	Employment	Public Places	Service Provision
8. Is there legislation on sexual harassment in:	No	Yes	No	No	No	No	No	No
9. Are there criminal sanctions for sexual harassment in employment?	Yes				No			

DOMESTIC VIOLENCE	SENEGAL				SERBIA			
1. Is there legislation that specifically addresses domestic violence?	Yes				Yes			
2. Is there a specialized court or procedure for cases of domestic violence?	No				No			
3. Does domestic violence legislation protect women in unmarried intimate relationships?	No				Yes			
	Emotional	Financial	Physical	Sexual	Emotional	Financial	Physical	Sexual
4. Does domestic violence legislation include the following types of abuse:	No	No	Yes	No	Yes	No	Yes	No
SEXUAL HARASSMENT								
5. Is there legislation that specifically addresses sexual harassment?	Yes				Yes			
6. Are there criminal sanctions for sexual harassment?	Yes				Yes			
7. Is there a governmental office tasked with addressing sexual harassment?	No				Yes			
	Education	Employment	Public Places	Service Provision	Education	Employment	Public Places	Service Provision
8. Is there legislation on sexual harassment in:	No	Yes	No	No	No	Yes	No	No
9. Are there criminal sanctions for sexual harassment in employment?	Yes				Yes			

DOMESTIC VIOLENCE	SIERRA LEONE				SINGAPORE			
1. Is there legislation that specifically addresses domestic violence?	Yes				Yes			
2. Is there a specialized court or procedure for cases of domestic violence?	Yes				Yes			
3. Does domestic violence legislation protect women in unmarried intimate relationships?	Yes				Yes			
	Emotional	Financial	Physical	Sexual	Emotional	Financial	Physical	Sexual
4. Does domestic violence legislation include the following types of abuse:	Yes	Yes	Yes	Yes	Yes	No	Yes	No
SEXUAL HARASSMENT								
5. Is there legislation that specifically addresses sexual harassment?	Yes				Yes			
6. Are there criminal sanctions for sexual harassment?	Yes				Yes			
7. Is there a governmental office tasked with addressing sexual harassment?	No				No			
	Education	Employment	Public Places	Service Provision	Education	Employment	Public Places	Service Provision
8. Is there legislation on sexual harassment in:	No	No	No	No	No	No	No	No
9. Are there criminal sanctions for sexual harassment in employment?	No				No			

Nigeria–Singapore

Pilot data on Protecting women from violence

DOMESTIC VIOLENCE	SOUTH AFRICA				SPAIN			
1. Is there legislation that specifically addresses domestic violence?	Yes				Yes			
2. Is there a specialized court or procedure for cases of domestic violence?	Yes				Yes			
3. Does domestic violence legislation protect women in unmarried intimate relationships?	Yes				Yes			
	Emotional	Financial	Physical	Sexual	Emotional	Financial	Physical	Sexual
4. Does domestic violence legislation include the following types of abuse:	Yes	Yes	Yes	Yes	Yes	No	Yes	Yes

SEXUAL HARASSMENT								
5. Is there legislation that specifically addresses sexual harassment?	Yes				Yes			
6. Are there criminal sanctions for sexual harassment?	No				Yes			
7. Is there a governmental office tasked with addressing sexual harassment?	No				Yes			
	Education	Employment	Public Places	Service Provision	Education	Employment	Public Places	Service Provision
8. Is there legislation on sexual harassment in:	No	Yes	No	No	Yes	Yes	No	No
9. Are there criminal sanctions for sexual harassment in employment?	No				Yes			

DOMESTIC VIOLENCE	SRI LANKA				SWEDEN			
1. Is there legislation that specifically addresses domestic violence?	Yes				Yes			
2. Is there a specialized court or procedure for cases of domestic violence?	Yes				No			
3. Does domestic violence legislation protect women in unmarried intimate relationships?	Yes				Yes			
	Emotional	Financial	Physical	Sexual	Emotional	Financial	Physical	Sexual
4. Does domestic violence legislation include the following types of abuse:	Yes	No	Yes	Yes	Yes	No	Yes	Yes

SEXUAL HARASSMENT								
5. Is there legislation that specifically addresses sexual harassment?	Yes				Yes			
6. Are there criminal sanctions for sexual harassment?	Yes				No			
7. Is there a governmental office tasked with addressing sexual harassment?	Yes				Yes			
	Education	Employment	Public Places	Service Provision	Education	Employment	Public Places	Service Provision
8. Is there legislation on sexual harassment in:	Yes	Yes	No	No	Yes	Yes	No	No
9. Are there criminal sanctions for sexual harassment in employment?	Yes				No			

DOMESTIC VIOLENCE	SWITZERLAND				SYRIAN ARAB REPUBLIC			
1. Is there legislation that specifically addresses domestic violence?	Yes				No			
2. Is there a specialized court or procedure for cases of domestic violence?	Yes				No			
3. Does domestic violence legislation protect women in unmarried intimate relationships?	Yes				No			
	Emotional	Financial	Physical	Sexual	Emotional	Financial	Physical	Sexual
4. Does domestic violence legislation include the following types of abuse:	Yes	No	Yes	Yes	No	No	No	No

SEXUAL HARASSMENT								
5. Is there legislation that specifically addresses sexual harassment?	Yes				Yes			
6. Are there criminal sanctions for sexual harassment?	Yes				Yes			
7. Is there a governmental office tasked with addressing sexual harassment?	Yes				No			
	Education	Employment	Public Places	Service Provision	Education	Employment	Public Places	Service Provision
8. Is there legislation on sexual harassment in:	No	Yes	No	No	No	No	No	No
9. Are there criminal sanctions for sexual harassment in employment?	No				No			

DOMESTIC VIOLENCE	TANZANIA				THAILAND			
1. Is there legislation that specifically addresses domestic violence?	No				Yes			
2. Is there a specialized court or procedure for cases of domestic violence?	No				Yes			
3. Does domestic violence legislation protect women in unmarried intimate relationships?	No				Yes			
	Emotional	Financial	Physical	Sexual	Emotional	Financial	Physical	Sexual
4. Does domestic violence legislation include the following types of abuse:	No	No	No	No	Yes	No	Yes	No

SEXUAL HARASSMENT								
5. Is there legislation that specifically addresses sexual harassment?	Yes				Yes			
6. Are there criminal sanctions for sexual harassment?	Yes				Yes			
7. Is there a governmental office tasked with addressing sexual harassment?	No				No			
	Education	Employment	Public Places	Service Provision	Education	Employment	Public Places	Service Provision
8. Is there legislation on sexual harassment in:	No	Yes	No	No	No	Yes	No	No
9. Are there criminal sanctions for sexual harassment in employment?	Yes				Yes			

TUNISIA / TURKEY

DOMESTIC VIOLENCE	TUNISIA				TURKEY			
1. Is there legislation that specifically addresses domestic violence?	No				Yes			
2. Is there a specialized court or procedure for cases of domestic violence?	No				Yes			
3. Does domestic violence legislation protect women in unmarried intimate relationships?	No				Yes			
	Emotional	Financial	Physical	Sexual	Emotional	Financial	Physical	Sexual
4. Does domestic violence legislation include the following types of abuse:	No	No	Yes	No	Yes	Yes	Yes	Yes

SEXUAL HARASSMENT	TUNISIA				TURKEY			
5. Is there legislation that specifically addresses sexual harassment?	Yes				Yes			
6. Are there criminal sanctions for sexual harassment?	Yes				Yes			
7. Is there a governmental office tasked with addressing sexual harassment?	No				No			
	Education	Employment	Public Places	Service Provision	Education	Employment	Public Places	Service Provision
8. Is there legislation on sexual harassment in:	No	No	No	No	No	Yes	No	No
9. Are there criminal sanctions for sexual harassment in employment?	No				Yes			

UGANDA / UKRAINE

DOMESTIC VIOLENCE	UGANDA				UKRAINE			
1. Is there legislation that specifically addresses domestic violence?	Yes				Yes			
2. Is there a specialized court or procedure for cases of domestic violence?	Yes				No			
3. Does domestic violence legislation protect women in unmarried intimate relationships?	Yes				No			
	Emotional	Financial	Physical	Sexual	Emotional	Financial	Physical	Sexual
4. Does domestic violence legislation include the following types of abuse:	Yes	Yes	Yes	Yes	Yes	Yes	Yes	Yes

SEXUAL HARASSMENT	UGANDA				UKRAINE			
5. Is there legislation that specifically addresses sexual harassment?	Yes				Yes			
6. Are there criminal sanctions for sexual harassment?	Yes				Yes			
7. Is there a governmental office tasked with addressing sexual harassment?	Yes				Yes			
	Education	Employment	Public Places	Service Provision	Education	Employment	Public Places	Service Provision
8. Is there legislation on sexual harassment in:	No	Yes	No	No	No	Yes	No	Yes
9. Are there criminal sanctions for sexual harassment in employment?	Yes				Yes			

UNITED KINGDOM / UNITED STATES

DOMESTIC VIOLENCE	UNITED KINGDOM				UNITED STATES			
1. Is there legislation that specifically addresses domestic violence?	Yes				Yes			
2. Is there a specialized court or procedure for cases of domestic violence?	Yes				Yes			
3. Does domestic violence legislation protect women in unmarried intimate relationships?	Yes				Yes			
	Emotional	Financial	Physical	Sexual	Emotional	Financial	Physical	Sexual
4. Does domestic violence legislation include the following types of abuse:	Yes	No	Yes	No	Yes	No	Yes	Yes

SEXUAL HARASSMENT	UNITED KINGDOM				UNITED STATES			
5. Is there legislation that specifically addresses sexual harassment?	Yes				Yes			
6. Are there criminal sanctions for sexual harassment?	Yes				No			
7. Is there a governmental office tasked with addressing sexual harassment?	Yes				Yes			
	Education	Employment	Public Places	Service Provision	Education	Employment	Public Places	Service Provision
8. Is there legislation on sexual harassment in:	Yes	Yes	No	No	Yes	Yes	No	No
9. Are there criminal sanctions for sexual harassment in employment?	Yes				No			

URUGUAY / UZBEKISTAN

DOMESTIC VIOLENCE	URUGUAY				UZBEKISTAN			
1. Is there legislation that specifically addresses domestic violence?	Yes				No			
2. Is there a specialized court or procedure for cases of domestic violence?	Yes				No			
3. Does domestic violence legislation protect women in unmarried intimate relationships?	Yes				No			
	Emotional	Financial	Physical	Sexual	Emotional	Financial	Physical	Sexual
4. Does domestic violence legislation include the following types of abuse:	Yes	Yes	Yes	Yes	No	No	No	No

SEXUAL HARASSMENT	URUGUAY				UZBEKISTAN			
5. Is there legislation that specifically addresses sexual harassment?	Yes				Yes			
6. Are there criminal sanctions for sexual harassment?	No				Yes			
7. Is there a governmental office tasked with addressing sexual harassment?	Yes				Yes			
	Education	Employment	Public Places	Service Provision	Education	Employment	Public Places	Service Provision
8. Is there legislation on sexual harassment in:	Yes	Yes	No	No	No	Yes	No	No
9. Are there criminal sanctions for sexual harassment in employment?	No				Yes			

South Africa–
Zimbabwe

Pilot data on Protecting women from violence

DOMESTIC VIOLENCE	VENEZUELA, R.B.				YEMEN, REP.			
1. Is there legislation that specifically addresses domestic violence?	Yes				No			
2. Is there a specialized court or procedure for cases of domestic violence?	Yes				No			
3. Does domestic violence legislation protect women in unmarried intimate relationships?	Yes				No			
	Emotional	Financial	Physical	Sexual	Emotional	Financial	Physical	Sexual
4. Does domestic violence legislation include the following types of abuse:	Yes	Yes	Yes	Yes	No	No	No	No
SEXUAL HARASSMENT								
5. Is there legislation that specifically addresses sexual harassment?	Yes				Yes			
6. Are there criminal sanctions for sexual harassment?	Yes				Yes			
7. Is there a governmental office tasked with addressing sexual harassment?	Yes				No			
	Education	Employment	Public Places	Service Provision	Education	Employment	Public Places	Service Provision
8. Is there legislation on sexual harassment in:	Yes	Yes	No	No	No	No	No	No
9. Are there criminal sanctions for sexual harassment in employment?	Yes				No			

DOMESTIC VIOLENCE	ZAMBIA				ZIMBABWE			
1. Is there legislation that specifically addresses domestic violence?	Yes				Yes			
2. Is there a specialized court or procedure for cases of domestic violence?	Yes				Yes			
3. Does domestic violence legislation protect women in unmarried intimate relationships?	Yes				Yes			
	Emotional	Financial	Physical	Sexual	Emotional	Financial	Physical	Sexual
4. Does domestic violence legislation include the following types of abuse:	Yes	Yes	Yes	Yes	Yes	Yes	Yes	Yes
SEXUAL HARASSMENT								
5. Is there legislation that specifically addresses sexual harassment?	Yes				Yes			
6. Are there criminal sanctions for sexual harassment?	Yes				Yes			
7. Is there a governmental office tasked with addressing sexual harassment?	Yes				No			
	Education	Employment	Public Places	Service Provision	Education	Employment	Public Places	Service Provision
8. Is there legislation on sexual harassment in:	Yes	Yes	Yes	No	No	Yes	No	No
9. Are there criminal sanctions for sexual harassment in employment?	Yes				No			

Acknowledgments

The project to develop the *Women, Business and the Law 2014* indicator set was led by Sarah Iqbal, under the general direction of Augusto López-Claros. Members of the core research team included Nayda Almodóvar-Reteguis, Yasmin Bin-Humam, Garam Dexter, Khrystyna Kushnir, Thibault Meilland and Paula Tavares. Assisting with data collection were Mike Chinoko, Maia Estelle D'Anna, Olusheun Olalekan Olaoshebikan, Lourdes Lizarraga Ortega, Chelsea Rubin, Katrin Anna Schulz, Mohammad Shouman, Rui Yang and Rana Imam Hassan Hosny Younes.

Mohammad Amin, David C. Francis and Judy Yang assisted in the data analysis. Mary Hallward-Driemeier and Tazeen Hasan collaborated in the preparation of the *50 Years of Women's Legal Rights* database. Assisting with data collection for the *50 Years of Women's Legal Rights* database were Shazia Akhter, Tatyana Chursova, Yulia Dovgaya, Abhinav Goel, Sarah Knapp, Erin F. Rogers, Lindsey Scannell, Zachary Walter and Ashley S. Zohar. The surveys for the pilot indicator on Protecting women from violence were prepared in collaboration with UN Women.

The report team is grateful for valuable input and comments provided by Melissa Johns, Jorge Luis Rodriguez Meza and Rita Ramalho, as well as colleagues from across the World Bank Group. The report was edited by AmadeaEditing with final editing by Paul Holtz, and design and graphics by Corporate Visions. The online *Women, Business and the Law* database (http://wbl .worldbank.org) is managed by Preeti Endlaw, supported by Varun V. Doiphode, Andres Baquero Franco, Kunal Patel, Vinod Vasudevan Thottikkatu and Hashim Zia. *The Women, Business and the Law 2014* report outreach strategy was executed by the communications team led by Nadine Ghannam which includes: Hyun Kyong Lee and Sushmitha Malini Narsiah, with support from Christopher Colford, Mary Donaldson and Xenia Zia Morales under the leadership of Nicole Frost.

Preparation of the report was supported by Switzerland's State Secretariat for Economic Affairs (SECO). The preparation of the pilot indicator on Protecting women from violence was supported by the Nordic Trust Fund for Human Rights. The preparation of the *50 Years of Women's Legal Rights* database was supported by the U.K. Department for International Development (DFID).

This report was made possible by the generous contributions of close to 800 lawyers, judges, academics, civil society representatives and public officials in 143 economies. Global contributors are organizations that have completed multiple surveys in their various offices around the world, or who have referred our surveys to their membership. Contact details for local partners are available on the *Women, Business and the Law* website at: http://wbl.worldbank.org

GLOBAL CONTRIBUTORS

Advocates for International Development

American Bar Association (ABA) Commission on Domestic and Sexual Violence

American Bar Association (ABA) Section of International Law

Employment Law Alliance (ELA)

Equality Now

German Women Lawyers Association (Bund Deutscher Juristinnen)

International Financial Law Review (IFLR)

International Models Project on Women's Rights (IMPOWR)

International Society of Women Lawyers (FIDA)

International Society of Women Lawyers (FIDA) Colombia Chapter

LANDESA Center for Women's Land Rights

MassPoint Legal and Strategy Advisory PLLC

The Protection Project

Society for Business and Professional Women (BPW) International

Women Against Violence Europe (WAVE) Network

ALBANIA

Alba Agolli
Refleksione Association

Sokol Elmazaj
Boga & Associates

Emel Haxhillari
Kalo and Associate

Monika Kocaqi, PhD
Refleksione Association

Arben Lena
Lena & Associates Law Firm

Aida Lico
Lena & Associates Law Firm

Artila Rama
Boga & Associates

ALGERIA

Radia Abdous
Ghellal & Mekerba

Larbaoui Malika
Bouchaib Law Firm

ANGOLA

Catarina Neto Fernandes
FBL Advogados

Carla Vieira Mesquita
Zenóglio Oliveira
Advoconsulting, SA.
Angola

ARGENTINA

Ursula Basset
Pontificia Universida
Católica Argentina

Carina Marcela
Castrillón
Estudio Bullo - Tassi -
Estebenet - Lipera -
Torassa Abogados

Graciela De Oto
Fundación Suma Veritas

Jorge Grispo
Estudio Grispo & Asociados

Leticia Andrea
Kabusacki
Harari & Kabusacki
Abogados

Diego Sebastián Kelly
Marval, O'Farrell & Mairal

Malcolm Leckie
Estudio Grispo & Asociados

Carlos Marín Rodríguez
Estudio Bulló - Tassi -
Estebenet - Lipera
Torassa Abogados

Gabriel Pablo Martinez
Niell
Estudio Grispo & Asociados

Laura Pautassi
Equipo Latinoamericano
de Justicia y Género - ELA

Enrique Mariano Stile
Marval, O'Farrell & Mairal

ARMENIA

Lara Aharonian
Women's Support Center

Maro Matosian
Women's Support Center

Liana Voskerchyan
GPartners

AUSTRALIA

Keira Brennan
Clayton Utz

Hedy Cray
Clayton Utz

Tess Lumsdaine
Freehills

Patrick Parkinson
University of Sydney

Susan Pearson
Pearson Family Lawyers

Noeline Rudland

Jane Wright
Freehills

AUSTRIA

Julian Feichtinger
CHSH Cerha Hempel
Spiegelfeld Hlawati, member
of Lex Mundi

Valerie Kramer

Elisabeth Schenkel
CHSH Cerha Hempel
Spiegelfeld Hlawati, member
of Lex Mundi

AZERBAIJAN

Aliagha Akhundov
Baker & McKenzie CIS Ltd.

Fuad Karimov
Kermur Specialized Bureau
of Advocates

Nurlan Mammadov
Baker & McKenzie CIS Ltd.

Mehriban Zeynalova
Clean World Social Union

BANGLADESH

Ishrat Ahmed
Siemens Bangladesh Ltd.

Salma Ali
Bangladesh National Woman
Lawyers' Association

Tania Amir
Amir & Amir Law Associates

Seema Karim
Amir & Amir Law Associates

Eva Quasem
Amir & Amir Law Associates

BELARUS

Sergei Makarchuk|
CHSH Cerha Hempel
Spiegelfeld Hlawati

Oksana Puchkovskaya
Stepanovski, Papakul and
Partners LLC

Nikita Tolkanitsa
CHSH Cerha Hempel
Spiegelfeld Hlawati

Natalia Ulasevich
Aleinikov & Partners

Liliya Vlasova
Vlasova, Mikhel & Partners

BELGIUM

Ian Forrester
White & Case LLP

Elvire Vignon
Cabinet d'avocats Vignon

BENIN

Cristel Akofa Gomez
Cabinet Gomez & Hermès

Vera Nkwate Ngassa

BOLIVIA

Carolina Aguirre Urioste
Bufete Aguirre Soc. Civ

Andrea Bollmann Duarte
Salazar, Salazar & Asociados
Soc. Civ.

Julieta Montaño
Oficina Jurídica Para la Mujer

Lorena Salazar Machicado
Salazar, Salazar & Asociados
Soc. Civ.

Sandra Salinas
C.R.& F. ROJAS- Abogados

Katia Uriona Gamarra
Coordinadora de la Mujer

BOSNIA AND HERZEGOVINA

Association of Women to Women (Udruzenje Zene Zenama)

Suvad Bakić
Wolf Theiss D.O.O. Sarajevo

Dina Duraković
Wolf Theiss D.O.O. Sarajevo

Feđa Dupovac
Attorney Office Spaho

Sead Miljković
Wolf Theiss D.O.O. Sarajevo

Amela Selmanagic
Wolf Theiss D.O.O. Sarajevo

Mehmed Spaho
Advokatska Kancelarija Spaho

Selma Spaho
Advokatska Kancelarija Spaho

Emir Spaho
Attorney Office Spaho

BOTSWANA

Yvonne K. Chilume
Chilume & Company

Tatenda Dumba
Armstrongs Attorneys
Notaries & Conveyancers

BRAZIL

Leticia Calderaro Batista
Centro Universitário do
Distrito Federal

Fábia Bertanha
Machado Meyer Sendacz e
Opice Advogados

Bruna Costa
Secretaria de Políticas para as
Mulheres da Presidência da
República

Moana Furletti
Papini Quadros e Quadros
Advogados Associados

Cibelle Goldfarb
BM&A Advogados

Sinara Gumieri
Anis – Instituto de Bioética,
Direitos Humanos e Gênero

Jorge Gonzaga Matsumoto
Machado Meyer Sendacz e
Opice Advogados

Carolina Ortolar
BM&A Advogados

Cristina Ortolar
BM&A Advogados

Juliana Paiva
Anis – Instituto de Bioética,
Direitos Humanos e Gênero

Fabiana Paranhos
Anis – Instituto de Bioética,
Direitos Humanos e Gênero

Camilla Arno Sant'Anna

Michele Silveira
BM&A Advogados

Mauricio Quadros Soares
Papini Quadros e Quadros
Advogados Associados

Naomy Christiani Takara

Marcela Tavares
Machado Meyer Sendacz e
Opice Advogados

Aline Yamamoto
Secretaria de Políticas para
as Mulheres da Presidência
da República

BULGARIA

Dimitar Dimov
Dimov&Tashev Law Firm

Katerina Partenova
Dimov&Tashev Law Firm

Radoslav Tashev
Dimov&Tashev Law Firm

BURKINA FASO

Patinde Marie Louise
Eléonore Belemlilga
Ministère de l'Eau, de
l'Assainissement et des
Aménagements Hydrauliques

Hamsetou Madeleine
Ouedraogo
Association Koom

BURUNDI

Dany-Axelle Ndayishimiya
Barreau de Bujumbura-
Burundi et consultant chez
Mkono & Co. Burundi

Lambert Nigarura
Barreau de Bujumbura-
Burundi et consultant chez
Mkono & Co. Burundi

Fabien Segatwa
Etude Me Segatwa

CAMBODIA

The Cambodian Center for
Human Rights

Sophal Chea
Better Factories Cambodia

Vandanet Hing
P&A Asia Law Firm

Veng Muoyky
P&A Asia Law Firm

Sokla San
P&A Asia Law Firm

Bun Huy Seng
P&A Asia Law Firm

CAMEROON

Che Collins
Voice of Grace Foundation
Cameroon

Désiré Makondo
DM & Partners

Isidore Baudouin Ndzana
PricewaterhouseCoopers Tax
and Legal

Neba Priscillia Lum
Voice of Grace Foundation
Cameroon

Patrick Menyeng Manga
The Abeng Law Firm

Ndonwi Wilfred
Voice of Grace Foundation
Cameroon

CANADA

Caroline Kim

Regina Martyn
Norton Rose Fulbright Canada
LLP

CHAD

Oscar d'Estaing Deffosso
PricewaterhouseCoopers Tax
and Legal

Guy Emmanuel Ngankam
PwC

CHILE

Juan Pablo Cabezón Otero
Estudio Jurídico Otero

Dolores Echeverría
Estudio Jurídico Otero

Natalia García Swaneck
Universidad del Desarrollo

Juan Ignacio Ipinza Mayor

Juana Méndez Barra
Corporación de Promoción y
Defensa de los Derechos del
Pueblo (CODEPU)

Gerardo Otero Alvarado
Estudio Jurídico Otero

Lucía Planet Sepúlveda|
Defesoría Laboral

Luis Andrés Ulloa Martínez
Carey y Cía Abogados

Viviana Uribe Tamblay
Corporación de Promoción y
Defensa de los Derechos del
Pueblo (CODEPU)

CHINA

Xue Bai
Times Commerce Law Firm

Ruiling Chen
Yingke Law Firm

Zhang Hongtao
Beijing Dacheng Law
Firm(Qingdao)

Xiaofei Li
Yingke Law Firm

Jeffrey Wilson
Jun He Law Offices

Sun Xiang
Beijing Dacheng Law
Firm(Qingdao)

COLOMBIA

Katherine Acuña
Universidad Sergio Arboleda

Paula Aguirre Ospina
Universidad Sergio Arboleda

María Margarita Bucheli Eraso

Andrea Caicedo Parra
Universidad Sergio Arboleda

Rafael Campo Díaz
Universidad Sergio Arboleda

Mario Castro Tarazona
Universidad Sergio Arboleda

Alberto José Esmeral
Universidad Sergio Arboleda

Carolina Gómez Osorio
Universidad Sergio Arboleda

José González Zuñiga
Universidad Sergio Arboleda

Natalia Andrea González
Universidad Sergio Arboleda

Juan Camilo Guevara Ortiz
Universidad de San
Buenaventura Cali

Fabián Andrés Hurtado
Oliveros
Universidad Sergio Arboleda

María Camila Jiménez Molina
Universidad Sergio Arboleda

Juan Carlos Moreno Peralta
Rodriguez Retamoso &
Associates

Elvira Isabel Osorio
Universidad Sergio Arboleda

María Adelaida Palacio Puerta
Universidad Sergio Arboleda

Nicolás Eduardo Riaño
Jiménez
Universidad Sergio Arboleda

Liliana María Rodríguez
Retamoso Rodriguez
Retamoso & Associates

María Paula Suárez Cock
Universidad Sergio Arboleda

CONGO, DEM. REP.

Pappy Kajabika

Ngay Guy Kalasi

Ridelphine Katabesha
Association des Femmes des
Medias du Sud-kivu AFEM/SK

Chouchou Namegabe
Association des Femmes des
Medias du Sud-kivu AFEM/SK

Dunia Zongwe

CONGO, REP.

Association Congolaise pour
le Développement Agricole
ACDA

Germaine Onanga née
Nguenoni
Comité National des Droits de
la Femme

Daldy Rustichel Youbou
Biagha

COSTA RICA

Rocío Amador Hasbun
Bufete Amador

Anna Karina Jiménez
Arias & Muñoz

Diana Pál-Hagedüs Ortega
Pál-Hegedüs & Ortega
Abogados

Marianne Pál-Hegedüs Ortega
Pál-Hegedüs & Ortega
Abogados

Paola Rivera
Arias & Muñoz

Graciela Soto
Arias & Muñoz

CÔTE D'IVOIRE

Abiba Coulibaly
Association des Femmes
Juristes de Côte d'Ivoire

Gnamien Emilienne Coulibaly
Association des Femmes
Juristes de Côte d'Ivoire

Julie Edoukou
Association des Femmes
Juristes de Côte d'Ivoire

Claude-Andrée Groga
Cabinet Jean-François
Chauveau

Koffi Marcelline Komenan
Association des Femmes
Juristes de Côte d'Ivoire

Patricia N'Guessan
Cabinet Jean-François
Chauveau

Véronique Ossohou-Kone
International Rescue
Committee Côte d'Ivoire

CROATIA

Women's Room–Center for
Sexual Rights

Marko Borsky
Divjak, Topić & Bahtijarević

Saša Divjak
Divjak, Topić & Bahtijarević

Marko Lovrić
Divjak, Topić & Bahtijarević

Ema Menđušić Škugor
Divjak, Topić & Bahtijarević

Karlo Novosel
Law Office Karlo Novosel

Davor Rukonić
Divjak, Topić & Bahtijarević

CZECH REPUBLIC

Barbara Adamcová

Jiri Balastik
Kocián Šolc Balaštík

Lenka Droscová
Balcar Polanský Eversheds

Radek Matouš
Balcar Polanský Eversheds

Sasha Stepanova
Kocián Šolc Balaštík

DENMARK

Elsebeth Aaes-Jørgensen
Norrbom Vindinq

Jacob Engelbrechtsen
Copenhagen University,
Denmark

Majken Johansen
Advokaterne

Annette Kronborg
Copenhagen University,
Denmark

Tina Reissmann
Plesner

DOMINICAN REPUBLIC

Guzmán Ariza Abogados y
Notarios

Merielin Almonte
Merielin Almonte Estudio
Legal

Marielle Garrigó
Pellerano & Herrera

Elisabetta Pedersini
Aaron Suero & Pedersini

Laura Pellerano
Pellerano & Herrera

Rosalía Prota
Pellerano & Herrera

Juan Manuel Suero
Aaron Suero & Pedersini

Ana Gisselle Valerio
Troncoso & Caceres

Ana Massielle Valerio
Thomas & Thomas

ECUADOR

Mariuxi Baquerizo

Daniela Chacón Arias
Prófitas S.A.

Juan Pablo Morales Viteri
Proyelítica

Wendy Reyes Chiriboga
Proyelítica

Raúl Riquelme Cardenas
Herrera Olalla & Riquelme
Abogados

EGYPT, ARAB REP.

Nevine Abou Alam
Ibrachy & Dermarkar Law Firm

Nanis Abou El Fotuh
Ibrachy & Dermarkar Law Firm

Sahar Abd Al-Sattar Emam
Menoufia - University Faculty
of Law

Sahar Emam
Menoufia University - Faculty
of Law

Rabha Fathy
Association of Egyptian
Female Lawyers

Marwa Omara
Telelaws

Abd Al-Rahman Quasem

EL SALVADOR

Christian Bará
Bufete Arias & Muñoz

David Ernesto Claros Flores
García & Bodán

Silvia Juárez
ORMUSA, Asoc. Organización
de Mujeres Salvadoreñas por
la Paz

Efraín Marroquín
Bufete Arias & Muñoz

Miriam Mixco
Gold Service, S.A. de C.V.

Violeta Molina Rivas
García & Bodán

Josué Rafael Reyes Campos
Bufete Arias & Muñoz

Kelly Beatríz Romero
Rodríguez
Nassar Abogados

Jaime Alberto Salinas Olivares
García & Bodán

Oscar José Torres Cañas
García & Bodán

Julio Vargas
García & Bodán

ESTONIA

Juulika Aavik
Advokaadibüroo
SORAINEN AS

Kaia Kuusler
Advokaadibüroo
SORAINEN AS

Karin Madisson
Advokaadibüroo SORAINEN A

Rando Maisvee
Eversheds Ots & Co.

Lauri Paulus
Law Office Legalia

Sandra Värk
Eversheds Ots & Co.

ETHIOPIA

Fikadu Asfaw
Fikadu Asfaw Law Office

Yodit Gurji
Fikadu Asfaw Law Office

Mahlet Mesganaw
Dagnachew Tesfaye Law
Office

Dagnachew Tesfaye
Dagnachew Tesfaye Law
Office

FIJI

Nicholas Barnes
Munro Leys

Shayne Sorby
Munro Leys

FINLAND

Jari-Pekka Alho
Krogerus Attorneys Ltd.

Jessica Brander
Dittmar & Indrenius

Petri Eskola
Backstrom & Co. Attorneys
Ltd.

Laura-Maria Lindström
Attorneys at Law Borenius

Raija-Leena Ojanen
Dittmar & Indrenius

Johanna Pakkanen
The Feminist Association
Union

Anna Polvenlahti
Krogerus Attorneys Ltd.

Jani Syrjänen
Attorneys at Law Borenius

Sami Tuominen
Attorneys at Law Borenius

FRANCE

Jérémie Blond
Cabinet Jérémie Blond

Aude Chloe Froment
Froment Marginale Associes

Marion Le Roux
Cabinet d'avocats Bredin Prat
AARPI

Virginie J.M. Tassin

GABON

Mano Itchola Alade
Scip Itchola & Agbanrin

Bernie Yala Tchimbakala
Cabinet d'Avocats Albert
Bikalou

GEORGIA

Boris Janjalia

GERMANY

German Women Lawyer's
Association, Commission on
Violence Against Women and
Children

Sibylla Flügge
Fachhochschule Frankfurt am
Main

Sibylla Gage-Lindner
Hessisches Sozialministerium
(Hesse Department of Social
Welfare)

Jan Tibor Lelley
Buse Heberer Fromm

GHANA

Emma Amakye
A&A law Consultant

Meredith Bambrick

Samuel Bryar

Hilary Gbedemah
The Law Institute

Funmi Iyayi
Integrated Legal Consultants

GREECE

Loukia Argyropoulou
General Secretariat for
Gender Equality, Ministry of
Interior

Ismini Assimakopoulou
KGDI

Anastasia Kelveridou
Kyriakides Georgopoulos &
Daniolos Issaias Law Firm

Effie Mitsopoulou
Kyriakides Georgopoulos &
Daniolos Issaias Law Firm

Viktoria Zioga

GUATEMALA

Roberto Carlos Ávila Del Cid
García & Bodán

Eduardo Calderón
Universidad Francisco
Marroquín

Fausto García
Universidad Francisco
Marroquín

Francisco Sagastume
García & Bodán

GUINEA

Yves Constant Amani
Anyray & Partners Guinea

HAITI

Girovna Brice
Cabinet Céant

Jean-Baptiste Brown
Brown Legal Group

Jean-Henry Céant
Cabinet Céant

Michèle Delerme
Banque de la République
d'Haïti

Marie Douchka Porcena
Cabinet Exumé

Frantz Elyzée
Association Nationale des
Institutions de Microfinance
d'Haïti

Jean Frisca Alexandre
Cabinet Exumé

Patrick Laurent
Cabinet Patrick Laurent &
Associés

Marie Josée Louisme
Office de Protection du
Citoyen et de la Citoyenne

Micosky Pompilus
Cabinet Chalmers & Chalmers

Carine Roenen
Fonkoze

Jean-Frédéric Salès
Cabinet Salès

Sibylle Théard Mevs
Théard & Associés

HONDURAS

Marcela Aguilar
Central Law Honduras -
Medina, Rosenthal &
Asociados

Gina María Aronne Laitano
Secretaría de Justicia y
Derechos Humanos

Alma Coello

Graciela Cruz
García & Bodán

Vivian Link

Ada Carolina López Aguilar
Secretaría de Justicia y
Derechos Humanos

Guadalupe Martínez Casas
Central Law Honduras -
Medina, Rosenthal &
Asociados

Ana Gabriela Mayes
Bufete Casco-Fortín, Cruz &
Asociados

Claribel Medina
Central Law Honduras -
Medina, Rosenthal &
Asociados

Jesus Humberto Medina-Alva
Central Law Honduras -
Medina, Rosenthal &
Asociados

Jazna Vanessa Oquelí
García & Bodán

Ana Romero

Roberto Williams Cruz
Bufete Casco-Fortín, Cruz &
Asociados

HONG KONG SAR, CHINA

Cynthia Chung
Deacons

Nga Kit (Christy) Tang

HUNGARY

Schalkház Éva Edit
Schalkház Law Office

Dézsi-Péterfy Ferenc
Dr. Péterfy Law Office

Tamás Mészáros
Dr. Rátky and Partners Law
Office

Attila Richter
Dr. Rátky and Partners Law
Office

Marianna Toth
Law Office of Marianna Toth

ICELAND

Gudrun Bergsteinsdottir
LOCAL Attorneys

Steinunn Holm Gudbjarsdottir
Borgarlogmenn sf. Holm &
Partners

Margrét Steinarsdóttir
Icelandic Human Rights
Centre

INDIA

Mohak Bhadana
Supreme Court of India

Shweta Bharti
Hammurabi & Solomon

Manjula Chawla
Phoenix Legal

Ritika Ganju
Phoenix Legal

Atul Gupta
Trilegal

Bina Jain
All India Women's Conference

Jyotika Kalra
All India Women's Conference

Sonia Kapoor
Hammurabi & Solomon

Rajas Kasbekar
Little & Co. Advocates &
Solicitors

Manoj Kumar
Hammurabi & Solomon

Pratyush Kumar
National Law University Delhi

Isha Mehta
Kesar Dass B & Associates

Bhargavi Mudakavi
Trilegal

Ajay Raghavan
Trilegal

Juhi Singh
Hammurabi & Solomon

Kanisshka Tyagi
Kesar Dass B & Associates

INDONESIA

Beauty Erowati Siswojo

Abdul Hamim Jauzie
LBH Apik's Federation

Lany Harijanti

Nursyahbani Katjasungkana
LBH Apik's Federation

Rusmaini Lenggogeni
Soewito Suhardiman
Eddymurthy Kardono

Elisabeth Lino
Soewito Suhardiman
Eddymurthy Kardono

IRAN, ISLAMIC, REP.

Shahrzad Majdameli
International Law Office
of Dr. Behrooz Akhlaghi &
Associates

IRELAND

Catherine Austin
Arthur Cox

Aisling Burke
Arthur Cox

Inge Clissmann
Inge Clissmann S.C
Kathleen Garrett
Arthur Cox

Leanne Cochrane
Northern Ireland Human
Rights Commission

Roisin Liddy
Law Library, Four Court,
Dublin

Elaine Mettler
Arthur Cox

Gill Woods
Arthur Cox

ISRAEL

Pnina Broder Manor
Naschitz Brandes & Co.

Ayala Filmus
Naschitz Brandes & Co.

Shoshana Gavish
S. Horowitz & Co.

Arnon Samburski
Naschitz Brandes & Co.

Ayelet Simon-Vekslar
Weinstock Zecler & Co.

ITALY

Giuseppe Battaglia Portolano
Cavallo Studio Legale

Enrichetta Sandra Bellini
Fornera
Business and Professional
Women International (BPWI)

Manuela Cavallo
Portolano Cavallo Studio
Legale

Andrea Gangemi
Portolano Cavallo Studio
Legale

Giliola Langher

Cesare Lombrassa
Studio Legale Lombrassa

Federica Midiri

Marilita Piromalli

Portolano Cavallo Studio
Legale

Giulia Quatrini
Portolano Cavallo Studio
Legale

JAMAICA

Maria Burke
DunnCox

Natasha Parkins
Institute for Gender and
Development Studies

Sharon Smith
Patterson Mair Hamilton

JAPAN

Kenichi Kojima
Ushijima & Partners

Ryoyu Naito
Naito & Associates

Tomonori Suwa
Haraguchi International
Law Office

Tomoko Tsuchida

Shin Ushijima
Ushijima & Partners

JORDAN

Amer Mohd Abu-Hassan
Abu-Hassan & Associates
Lawyers & Consultants

Mahasen Al-Jaghoub
University of Jordan

Omar Aljazy
Aljazy & Co. (Advocates &
Legal Consultants)

Tarik Arida
Arida Law Firm

Laith Nasrawin
Aljazy & Co. (Advocates &
Legal Consultants)

KAZAKHSTAN

Zulfiya Akchurina
Grata Law Firm

Tatyana Gustap
Aequitas Law Firm

Marina Kolesnikova
Grata Law Firm

Askar Konysbayev
Grata Law Firm

Shayakhmet Zharkimbayev
Grata Law Firm

KENYA

Jane Kamangu

Angela Kimani
Kaplan & Stratton Advocates

Rose Kimotho
Kenya National Commission
on Human Rights

Rosemary Mugwe

Roselynn Musa

Helene Namisi
Namisi & Company Advocates

Christina Ndiho
Kaplan & Stratton Advocates

Jacqueline Nyabwa
Anjarwalla & Khanna
Advocates

Sonal Sejpal
Anjarwalla & Khanna
Advocates

KOREA, REP.

Chun Wook Hyun
Kim & Chang

Marian Im
Kim,Choi & Lim

Hun-gap Jo
Kim,Choi & Lim

Bo Moon Jung
Kim & Chang

KOSOVO

Sokol Elmazaj
Boga & Associates

Sabina Lalaj
Boga & Associates

Delvina Nallbani
Boga & Associates

Kujtesa Nezaj-Shehu
SDP KOSOVË

Nita Shala
Kosovo Legal Group

Xhevdet Shala
Kosovo Legal Group

Besa Tauzi
Boga & Associates

KUWAIT

Ola Saab
Curtis, Mallet-Prevost, Colt
& Mosle Ltd. (in association
with Mashora Advocates and
Legal Consultants)

KYRGYZ REPUBLIC

Lenara Mambetalieva
Promotion of Foreign
Investment to Kyrgyzstan,
Geneva

Natalia Molodanova
Veritas Law Agency

Aisanat Safarbekkyzy
Grata Law Firm

Elvira Sharshekeeva
Grata Law Firm

LAO PDR

Sithong Chanthasouk
Foreign Trade Policy
Department, Ministry of
Industry and Commerce,
Lao PDR

Jan Edwards
Edu-research Consulting

LATVIA

Andis Burkevics
SORAINEN

Juris Dilba
Resource Centre for Women
"Marta"

Jelena Kvjatkovska
Law Office Rode & Partners

Evija Mikelsone
SORAINEN

Lāsma Rugāte
SORAINEN

Janis Taukacs
SORAINEN

LEBANON

Leila Alem Hammoud
Alem & Associates Law Firm

Melkar El Khoury

Maryline Kalaydjian
Badri and Salim El Meouchi
Law Firm, member of
Interleges

Joelle Khater
Etude Badri et Salim El
Meouchi

Antoine Sfeir
Badri and Salim El Meouchi
Law Firm, member of
Interleges

LESOTHO

Litsabako Kali

Bokang Makututsa

Mamosa Mohlabula-Nokana

Nthoateng Russel

Lindiwe Sephomolo
Federation of Women
Lawyers

Tomas Thakalekoala

LIBERIA

Mohamedu F. Jones
Liberian Legal International
Inc.

LITHUANIA

Viktorija Čivilytė
Budvytis, Civilis and Partners,
Law Firm

Audrone Kisieliene
European Innovation Centre

Liudmila Mecajeva
Social Innovation Fund

Marius Navickas
Budvytis, Civilis and Partners,
Law Firm

Algirdas Pekšys
SORAINEN

Vilius Velica
Mykolas Romeris University

Agnietė Žukauskaitė
SORAINEN

MACEDONIA, FYR

Association for Emancipation,
Solidarity and Equality of
Women

Emilija Kelesoska Sholjakovska
Debarliev, Dameski &
Kelesoska Attorneys at Law

Elena Miceva
Debarliev, Dameski &
Kelesoska Attorneys at Law

Valerjan Monevski
Monevski Law Firm

MADAGASCAR

Johanne Francia
Andria-Manantena

Olivia Alberte Rajerison
Cabinet d'Avocats Rajerison

Bebisoa Zafindravaka
Cabinet John W. Ffooks & Co.

MALAWI

Masauko Chamkakala
Churchill, Norris & Foster Law
Consultants

Mike Chinoko
Malawi Law Commission

Martha Chizuma-Mwangonde

Tisungane Makato
Ministry of Justice and
Constitutional Affairs

Burton Mhango
Mbendera & Nkhono
Associates

Mercy Mulele
MTM Law Chambers

Rachel Sophie Sikwese
High Court of Malawi

Chikosa Silungwe
The Mizumali Foundation

MALAYSIA

Messrs Shearn Delamore
& Co.

Suryna Ali

Ren Chung Yu
Women's Aid Organisation
(WAO)

Nathan Jackson
Solidiance

Zaleha Kamaruddin
International Islamic
University Malaysia

Lauren Low
Messrs Zain & Co.

Hui Ming Teh
Solidiance

Sivabalah Nadarajah
Messrs Shearn Delamore & Co

Umar Oseni
International Islamic
University Malaysia

Ming Wang Lim
Messrs Zain & Co.

Hakimah Yaacob
International Shariah Research
Academy for Islamic Finance
(ISRA)

MALI

Mamoudou Samassekou
Faculté de Droit Privé de
l'Université de Sciences
Juridiques et Politiques de
Bamako

MAURITIUS

Najibah Emamally
Wortels Lexus

Fayaz Hajee Abdoula
BLC Chambers

Jason Harel
BLC Chambers

Siv Potayya
Wortels Lexus

Bhavna Ramsurun
BLC Chambers

MEXICO

Vanessa Casas Vessi
Barrera, Siqueiros y Torres
Landa, S.C.

Juan Carlos De la Vega
Santamarina y Steta, S.C.

Mary Carmen Fuertes Abascal
Barrera, Siqueiros y Torres
Landa, S.C.

Laura Elena García González
Sanchez, Nuñez y Asociados,
S.C.

Paola Florencia López
Jiménez
Barrera, Siqueiros y Torres
Landa, S.C.

Luis Francisco Núñez Garrido
Sanchez, Nuñez y Asociados,
S.C.

Alan Tirzo Ramírez Cassaza
Barrera, Siqueiros y Torres
Landa, SC

Fernando Rodríguez Cortina
Barrera, Siqueiros y Torres
Landa, S.C.

Luis Adrián Rosas Ortega
Barrera, Siqueiros y Torres
Landa, S.C.

Paola Sánchez Hernandez
Barrera, Siqueiros y Torres
Landa, S.C.

Cecilia Stahlhut Espinosa
Barrera, Siqueiros y Torres
Landa, S.C.

Francisco Udave Treviño
Santamarina y Steta, S.C.

MOLDOVA

Gheorghe Avornic
Avornic & Partners

Marin Domente
Avornic & Partners

Alexandru Munteanu
Intreprinderea
cu Capital Strain
PricewaterhouseCoopers
Legal SRL

Ilona Panurco
PricewaterhouseCoopers
Legal

MONGOLIA

Otgon Altankhuyag

Odonchimeg Chuluunbat
National Center Against
Violence

Enkhjargal Davaasuren
National Center Against
Violence

Munkhsaruul Mijiddorj
National Center Against
Violence

Muugi
National Center Against
Violence

Arvintaria Nordogjav
National Center Against
Violence

Bolormaa Volodya
Grata Law Firm

MONTENEGRO

Jelena Danilovic
Karanovic & Nikolic Law Office

Jadranka Jerkovic
Karanovic & Nikolic Law Office

Iva Paic
Karanovic & Nikolic Law Office

Branimir Rajsic
Karanovic & Nikolic Law Office

MOROCCO

Moulay El Amine El
Hammoumi Idrissi
Hajji & Associés

Reda Gzouli
Cabinet Gzouli & Associés

Amin Hajji
Hajji & Associés

Ali Lachgar Essahili
Lachgar Essahili Law Firm

Aatifa Timjerdine
Association Démocratique des
Femmes du Maroc

MOZAMBIQUE

Amina Abdala
GLM-Gabinete Legal
Moçambique

Eduardo Calú
Sal & Caldeira, Advogados,
Lda.

Edurne Monreal Garcés

Gimina Mahumana
Sal & Caldeira, Advogados,
Lda.

Diana Ramalho
Sal & Caldeira, Advogados,
Lda.

NAMIBIA

Nekwaya Eliaser
Government Attorney Office

Petrine Hango
Titus Ipumbu Legal
Practitioners

NEPAL

Bidya Bhattarai
Beyond Beijing Committee

Pratima Burma
Gandhi and Associates

Ankita KC

Rishu Mulepati
Gandhi and Associates

Rakshya Paudyal
Beyond Beijing Committee

Surendra Pokharel

Laxmi Prabha Shrestha
Beyond Beijing Committee

Deepak Raj Joshi
Gandhi and Associates

Balkrishna Sharma

Renuka Devi Sitaula

NETHERLANDS

Eugenie Nunes
Boekel De Nerée N.V.

Rekha Rambali-Jhagroe
Schut van de Ven
Notariskantoor B.V.

Nanouck Schmeitz
Boekel De Nerée N.V.

NEW ZEALAND

Phillipa Muir
Simpson Grierson

NICARAGUA

Blanca Paola Buitrago Molina
García & Bodán

Karen Amelia Cerrato
Espinoza
Alvarado y Asociados

Yuri Fernando Cerrato
Espinoza
Alvarado y Asociados

Luz Marina Espinoza Ruiz
Alvarado y Asociados

Azahalia Solís Román
Movimiento Autónomo de
Mujeres

Carlos Eduardo Téllez Páramo
García & Bodán

NIGER

Balkissa Dialo
Association des Femmes
Juristes du Niger à Niameyt

Wassa Djataou
SWAA-Niger

Ibrahim Djermakoye
Cabinet I. Djermakoye,
Avocats

Ibrahim Haby
Coordination des ONG et
Associations Feminines
Nigeriennes (CONGAFEN)

NIGERIA

Adejumoke Ademiluyi
Udo Udoma & Belo-Osagie

Joseph Eimunjeze
Udo Udoma & Belo-Osagie

Mary Ekemezie
Udo Udoma & Belo-Osagie

Folake Elias Adebowale
Udo Udoma & Belo-Osagie

Ibiyemi Fashina
MacStellos Consulting

Oluwabukola Iji
SPA Ajibade & Co.

Kafayat Jumoke Lambo
Udo Udoma & Belo-Osagie

Nkeiruka Mgbeoji
Blackfriars LLP

Ozofu Ogiemudia
Udo Udoma & Belo-Osagie

Osai Ojigho
Alliances for Africa

Olaoye Olalere
SPA Ajibade & Co.

Adebisi Oyelade
F.O. Fagboghungbe & Co.

Folakemi Praise
Margsolu Legal Practitioners
& Consultants

NORWAY

Berit Stokke
Thommessen

OMAN

Kamilia Al Busaidy
Cutirs, Mallet-Prevost, Colt
& Mosle LLP

Sarah Al Sharji

Azzan Al Yahmadi
Said Al Shahry Law Office
(SASLO)

PAKISTAN

Zeeshan Ashraf
Meer & Hasan

Salim Hasan
Meer & Hasan

Hina Hafeezullah Ishaq
shaq & Sayed

Wahid Khan
Women Shade

Farah Nawaz Azam
Ishaq & Sayed

Amir Siddiq
Ishaq & Sayed

PANAMA

Eliecer Almanza Carrasco

María Judith Arrocha de la
Rosa
Despacho Legal Arrocha de la
Rosa Abogados (ADELAR)

Nelly Cedeño de Paredes
Organo Judicial

PAPUA NEW GUINEA

Clayton Joseph
Ashurst LLP

Jeff Shepherd
Ashurst LLP

Derek Wood
Ashurst LLP

PARAGUAY

Ysmael Reinerio Gaona Villaba
Aprevim Paraguay

Alicia Marti
Aprevim Paraguay

María Esmeralda Moreno
Moreno Ruffinelli & Asociados

Romina Paiva Godoy

Rodolfo G. Vouga
Vouga & Olmedo Abogados

PERU

Tania Díaz Delgado
Universidad Católica San
Pablo

Clea Guerra
Centro de la Mujer Peruana
Flora Tristan

Claudia Cecilia Morán Morales
Poder Judicial de Perú

Ana María Olguín Britto
Universidad Católica San
Pablo

Lidia Vilchez Garcés
Estudio Ferrero Abogados

PHILIPPINES

Kenneth Chua
Quisumbing Torres, member
firm of Baker and Mckenzie
International

Leslie Dy
SyCip Salazar Hernandez &
Gatmaitan

Joan Mae S. To
SyCip Salazar Hernandez &
Gatmaitan

Paolo Tolentino
Quisumbing Torres, member
firm of Baker and Mckenzie
International

POLAND

Wojciech Babicki
Miller, Canfield, W. Babicki,
A. Chełchowski i Wspólnicy
Sp. K.

Małgorzata Grzelak
Squire Sanders Świecicki
Krzesniak sp.k.

Monika Kamińska
University of Warsaw, Faculty
of Law and Administration

Michal Niemirowicz-Szczytt
bnt Neupert Zamorska &
Partnerzy S.C.

Grzegorz Piliszek

Dominika Wagrodzka
bnt Neupert Zamorska &
Partnerzy S.C.

Monika Wołłk-Łaniewska

Mariola Wolska-Wasiak
Squire Sanders Świecicki
Krzesniak sp.k.

Malgorzata Zamorska
bnt Neupert Zamorska &
Partnerzy S.C.

PORTUGAL

Maria Shearman de Macedo
AMCV

Maria Da Gloria Leitão
Cuatrecasas, Gonçalves
Pereira

Ricardo Lopes
Franco Caiado Guerreiro &
Associados

Paula Luz

Tânia Pinheiro
Franco Caiado Guerreiro &
Associados

PUERTO RICO (U.S.)

Lourdes M. Rodríguez-Morera

ROMANIA

Iulian Berbece
POP PEPA SCA

Roxana Dobrila
Gilescu & Partenerii

Flora Drăgan
POP PEPA SCA

Ioana Dumitru
Popovici Nitu & Asociatii -
Attorneys at Law

Luminita Gheorghe
Wolf Theiss & Asociatii

Ileana Glodeanu
Wolf Theiss & Asociatii

Alexandra Măieț
POP PEPA SCA

Smaranda Mandrescu
POP PEPA SCA

Ruxandra Musat
Wolf Theiss & Asociatii

Mirela Nathanzon
Gilescu & Partenerii

Vlad Neacsu
Popovici, Nitu & Asociatii -
Attorneys at Law

Irina Sorescu
CPE- Center for Partnership
and Equality

Cristina Vedel
POP PEPA SCA

Mihai Vlasceanu
Wolf Theiss & Asociatii

RUSSIAN FEDERATION

Valery Getmanenko

Yulianna Vertinskaya

RWANDA

Pamela Abbott
University of Aberdeen

Désiré Kamanzi
ENSafrica Rwanda

Frank Karemera
Kigali Allied Advocates

Alvin Mihigo
R & Partners Law Firm

Vera Nkwate Ngassa

Hervé Ntege
ENSafrica Rwanda

SAUDI ARABIA

Shahd Abduljawwad
Bafakih & Nassief

Arwa Aulaqi
Bafakih & Nassief

Alioune Dione
Ministère de la Femme
de l'Enfance et de
l'Entreprenariat Féminin

Karim Fawaz
Clyde & Co.

Sara Khoja
Clyde & Co.

SENEGAL

Boubacar Diakité
Géni & Kébé SCP d'Avocats

Magatte Fall Dieng

Mohamed Dieng
Géni & Kébé SCP d'avocats

Yankhoba Ndiaye
Géni & Kébé SCP d'Avocats

Ababacar Sadikh Niang
Tribunal Regional de
Tambacounda

Fakha Touré
Géni & Kébé SCP d'Avocats

SERBIA

Autonomous Women's Center

Dragoslav Bijelić
Law office Milošević

Olga Cvejić Jančić
Singidunum University
Belgrade, Faculty of European
Legal and Political Studies-
Novi Sad

Jovana Tomić
Živković Samardžić Law Office

Milica Vesic
Joksovic, Stojanovic and
Partners

SIERRA LEONE
Aiah Allieu
Ministry of Justice, Sierra
Leone

John Kallon
Ministry of Labor and Social
Security, Sierra Leone

Victor Massaquoi
Livelihood Program for
Disadvantaged Youth

Monfred Momoh Sesay
Ministry of Justice, Sierra
Leone

Charles Vandi
Ministry of Social Welfare,
Gender and Children's Affairs,
Sierra Leone

SINGAPORE
Jean Gan
Association of Women for
Action & Research (Aware)

Lay Lian Kee
Rajah & Tann LLP

Michelle Lee
Rajah & Tann LLP

Corinna Lim
Association of Women for
Action & Research (Aware)

Francis Xavier
Rajah & Tann LLP

SLOVAK REPUBLIC
Iveta Abelovská
Abelovsky & Sulva Legal s.r.o.

Ľudmila Dohnalová
CHSH Šiška & Partners s.r.o.

Igor Šváby
B & S Legal s.r.o.

Maroš Terkanič
Abelovsky & Sulva Legal s.r.o.

SLOVENIA
Damijan Gregorc
Law firm Miro Senica and
attorneys, d.o.o.

Suzana Kralijić

SOUTH AFRICA
Richard Bollaert
Nowitz Attorneys

Chantelle de Sousa
Soliticitors' International
Human Rights Group

Karen Fulton
Bowman Gilfillan Inc.

Chantal Kur
The Mediation Clinic and
Divorce Mediations

Lusanda Raphulu
Bowman Gilfillan Inc.

Ziona Tanzer

SPAIN
Enrichetta Sandra Bellini
Fornera
Business and Professional
Women International (BPW)

Virginia de la Cuadra Galera

Ivette Garrido Gea
Gómez-Acebo & Pombo

Lourdes Martín Flores
Uría Menéndez

Amparo Martínez Miró

Isabel Rodríguez Leon
Uría Menéndez

Pablo Santos Fita
Gómez-Acebo & Pombo

Julio Soler

SRI LANKA
Sharmela de Silva
Tiruchelvam Associates

Savitri Goonesekere
University of Colombo

Shamalie Jayatunge
Tiruchelvam Associates

Ramani Muttettuwegama
Tiruchelvam Associates

SUDAN
Yassir Ali
AIH Law Firm

Aziza Ismat Hassanien
AIH Law Firm

Fayha Sanosy
AIH Law Firm

Rayan Ati
Omer Abdelati Law Firm

SWEDEN
Roks, The National
Organisation for Women's
and Young Women's Shelters

Geraldine R. Bjallerstedt

Melanie Gutman

Ajda Hosseini

Jonas Lindbald
Advokatfriman Vinge KB

Åsa Torkelsson

SWITZERLAND
Kecia Barkawi
|Valueworks AG

Caroline Raeber-Piraud
Valueworks AG

Peter Reinert
Baker & McKenzie Zurich

TAIWAN, CHINA
Sophia Hsieh
Tsar & Tsai Law Firm, member
of Lex Mundi

Melanie Lo
Lee, Tsai & Partners,
Attorneys-at-Law

TAJIKISTAN
Aisanat Safarbekkyzy
Grata Law Firm

Kanat Seidaliev
Grata Law Firm

TANZANIA
Hilda S. Dadu
Tanzania Women Lawyers
Association (TAWLA)

Khalifa Kiango
Zenith Attorneys

Mectrida Rweyemamu
Zenith Attorneys

THAILAND
Rachanatorn Laohaphan
Price Sanond Prabhas &
Wynne

Vomramai Patomrat
Price Sanond Prabhas &
Wynne

Aroonee Sirivadhna
Association for the Promotion
of the Status of Women

Pramote Srisamai
Deacons

Andrew Wynne
Deacons

TOGO
Ehonam Yvette Gamisso
SCP Aquereburu & Partners

TUNISIA
Béchir Ghachem
GLA

Wael Haffar

Aziz Sammoud
CAG Law Firm

TURKEY
Nebahat Akkoc
KAMER

Duygu Alkan
ADMD - Mavioglu & Alkan
Law Office

Susen Aklan
Serap Zuvin Law Offices

Ayca Bayburan
ADMD - Mavioglu & Alkan
Law Office

Deniz Bayram
Mor Cati Women's Shelter
Foundation

Burak Benli

Duygu Beyazo
Serap Zuvin Law Offices

Eda Berat Deniz
ADMD - Mavioglu & Alkan
Law Office

Ayse Nur Gedik
KAMER

Melis Oget Koc
Serap Zuvin Law Offices

Batuhan Sahmay
Bener Law Firm

Zeynep Serim
Bener Law Firm

Pelin Tırtıl
Bener Law Firm

Ali Yurtsever
ADMD - Mavioglu & Alkan
Law Office

Serap Zuvin
Serap Zuvin Law Offices

UGANDA

Primah Atugonza
Masembe, Makubuya, Adriko,
Karugaba & Ssekatawa
Advocates

Stella Biwaga
Uganda Association
of Women Lawyers
(FIDA-Uganda)

Charles Kalumiya
Kampala Associated
Advocates

Brigitte Kusiima
Shonubi, Musoke & Co
Advocates

Rachel Musoke
Masembe, Makubuya, Adriko,
Karugaba & Ssekatawa
Advocates

Emma Ssali
Uganda Association
of Women Lawyers
(FIDA-Uganda)

UKRAINE

Oleksiy Kononov
University of Buraimi

Syatoslav Kushnir

Vitaly Makhinchuk
Gestors

Valeriya Malaya

Volodymyr Monastyrskyy
LLC Salans

Oksana Orlova
LLC Salans

Peter Zenon Teluk
Squire, Sanders Ukraine LLC

Andriy Tsvyetkov
Gestors

UNITED ARAB
EMIRATES

Raya Abu Gulal

Preeti Tolani

UNITED KINGDOM

Anne-Marie Glover
Coram Chambers

Michael Leftley
Addleshaw Goddard LLP

Tarai Makawa
Peters & Company Solicitors

Deborah Manoovaloo
Jessamine

Dinu Suntook
Addleshaw Goddard LLP

UNITED STATES

Hdeel Abdelhady
MassPoint Legal and Strategy
Advisory PLLC

Areej Faiz

Demian McGarry
McGarry Law Firm, PLLC

Elena Paraskevas-Thadani
Littler Mendelson

Mary Rothwell Davis
Sanctuary for Families Center
for Battered Women's Legal
Services

Michael Stone

URUGUAY

Álvaro Carrau
Estudio Bado, Kuster, Zerbino
& Rachetti

Guillermo Duarte
Bergstein Abogados

Analía Fernández
Bergstein Abogados

UZBEKISTAN

Anvar Ikramov
Ashur Law Firm

Sayora Khakimova
Sasol Synfuels International

Nodir Yuldashev
Grata Law Firm

VENEZUELA, RB

Pedro Pablo Calvani Abbo

Dorialbys De La Rosa
COFAVIC

Gilberto Jorge
Palacios, Ortega y Asociados

Gabriela Longo V.
Palacios, Ortega y Asociados

Georgina Morales Landazábal

Liliana Ortega Mendoza
COFAVIC

José Manuel Ortega Pérez
Palacios, Ortega y Asociados

Luis Esteban Palacios
Palacios, Ortega y Asociados

Ricardo Rojas Gaona
Rojas Gaona & Bandres

VIETNAM

Thi Hien Bui
Kelvin Chia Partnership

Andrew Lai
Kelvin Chia Partnership

Matthew Matheson
DFDL Mekong Law Group

Thanh Nguyen Tran
DFDL Mekong Law Group

Vu Anh Thu
Mayer Brown JSM (Vietnam)

Dang Thi Tuong Vi
PBC Partners

Benjamin Yap
PBC Partners

WEST BANK AND GAZA

Maha Abu Dayyeh
Women's Center for Legal Aid
and Counselling

Ashraf Abu Hayyeh
Women's Center for Legal Aid
and Counselling

Mohanad Kababji
Kababji Law Office

Luna Orayquat

YEMEN, REP.

Abdulkader Al-Hebshi
Advocacy & Legal
Consultations Office (ALCO)

Gamal Mohammed Aljabi
Aljabi Firm

Gehad Al-Sanabani
Q&A Law Office

Nabil Alshami
LSC

Noora Al-Wali
Law Offices of Sheikh Tariq
Abdullah

Ahmed Arman

Muath Saleh
Dr. Hamzah Shaher Law Firm

ZAMBIA

Jay Mutale Chisanga
Corpus Legal Practitioners

Mabvuto Sakala
Corpus Legal Practicners

Beatrice Simwapenga
Hamusonde

ZIMBABWE

Precious Chakasikwa

Slyvia Chirawu
Women and Law In Southern
Africa

Chatapiwa Malaba

Nyasha Timba
Kantor and Immerman